# THE MOST EXCLUSIVE CLUB

ALSO BY LEWIS L. GOULD

*Wyoming: A Political History, 1868–1896*

*Progressives and Prohibitionists:*
*Texas Democrats in the Wilson Era*

*The Presidency of William McKinley*

*Lady Bird Johnson and the Environment*

*The Presidency of Theodore Roosevelt*

*1968: The Election That Changed America*

*Reform and Regulation:*
*American Politics from Roosevelt to Wilson*

*Lady Bird Johnson: Our Environmental First Lady*

*America in the Progressive Era, 1890–1914*

*The Modern American Presidency*

*Grand Old Party: A History of the Republicans*

*Alexander Watkins Terrell:*
*Civil War Soldier, Texas Lawmaker, American Diplomat*

# THE MOST EXCLUSIVE CLUB

## A History of the
## Modern United States Senate

# LEWIS L. GOULD

A Member of the Perseus Books Group
New York

Copyright © 2005 by Lewis L. Gould

Published by Basic Books,
A Member of the Perseus Books Group

Books published by Basic Books are available at special discounts for
bulk purchases in the United States by corporations, institutions, and
other organizations. For more information, please contact the Special
Markets Department at the Perseus Books Group, 11 Cambridge Center,
Cambridge, MA 02142, or call (617) 252-5298 or (800) 255-1514, or
email special.markets@perseusbooks.com.

Text design and composition by Trish Wilkinson
Set in 11-point Goudy

Library of Congress Cataloging-in-Publication Data

Gould, Lewis L.
    The most exclusive club : a history of the modern United States
Senate / Lewis L. Gould.
        p.   cm.
    Includes bibliographical references and index.
    ISBN-13: 978-0-465-02778-1 (hardcover : alk. paper)
    ISBN-10: 0-465-02778-4 (hardcover : alk. paper)  1. United States.
Congress. Senate—History—20th century.  I. Title.
K1161.G68 2005
328.73'071'09—dc22                                        2005019310

05   06   07   08   /   10   9   8   7   6   5   4   3   2   1

# Contents

*Introduction*                                                    *vii*

CHAPTER ONE
Great Old Personages: The Senate in 1900              1

CHAPTER TWO
The President and the Senate Four                        17

CHAPTER THREE
La Follette Challenges the Senate                         33

CHAPTER FOUR
John Worth Kern and the New Freedom                53

CHAPTER FIVE
The Senate and the League of Nations                   73

CHAPTER SIX
Spearless Leaders in the 1920s                             93

CHAPTER SEVEN
The Senate in the Depression                              113

CHAPTER EIGHT
The New Deal and the Conservative Club              135

CHAPTER NINE
The Senate in Wartime                                       155

CHAPTER TEN

The Senate at Mid-century                                            175

CHAPTER ELEVEN

The Senate Club in the Age of Joe McCarthy                           195

CHAPTER TWELVE

Pawed All Over: Lyndon Johnson and the Senate                        213

CHAPTER THIRTEEN

Mike Mansfield's Senate                                              233

CHAPTER FOURTEEN

"Juggling Too Many Balls"                                            257

CHAPTER FIFTEEN

A Ruder Senate                                                       277

CHAPTER SIXTEEN

Republican Ascendancy at Century's End                               295

Conclusion: The Senate and Its Future                                313

*Notes*                                                              *321*
*Suggestions for Further Reading*                                    *373*
*Acknowledgments*                                                    *379*
*Index*                                                              *383*

# Introduction

A s an idea, the United States Senate came into existence in 1787. The Framers of the Constitution created a second house for Congress in order to provide a legislative check against the potential tyranny of unrestrained majority rule. Unlike members of the House of Representatives, who were popularly elected and held two-year terms, senators would be selected by state legislatures, not by the people directly, and would serve in six-year terms. From its founding, the Senate was conceived as both a counterweight to excessive executive power and a source of restraint on popular but perhaps unwise policy initiatives. As James Madison put it, in addition to its role as a check on the executive, the Senate would "protect the people against the transient impressions in which they themselves might be led."[1]

The Senate started its proceedings in April 1789. At the outset, the House of Representatives seemed to be the more powerful branch. But over the course of the nineteenth century, because their terms were longer and their number smaller, senators came to look down on members of the House as lesser beings. Because of the bicameral nature of the Congress and the legislative process, which requires cooperation between the houses of Congress for legislation to be enacted, tensions between the House and Senate have been a persistent feature of the history of Congress. One former House member told an interviewer in the 1980s, "I hated the Senate from the very first day I was in the House."[2]

By the start of the twentieth century, in the eyes of the public the Senate had eclipsed the lower chamber as the more prestigious and celebrated body in the legislative process. And indeed, the Senate plays a number of crucial roles within the political system. Treaties have to receive the upper chamber's advice and consent to go into effect. As a result, the upper house exerts (and even more often claims to exert) an influence equal to that of the White House in the shaping of foreign policy. Likewise, all nominees to federal offices and judgeships must gain Senate confirmation. That has created a codependence between the legislative and executive in how these important appointments will be determined. In recent years, however, the Senate's role in the approval and rejection of judicial nominees has become a source of greater friction within the chamber and between it and the White House.

The unique and powerful role of the Senate is reflected in the way it has been written about over the years. Biographies of senators abound; books on individual members of the House are harder to come by. Senators can leave their mark on the life of their institution, whereas even talented House members find it difficult to make their names stand out among those of hundreds of their contemporary colleagues. In the historical memory, as in the life of Washington, D.C., senators have just seemed more important in the life of the nation.

For this reason it is not surprising that a tone of reverence has often characterized accounts of the Senate by both scholars and journalists. These narratives have fostered a sense of enduring legislative greatness in the upper house. In that vanished past, giants stalked the floor of the institution. Their eloquent speeches attracted adoring audiences, collegiality reigned, and bipartisanship ensured judicious compromises. History has blended into legend because so much of the writing about the Senate has been concentrated on discrete incidents of major historical importance or key actors in the legislative drama. And of course, veneration of the Senate goes back to the origins of the word and the concept of Senate in the Roman republic and the Latin language. The word "Senate" comes from the Latin word for Senate, *Senatus*, which derives from *senex*, Latin for "old man." The first U.S. president, George Washington, refused a crown, refused empire, and thus set the nation on the path of republican and democratic values.

The U.S. Senate's pivotal role in the government ensures that it remains one of the most examined and studied legislative bodies in the world. Its proceedings appear on cable television; its committee hearings are open to press and public. With on-line resources, a citizen can follow debates and track votes with the click of a mouse. Political scientists and historians conduct interviews, pore over archives, and look for trends and significance in how the chamber has developed.

Yet no book exists that treats the twentieth-century history of the Senate as a cohesive unit. During that time, a small, individualistic chamber of 1900 became a complex, sophisticated institution that now employs thousands of people, attracts intense media scrutiny, and stands second only to the president as a focus of life in Washington. It seemed time to do for the Senate what has been done for presidents, the Supreme Court, and other key institutions—provide a narrative that looks at the chamber over the span of the last century.

When I embarked on the research for this book, it was with the belief that the upper house had compiled a record that, with some notable exceptions, brought enduring credit on the institution. My goal was to discern and narrate the qualities that had made the Senate such a vital part of congressional history. What had made the Senate—"the most exclusive gentlemen's club in Washington," as it was called during the 1950s—so valuable to the country?[3]

Indeed, there have been periods of intense activity and high drama. During the first term of Woodrow Wilson, for example, the Democrats, under their leader, John Worth Kern of Indiana, enacted such laws as the Federal Reserve Act, the Underwood Tariff, and legislation to restrict child labor. Later in the Wilson presidency, the dispute about the League of Nations in 1919 and 1920 provided a high-minded debate about the future of foreign policy.

At the height of the New Deal of Franklin Delano Roosevelt, members worked with their House counterparts to create Social Security, engage pressing problems of relief during the Depression, and accord organized labor the right to bargain collectively in the Wagner Act. The 1950s brought significant struggles over the issues of anti-Communism and the Cold War as the chamber reacted to the initiatives of Harry S. Truman and Dwight D. Eisenhower. In the Mike Mansfield era, the Senate passed the Civil Rights Act of 1964 and the Voting Rights Act of 1965, not to mention other Great Society measures. At the other end of the political spectrum, during the presidency of Ronald Reagan, in 1981–1982, Congress moved promptly to enact the new administration's program of tax cuts and increased defense spending.

The Senate's failings over the last century are, however, even more striking. The lawmakers must be rated poorly on such major social questions as race, economic inequality, the role of women in society, and health care. For protracted periods—at the start of the twentieth century, in the era of Theodore Roosevelt, during the 1920s, and again for domestic issues in the post–World War II era—the Senate functioned not merely as a source of conservative reflections on the direction of society but as a force to genuinely impede the nation's vitality and evolution. The power of the southern bloc in the Senate from the early 1920s to the early 1960s meant that a substantial portion of the nation's population, its African-American citizens, lacked political representation. Likewise on such matters as health care and the rights of labor, the Senate stood as a bulwark of vested economic power rather than as an advocate for the interests of American citizens.

The Senate's record in "advising" the executive branch on foreign policy has been similarly mixed. Some traditional criticisms in this area are misplaced. It was President Wilson's mistakes, more than Senate intransigence, that accounted for the defeat of the League of Nations. Following on that episode, the members of the chamber reflected the isolationist sentiment of the 1920s and 1930s to hold back presidents from undue overseas involvement that might repeat the perceived errors of American neutrality from 1914 to 1917. The Senate's isolationism blocked Franklin D. Roosevelt from meeting the challenge of the dictatorships in Europe and the Japanese in the Pacific with more effectiveness.

Nowhere have the obstructionist impulses of the Senate been more clearly manifest than in the troubled history of the filibuster in the twentieth and early twenty-first centuries. Always available to a determined minority, the principle of unlimited debate and the possibility of its use shaped how sponsors of controversial legislation framed their appeals and considered the chances of ultimate success.

The filibuster attained its greatest notoriety after World War II, when Strom Thurmond, Richard B. Russell, and other Southerners used the technique to block civil rights measures. It became a chronic weapon during the 1970s when the post-cloture filibuster ensured that senators could keep on talking even after debate had been closed by calling for a vote (the meaning of "cloture"). Since 1995, the use of the filibuster against judicial nominations has again excited partisan passions. Though it is always possible to cite specific cases where the filibuster could be justified as a means of stopping bad legislation, the reliance on this anti-majoritarian device has been an unhealthy development for the Senate. The existence of two legislative chambers and the procedural slowness of the Senate provide enough time for mature deliberation about proposed laws. Requiring super-majorities—more than 51 percent—for democratic action is contradictory and unwise.

While becoming somewhat disillusioned about the overall record of the Senate as a legislative body in the course of my research, I also grew increasingly skeptical about the historical verdict on some of the celebrated giants of the upper house. Such figures as Robert La Follette, William E. Borah, Robert Taft, and Lyndon Johnson had achieved mythic status among historians and the reading public. Many books have been devoted to their careers, and contemporary senators often model themselves on these putative giants. Some senators, such as Harry S. Truman, John F. Kennedy, and Lyndon Johnson, went on to hold the office of president; their subsequent reputations in that role have often influenced opinions about their performance as lawmakers.

Yet under scrutiny, the qualifications of some of these senators for greatness came into question. This was scant surprise for a figure such as John F. Kennedy. Although he remains a hero in the popular imagination, scholars have long known that Kennedy was a part-time senator more committed to his own sexual and political ambitions than to the tedium of creating legislation. More surprising were the facts that emerged about other senators who had previously seemed so central to the unfolding of Senate history.

The career of the Idaho Republican William E. Borah as an advocate for progressive causes and isolationism in foreign policy seemed to consist mostly of windy speeches and abandoned initiatives. Despite all the attention historians have given him, when viewed close up, Borah seemed an empty suit, albeit one of a far-western cut. Robert A. Taft, who has a memorial to his prowess as a lawmaker in Washington, also came to seem less imposing. Aside from the Taft-Hartley Law of 1947, the Ohio Republican's impact on legislation seemed marginal and his judgments on foreign policy erratic at best.

The subject of notable biographies by Robert Dallek and Robert Caro, Lyndon Johnson has exerted an extraordinary hold over the public imagination in recent years. Closer scrutiny of his record reveals that he did indeed overawe his colleagues and increase the authority of the office of majority leader. In the long history of the upper house, however, Johnson's intensity impressed his colleagues not as a model for future leaders but as an example to be avoided. As a result, Johnson's successor, Mike Mansfield of Montana, had a greater effect on how the Senate operated and how the role of majority leader developed.

Just as some of these famous senators appeared to be less crucial to the history of the Senate than I had once thought, other legislators emerged out of obscurity to assume a larger place in the narrative. John Worth Kern, an Indiana Democrat, led his party during Woodrow Wilson's first term. Through his deft management of his caucus, Kern enabled the president to get his New Freedom program enacted despite Republican taunts that the Democrats lacked the capacity to govern. Though he served only a single term, Kern had more effect on the history of the Senate and the nation than many who stayed in Washington through three or four election cycles.

Later in the century, a conservative southern Democrat named James B. Allen, who served from 1968 to 1978, helped formulate new techniques for extending the life of filibusters even after his colleagues had voted to close down debate. A master of the Senate rules, Allen frustrated attempts to enact liberal legislation during the 1970s and instructed other senators of all ideological hues how they might imitate his example. Similarly, other lawmakers of historical importance, such as Henry Cabot Lodge, Sr., Alben Barkley, and Mike Mansfield, came to impress me as even more constructive figures.

One striking—and recurring—theme of Senate history that emerged in the course of my research was the prevalence of alcoholism. There are some clear-cut examples of a senator's alcoholism affecting job performance. But more often, the culture of alcoholism that pervaded the Senate through much of the twentieth century took its toll in the form of diminished judgment, erratic behavior, and recurrent health problems.

In many ways, the history of the Senate can be viewed as the history of small clubs or groups within the much larger club of the chamber itself. The Senate began the twentieth century with its fate in the hands of a small group of Republicans called "The Four." Led by Nelson Aldrich of Rhode Island, the Four included William Boyd Allison of Iowa, Orville H. Platt of Connecticut, and John Coit Spooner of Wisconsin. At first they cooperated with President Theodore Roosevelt, but they resisted his program of railroad regulation and greater government supervision of corporations. During the next decade the power of these individuals ebbed under the pressure of progressive reformers such as Robert La Follette of Wisconsin and Albert J.

Beveridge of Indiana. For the next two decades, leadership fluctuated among parties and individuals from Kern and the Democrats between 1910 and 1917 to Lodge and other Republicans in the 1920s.

The onset of the Great Depression and the emergence of the New Deal helped bring into existence the Club, whose members were Southerners and conservative Republicans. Fears about civil rights, government regulation, and social change held together a group led by Richard Russell of Georgia, Harry Byrd of Virginia, and Robert A. Taft of Ohio that would shape the Senate's course through the mid-1960s.

By the late 1960s the grip of the Club loosened. Its members were getting old, the rise of the civil rights movement undercut its power, and more liberals were coming to the Senate during the presidencies of John F. Kennedy and Lyndon Johnson. Concerns that an inner circle dominated affairs in the chamber gave way to complaints that senators were freelancers no longer respectful of the customs of the institution. In the next forty years, the Senate responded to the pressures of television, the rising costs of campaigning, and increasing partisanship. In the process, the Senate gradually came to behave more like the House of Representatives. Since the 1890s, the House had been a place where majorities worked their will and had their way. Long-standing procedures and institutional barriers to majority power in the Senate such as filibusters, the power of committee chairs, and the ability of senators to delay judicial nominations came under attack as undemocratic and outmoded. Republican senators, more often in the majority after 1980, valued victory in specific cases more than respecting the continuity of Senate practices, as their attitude toward the filibuster demonstrated: The Republicans and southern Democrats had supported it when it suited them but turned against it when Democrats began using it to block nominations of conservatives as judges.

Central also to the evolution of the Senate over the past century has been the effect of the increasing costs of senatorial elections. Direct election of senators, a salutary reform that was brought about by passage of the Seventeenth Amendment in 1914, carried with it the unintended consequence that individual candidates increasingly had to pay for statewide campaigns. After World War II, with the rise of television and its expensive demands, candidates and eventually incumbents found themselves ever more dependent on incessant fund-raising. The mass media thus became for senators both a means to enhance their reach with the public and a burden that required time away from making laws in favor of collecting donor checks. Being a member of the "world's greatest deliberative body" provides access to important power, but the price of admission is high. Election campaigns in large states can cost more than $20 million and demand prodigious individual effort from the candidate.

Despite the significant changes in the way the Senate operates, unfortunate continuities persist. Throughout the twentieth century the chamber remained almost exclusively white and male. It wasn't until the 1990s that women appeared for the first time in more than token numbers—reaching a peak of fourteen in 2005. During the twentieth century only two African Americans, one Native American, and a handful of Hispanics and Asian Americans won election to the upper house. Of course, the Senate mirrored the marginalization of women and minorities in American life, and the absence of diversity in the makeup of the chamber also contributed to the body's inability to address these injustices.

A profound sense of crisis now surrounds the Senate and its members. Critics allege that it is an undemocratic place where the national interest receives only fitful attention. There are allegations that members of both parties spend more time on getting reelected and dispensing pork-barrel subsidies to well-heeled constituents than they do on debating and discussing the major issues before the nation. Where does this sense of an embattled, partisan Senate come from? What were its origins in the history of the institution? Can the Senate's continued existence as part of American government be justified?

The Senate is a fascinating human institution. Its history in the twentieth century is rich in compelling personalities, dramatic moments of lawmaking, and several seasons of silliness. Despite the many qualms I have developed in writing this book about the Senate's performance in the past one hundred years, I believe that the upper house provides something crucial to the political system. If the Senate were to be abolished, as some of its sternest critics have advocated, something unique would disappear from the way in which Americans govern themselves.

## CHAPTER ONE

# Great Old Personages:
# The Senate in 1900

T HE DAY BEGAN WITH FLOWERS. WHEN THE UNITED STATES SENATORS assembled for the start of legislative business on December 3, 1900, they found their chamber transformed into a great "fragrant bower." The abundance of blossoms and sprays, personal tributes to senators from friends and family, adorned one of Washington, D.C.'s grandest social occasions. From the gallery of the Senate an invited audience of foreign military attachés in their resplendent uniforms, handsomely gowned women, and the diplomatic corps in formal dress observed the renewal of congressional work. At exactly noon, William P. Frye of Maine, the president pro tempore—by custom the senator of the majority party with the longest record of continuous service—gaveled for order. For the ninety members of the upper house from all the forty-five states, another session was under way. It would last until their mandated adjournment on March 3, 1901, and so would bridge the nineteenth and twentieth centuries.

In the new century, this most exclusive club in the world would find itself grappling with great questions of empire and democracy, war and peace, capital and labor, race relations and women's rights, fascism and Communism, terrorism and human rights.[1] Amid the flowers and festivities of this December 3, 1900, the senators also came prepared to work. Senator Frye had alerted members of the Republican majority that he hoped "to see each Senator in his seat on the morning of the first day of the session" in order to take

1

up the first order of business: shipping legislation to promote the American merchant marines, which had been in a depressed state since the Civil War.[2]

The senators met in the chamber that the Senate had been using since 1859. The room was 113 feet long, 80 feet wide, and 36 feet high. On the north side was the platform on which the vice president's desk rested, along with the desks and tables of the secretary and the staff. Arranged in semicircles in front of the presiding officer were the chairs for the individual senators. Ever since the two major parties had emerged as partisan rivals in the 1850s, the Republicans had been to the left of the presiding officer and the Democrats to his right.[3]

The Senate chamber looked imposing with its ornaments and busts of vice presidents and other worthies from American history, but George H. Haynes, a distinguished historian of the Senate writing in 1938, called it "one of the most unimpressive national legislative chambers on the face of the earth." In the years before air-conditioning was installed, in 1929, it was certainly one of the most unpleasant places to produce legislation or indeed do anything at all. The sweltering, swamplike Washington summers made the Senate a cauldron in which exhaustion and illness became endemic. Orville H. Platt, a prominent Republican, said in the 1880s: "While we remain we must live in a dungeon. This Chamber is an architectural failure."[4]

On that festive December 3, 1900, no one would have been rude enough to criticize the inadequacies of the Senate's physical setting. Party warfare had paused for a moment and collegiality reigned. The tough politicians who understood what it took to win their way to the Senate appreciated each other's struggles. Most senators "appeared in what the fashion journals describe as full afternoon costume." Backslapping, hearty laughs, and masculine fellowship were the order of the day.[5] In many respects, the upper house of Congress was another in a series of male organizations to which all the senators had belonged at one time or another since their boyhood days. Debating societies, literary associations, military units, and political parties, all these bodies taught nineteenth-century American men how to conduct business, interact with colleagues, and present ideas. Most new arrivals in the Senate fell easily into the bonding rituals of the chamber and accepted the internal rules about how to behave. It was natural for outsiders to label the Senate an exclusive club, especially since only two men from each state could hope to be members at any one time.[6]

The holiday spirit of Washington upon the reconvening of Congress reflected the self-confidence of the United States on the brink of the twenti-

In the early twentieth century, the Senate was a world of its own within Washington. The Senate pageboys, who did errands for the members, are shown throwing snowballs after a winter storm. (LIBRARY OF CONGRESS)

eth century. To the middle class and those made wealthy in the post–Civil War era, the nation in December 1900 seemed prosperous and assured of greatness. Defeating Spain in the Spanish-American War of 1898, the United States had suddenly become a major world power, adding the protectorates of Cuba, Puerto Rico, and the distant Philippines to what was beginning to look like a budding empire. Speaking through his popular character, the working-class Irish immigrant Mr. Dooley, the humorist Finley Peter

Dunne caught the spirit of the times in this watering-hole dialogue. "We're a gr-reat people," said Hennessy. "We ar-re that," said Mr. Dooley. "We ar're that. An th'best iv it is, we know we ar're."[7]

As Mr. Dooley hinted, beneath the surface of national self-congratulation, all was not well with the United States. The severe economic depression of the 1890s with its widespread misery and grinding unemployment had called the nation's institutions into question. The brief, successful war with Spain had triggered an intense debate about whether the United States should become a world power. Imperialists, most notably within the Republican Party, argued that the country should play a commanding role in the struggle for international ascendancy. Their opponents, many of them Democrats, countered that self-government could not be extended beyond the nation's borders.

The 1890s, with their economic depression and social unrest, had raised the specter of socialism and threats to internal stability. Although the danger of a revolutionary upheaval diminished after the return of prosperity in 1898, middle-class Americans wondered whether the country was on the right track. A newspaperman, Ray Stannard Baker, spoke for many of them when he wrote, "We can feed ourselves, we are great and powerful; but we have our own galling Negro problem, our rotten machine politics, our legislative bribery, our municipal corruption, our giant monopolies, our aristocracy of mere riches, any one of which is a rock on which the ship of state, unless skillfully navigated, may go to its destruction."[8]

As Americans grew skeptical about how their system worked, or didn't, the Senate came in for particular scrutiny. Senator George Frisbie Hoar of Massachusetts acknowledged, "It cannot be doubted that there is a widespread and growing impatience with the condition of things in the Senate." For many Americans, the upper house of Congress appeared isolated and removed from their daily concerns. It was, so the conventional wisdom went, a club for millionaires who had bought their way into prominence. When the distaste for political parties and partisanship grew after 1896, the Senate loomed as an inviting target. Critics called it undemocratic and far from representative.[9] If change was to come, the Senate seemed the last place where it could happen. These ninety politicians, mostly attorneys over the age of fifty, believed they represented the sober second thought in national affairs. If some elements in society called for more government regulation of the economy or greater rights for the disadvantaged, it was the job of the Senate to be skeptical and scrutinize those claims.[10]

By 1900 the House of Representatives had become an institution where a determined majority in either party could pass whatever legislation it supported. In 1890, Speaker of the House Thomas B. Reed had persuaded his Republican colleagues to adopt rules that prevented the minority from staying away to create the absence of a quorum. With dominance of the committees and a cohesive caucus of majority members, the Speaker could see to it that the party's agenda was adopted. The minority could speak in protest and make its case to the public. What the minority could not do was to preclude action that the majority espoused. That was the task and the special role of the Senate.

The United States in 1900 faced new issues about the role of government that senators had to address. Ever since the founding of the Republic, the debate about economic policy had focused on how best to promote the growth of the productive sectors of society. From Jefferson to Cleveland, Democrats had favored small government, state rights, and economy in expenditures. This was how the government would allow autonomous individuals to realize their full potential. The Republicans, since the party's founding in the 1850s, had endorsed a strong national government that promoted the expansion of business through protective tariffs, subsidies to businessmen and farmers, and stimulation of overseas trade. The Republicans had been the activists in politics; Democrats were the party of caution and conservatism.[11]

By the 1890s the political ground had shifted. As industrialism spread across the land, the injustices of that economic change appeared. Workers suffered industrial accidents. Children labored in factories and mills for long days in deplorable conditions. Big business reshaped communities and the social relations within them. In towns and states, advocates of reform asserted that government should concern itself not just with promoting growth but also with regulating the conduct of business in the public interest. These policy demands posed new issues for the national government. Cries arose that government should enact stronger, more effective legislation to curb the ills of business.[12]

These sentiments had not yet formed into a national consensus on positive action. When they did so, advocates of reform faced a powerful impediment in the Senate. There the power of the Republican majority worked against programs to shift the balance of power in society. As it existed in 1900, the upper house had little sympathy for those Americans whom the rise of large corporations had disadvantaged. Even the Democrats were less than excited about using federal power to right the wrongs of industrialism. In their minds, a government strong enough to control a dishonest corporation might also be powerful enough to restrict racial segregation in the South. The best approach, these conservative Democrats contended, was to foster small government and preserve state rights. Senators of both parties were not disposed to take up the problems of industrialism and those it had damaged. As the Senate launched the short session that would end in March 1901, the lawmakers were most engaged with problems of managing the new American empire. Issues of domestic reform remained on the outer edge of their concerns.[13]

The Senate had been founded in large measure not to engage the pressing issues of society with any degree of urgency. The senators who showed up that December morning in 1900 were part of a tradition that stretched back almost 112 years, to the first session of the Senate on April 6, 1789. In the ensuing century, the institution had become one of the most celebrated and controversial features of American political life. By 1900 it appeared that the upper house was as important as or perhaps even ascendant over the presidency. A chorus of complaints about this situation appeared in the popular press. "The Senate thinks highly of itself because it is really overshadowing because it is the most powerful element of the government," wrote a journalist in 1903. Yet a newspaper editor could also say in 1897 that "the Senate ranks lower in popular estimation today than it has at any time in the history of the country." Powerful and disputed, revered and yet under attack, the Senate had come a long way from the compromises and innovations that attended its creation at the Constitutional Convention in Philadelphia in 1787.[14]

The Framers of the new Constitution believed that a second legislative chamber, not popularly elected, was required to provide balance against the House of Representatives and to check executive power. They decided to allocate to each state two senators, each serving a six-year term. The senators were to be chosen by state legislatures from among their members, forming a body that came to be known over time as the upper house. To offset the power of the president in foreign affairs, treaties would have to receive Senate approval from two thirds of members present and voting. In the selection of federal judges, presidents nominated and the Senate would then confirm or reject the choices. In the case of impeachment, the House of Representatives would present charges, and the members of the Senate, with the Chief Justice of the United States presiding when a president was the accused, would conduct the trial.[15]

The larger purpose of the Senate was revealed in the famous anecdote, told repeatedly in the Senate literature, about a conversation between Thomas Jefferson and George Washington. Jefferson had not been in the United States when the Constitution was written. He asked Washington what led the future president to accept the idea of a Senate. Washington responded, "Why did you pour that coffee into your saucer?" Jefferson answered, "To cool it." To which Washington replied, "Even so, we put legislation into the senatorial saucer to cool it." And so the Senate became part of the new government that went into operation during the spring of 1789.[16]

In practice, preserving the rights of the states, especially the smaller ones, was the great unsolved problem of the infant United States. More than six hundred thousand African Americans labored in bondage, most of them in the South. They represented a continuing dilemma for the Framers of the Constitution. As a result, the problem plagued the Senate as well. The presence of slavery and the race issue meant that the deliberations of the Senate had the potential to disrupt the new union at any time. Throughout its ensuing history, the upper house would be forced, for the most part against its will, to confront the problem of the status of African Americans in the nation. Many of the procedural tangles and obscure controversies that tied the Senate in knots over the years arose from the serious divisions within the country about race.

For the first thirty years of its existence, the Senate did not assume a preeminent position in the nation's affairs. After the War of 1812, however, the slavery question gained additional salience as the nation expanded westward after the 1803 Louisiana Purchase, and the role of important lawmakers who argued about the place of human bondage in the newly opening lands thrust the upper house into the nation's consciousness. Such giants as Massachusetts' Daniel Webster, Kentucky's Henry Clay, and South Carolina's John C. Calhoun participated in the great compromises that in 1820, 1833, and 1850 were attempts to resolve the looming sectional crisis. The nation's newspaper readers followed the drama on the Senate floor with rapt attention as senators engaged in complex legislative maneuvers and elevated rhetoric. Schoolchildren in the North learned by heart Webster's reply in 1830 to his southern colleague Robert Hayne of South Carolina, who had spoken in favor of state rights—a coded reference to the right to maintain slavery. Concluding his affirmation of American nationalism, Webster proclaimed, "Liberty and Union, now and forever, one and inseparable."[17]

The apex of the Senate's impact on the United States in the nineteenth century occurred during the debates that produced the Compromise of 1850. The Mexican War of 1846–1848 had left major sectional issues relating to the slavery question unresolved. Should slaveholders be allowed to take their slaves into territory of the Southwest seized from Mexico? Could the federal government restrict slavery from establishing itself in California and parts of what are now Arizona, New Mexico, and Utah? In 1850 that explosive problem came before the Senate for settlement.

The wily and charismatic Henry Clay, from the border state of Kentucky, endeavored to frame a set of measures that would avert a confrontation between North and South. Webster and Calhoun entered the struggle with notable speeches. Calhoun, dour and fanatical, asserted the rights of the South against the perceived aggression of the North against slavery. Webster risked his political career to speak for compromise and moderation. In the end, Clay's comprehensive solution gave way to the efforts of Stephen A. Douglas of Illinois to pass the separate legislative elements of what Clay had proposed. Although the resulting enactments only delayed the sectional strife for a few years, they became enshrined in Senate lore. The Compromise of 1850 was regarded as a moment when the towering figures of the upper house exercised their greatest influence on events.[18]

The early years of Senate history also produced a procedure, the filibuster, that has become a unique feature of the institution's history. Derived from French, Dutch, and Spanish words for "freebooters," the term became associated with lengthy speeches to delay votes in the mid-nineteenth century. The idea that senators may speak for as long as they wish on a particular subject is part of the intrinsic character of the upper house. Yet the right of unlimited debate did not exist in that form until the middle of the nineteenth century. In 1806, the right to ask for the previous question and thus end debate was put aside, largely because it was not much used. Once senators had the prerogative to speak without limit, they came to admire the idea. Then the concept of unlimited debate was challenged when Henry Clay in 1841 proposed an "hour rule" to cut off discussion and go to a vote. John C. Calhoun and his southern allies saw an implicit threat to slavery in the proposal and blocked its adoption and the idea of the previous question. They feared that a majority might pass measures to curb some of the privileges that slavery had under the Constitution. Despite periodic attempts to impose limits on discussions (known as "cloture" in parliamentary parlance), the tradition then became well established as many senators found in the tactic a useful weapon. Sometimes, senators worked out informal understandings to limit debate in what foreshadowed the unanimous-consent agreements of the late nineteenth and twentieth centuries.[19]

The Senate remained a focus of national attention during the tumultuous years of Civil War and Reconstruction, after the southern members departed in 1861 and the Republicans held sway for the remainder of the decade. The chamber echoed to impassioned debates over the future of African Americans and their role in society as lawmakers adopted the Thirteenth Amendment to outlaw slavery in 1865, the Fourteenth Amendment to establish national citizenship in 1868, and the Fifteenth Amendment to guarantee all male citizens the right to vote in 1870.

A major test for the Senate came with the 1868 impeachment trial of Andrew Johnson, who had succeeded to the presidency after Abraham Lincoln's assassination. The Republican House had brought charges because of the Southerner Johnson's obstruction of the government's post–Civil War Reconstruction program in the South. The prosecution fell one vote short of the two-thirds needed for conviction and removal from office. In time, the episode came to be seen as an example of congressional overreach and an incident in Senate history that should not be repeated.[20]

By 1877 and the end of Reconstruction, observers commented that the Senate had less room for the political orators of an earlier time. Now the upper house became the preserve of businessmen and lawyers who won their seats because of their personal fortunes or their close connections with corporate power. The pool of available candidates comprised men with ties to wealth and influence in their states, and the parties screened who should be eligible for election by the state legislatures. Individualists or men of outstanding reputations now had less chance.

As a result of the changes in its membership and working habits, the Senate's business became more routine. The talents of the florid orator yielded to the skill of the partisan leader who settled issues in the Senate cloakroom. Floor debate evolved into a ritual meant for public consumption. The caucus and the party counted for more than individual ability in managing the Senate.

Critics of the new Senate focused on the way senators were elected. The manner of choosing senators had been set out in the Constitution and had now become a fixed ritual in partisan life. When the term of an incumbent

ended, both houses of the state legislature met in joint session and cast ballots to retain the sitting lawmaker or to elect a successor. The first person to
receive a majority of the votes in the legislature won the six-year term.[21]

A successful candidate often needed only to win the votes of half or
even just a plurality of his party's caucus in the legislature. All members of
the party would be bound to vote for him during the actual tally. The possibility of influencing or bribing a small number of legislators proved too
tempting for many an unscrupulous politician, and dubious senatorial elections abounded. When a question arose as to whether an election had been
fair and honest, the Senate itself made the decision whether a particular
election had been correctly conducted and the aspiring senator was entitled to a seat. The partisan alignment usually dictated how the Senate ruled
in each case. By 1900 the Republicans held fifty-six seats to twenty-three
for the Democrats and ten for third parties. Early in that year, the Senate
declared that the recent election of William A. Clark, the owner of silver
mines in Montana and a Democrat, had been so tainted with fraud that it
declared his seat vacant.[22]

On other occasions legislatures deadlocked and failed to choose a senator
at all, which is what happened to Wyoming and Montana in the mid-1890s.
Between 1899 and 1903, Delaware had only one senator because of the persistent ambition of one wealthy politician. A Republican with much money
but little virtue, J. Edward Addicks spread cash through the system of that
small state. His ambitions kept Delaware lawmakers stalemated and ensured
that the seat went unfilled. In 1906, the *Washington Post* opined, "The
Delaware legislature is in session again, going through the usual performance
of chasing Mr Addicks away from the Senatorial trough."[23]

In the wake of these embarrassments, the Senate gained a reputation as a
place where money determined the outcome of elections and legislation. A
popular anecdote caught the spirit of this point of view. The story went that
President Grover Cleveland was roused one night by his wife, who said,
"Wake up, Mr. Cleveland, wake up, there are robbers in the house." The
sleepy chief executive replied, "I think you are mistaken. There are no robbers in the House, but there are lots in the Senate." Real-life senators knew
how extensive a role corruption played in their deliberations. Maine's Senator Frye, who had been in the chamber since 1881, told a friend in 1899,
"You do not believe that a man should buy a United States Senatorship, nor
do I, yet there are several in our distinguished body who hold their seats
by purchase."[24]

The persistent corruption and chaos when legislatures chose senators led to calls for the direct election of members by the people of their states, a change that required an amendment to the Constitution. The Constitutional Convention had believed that legislative elections would produce better senators who could represent the opinion of the states and act as a check upon the House. By the early twentieth century, however, that argument seemed more and more out of touch with national realities and the actual squalid performance of legislatures in choosing senators. As the editors of the reform journal *The Nation* put it in 1902, "To hold the people incapable of electing Senators is an insidious reflection upon the dignity of a nation whose political creed is the sovereignty of the people." The House duly passed a direct-elections amendment several times around the turn of the century, knowing full well that their senatorial counterparts would reject the change. In 1902 Massachusetts Senator George Frisbie Hoar called the reform "half a joke."[25]

In 1900, the upper chamber was exclusively white and male. There had been only two African-American senators during the Reconstruction period a generation earlier. Hiram Revels of Mississippi had served for two years, and then Blanche K. Bruce, also of Mississippi, had represented the state for a full term during the 1870s. The last black congressman of the nineteenth century, George H. White of North Carolina, was leaving Congress after his term expired in 1901. Few white Americans thought that it was wrong to have a Congress in which a large portion of the population had no representatives.

With the issues of the Civil War and its aftermath fading from the consciousness of most white Americans, neither Democratic nor Republican senators gave much attention to minority rights during the first two decades of the century. Most senators looked upon Reconstruction as an unwise experiment in multiracial government that, by their lights, had been a disastrous failure. Even with the national consensus favoring their racial bigotry, southern senators remained quick to bristle at any perceived slights to their segregated way of life.[26]

The Senate had even less to offer American women. In the political environment of 1900, women sitting as members in the upper house would have been unthinkable. Women could vote in a handful of western states, but any influence they wielded in Washington took place behind the scenes in a social capacity. Secretaries and clerks were mostly male. Capitol Hill was a masculine preserve. For legislators' wives there was an endless round of visits and social occasions where, as one congressional wife put it, "official position regulates society."[27]

The impression that the Senate was a rich men's club, so pervasive in 1900, was based on about twenty members whose wealth was well known, including James S. McMillan of Michigan, Chauncey Depew of New York, Marcus A. Hanna of Ohio, and Nelson W. Aldrich of Rhode Island. Republicans dominated the list, since Democrats tended to come from the more impoverished South. For some of the rich senators, their holdings and their abilities translated into real power with their associates. Others with fewer legislative skills found themselves on the fringes of decision making.[28]

The 1890s brought political turbulence to the Senate. After winning control of the White House and Congress in the 1888 elections, Republicans saw their majority in the House vanish and their hold on the upper house weaken two years later. Cleveland, a Democrat, then won a second term in 1892 and the Democrats regained mastery of both houses of Congress that same year. The Panic of 1893 and the resulting depression in 1893 devastated the Democrats, and they suffered crippling reverses in the 1894 congressional elections. Republicans took back the House but could not form a majority in the Senate over the combined votes of the Democrats and the agrarian-based Populists. Two years later, in 1896, the Republicans regained a majority and their numbers expanded in 1898 and 1900 to establish a firm dominance in the upper chamber.

During the presidency of William McKinley (1897–1901), the Republicans proved cohesive and purposeful in their legislative program. They raised tariff rates in the Dingley Tariff of 1897; waged a successful war with Spain, taking responsibility for Cuba, Puerto Rico, and the Philippines; and put the nation on the gold standard in 1900. The return of prosperity after the hard times of the 1890s lifted the Republicans into what seemed to be a firm ascendancy on Capitol Hill. The prospects for a constructive second term for McKinley appeared bright as 1900 ended.

In addition to passing legislation, the Senate had two other constitutionally mandated tasks that gave it a privileged role in government. "Without the assent of the Senate," wrote Henry Cabot Lodge, "no bill can become law, no office can be filled, no treaty ratified." Its responsibility to "advise and consent" to treaties meant that senators had to be consulted in the shaping of foreign policy, whether presidents liked it or not. When the White House failed to work with the Senate, political reverses followed. Three years earlier, during the first months of the McKinley administration, the Senate had turned down a treaty with Great Britain to arbitrate international differences between the two countries.[29]

In 1900, the same point was driven home to President McKinley and his secretary of state, John Hay. To make possible the construction of a canal across Central America, Hay had renegotiated a half-century-old treaty with Great Britain, the Clayton-Bulwer Pact, which gave the British government the right to approve or disapprove such an isthmian waterway. In the Hay-Pauncefote Treaty (named after the British ambassador in Washington, Julian Pauncefote), the secretary of state had provided for a canal that would not be fortified and would be open to vessels of all nations. The Senate, led by Henry Cabot Lodge of Massachusetts, erupted in opposition to this perceived abridgment of American rights.[30]

Much to the disgust of Hay, the pact was ratified with amendments that the British could not accept. London rejected the treaty, and the administration had to start over to craft a document that the Senate could endorse. That outcome would not be achieved until late 1901, after McKinley was dead and Theodore Roosevelt was the new president. As for John Hay, he learned to hate the upper chamber for its intrusive role in foreign affairs. "A treaty entering the Senate," he wrote, "is like a bull going into the arena. No one can say just how or when the final blow will fall—but one thing is certain—it will never leave the arena alive."[31]

The Senate's other constitutional functions—trying the cases of federal officers who had been impeached and the confirmation of presidential cabinet, military, and judiciary appointments—were less controversial than they would later become. There had not been an impeachment case against a federal official in a quarter of a century, and the trial of President Johnson was also a fading memory.

The selection and confirmation of members of the cabinet took place very rapidly when a new administration came in or when changes were made. No elaborate hearings occurred, there was little in the way of background checks, and there was no Federal Bureau of Investigation to undertake probes of possibly criminal pasts either. Senators relied on their network of contacts within the party to decide whether a cabinet member was qualified. As a result, confirmation of choices for what was called the president's "official family" might be done in a matter of days.

Diplomatic nominations and military appointments and promotions were usually handled in the same expeditious manner. President Cleveland had experienced the rejection of two Supreme Court nominees in 1894, but the issue was not one of policy or ideology. The president had failed to consult with the appropriate New York senator. The lawmaker then invoked the concept of "senatorial courtesy," which gave a member veto power over a nominee when the individual was personally distasteful to him.[32]

For senators the most burdensome aspect of making judicial and legal selections involved patronage, the designation of favored candidates for government positions. Lawmakers had to sift through voluminous letters of recommendation in favor of a candidate and equally strong documents against particular aspirants in choosing district attorneys and judges to recommend to the White House. Then there were the collectors of internal revenue, land office employees, and minor offices in profusion. "The candidates for these federal offices are more numerous than the leaves in Valambrosa," complained Julius Caesar Burrows of Michigan in 1896, "and some deserving ones must be disappointed." (Imagine a senator a century later throwing out a reference to John Milton's *Paradise Lost* in a letter to a constituent!) All these documents poured into the Capitol. More arduous was meeting and interviewing the candidates for United States marshal, collector of internal revenue, and district attorney. Each of these potential officeholders was certain that if he could just sit down with the senator from his state, his success would be assured. In a political system in which the parties still wielded great influence, patronage was an intricate system of reward and punishment that absorbed senatorial time and energy. Because the McKinley administration would continue into a second term with its previous appointments largely intact, there was a little less patronage pressure than had been the case four years earlier.[33]

The last session of the Fifty-sixth Congress proved very productive for the Senate and the White House. In three months of work, Congress passed the Platt Amendment, which regulated American relations with Cuba; created a civil government for the Philippines; and approved legislation to reorganize the army after its disappointing performance in Cuba and the Philippines. The issue of the merchant marine remained unresolved in the decade and a half before World War I. The McKinley White House cooperated with Capitol Hill in these endeavors, and an era of legislative-executive harmony seemed possible as the new century opened. The editors of the *Philadelphia Press* said that "no executive in the history of the country . . . has given a greater exhibition of his influence over Congress than President McKinley."[34]

One reminder of the Senate's tradition of unlimited debate and filibusters surfaced at the close of the session. Lawmakers routinely allocated
government "pork" on pet projects, and the rivers and harbors appropriation bill, usually passed within days or hours of adjournment, was a recurrent event. Western senators, certain that the East and Middle West did
better in the competition for federal dollars, wanted more money for irrigation projects in their arid region. Thomas H. Carter, a Montana Republican, talked the rivers and harbors bill to death to make this point. In this
period, filibusters were most effective at the end of a session, when the
clock and a mandated date for adjournment helped the protesters achieve
their goals. During the next ten years similar talkathons would be customary for political parties. Yet they were more of an annoyance than lightning
rods for partisan discord.[35]

As his second term began, President McKinley had significant influence
in the upper house. He had assiduously courted lawmakers over his first four
years in office. As a former member of the House, he understood congressional sensibilities as few other presidents have. During the negotiations for
a peace treaty with Spain in 1898, he had recruited senators from both parties to serve on the delegation that went to Paris to end the war. That strategy had helped to secure narrow approval of the peace document in the
Senate during early 1899. Senator Frye, one of the members in the delegation, recalled what happened when the president asked him to go to Paris.
McKinley stipulated to Frye that he "should give a good excuse" for not
serving his country. When the senator responded that he wanted to "fish
and hunt through September and the first half of October," McKinley "was
not satisfied with this. Strange isn't it?" Through his deft persuasive abilities and his willingness to stroke senatorial egos, McKinley strengthened
the power of his office and achieved many of his legislative goals.[36]

Even a subtle and effective president such as McKinley hit limits when
he tried to move the Senate. The White House sought approval for a strategy to lessen the political damage of the protective tariff in national politics. That goal involved the ratification of several reciprocity treaties.
These pacts had negotiated tariff rates on goods that the United States im-
ported. In return for making the goods of such countries as France, Argentina, and Jamaica more available to American consumers, these trading
partners would provide concessions for the goods Americans exported to
them. Because the treaties threatened the protective system in which many

Republicans believed and that many industries favored, the Senate majority was cool to the idea. During the short session of 1900–1901, the upper chamber refused to act on the issue. The administration planned to bring the treaties up again when lawmakers returned in December 1901. Protectionists worried that the popular McKinley was going to press them to accept the new policy at that time.[37]

To drum up Senate support for his reciprocity policy, McKinley attended the Pan-American Exposition in Buffalo, New York, in early September. On September 5, he spoke out for opening markets, expanding the nation's trade, and by implication endorsing the treaties. The speech was well received. The next day, while McKinley was receiving guests in the Temple of Music, an anarchist named Leon Czolgosz shot him. McKinley died eight days later. Theodore Roosevelt was now the twenty-sixth president.

Although Roosevelt had been governor of New York and was a national hero for his exploits during the Spanish American war, he had limited experience with Congress and its ways. He had served three terms in the New York Assembly two decades earlier and had spent six years in Washington from 1889 to 1895 as a member of the Civil Service Commission. From that latter perspective, which involved how patronage was handled, he had seen Capitol Hill at its most sordid. As vice president, he had presided briefly over the Senate in March 1901, writing, "I have really enjoyed presiding over the Senate for the week the extra session lasted." Because the vice president only voted in the event of a tie, Roosevelt, like other occupants of his office before him, found the job of presiding over the Senate not a demanding one. Once McKinley's cabinet nominees had been confirmed in early 1901 and other routine business discharged, the Senate adjourned. Facing four years of tedium as the presiding officer in the upper house, Roosevelt thought about studying law, since he would have so much free time. When, in June 1901, McKinley ruled out any talk of a third term, Roosevelt spent much of the summer looking ahead to a race for the White House in 1904. Then came Buffalo and Roosevelt's elevation to the presidency.[38]

With the energetic and youthful Roosevelt in the White House and the conservative Senate on Capitol Hill, political observers relished the prospect of a clash between the new president and the men who ran the upper chamber. An Ohio newspaperman, Murat Halstead, wrote, "I shall not feel sorry if some of the great old personages in the Senate, made up largely of stuffing with patronage and money, find their innards ripped up in due time."[39]

## CHAPTER TWO

# The President
# and the Senate Four

THE REPUBLICAN SENATE SURVEYED THEODORE ROOSEVELT WITH
unease as the new president settled into the White House in the autumn of 1901. The senators were accustomed to a leisurely pace of lawmaking without incessant importuning from the White House. They did not
look forward to urgency and crisis as part of their business. "The air of the
Senate, like that of all high altitudes, is clear and calm," wrote the journalist Condit Crane. "Beneath are the clouds and storms; here prevails the
serenity of remoteness and permanence." This new, charismatic president
might upset the measured routines by which the upper house lived.[1]

At the same time, the Senate had much to teach Theodore Roosevelt
about the power of the Republican leaders to compel even an energetic
president to defer to their wishes. As he confronted the political and constitutional barriers that the Senate posed to any chief executive, Roosevelt
learned about the limits of his power as an unelected president. The experience sharpened his resolve to gain power in his own right so that he might
battle the upper house on more equal terms. That goal required him to
learn how the Senate conducted its business and how the interplay of personalities and issues worked to make the Republican leaders so important.
From 1901 to 1904 Roosevelt and the Senate felt each other out in readiness for the disputes over government regulation of business that would lie
ahead if he gained a second term.

In 1901, being a U.S. senator was by no means a full-time job. Congress assembled each year in early December. In odd-numbered years, the session had no fixed time limit and could stretch through the spring and into the early summer before the heat of the city caused everyone who could to flee for cooler climes. Sessions in even-numbered years occurred after a presidential or congressional election, and in the first three decades of the twentieth century, presidential inaugurations fell on March 4, so sessions that opened in even-numbered years by law had to adjourn before March 4 of the following year. These "short sessions" often became a conclave of defeated members, or "lame ducks" who had become cut off from their constituents and suffered repudiation at the polls.[2]

While the new president and the Senate leaders were making big decisions in the late fall of 1901, the freshman members of the Senate sought to learn about Washington and its customs. The capital had its ways, and every arriving lawmaker had to master them. Finding a place to live during a session was not easy. The $5,000 annual salary (about $125,000 in 2005 dollars with no income tax) was seven or eight times what an industrial worker could bring home, but life in the District of Columbia was expensive. Such plush establishments as the Portland Hotel near Dupont Circle and the Arlington Hotel attracted senators. More affluent members, such as James S. McMillan of Michigan, had lavish homes in the city's most fashionable districts. For less wealthy senators, leaving their families at home and living alone in Washington was the only affordable answer.[3]

When they went to work, new senators discovered that they each had the services of a single secretary and $1,500 a year for expenses. Only the most powerful figures could claim spacious offices in the United States Capitol as their base of operations. Others had to work out of dark, dingy offices in the basement, if they were lucky enough to get such a space at all. The Senate rented offices in a run-down Washington structure called the Maltby Building. Although it provided some badly needed space, District of Columbia authorities had labeled the facility a fire hazard. At this time, senators lacked the large staffs and extensive support systems that arrived in the middle of the twentieth century.[4]

To supplement their salaries, men who were not wealthy practiced law during the congressional recesses, ran their businesses, and in some cases lived by writing. Albert J. Beveridge of Indiana noted in 1903 that the *Saturday Evening Post* had paid him more than $30,000 for the articles he had composed for its pages since 1899. In modern terms, that amount would represent hundreds of thousands of dollars. The ethical rules were still being worked out. Joseph B. Foraker, an Ohio Republican, did unpublicized legal work for the Standard Oil Company. When his relations with the company were revealed in 1908, the disclosures helped end his political career.[5]

In 1901 there were no conflict-of-interest rules, public-disclosure procedures, and ethical requirements such as exist in the modern Senate. Members often crossed moral lines and behaved in ways that today would trigger an investigation of their conduct. No rules existed about revealing financial holdings, and so senators owned stock in companies whose interests they pushed on Capitol Hill. Nelson Aldrich of Rhode Island had control of street railways in Providence that profited from the way he wrote tax and regulatory laws. Wisconsin's John Coit Spooner was just one senator who owned railroad securities; Francis E. Warren of Wyoming operated sheep ranches and kept tariff rates high on the wool his foreign competitors grew. A wry colleague called Warren "the greatest shepherd since Abraham." In their minds, senators separated personal and public business when they voted, or thought that they did. Yet the temptation to profit was always there. The insider saying in Washington was that a Senate seat was worth $60,000 per annum to its occupant.[6]

When the pressures of the Senate's business became too intense, members sought refreshment in the "thirst parlor" that operated openly in the Capitol. Louis Ludlow, a newspaperman who first started covering Congress in this period, recalled that "one of the first notes that greeted my ear" when he reached the building "was the clinking of glasses." Other senators brought alcohol onto the floor in glasses that were supposedly filled with tea. A former Senate page, J. Franklin Little, recalled seeing "senators and congressmen so piss-assed drunk they have to have somebody to help them." Among them was Charles A. Culberson of Texas, who became known as "the senator from Battle Creek" for his frequent trips to dry out at a Michigan sanitarium after his binges, and Beveridge was later nicknamed "Beverage."[7]

Senators had other fleshly pleasures available. Washington in those years had a "red light district within one square mile of the White House grounds." J. Franklin Little observed that some members had dalliances closer to home in the Capitol: "I've seen them come out with their pants down." Washington was still a small town with moderate vices. It would be another century before a Republican senatorial candidate had to drop out of a race in 2004 when his taste for sex clubs with whips, chains, and cages was disclosed.[8]

As the more prestigious of the two branches of Congress, the Senate attracted the greatest share of gossip and speculation. Tongues wagged when Edward O. Wolcott of Colorado won $12,000 on the turn of a faro card at a European casino. With its smaller size, more exciting personalities, and reputation as a place for interesting debate, the upper house was easier to comprehend as an institution. The representatives, no matter how colorful or controversial they might be, commanded less respect than did the two senators from each state. To members of the Senate went better treatment from hotels, deference when they moved around the city, and more coverage from the press. As one commentator about Congress put it in 1899, "The sight of a Congressman talking with his Senator reminds one of a good little boy being sent on an errand—he looks so pleased to do as he is told."[9]

Because of the attention lavished upon them, senators developed a heady sense of self-importance. Fred Dubois of Idaho said, "There is no office I would have except that of Senator," and senators spoke of being "promoted" or "translated" to the upper house, much to the disgust of representatives. "There is more independence of thought and action in the Senate than in the House," wrote the journalist Henry L. West in 1901, a judgment with which senators would readily have agreed. Members also viewed with disdain the prospect of accepting a cabinet position and leaving the Senate. John Coit Spooner said of such choices that "the Senate is a much more independent, and I think lofty position than a position in the Cabinet."[10]

New senators had to learn the intricacies of the body's written rules and the folkways of a group steeped in self-imposed traditions. At this time, there was no firm custom as there would be later in the century against freshmen making speeches during their first session, but at the same time some recognition of the Senate's patience was expected. Albert J. Beveridge arrived in late December 1899 as an incoming member. He made a well-received speech on imperialism on January 9, 1900. The public acclaim that greeted his flag-waving oration further swelled the new senator's already ample sense of self-importance. Several months later, when he spoke again on the issue of trade with Puerto Rico, his colleagues had had enough of this overbearing manner. As Beveridge began his remarks, one by one the members hazed him when they walked noisily out of the chamber. The next day a Democratic senator delivered a parody of Beveridge's pompous speaking style.[11]

Within the confines of the clubby atmosphere, tempers sometimes boiled over when senators disliked each other. During the summer of 1902, as Congress neared adjournment in the oppressive heat, Joseph Weldon Bailey, a volatile and temperamental Texan, took offense when Beveridge criticized his Lone Star State colleague for an attack on a State Department official. After an exchange of words, Bailey said that if Beveridge would not withdraw his comments, "then, damn you, I'll make you!" The Texan lunged for the throat of his adversary, but other senators intervened and nothing further happened.[12]

Another sensational encounter took place between Benjamin "Pitchfork Ben" Tillman of South Carolina and his state's other senator, John L. McLaurin. Tillman was a one-eyed racist with a hot temper who got his name from threatening to stick Grover Cleveland in his "fat ribs" with a pitchfork in the 1890s. In 1902 his assault on McLaurin led to a fistfight on the floor, and the Senate censured the two combatants. The resulting scandal caused Theodore Roosevelt to bar Tillman from White House functions for his lack of decorum and respectability.[13]

Dealing with the clash of personalities and conducting legislative business was the job of the leadership in both parties. For the Democratic minority, their days of controlling the upper house in the early 1890s were a fading memory. In fact, at the start of the Roosevelt presidency the Democrats lacked a strong leader of their delegation. Arthur Pue Gorman of Maryland had played that role for the preceding ten years, but he had lost his seat in 1899 and would not return for three years. In the meantime, the opposition party struggled to present a united face to the GOP majority.

The Democrats still split along the lines that had sundered their party during the 1890s. Eastern senators in the "Democracy" believed in the gold standard for the currency. The inflationary policy of coining silver into money at an appropriate ratio with gold commanded Democratic adherents from the agrarian South and West, where inflation would raise crop prices and make debts easier to pay. Free silver, as this policy was then called, became a fading issue once gold was discovered in South Africa and the Yukon. Yet, even the success of the Republican majority in enacting the Gold Standard law in 1900 did not diminish the enthusiasm for silver among Democratic senators, an allegiance that would continue for decades.[14]

The main source of Democratic strength in and out of Congress was the South. The still-strong passions engendered by the Civil War and the race issue made the Democratic Party, "the party of the fathers," the only choice for white voters in most sections of Dixie. Local politics in that region produced some turnover among Democrats, but cannier leaders recognized how seniority in Congress could work to their advantage. For their part, the Republicans viewed the southerners with genial disdain. When asked his opinion of the senators from Dixie, a Colorado Republican replied, "Well, they seem to be a lazy, tobacco-chewing casual lot of fellows, but they are so d--d rotten poor, I'm proud of 'em."[15]

The stereotype of the southern senators—grandiloquent, verbose, and racist—had not yet become a Washington cliché, but the elements of the image were coming together. Joseph Weldon Bailey arrived in 1901 after ten years in the House. He was one of the great orators on the floor of that day, but he also had an extravagant lifestyle underwritten by a thriving corporate law practice. A British visitor, the Fabian socialist Beatrice Webb, found him "a cad of the worst description, a strange combination of low class actor and rowdy stump orator." Living beyond his means, with fancy horses and large estates, preaching the stale doctrines of state rights and small government to keep blacks in their place, Bailey would be the quintessential Democrat for the next dozen years.[16]

Real power, of course, lay with the Republican majority and its deferential allies on the Democratic side. A one-term Republican from Oregon, Joseph Simon, told a friend after a year in office that "it is very difficult for a new Senator to get very deep inside of the little ring that controls legislation in the Senate and, practically, the legislation of the country. This little coterie of Senators is extremely jealous of its power and will not permit an addition to its number." As the New York Times observed, "in the Senate the leaders have risen to their places because they can lead, and have solidified their leadership by their strategic positions."[17]

The embodiment of the ruling insiders was Nelson Wilmarth Aldrich of Rhode Island. He dominated the inside group called The Four and was depicted in the press as a "chess player with men." By 1901, Aldrich was approaching his sixtieth birthday and had been in the upper house for twenty years. "A handsome man with piercing eyes and a flowing white mustache," Aldrich had a safe seat in his tiny state. He disdained electoral politics and allowed his followers to ensure that he was returned to office every six years. Devoted to the promotion of business enterprise and to the protective tariff that raised customs duties on imports to help American firms, he took little account of public opinion either in Rhode Island or nationally. As an aide wrote after his death, "Aldrich at heart believed that the masses of people did not know what they wanted or what was best for them in the way of legislation."[18]

The Republican leaders of the Senate (left to right, O. H. Platte, John C. Spooner, William B. Allison, and Nelson Aldrich) map out strategy on the verandah of Nelson Aldrich's Rhode Island mansion during the summer of 1903. (SENATE HISTORICAL OFFICE)

Admirers liked to portray Aldrich as a far-seeing statesman. He rarely spoke on the floor and allowed associates to make the public show. He was apt to leave the intense work to his colleagues while he formulated grand strategy. An irritated Orville H. Platt of Connecticut, one of The Four, exploded in early 1905 when Aldrich made an unscheduled trip abroad, leaving Platt to manage the Senate: "I think it inexcusable for Aldrich to go off to Europe as he did, but he is always doing inexcusable things." A narrow conception of the needs of society, based on his Rhode Island experience, formed his principles. As long as the protective tariff remained in place, the national welfare would be safe. Social inequities arose from natural forces and could not be changed through legislation. Whatever existed was right, and the Senate should leave reform alone. The plight of child labor or unsafe working conditions for industrial employees were dilemmas that could be ignored.[19]

The three other members of the ruling quartet shared Aldrich's conservatism but had more human qualities than their leader. Platt had been in the chamber since 1879. Something of an intellectual, Platt read the classics with his wife in the evening. Other senators looked to him for guidance and regarded him as the most principled member of the hierarchy. He was, wrote a colleague, "capable in more ways than any other man in the Senate of doing what the exigencies of the day from time to time put upon him." Platt defended the protective tariff with enthusiasm but had a larger sense than Aldrich did of how times were demanding a bigger role for government.[20]

The other two Republican leaders hailed from the Middle West. William Boyd Allison of Iowa once had presidential hopes that William McKinley extinguished in 1896. He was seventy-two in 1901, with white hair and a beard, and a stoical look that reflected his innate caution. The Washington joke was that Allison could walk on pianos from Des Moines to Washington and never strike a note. As the new century began, he faced a rising tide of discontent in his home state, where unhappiness with high tariffs emerged.[21]

Some of Allison's constituents, fearful of the power of big business, believed that the price of consumer goods they purchased rose because of the tariff. Meanwhile, the farm products of the "golden buckle on the corn belt" such as wheat and other grains enjoyed no support and protection from foreign competitors. The "Iowa Idea" of some of Allison's opponents was to lower tariff rates on goods that large American businesses made and sold overseas at reduced prices to foreign consumers. That would help American consumers, Iowans contended. Allison responded to these pressures, and tensions over the tariff created some strain among the ruling four senators as soon as Theodore Roosevelt became president.[22]

John Coit Spooner of Wisconsin rounded out the leadership quartet. With his thick hair, high forehead, and pince-nez glasses, he looked like the high-powered railroad lawyer he had been in the Badger State. He had been in Washington for a single term from 1885 to 1891 but lost in the Democratic landslide of 1890. He spent part of the next six years as one of the attorneys for the receivership of the Northern Pacific Railroad, which had failed in the Panic of 1893. The job paid him more than $100,000. Elected to the Senate again in 1896, he moved into a leadership spot as chairman of the Committee on Rules, whose duties included the allocation of offices among his fellow senators. He once complained, "I am utterly weary of being the room clerk of the Senate."[23]

Spooner led the Republicans on the floor. Theodore Roosevelt called him a "Senate lawyer," and he was renowned as an expert on senatorial procedure and constitutional law. In debate, he often demolished the Democrats. At home in Wisconsin, however, he faced the rising power of Governor Robert M. La Follette and the progressive movement. In time, that opposition persuaded Spooner to leave the Senate. For the moment, he and his colleagues dominated the upper house.[24]

The Republican majority was more than the sum of these four men, however. Such important figures as George Frisbie Hoar and Henry Cabot Lodge, Sr., of Massachusetts; Marcus A. Hanna of Ohio; and Eugene Hale and William P. Frye of Maine provided significant direction for the way the Senate worked. A senator such as Hale enjoyed great influence on naval affairs because he specialized in that issue so close to the heart of his sea-going voters. Until his death in 1902, James S. McMillan was an important adjunct of the leadership with his poker games at his "School of Philosophy" club in his palatial home on Vermont Avenue. The Republicans played hard for low stakes. While the chips clicked and the cards were dealt, the party's strategy for the next day and the remainder of the session would emerge.[25]

The formal mechanism for wielding power among Republicans was the party's caucus, or conference, to which all GOP senators belonged, chaired by Allison. Out of that group flowed the eleven-member Republican Steering Committee, which set policy for the majority. Aldrich and his allies dominated Steering's decisions and also controlled the Committee on Committees, which assigned members to the various committees. From these vantage points they held sway over the major committees. Aldrich headed Finance, which oversaw tariffs. Allison chaired Appropriations, and Spooner directed Rules. The Republican majority was cohesive, purposeful, and efficient in its control. There seemed to be little chance that its authority would be threatened by the Democrats. As Thomas Collier Platt, a Republican of New York, wrote Allison in July 1899 about the issues before the Grand Old Party, "I am with and for the Government, and I consider the interests of the Government as embodied in you and Senator Aldrich. What you say goes. Kindly keep me posted as to what you do, so I may not go astray."[26]

The Four believed that presidents did best when they followed the lead of the Senate. For that reason, Theodore Roosevelt and the chamber were a philosophical mismatch. The pretensions of the upper house to a serious role in foreign affairs struck Roosevelt as insane. "I do not much admire the Senate," he wrote in 1905, "because it is such a helpless body when efficient work for good is to be done." In private, he criticized senators. In gossipy Washington, presidential aspersions soon got back to their targets. Lawmakers did not appreciate hearing that they had been called "criminals" or "scoundrels" by the chief executive. In the case of Hale of Maine, Roosevelt told one the members of his Cabinet in 1908 that the senator was "a horrible, bigoted, narrow minded selfish voluptuary."[27]

During the autumn of 1901, the Republicans in the Senate and the new president eyed each other with wary skepticism. Roosevelt wanted to be elected in his own right in 1904, and a battle with the Senate would not aid that goal. The Republican leadership had not approved of McKinley's tariff reciprocity campaign in 1901, and they hoped that the trade treaties would be shelved. Yet on taking office Roosevelt pledged to continue McKinley's programs. It soon became evident that the new president's vow was subject to many interpretations. When he encountered opposition about reciprocity treaties from the heavyweights on Capitol Hill, Roosevelt retreated.

The new president consulted widely with senators during the first days of his administration about his annual message to Congress. The document would represent his first formal statement of where he wanted the country to go. Aldrich recommended that the president should refer to the treaties but offer no formal recommendation. In public, the Republican leader warned against "tinkering with the Tariff" through "the negotiations of reciprocity." He delivered the same message to the White House in private. As a result, Roosevelt made only a passing mention of the treaties in the message in December, and they died, never to be revived. For the next four years, Roosevelt struggled to regain the political initiative with the Senate that he had forfeited.[28]

During the first year of his presidency, Roosevelt found more reasons not to cross the Senate. When he tried to push a bill granting Cuba, nominally independent but in fact an American protectorate, lower tariff rates on tobacco and sugar, the president ran into resistance from lawmakers beholden to domestic producers. A journalist reported that the episode left hard feelings among senators "who think T.R. too much president, & complain that he doesn't lie down and let senators walk over him." Despite his tough stance, Roosevelt lost this battle, though Cuba eventually received its tariff concessions.[29]

On the issue of tariff protection itself, Roosevelt and The Four agreed that it would be wise during the congressional campaign of 1902 not to stress such a divisive subject. By late summer Roosevelt decided that a conference with the leadership would be prudent. Just before he left on a tour of the Midwest, he summoned the four leaders, plus his friend Henry Cabot Lodge, to his house in Oyster Bay, New York. According to later political lore, the young chief executive and the congressional leaders agreed on September 16, 1902, that Roosevelt could speak as he pleased on issues other than the tariff. He was free, for example, to argue for regulation of large corporations. On the tariff, however, he would defer to the views of the senatorial elders. The episode became famous as the moment when Roosevelt yielded to the Senate leaders to ensure his election in 1904.[30]

The real story was more complex. Roosevelt agreed that the tariff should not be the main focus of his speeches on regulating corporations. Since the president did not understand the ramifications of protection and the tariff, except in a political sense, it suited him to concentrate on restraining corporations, where he felt comfortable. That strategy served his goal of keeping the Senate quiet and preventing any alternative candidate from appearing to threaten his nomination.

The 1902 elections brought little change in the composition of the Senate. Both parties gained two seats as the last four members of the Populist Party who had been elected in 1896 were replaced. For the upper house itself, the most important result of the voting was that Joseph G. Cannon of Illinois replaced David B. Henderson as Speaker of the House of Representatives when Congress reconvened in December. "Uncle Joe" Cannon, as he was known to his colleagues, was perhaps even more conservative than any of The Four. He operated from a strong sense of institutional loyalty to the House. As he told reporters in 1905, he was "heartily tired of the Senate dominating both houses of Congress." Over the next seven years, Cannon asserted the power of the lower house against even the leaders of his own party in the Senate.[31]

During the short session that followed the 1902 elections and as the adjournment date of March 3 neared, the Senate faced an end-of-session filibuster by Indiana Republican Albert Beveridge against a bill to admit New Mexico, Arizona, and Oklahoma as states. By the close of the session there were several other filibusters. The session expired with much left undone, including authorization of a canal across Central America. Roosevelt called lawmakers back after March 4 to resolve that matter. In an ironic comment on the process, Republican William E. Mason of Illinois, whose term was expiring and who himself was filibustering, urged his colleagues, "Amend your rules so that a majority can transact your business. This is a government of majorities." The plea had no effect and the filibuster remained as a problem that no senator of either party wanted to address.[32]

The Democratic Party gained control of the Maryland legislature in early 1902, and Arthur Pue Gorman was returned to Washington, where he resumed the post of minority leader. When the Senate reconvened for the Fifty-eighth Congress in March 1903, Gorman became chair of the Democratic conference. There was even talk that the Marylander might use the leadership of the minority as a means of getting the Democratic presidential nomination in 1904. That was unlikely because the Democrats in the Senate were so fractured over foreign and domestic policy that getting them to move in the same direction would test all of Gorman's abilities.[33] The brief 1903 session had been called to consider the treaty with Colombia allowing the United States to construct a canal across the Isthmus of Panama, which was Colombian territory. Once the treaty won approval on March 17, 1903, the Senate adjourned until it met in another special session in November. In that conclave, another treaty, with the Panamanian government, which had revolted against Colombian rule, was discussed. The rebels, encouraged by Theodore Roosevelt, had agreed to the pact with the United States to make a canal possible. Gorman decided that Roosevelt's use of executive power provided a winning issue for the Democrats. They would assail the "dictatorial" methods of the president that had led to this foreign-policy success. As it turned out, the seizure of Panama was popular and Americans cared more for the result than the methods used to oust Colombia as a player in the process.[34]

On December 12, 1903, twenty-seven of the thirty-three Democratic senators met in the Minority Caucus Room to form a strategy. To beat the administration and the fifty-seven Republicans and block the treaty, the Democrats had to act together. Gorman proposed that if two-thirds of the caucus members voted in favor of a resolution on a disputed issue, the decision should compel all Democratic senators to vote that way. From the leader's point of view, such a tactic would demonstrate cohesion, even though it meant restricting the right of a senator to vote as he pleased. After several days of debate the Democrats adopted the rule but provided dissenters a loophole in the event a constitutional issue was raised, the interest of constituents was involved, or the state legislature sent them instructions. The practical result was that nothing changed for the Democrats in the Senate, as Gorman soon discovered.[35]

On the Panama Canal issue, disunity ruled among the Democrats. Public opinion supported Roosevelt for blocking Colombia and sparking a revolution in Panama. Few Democrats wanted to be on the wrong side of the issue. The treaty sailed through in February 1904 by a vote of 66 to 14. Gorman had been embarrassed and his leadership called into question. The Democrats continued as a powerless minority in the chamber. An abashed Gorman wrote in his journal that his effort to unite Senate Democrats against Roosevelt over Panama had "Ended in Smash."[36]

Since 1904 was a presidential election year, the upper house adjourned on May 7 and awaited the results of the voting in November. One prominent Republican senator, Mark Hanna of Ohio, had been a potential challenger to Roosevelt's nomination. After he got to the White House, Roosevelt had been very suspicious of Hanna, who had been McKinley's good friend and political ally and backer. Roosevelt feared that Hanna might use his organizational base within the party to challenge him for the nomination. Enemies of Hanna fed these presidential suspicions. There was an undeclared struggle between the two men, with Roosevelt doing most of the fighting, during 1902–3, but it is not clear that the Ohio senator ever had any intention of challenging the incumbent.[37]

In any case, Hanna died in mid-February 1904 after a brief illness. Any hope on the part of conservative Republican senators that he might declare against Roosevelt had long since evaporated, and they had to be content with placing one of their own on the ticket to balance the uncertainties of Roosevelt. The Republican National Convention looked to the Midwest and the upper house for its choice for vice president. The gesture was also designed to placate the business community, where suspicions of Roosevelt's "radicalism" simmered. Charles W. Fairbanks of Indiana was, in the words of one Republican, "almost as timid as was the boy who was afraid to say boo to the goose." At six feet seven, Fairbanks was imposing in size but not in political energy or charisma. His dullness made him a pleasing choice for senators who feared "that if Roosevelt is elected he will 'do things.'"[38]

During his first term, Roosevelt had cooperated with the Senate leadership and, under their adroit flattery, had even come to enjoy the experience. He found that Aldrich, Platt, Spooner, and Allison were practical men who kept their word even when they disagreed with the White House.

Roosevelt enjoyed it when people deferred to him, and The Four kept their qualms about the president carefully concealed. Both sides discovered reasons for entente, and a spirit of cooperation and fellowship blossomed, so Roosevelt could write in March 1903 that "with every one of these men I at times differ radically on important questions, but they are the leaders and their great intelligence and power and their desire in the last resort to do what is best for the government make them not only essential to work with, but desirable to work with." The legislative-executive rapprochement was fragile, however, and, in his passion to be elected in his own right, Roosevelt was kidding himself. The good will between White House and Senate depended on Roosevelt's readiness to accept what Capitol Hill, and especially The Four, told him was possible and right. Should he expand his policy agenda during the second term, confrontation with the Senate would become more likely.[39]

The election was a walkover for Roosevelt. The Democrats selected as their presidential nominee a colorless and inept state judge from New York named Alton B. Parker. "I was afraid that when the campaign began that possibly Parker might develop some unexpected strength," said Jonathan P. Dolliver of Iowa, "but so far he appears to be a blank cartridge." Roosevelt did not campaign, as was the custom for incumbent presidents. Instead, senators from the inner circle helped make the Republican case for retaining Roosevelt. Orville Platt told a Rhode Island audience that the president had been "tried and found true and faithful, and able." The American people, the senator went on, "like him, believe in him, admire him, and are growing more and more to love him."[40]

Behind this friendly rhetoric lingered suspicions. The leadership in the upper house feared what Roosevelt would do to assist the growing number of reformers within the Grand Old Party. Spooner fretted that "the tidal wave of populism and radicalism" of the 1890s had "certainly reached Washington within the last year, and the geyser seems to be bubbling over in the White House yard." The campaign offered few clues as to where Roosevelt might go in another term, and a sense of wary anticipation permeated the party as the election approached.[41]

Beyond the Senate, forces for change were gathering momentum. When Congress failed to act on an amendment to provide for direct elections of senators, states took steps of their own. In the South, Democrats held primaries in which the candidate with the highest number of votes for a senatorial vacancy would be the choice of the legislature. Legislators in Oregon adopted a law in 1901 whereby a future legislature would have to select the candidate who had received the most votes in the general election as a senatorial choice. In the first election in which the system was tried, the Oregon legislature nevertheless chose an aspirant who had not won the most popular votes. Accordingly, a second primary law, adopted in response to this development, made the link between voting for a candidate and the election of a senator more explicit. Oregon's experience showed clearly that popular sentiment was turning toward direct elections.[42]

Two developing scandals further eroded public confidence in the probity of the upper house. First, Senator John H. Mitchell of Oregon was implicated in fraud related to the management of public lands, and as the evidence against him accumulated, an indictment after the 1904 election appeared certain. Then, Joseph R. Burton of Kansas was indicted and convicted of postal fraud. The case worked its way through the appeals court during 1904. Charges of bribery and undue influence involving other senators circulated in Washington.[43]

The clubby Senate, led by The Four, stood at the apex of its power relative to both the president and the House in the early twentieth century, but its moment of triumph would be brief. Popular discontent with the way the Senate operated would soon put the chamber under political siege. Meanwhile, tensions with the activist president who wanted to make his historic mark on the country would erupt. These clashes between the White House and Capitol Hill would feed the perception that the Senate had, in the words of a magazine of the day, "been built up as an enduring and unchangeable power, always grasping for new privileges, not directly responsible to the electors, concerned chiefly for its prerogatives and the protection of special interests." The implications of that harsh judgment would be played out during the decade in which Theodore Roosevelt and William Howard Taft occupied the White House. In the process, the nature of the Senate would be changed in what reformers hoped would be a fundamental manner. These advocates of a new Senate would learn, however, that transforming the upper house was a more demanding political task than simply revising the way senators were chosen.[44]

## CHAPTER THREE

# La Follette
# Challenges the Senate

A FTER THEODORE ROOSEVELT'S LANDSLIDE ELECTION VICTORY IN 1904, talk of an impending collision between the popular president and the Senate leadership of his own party filled Washington. Roosevelt wanted to be a more assertive chief executive in the four years left to him in the presidency. His announcement on election night in 1904 that he would not be a candidate four years later left the clock running on his prestige and effectiveness. If he wished to regulate the railroads and accomplish other reforms, he had to move quickly.

This presidential energy ran up against Nelson Aldrich and Orville Platt, who distrusted government interference in the economy. They persuaded Roosevelt to defer any changes in the tariff until after the next congressional elections, if then. Roosevelt had no problem with that, since the tariff issue bored him. On the hot topic of regulation of the railroads, which was currently very popular in the Middle West, senators knew that Roosevelt wanted action, but they hoped to diffuse his energies and postpone attempts to strengthen the power of the Interstate Commerce Commission to oversee railroad rates.

Roosevelt was not about to go slow. "On the interstate commerce business, which I regard as a matter of principle, I shall fight," he wrote in January 1905. "On the tariff, which I regard as a matter of expediency, I shall endeavor to get the best results I can, but I shall not break with my party."

This intention aroused resistance, and the *New York Herald* reported that "some men in the republican party even now are seriously discussing the formation of a 'conservative' wing of the republican party for the purpose of fighting the president and his measures."[1]

The latent tension between the Senate and the White House appeared first on a foreign policy issue. During the short session of 1904–1905, Roosevelt sent ten arbitration treaties to Capitol Hill. These pacts looked to settle future differences with nine European countries and Mexico through peaceful talks. As written, each document stated that the president could at various stages work out a "special agreement" during the negotiations. Sensing executive usurpation of its historic role in treaty making, the Senate rebelled. Even such a staunch personal friend of the president's as Henry Cabot Lodge insisted that these "agreements" were in fact treaties that the Senate must approve. Resistance to his authority in foreign policy angered Roosevelt, who fired off a testy letter to the chairman of the Senate Foreign Relations Committee, which he also released to the press. In it he called the Senate's position "a step backward." Lawmakers complained of "Executive interference" and by a vote of 50 to 9 went ahead with the language asserting the Senate's role that Roosevelt disliked. The president then withdrew the treaties.[2]

The incident left hard feelings on Capitol Hill. A friend of the president, James R. Garfield, said that "The Senate is in a bad mood & there is a danger that all general legislation may be held up." Senator Jacob H. Gallinger of New Hampshire, an influential conservative, wrote that Roosevelt "has started out to dominate (if not intimidate) the Senate, but he will find that more of a job than he thinks." Roosevelt was equally upset. In private he "spoke bitterly about the Senate and its attitude."[3]

For the Senate the public venting of anger against the White House came when its own reputation was under attack in the press. The convictions of Senator John H. Mitchell of Oregon and Joseph R. Burton of Kansas moved journalists to focus again on Senate ethics.[4] Bad as it was to have two guilty senators, other embarrassments for the chamber came during early 1905. In Connecticut, Morgan Bulkeley won a seat amid charges that he "openly avows his belief in purchasing votes" in the legislature. A clergyman said that his selection "marks the lowest ebb of Connecticut politics within the memory of man." The editor of the *Hartford Courant* lamented to Orville Platt that "it doesn't seem as if the gentlemen who make up what is so frequently called through the country the rich men's club of America realized the delicacy of the position of the United States Senate."[5]

Later in the year a probe into the Equitable Life Assurance Company and its majority stockholder James Hazen Hyde led to more troubling news involving Senator Chauncey M. Depew of Connecticut, who was one of the great after-dinner speakers of the era and something of a blowhard. Widely regarded as the instrument of the "Easy Boss" of the state, his senatorial colleague Thomas Collier Platt, Depew was enriched through a clandestine retainer of $20,000 per year from the Equitable. He also had an interest in lucrative real estate loans that the Equitable made. The spectacle of a senator as the paid agent of an insurance company was distasteful to many observers. These revelations led one New York clergyman to write to Jonathan P. Dolliver of Iowa, "The whole country is waiting for a leader in the Senate. It is a national misfortune that most of your colleagues are looked upon as agents for the great corporations. Many of your leaders have accepted the retainers from the large corporations, and in the nature of the case are not free men."[6]

In April 1905 the first crack in the position of The Four occurred when Orville Platt died. As midwestern sentiment for railroad regulation mounted in 1905–6, Allison and Spooner increasingly distanced themselves from Aldrich, who was growing more and more conservative and becoming a lightning rod for discontent about the Senate.

In January 1905, the Wisconsin legislature chose the governor, Robert M. La Follette, as the state's new junior senator. As one of La Follette's enemies put it on the day the voting took place, "within an hour the political villainy would have been consummated" or, in other words, the reformist governor would be elected. Claiming the pressure of state business, La Follette did not go to Washington to take his seat until the Senate assembled in December 1905 for its regular session. Once there, his presence signaled a crucial change in the nature of the Senate, one that would shape the next decade.[7]

Robert La Follette was fifty when he came to Washington. He had served in the House in the late 1880s and then had gone home to practice law and seek state office. A bribe attempt by a wealthy Republican in 1891 soured him on the regular Republicans. He built a following among dissenting Republicans that put him into the governor's chair in 1900. La Follette,

Robert La Follette, the fiery Progressive reformer from Wisconsin, read the roll call of the votes of his Senate colleagues to his audiences on the campaign trail and sought to use his Senate base as a springboard to the presidency. (*LA FOLLETTE'S AUTOBIOGRAPHY*, 1913)

or "Battle Bob" as his friends called him, assailed the railroads, conservative politicians, and accumulated wealth. With a shrewd eye for publicity and a red-hot speaking style, La Follette captured national attention with the "Wisconsin Idea," whereby the University of Wisconsin fed policy ideas to the governor and the legislature. By 1904 his ambition to be president led him to see the Senate as a logical next step. On the wall of his study at his Wisconsin farm hung words from Robert Browning that, the senator told friends, summed up his credo as a politician and national leader: "Never dreamed, though right were worsted, wrong would triumph/Held we fall to rise, are baffled to fight better/Sleep to wake." That was the spirit that La Follette carried to Washington.[8]

For the Senate to serve as the springboard for La Follette's presidential hopes, he looked to the same methods that had served him so well from Wausau to Green Bay. On the stump, the short, dynamic governor would read out the voting records of his foes to crowds around the state. Now the

Senate offered a new field for this technique. Bristling with animosity toward his perceived foes and convinced of his own rectitude, La Follette intended to show his new colleagues that he did not plan to become conservative after "a few months in the Senate refrigerator," as he put it in his memoirs.[9]

Few senators were less suited to the men's club ethos of the Senate. La Follette could accept and wanted deferential followers but was always suspicious of the loyalty of colleagues in a political fight. Working alone fit his aloof, distrustful nature. Appeals to "go along to get along" meant nothing to La Follette if they entailed submerging his aims in the interest of some common result. He would always be willing to use the Senate for his own ends, but never really adapted to the customs and rituals of the place. One contemporary of La Follette offered a detached view of La Follette's operating style. Herbert Parsons, a New York congressman, wrote in 1911: "Senator La Follette is not a worker at his congressional duties. He is a grand-stand player, taking up certain issues and handling them effectively. But so far as the day in and day out work is concerned, he is little of a factor."[10]

La Follette came to the Senate just as a major confrontation was brewing between the White House and the upper chamber about regulating the railroads. In the first decade of the new century, consumer and commodity prices rose as an increasing gold supply and a growing population fed inflation. When railroads raised their rates, shippers and consumers complained about the impact on their localities. Across the South and Midwest, voters increasingly demanded government remedies to higher rail rates; meanwhile, commercial associations and industry groups lobbied Congress. Theodore Roosevelt believed that the federal government should regulate the railroads to stave off more dramatic solutions such as public ownership of railway lines.[11]

Roosevelt's solution involved giving greater power to the Interstate Commerce Commission. That regulatory body, founded in 1887, had seen its authority erode during the 1890s because of unfavorable court rulings, lack of congressional sympathy, and apathy from the White House. Now seemed the right time to give the ICC more discretion to say when a railroad rate was too high and give it the power to impose a fairer rail rate. Roosevelt proposed in his annual message of 1904: "The government must in increasing degree supervise and regulate the workings of the railways engaged in interstate commerce." Conservatives saw such language as a first step on the road to socialism and government ownership of the railroads.[12]

Politicians knew that advocating lower railroad prices was a winner. A regulatory bill passed the House in February 1905 by 326 to 17. House members, certain that the Senate would move with caution, could with impunity vote for the popular idea of railroad regulation. The upper chamber, bowing to Aldrich and his allies, some with ties to the rail companies, decided that such legislation "ought not to be passed in the Senate without full opportunity for consideration and debate." And so during the summer the Senate Interstate Commerce Committee held public hearings to allow railroad executives the chance to make their case against regulation. But the hearings exposed the secret ways that the industry had pressured Congress and manipulated public opinion. Meanwhile, Roosevelt swayed public opinion through a series of speeches around the country making the case for government regulation.[13]

Once Congress was back in session, the railroad bill, now called the Hepburn bill, for Congressman William P. Hepburn of Iowa, passed again, by a vote of 346 to 7. There was strong support in the House, but members also had a free vote, since again they knew the measure would be decided in the Senate. Democrats gave the administration many votes in the House and were likely to repeat the process in the Senate. Republicans, on the other hand, while they talked of supporting the president also spoke of amending the bill to lessen the threat to the railroads.[14]

The main Republican advocate of the Hepburn bill was Jonathan P. Dolliver of Iowa. Long an Allison protégé, he had become sympathetic to railroad reform, because of pressure from his constituents but also because he believed that the excesses of the rail lines had to be restrained. He and Aldrich had by now become open enemies after some testy exchanges on the floor. To win approval of the bill, Dolliver had been negotiating with Democrats on the Interstate Commerce Committee to have the bill reported to the full Senate for debate. "It is now up to the Senate to beat it if they can," Dolliver wrote with what proved to be overconfidence. "I do not think they can."[15]

Dolliver, however, underestimated the wily Aldrich. After Dolliver won an eight-to-five vote in the committee to send the bill forward, Aldrich made a deal with several Democrats to have "Pitchfork Ben" Tillman of South Carolina manage the measure on the floor. The racist Tillman had been censured in 1902 by the Senate and barred from the White House after a fistfight with a colleague on the Senate floor. For the president now to have to deal with Tillman would complicate White House efforts to get a Senate majority for the Hepburn measure. A bitter Dolliver wrote, "If the railroad fellows had employed a pack of d--d fools to make the worst possible mess of their case they could not have improved on the present situation."[16]

The Senate received the Hepburn bill on February 26, 1906, and debate focused on the extent to which federal courts could review the rate decrees of the ICC. Conservatives hoped that jurists would water down the effect of government regulation. Proponents of the bill sought to limit the judicial role to circumvent this difficulty. As so often happens in the Senate, the battle on the merits of the measure was waged in the constitutional argument about the role of the courts. During March, Roosevelt negotiated with Republican senators about language to resolve the matter of court review.

To get the bill through, the president saw that he would have to win Democratic votes. That meant working with Tillman. To avoid embarrassment to the White House and the senator, Roosevelt turned to an intermediary, a former New Hampshire senator, William E. Chandler, who had become a friend of Tillman's from their days as Senate colleagues. Could Roosevelt and Tillman find twenty-six Democratic votes for the amended bill to go with the twenty Republican members on whom Roosevelt could rely?

As the Senate prepared for the Hepburn bill debate in early 1906, a series of muckraking articles titled "The Treason of the Senate" by David Graham Phillips began to appear in William Randolph Hearst's *Cosmopolitan*. In them, Phillips accused Depew, Aldrich, Thomas C. Platt, Joseph Weldon Bailey, and other senators of betraying the public interest by favoring the moneyed interests that kept them in power. "Treason is a strong word," he wrote, "but not too strong, rather too weak, to characterize the situation in which the Senate is the eager, resourceful, indefatigable agent of interests as hostile to the American people as any invading army could be."[17] Written in an overheated style, the articles were longer on rhetoric than on documented facts, but the cumulative effect was to intensify popular suspicion of the Senate and its members' motives. To counteract their impact, David S. Barry, a Republican journalist who was close to Aldrich, was enlisted to write a series of rebuttals under the title "The Loyalty of the Senate." Lawmakers themselves had articles ghostwritten and delivered speeches denouncing Phillips and his accusations.[18]

These developments did not please Theodore Roosevelt. While at heart he may have shared the sentiments that Phillips expressed about many in the upper house, the president knew that sustained denunciation of the Senate was not serving the interests of the Hepburn bill and other regulatory legislation that the body was considering. Investigative reporters, Roosevelt decided, "are all building up a revolutionary feeling which will most probably take the form of a political campaign."[19]

To preserve his position with the Senate in the negotiations over railroads and to blunt the force of the Phillips series, on April 14, 1906, Roosevelt delivered his now famous speech attacking the tactics of journalists he labeled "muckrakers." He borrowed an image from John Bunyan's *Pilgrim's Progress* of the man who spent so much time raking the muck on the floor that he missed the heavenly crown above. By assailing investigative reporters, Roosevelt hoped to placate the Republicans who disliked the Hepburn bill, but while the president was concentrating on wooing the conservatives, Robert La Follette was about to complicate the situation even more.[20]

The Wisconsin senator had watched the debate over the railroad measure and kept silent, as befitted a new member. Unhappy with the direction the bill was taking, he decided to offer nine amendments that would, he said, improve the proposed law. He had another motive. If he made the senators vote on these changes, he would create roll-call tallies that he could then turn to his advantage on the stump that summer. Members in the upper house preferred voice votes or agreements that left no paper trail of how they had voted. La Follette was determined to put them on the public record. So on April 19, five days after Roosevelt's speech about muckrakers, La Follette began remarks that consumed eight hours over three days of debate.

The opening moments of his oratory brought high drama. La Follette started at midday, following a heated exchange between an Illinois senator and Tillman over the race issue that left the chamber in an agitated state. When La Follette began, some senators went off to lunch. Others made their dislike of him obvious by leaving the chamber. Noting these ideological departures, the speaker spoke to the fascinated gallery:

> I cannot be wholly indifferent to that fact that Senators by their absence at this time indicate their want of interest in what I may have to say about this subject. The public is interested. Unless this important subject is rightly settled, seats now temporarily vacant may be permanently vacated by those who have the right to occupy them at this time.

The visitors applauded La Follette's words, and the chair admonished them to observe Senate rules about keeping their opinions to themselves. As it turned out, over the next few years La Follette's prediction seemed to come true, since many of his tormentors retired or were defeated. And so, this moment when senators "hazed" their colleague came to symbolize La Follette's impact on the institution. However much senators might deny that La Follette had been rebuked, the episode went down in the lore of the Senate. Variants of it would appear decades later in Frank Capra's 1939 film *Mr. Smith Goes to Washington* and Allen Drury's 1959 novel *Advise and Consent*. But melodrama was not the point of La Follette's tactic. The fate of his amendments was less important than the effect of votes now being recorded for later use on the campaign trail. La Follette was the first senator of the twentieth century to see the legislative process as a phase of electoral politics where their votes could help defeat your opponents.[21]

While "The Treason of the Senate" and La Follette's remarks dominated the headlines, Theodore Roosevelt had to abandon his attempt to forge a Democratic-Republican coalition on the Hepburn bill. The alliance simply did not give him the votes he needed. And so he went back to the leadership and made the best deal he could, an about-face that led Democratic senator Bailey of Texas to observe, "Let us have no more talk in the Senate and in the country about this 'ironman'; he is clay, and very common clay at that." Roosevelt endorsed a compromise that Aldrich and Allison had worked out concerning judicial review of the orders of the ICC. The language pleased Aldrich, and Roosevelt got his bill. Senators voted 72 to 3 for the bill on May 18, 1906, and a conference committee hammered out the final wording, which both houses approved a month later. The conservatives believed that Aldrich had won out and that the law "goes out of the Senate much improved," but it was Roosevelt who garnered public credit for the new law and for his efforts to achieve still more to protect consumers and the middle class.[22]

Roosevelt saw this campaign succeed in two other areas. In response to disclosures about unsafe and disgusting conditions in the meatpacking industry, sparked by Upton Sinclair's novel *The Jungle*, lawmakers added a meat inspection amendment to the Agricultural Appropriation Act in 1906. At the same time, the public outcry over meat quality helped move the Pure Food and Drug Act, sponsored by consumer groups, out of the Congress. Again, Roosevelt received public credit for the accomplishments

of the session, much to the dismay of his senatorial critics. *Collier's* magazine captured the consensus: "It has been a great Congress, but perhaps
with the quality of those men who have greatness thrust upon them. Its
best work has been done with apparent reluctance, under the spur of Presidential insistence and the lash of an imperious public opinion."[23]

For La Follette, the end of the session meant that he could try out his
strategy of reading the roll calls in public. He began an extensive summer
tour of the Middle West, where he reported that the response was all that
he could have wished. After a speech in Iowa in early July, he told his family, "It *goes* & some Senators will find a back fire to look after. I suppose
they will think I am the meanest fellow ever to 'go and tell.'"[24]

The La Follette strategy did anger those of his colleagues who were the
targets of his assault. To offset the attacks, the conservatives made speeches
praising each other. They also enlisted their political allies to keep the Wisconsin senator out of their states and away from any official Republican
campaign appearances. As Shelby M. Cullom of Illinois groused, "I would
about as lief be beaten for the Senate as to have the son-of-a-gun come
about." When La Follette returned to the Senate in December, he informed
his wife and political partner, Belle, that "there is a great deal of soreness
toward me I hear but I think they are in doubt about how to get at me." For
all of his fulminations against how the Senate operated, La Follette was
quite willing to rely on the collegial practices of the Senate club to protect
him against political retaliation such as loss of committee assignments.[25]

Senators saw no need, however, to grant Theodore Roosevelt the same
leeway. By now, Washington insiders understood that the president and the
upper house were definitely at odds. Lawmakers complained about Roosevelt's frequent formal messages to them urging more action. The British
ambassador reported home that the president "sends too many Messages,
and they are too long, and the tone of them is resented as didactic if not
dictatorial." The Democrats didn't trust him after the Hepburn Act, and
the Republicans who defended Roosevelt often found themselves the target
of his barbs.[26]

Senators pointed to Senator Joseph B. Foraker of Ohio as a vivid example
of what might happen to a presidential critic. After cooperating in Roosevelt's first term, Foraker and Roosevelt had fallen out over the Hepburn
Act, when Foraker was one of three votes (and the only Republican) against
the measure. Then, in August 1906, a shooting episode occurred in Browns-

ville, Texas, and townspeople blamed African American soldiers stationed at a nearby post. Roosevelt concluded in haste that all the troops had knowledge of the incident and peremptorily discharged them from the service. Foraker came to the defense of the black soldiers and challenged the fairness of Roosevelt's actions. A bitter feud erupted. A dramatic confrontation flared at the annual dinner of the Gridiron Club, in January 1907, and Foraker became the object of presidential wrath. Roosevelt opposed the Ohio senator's efforts to win the 1908 Republican presidential nomination. When Foraker's ties to Standard Oil were exposed, the president helped to defeat him for reelection to the Senate that same year.[27]

But the Foraker-Roosevelt quarrel was a sideshow compared to the struggle between the president and Nelson Aldrich for control of the political agenda in 1907–8. The Four had by now dwindled to a single member. Spooner left the Senate in 1907 and Allison's health was failing. He died in 1908. Aldrich and his conservative allies within Republican ranks also faced rebellious younger senators such as Dolliver and Beveridge, who saw themselves as agents of the White House in the upper house. Aldrich's greatest asset was the suspicion of Roosevelt that permeated the chamber. Mabel Boardman, a close observer of the Washington scene, wrote, "I do not think today, save for Senator Lodge and possibly a few western senators like [Jonathan] Bourne he has a sincere friend in the Senate. This has been caused not so much by his policies as his methods."[28]

In his contest with the upper house over public perceptions, however, Roosevelt was winning. Aldrich and Speaker of the House Joseph G. Cannon came to be seen as the leaders of reactionary resistance to Roosevelt's popular programs. The Democrats saw an opportunity, and in the 1906 elections emphasized that they, unlike the Republicans, supported Roosevelt on the regulation issue. Still a faithful Republican, Roosevelt rejected this notion in letters he wrote to help his party during the campaign, and in the fall election, the Democrats gained seats in the House, but not the Senate.[29]

The lame-duck session of 1906–7 produced further evidence of Republican Senators' displeasure. Western members sought to curb Roosevelt's power over public lands in their region, where the White House had been implementing conservation policies. The agricultural appropriations bill contained a restrictive rider that would have limited the executive's authority to create new forest reserves in Oregon and five other states in the

West. Unable to veto the bill with the end of the session approaching, Roosevelt instead created twenty-nine new reserves in the days just before the Senate adjourned. This display of presidential defiance made relations between the Senate and the president even chillier.[30]

Throughout 1907, Republicans in and out of the Senate looked to the next presidential election for relief from Roosevelt. Several lawmakers cherished dreams that their candidacies might catch fire. Foraker hoped to control the Ohio delegation and build on his popularity with black voters in the South, but since his quarrel with Roosevelt had soured their relations, Foraker had no chance to win the president's crucial endorsement. On the Progressive side of the party, La Follette believed that his reform ideas would bring him the nod. Party regulars, however, regarded him with distaste, and his campaign never produced converts outside Wisconsin. By late 1907 it was evident that Roosevelt's personal choice for a successor, William Howard Taft, the secretary of war, was the front-runner.

Not content with endorsing Taft, Roosevelt also intended to make his last long session of Congress as president a productive one. In his annual message and others that followed during the early months of 1908, he presented Capitol Hill with proposals for political and economic reform that conveyed little sense that his term was ending in a year. Roosevelt requested antitrust legislation, action on the nation's ailing banking system, a workmen's liability law, and greater appropriations for the navy to modernize the fleet. The result was a series of running battles between the White House and the weary legislators.

The first of these battles came over Roosevelt's efforts to build up the fleet to help make the nation a world power. In the upper house, Beveridge had agreed to serve as the floor leader to secure funds to build four new battleships. By 1908, the once imperialistic Beveridge had taken up Progressive causes. He advocated lowering the tariff and he was the champion of regulating child labor. Becoming a reformer had not lessened Beveridge's own high opinion of himself, and Washington insiders often chuckled over his conceit. According to one account, the Indiana senator sat to have his formal portrait painted. For the lady artist to have a correct idea of the figure he cut during debate, "he insisted upon making & acting for her in the studio his speech in the Senate" about child labor "during which he tore off his collar, cravat & rampaged about the studio with amazing activity and violence."[31]

When the naval appropriations bill came to the floor for debate, Beveridge, Dolliver, and La Follette went at Aldrich head on. They resisted efforts to pare down the president's request in the face of opposition from conservatives who did not think the country needed a large navy. The president's allies succeeded in getting funds for at least two battleships every year. They did not get all that Roosevelt had asked for, but the White House was satisfied with the principle of regular annual increases in the number of ships to be launched. More important, Roosevelt's allies had faced down Aldrich and not been overwhelmed. Beveridge and the Republican leader had several angry exchanges during the debate. Newspaper reporters decided that "the young Republicans from the West" had "forced the Senate oligarchy into a defensive position and put an end to the method of silent rule." The impact of this skirmish would become apparent a year later when the upper house took up revision of the tariff.[32]

The spring of 1908 brought an even more sensational confrontation, this time between La Follette and Aldrich. Because of banking failures that triggered the Panic of 1907, the White House pushed for remedial legislation to forestall another crisis for the fragile monetary system. The Aldrich bill, as the Aldrich-Vreeland bill became known, made some modest changes and laid the groundwork for further action on how banks operated. Its most important feature was a proposed investigation of the overall banking problem. Favorable to the more powerful banks, it seemed to the White House the most that could be achieved. And it was a compromise that would enable Congress to adjourn by the end of May. The conference report that embodied these negotiations came up in the Senate days before the agreed-upon adjournment on May 30.[33]

For La Follette, the conference report represented an outright betrayal of the public interest. Ever the foe of concentrated economic power, he vowed to block passage of the compromise measure and demonstrate to the country who was the real advocate of controlling big business. La Follette began speaking on May 29 and held the floor, with the help of other opponents of the bill, in one of the most controversial filibusters of the period. After speaking for eleven hours, the Wisconsin senator needed nourishment to keep going. As a vegetarian, La Follette relied on a concoction of milk and eggs during his long ordeal. A glass containing this mixture was brought to his desk. He swallowed some and then screamed to his colleagues and the gallery, "Take it away, it's 'drugged.'" The brew was indeed undrinkable, but it had gone bad because of the heat of the Senate in the days before air-conditioning and the long trip from the kitchen where the drink had been prepared. There had been no attempt to kill La Follette, but the moment made for great political theater.[34]

The filibuster that La Follette led against the Aldrich-Vreeland Act came to a dramatic end the next day. The two allies of La Follette in the extended debate were William J. Stone, a Missouri Democrat, and Thomas P. Gore of Oklahoma, also a Democrat. Stone spoke, then yielded to Gore, who was blind, and the Oklahoman began. After two hours, Gore paused, expecting his Missouri colleague to take over, but Stone had left the floor, a fact that Gore could not see, and the Republican leadership moved quickly to bring a vote. Aldrich had already obtained an agreement from his colleagues that a roll-call vote would start whenever debate concluded. The vice president, Charles W. Fairbanks, who was presiding, immediately called for a vote on the conference report and Aldrich demanded a roll call. Once the voting had started, it could not be stopped. Aldrich had outmaneuvered his opponents by capitalizing on Gore's blindness. It was a move that left a bad taste in the mouths of Aldrich's opponents.[35]

The La Follette episode led to significant procedural changes in how the Senate managed filibusters. To obtain some rest for himself and to wear out the majority, the Wisconsin senator had relied on frequent quorum calls in which, under the rules, senators were supposed to come to the floor and answer to their names. Aldrich obtained a ruling from the chair that quorum calls could only occur when the Senate moved on to some other subject than the one that was the present business, a change that would make it easier to manage future filibusters. In an important way the Senate had taken a few tentative steps toward regulating filibusters. In the next few decades, however, Aldrich's action in curbing filibusters was not repeated by other senators.[36]

The Senate adjourned on May 30 so that both parties could wage the 1908 presidential election campaign. The contest between the Democratic candidate, William Jennings Bryan, and William Howard Taft resulted in a victory for the Republicans and their continued domination of the Senate. The Grand Old Party had sixty-one seats to thirty-one for the Democrats. The addition of New Mexico and Arizona to the Union over the next four years expanded Senate membership to ninety-six. What seemed to be a comfortable working majority for Aldrich and the conservatives, however, was more fragile than it seemed. Republican dissidents such as Dolliver, Beveridge, and La Follette had seven or eight allies who were restless under Aldrich. If these members defected on an issue such as the tariff, Aldrich could find himself with a much narrower margin in the upper house. With high tariffs seen as favoring business and middle-class voters restive about the effect of custom duties in raising prices, Republicans in the Senate were split on the issue of whether tariff rates should come down.

During the 1908 contest, the Republicans promised to revise the tariff but carefully did not specify in what direction changes might be made. The general assumption was that some downward movement in tariff rates would be in order. Certainly that was the feeling of Taft when he took office. He had decided to call a special session of Congress in the spring of 1909 to redeem the pledge his party had made to address the tariff. Progressive and conservative Republicans regarded Taft as an unknown quantity and each hoped to sway the new chief executive to their side.

It soon became apparent that Taft was not an adroit politician when it came to Congress. He kept important lawmakers waiting for hours to see him, he often changed his mind about policy decisions, and he developed personal animosities toward several senators, including Beveridge and La Follette. Over time, the president found himself more and more in sympathy with Aldrich and conservatism. The progressives became more alienated, and an atmosphere of bitterness infused their relations. In general, Taft had few friends in the Senate.[37]

Starting a tariff debate in the spring that would drag on into the summer also posed risks for the new administration. In the stifling heat of the Washington summer, the Senate chamber could become a virtual sauna for those trapped in the debates. As the wrangling wore on, Beveridge wrote a friend, "It is a hundred degrees here and sitting, and fighting and thinking for ten hours at a stretch with the temperature 104 and 105 degrees in the Senate Chamber, and then sitting up and working all night, is just about killing me."[38]

The first part of the tariff battle went according to White House plan: The House of Representatives, under the secure control of Speaker Cannon, produced a bill—often called the Payne bill, for the chairman of the Ways and Means Committee, Sereno E. Payne—that lowered tariff rates on agricultural products and some key industries. The bill went through the House with lower tariffs on lumber, iron, and sugar. Cattle hides and coal were placed on the free list, which meant no tariff would be assessed. Now the bill headed for the Senate.[39]

Aldrich had a delicate task ahead. He had to hold the votes of the eastern protectionists unhappy about free coal and placate senators from western states who wanted a tariff on hides. To put together a working majority, in the Senate version of the bill Aldrich raised rates back toward the levels of the Dingley Tariff of 1897. Cattle-hide duties were Aldrich's way of placating the key bloc of western-range senators who represented ranching interests. The midwestern rebels, now called Insurgents, were outraged at this turn of events. They divided the bill up by the various schedules and launched coordinated attacks on what Aldrich had offered. The most controversial items, wool, cotton, sugar, and others, became the targets for acerbic criticisms.[40]

The debate soon got personal. La Follette complained that Aldrich "brings in a great bill here for revision of the tariff, keeps everybody in the dark with respect to all the important facts upon which that revision should be made, and is silent when he should speak." Dolliver charged that "the American people expect us, if it can be done, to reduce the schedules of the Dingley tariff act somewhat." Aldrich replied that the Insurgents were party rebels who were doing the work of the Democrats. Of Beveridge he said, "The Senator from Indiana does not speak for the Republican party." The criticism of Aldrich in turn was so scathing that the Democrat "Pitchfork Ben" Tillman observed with mock solicitude once when the Republican leader was off the floor, "He has been pelted and bombarded from all directions, and I do not wonder he should sometimes get out of the range of fire."[41]

The Senate finally passed the bill on July 8 by a vote of 45 to 34. Ten Insurgents voted against the measure, and its fate now lay in the hands of a conference committee. In that panel, President Taft hoped to wield his influence to get a bill that fulfilled the implicit promise of the 1908 campaign to revise tariff rates downward. He lobbied with the conferees for reductions in oil, coal, wood pulp, lumber, scrap iron, and, most important, cattle hides. Taft stood resolute against the western senators on the hides issue and pushed the panelists writing the final version to find a consensus on which Republicans could agree. Convinced that the resulting Payne-Aldrich Tariff was the best he could do, Taft turned away suggestions from La Follette and other Insurgents that he should veto the bill. In early August the Senate adopted the conference report, with seven Insurgents voting no. The bill passed and Taft signed it into law.

The fight over the tariff left deep scars within the Republican majority in the upper house. "To be a protectionist," said Beveridge, "does not mean that we are to be extortionists." Taft identified with the regular Republicans who had supported his bill. He called it "the best tariff bill that the Republican party ever passed" and indicated that loyal party members should endorse it. The verdict among the Insurgents was that the president "seems to have surrendered absolutely to Aldrich."[42]

Discord between the Insurgents and the regulars in the Senate extended into 1910 and eroded the party's chances for success in the fall elections. Taft endeavored to withhold patronage from his rivals, a tactic that did little to wound them at home but increased their resentment toward him. The rhetoric on both sides became more bitter. Kansas Republican Joseph L. Bristow charged that Taft would not do anything "that is not in absolute accord with the purposes of Aldrich, Cannon, [New York Senator Elihu] Root and [Vice President James S.] Sherman." Even when House Republicans took away some of the power of Speaker Cannon in March 1910, discontent about the stern rule of Aldrich persisted in the press.[43]

With the midterm election on the horizon, the congressional Republicans and the president found some common ground during the spring and achieved the passage of some reform measures. The Mann-Elkins Act extended the power of the Interstate Commerce Commission over railroads. In the closing days of the session, lawmakers enacted laws on postal savings, limits on campaign contributions, and legislation to spur conservation. But problems remained. A dispute between Secretary of the Interior Richard A. Ballinger and the head of the Department of Agriculture's Forest Service, Gifford Pinchot, over forest reserves and coal lands policy led to a congressional investigation that kept the political situation in turmoil throughout the session.

By the summer of 1910, it was apparent that the Republicans faced a disgruntled electorate. The rising cost of living, blamed on the tariff, gave the Democrats an opening that they exploited with relish. Most of the Insurgent Republicans who had to face the voters came from states where the Democrats were weak and so they had few worries about defeat. In the case of Albert Beveridge, however, his position in the hotly contested state of Indiana was precarious. The Democrats ran a strong candidate, John Worth

Kern, against him while his own party provided him with only tepid endorsement. Beveridge went down before the Democratic tide.

Another significant loss for the Insurgents was Jonathan P. Dolliver. He did not face the voters, but his exertions on the Payne-Aldrich bill had weakened his health. He died from heart failure in September. With Beveridge gone and Dolliver dead, the leadership role fell to La Follette, whose prickly personality and presidential ambitions made it difficult for other Republican dissidents to follow him enthusiastically.

The election results produced a dramatic drop in the Republican Senate majority. Democrats gained ten seats in the upper house, leaving the Republicans with a 51–41 margin. If the Insurgents were to defect as a group on any bill, then the Republican hold on the Senate's agenda would be in doubt. Aldrich had already declared that he would not seek reelection in 1910, and so the era of his dominance was passing. The Republicans entered the second decade of the century without a commanding figure to direct their fortunes in the upper house.

For someone who had been such a source of discord and controversy, Aldrich left few long-term traces of his presence on the national scene. He had outdueled Roosevelt on the Hepburn bill only to have the courts side with the president and the Interstate Commerce Commission in interpreting the statute. The Payne-Aldrich Tariff lasted only four years before Woodrow Wilson and the Democrats replaced it in 1913. Aldrich did make a very constructive contribution to the debate about the future of the banking system, but most of that took place after he had left the Senate itself from his work on the National Monetary Commission, which set the stage for enactment of the Federal Reserve Law in 1913. Within a few years, Aldrich seemed a figure out of the past who had once been important but who left little enduring impression on the Senate.

La Follette also found that the election of 1910 had reduced his importance after a four-year run in the political spotlight. His ability to act as a political outsider had been facilitated by the large Republican majority, which allowed him to criticize without having to make partisan decisions. Once the balance in the upper house became more even between the two parties, the Wisconsin legislator had to choose to move closer to the Democrats or the Republicans. Since he hoped to get the nomination of the Grand Old Party in 1912, there were limits on how far he could go in the direction of rebellion. In the six years after 1910, La Follette was not as central a figure for the Senate as he had earlier been. Nonetheless, he had demonstrated how a maverick solon could turn the procedures of the body to his own advantage and achieve a national reputation. That lesson would impress other senators and become a model of how to use the upper house to achieve national recognition and power.

As for the Senate itself during the first decade of the twentieth century, its record was notable largely for the issues it left unaddressed and unresolved. The festering problem of racial injustice intruded only by accident, as in the Brownsville episode. Of the social inequities that plagued the country, the Senate was unconcerned and probably contributed to making them worse. On railroads, tariffs, and banking policy, the upper house adopted compromise measures or conservative solutions that represented little meaningful progress. The chamber left the urgent dilemmas of the United States during the age of reform for subsequent generations of senators to engage.

CHAPTER FOUR

# John Worth Kern
# and the New Freedom

FOR THE SENATE, A CREATIVE BURST OF ENERGY OCCURRED IN THE SIX
years following the Democratic election victories in 1910. In that span,
the upper house adopted a constitutional amendment for the direct election of senators, approved the Federal Reserve Act, passed the income tax,
and enacted the social justice legislation that President Woodrow Wilson
proposed.

The service of the new Democratic senators who won seats in 1910 began in April 1911, when President Taft summoned lawmakers into a special
session. The session's main purpose was to deal with the president's proposal for a reciprocal tariff agreement with Canada. When they assembled
for that task, the senators soon faced a showdown on the constitutional
amendment to provide for direct election of senators.[1]

Since 1905, states had sought various ways to require legislatures to accept the winner of a party primary as their choice for the Senate. As these
procedures evolved, they generated pressure on the Senate to adopt an
amendment for the direct election of senators. Adding to the urgency that
members felt was mounting evidence of corruption in the way some states
chose senators. For example, when John Coit Spooner left the Senate in
1907, the governor of Wisconsin appointed Isaac Stephenson to succeed
him. Two years later, the elderly, wealthy Stephenson won the Republican
primary for a full term. His opponents charged that he had spread money

around during the primary contest to make sure of his victory. Challenges to the legality of his election went before the Senate.[2]

Yet what happened in Wisconsin stirred less popular clamor than did the controversy over the election of William Lorimer of Illinois in 1909. Once the "Blond Boss" of Chicago politics, Lorimer had faded as a player in the city's public life, but then was unexpectedly chosen for the Senate after the legislature had deadlocked over other hopefuls. Lorimer became a conservative ally of Nelson Aldrich in Washington.[3]

Then the scandal broke. In late April 1910, a Democratic member of the Illinois Assembly told a Chicago newspaper that he had been bribed to vote for Lorimer. Banner headlines made the charge a national controversy. A Senate subcommittee of the Senate Privileges and Elections Committee looked into the matter and exonerated Lorimer of wrongdoing. In December 1910, the full Senate confirmed that result by a vote of 46 to 40, but that ballot was not the end of the Lorimer battle. His enemies continued to gather evidence of scandal in his election, and the battle over his right to hold the seat raged in the national press.[4]

Meanwhile, proponents of direct elections pressed for action on the amendment. Joseph L. Bristow of Kansas had been pushing the amendment for two years without making much progress. In the wake of the Lorimer affair, the Judiciary Committee agreed to name a subcommittee to consider the resolution to adopt the amendment at the end of December 1910. Their deliberations led to language about direct election in a proposed amendment but with important new wording. Southern senators, fearful that the federal government might enforce the voting rights of African Americans, wanted a concession. They insisted on adding a provision that would strip the Congress of the power to provide rules for senatorial elections, as specified in the Constitution, and would cede it to the states.[5]

The always lurking race issue now flared up. Republicans sought to amend the Bristow resolution by deleting the wording that the South wanted about Senate elections. Concern for African-American rights was one element in their thinking. In addition, conservatives who disliked direct elections knew that the removal of the provision about state control of Senate elections would make southerners less likely to vote for the underlying principle. On the floor, Republicans complained that ceding jurisdiction over Senate contests to the states "would give substantial though limited sanction to the disfranchisement of Negroes in the Southern states." In February 1911, the

Republicans' wording for the amendment was adopted. The resolution for a constitutional amendment then failed to obtain a two-thirds majority.[6]

With Taft's special session, the direct-election amendment reappeared, as its proponents seized the chance to see it passed in a more sympathetic Senate. Bristow proposed to his colleagues that they drop the language about states controlling Senate elections and just support the principle of having the voters elect senators. There was a tie on this vote, and Vice President James S. Sherman cast the deciding ballot in favor of Bristow's position. Both houses had now approved the amendment, but southerners in the House insisted on removal of the election control provision from the Constitution. Eleven months passed before the House yielded and agreed to the Senate version, on May 11, 1912. The amendment then went to the states for ratification.[7]

The larger purpose of the amendment, in the minds of Bristow and Idaho's William E. Borah, was that direct elections could be "the most effective means of taking from organized wealth the control of the Senate, and indeed our national politics." The quality of the upper house would also be improved once the people themselves would choose their senators. The fervor to have senators elected in this way grew out of the dislike for political parties that animated middle-class Americans during these years. Having legislatures designate senators was inherently undemocratic; now the people would rule. Once the amendment was ratified, as everyone knew it would be, this political optimism would be put to the test.[8]

The convening of the special session also compelled both parties to select new leaders. The Republicans' task was to find a credible successor to Aldrich. The conference chose an aging conservative, Shelby M. Cullom of Illinois. Rather than conciliate the Insurgents, whose votes the Grand Old Party needed to stay in power, the Republicans declined to give Bristow and La Follette seats on the prestigious Finance and Commerce committees.[9]

The Democrats had their internal differences as well. Joseph Weldon Bailey had become so tainted with scandal in Texas that he was planning to leave the Senate before his term expired. But Bailey's decline did not lead to success for the more reform-minded Democrats. The progressives in the party found to their dismay that Thomas S. Martin of Virginia, another member of the party's old guard, had rounded up enough pledges before the meeting to assure his victory. John Worth Kern forced a roll-call vote, which Martin won 21 to 16. Kern then issued a statement to the press predicting that the number of reform Democrats "will be increased in the natural course until the progressive spirit thoroughly permeates the Democratic minority." The outcome of the vote revealed that Kern would likely be the future leader when the Democrats regained control of the upper house.[10]

Partisan squabbling dominated the last two years of Taft's presidency. The White House won approval of the Canadian reciprocity agreement only to have voters in Canada reject the existing government and thereby the reciprocity agreement as well. Capitalizing on their control of the House, Democrats passed bills to lower the tariff on such items as wool and cotton goods. Democrats and insurgent Republicans endorsed these measures in the upper chamber, whereupon Taft vetoed them. In foreign policy, the president submitted international arbitration treaties that failed to win endorsement. Meanwhile, continued doubts about the legality of William Lorimer's election sparked a second probe of his fitness to serve. After months of inquiry and negotiation, the Illinois senator was ousted in the spring of 1912 by a vote of 55 to 28. One newspaper said that the Lorimer case had provided the nation with "a new Senate—new in spirit, in purpose, in honest progressivism, in worthy respect for national sentiment and simple decency."[11]

Presidential politics provided a fascinating backdrop to the 1911 special session. Theodore Roosevelt and William Howard Taft were engaged in an undeclared war for control of the Republican Party. Would the former president challenge the incumbent for the nomination in 1912? Another Republican, Senator Robert La Follette, launched an unsuccessful bid for his party's nomination. Taft defeated Roosevelt for the Republican nomination, whereupon the loser bolted to form his own Progressive Party.

The Republican split, coupled with the selection of Woodrow Wilson as the Democratic presidential nominee, meant that the long period of Republican dominance of the Senate—since 1896—was going to end. Knowing that Wilson was likely to win against the divided Republicans, the Democrats decided not to act on the judicial and military nominations that Taft, now a lame duck, was submitting for Senate action. Instead they resolved to talk these candidates to death as the clock ran out. An exasperated Henry Cabot Lodge, Sr., Republican of Massachusetts, complained, "The Democrats have filibustered at every executive session."[12]

By March 1913, Woodrow Wilson had become the first Democratic president in sixteen years. In theory, the new chief executive and the Senate should have found harmony in their political goals. Few politicians have been elected president with a better idea of how Congress worked in theory than Wilson. As a young man he had written *Congressional Government*, the first academic study of the legislative branch, published in 1885. While the book delved into the functions of Congress in a perceptive manner, Wilson had examined Congress from a distance as a graduate student at Johns Hopkins University. He had not made the short trip from Baltimore to Washington to observe lawmakers in action. Accordingly, his firsthand knowledge was limited, and, as time would reveal, Wilson had only minimal respect for congressional feelings. By 1912, he had decided that presidents could do much to sway the legislature to achieve the goals of an administration. The chief executive, he wrote, "must be prime minister, as much concerned with the guidance of legislation as with the just and orderly execution of law."[13]

Wilson had strong majorities in both houses to help him work his will as a new president. The House had a solid margin for the Democrats, but the edge was smaller in the Senate. There Wilson's party had a 51–44 advantage, with one Progressive senator, Miles Poindexter of Washington. Some insurgent Republicans could help the administration make good on Wilson's campaign pledge to enact tariff legislation. Since the Democratic platform had promised lower tariffs, Wilson planned to call lawmakers into a special session in April 1913. The Democratic leader would be crucial to the passage of a tariff bill and to changing the party's reputation, formed in the Cleveland administration, of being too inept to govern. The incumbent Democratic leader, Thomas Martin of Virginia, was seen as too conservative to be a forceful advocate of Wilson's reform program.[14]

Defying their previous record of futility, the Democrats selected a strong candidate, John Worth Kern, as the chair of the Democratic caucus on March 5, 1913, a post that would later be known as majority leader of the Senate. Because Kern served only one term and then died, he is now a mere footnote to history and a forgotten figure in Democratic lore. A biography appeared after his death in 1917 and a dissertation on his career was completed nearly six decades later. In his day, however, he played a key part in the evolution of the role of majority leader. More important, he supplied the energy and direction that made the Senate a partner in the achievement of the program of tariff reduction, banking reform, and trust regulation Wilson called the New Freedom.[15]

Kern, now sixty-three, had been a fixture in Indiana politics since the 1870s. His record showed occasional victories and persistent losses. So crucial was the Hoosier State to Democratic hopes of winning the White

John Worth Kern, the Democratic leader from 1913
to 1917, was instrumental in bringing the Democrats
together to enact Woodrow Wilson's New Freedom
program. (LIBRARY OF CONGRESS)

House that he was chosen as William Jennings Bryan's running mate in
1908. Kern's deeply rooted progressivism included support for labor unions
and social justice as when in 1913 he defended the labor leader Mary Harris, "Mother Jones," from political attacks. Known as "Uncle John" to his
colleagues, he was a hard worker, a heavy smoker, and a quiet, conciliatory
leader. His steel glasses, neatly cropped beard, and thin face gave him the
look of a schoolmaster, but Kern was a tough fighter in the cut-and-thrust
of running the Senate.

Key to Kern's success was control of the Democratic conference (composed of all Democratic senators), as control of the Republican conference had been to Aldrich's. Of the fifty-one Democrats in 1913, thirty-one were progressive in their outlook toward reform legislation and the operation of the Senate. Despite some concessions to the conservatives, progressives dominated the Steering Committee, leading to the appointment of fellow progressives as chairmen of key committees. The Kern forces also arranged the rankings on the various committees and moved reformers ahead of conservatives with more seniority. Kern gave Democratic conference members the right to select their chairman and to name senators to the Steering Committee. As Kern told reporters after announcing these changes on March 15, 1913, his goal was to make "this great body Democratic not only in name but in practical reality." In that way, he continued, "the charge, so often made, that it is controlled by a few men through committee organization and otherwise shall have no basis in fact."[16]

Success for Kern was hard-fought. Long years in opposition had made the Democratic senators balky and hard to manage. Frequent absences from the floor, especially during the sweltering summer, meant that Kern could not always rely on his colleagues. With only a seven-seat majority, the defection of three Democrats could and on a few occasions did place the party's control in jeopardy. "Uncle John" resorted to cajoling, sarcasm, and some arm-twisting to persuade his charges to be present for votes on the tariff and other "must" legislation from the White House.[17]

So harried did Kern become that he asked the conference to create the position of party whip on May 28, 1913. Based on a similar position in the British Parliament, the whip would make sure that members were present when decisive votes took place. A freshman senator, J. Hamilton Lewis of Illinois, a Chicago attorney and stem-winding speaker, took up the post and held it for one term, before he lost his seat. When he returned to the Senate in the 1930s he resumed the assignment. Lewis was a snappy dresser whose clothes, said one newspaper account, have "always been of the latest cut and style, his cravats gorgeous, his socks ditto, and his gloves and hat absolutely a la mode." The debonair Lewis took a relaxed approach to being whip and did not help Kern much with rounding up votes. His elevation did make the whip post a continuing part of the leadership, though. The Republicans followed suit in 1915 when they elected James W. Wadsworth of New York as their whip.[18]

The Democrats under Kern stressed economy in the internal operations of the Senate and a desire to limit the privileges of members. When the new Senate office building (now the Richard B. Russell Building) opened in 1909, it had bathing facilities for senators that included a masseur and three assistants. The Democrats decided in 1913 to close down these amenities as a way of saving taxpayer money. Democrats in those years prided themselves on being the party of frugality as compared with the extravagance they imputed to their Republican rivals. The baths would not be reopened until the Republicans returned to power after World War I. One change that all senators applauded was the opening of an electric railway connecting the new building with the Capitol, making it much easier for senators to get to the chamber for votes and meet constituents in their offices.[19]

The sense that the Senate was an exclusive, private club persisted despite the reform spirit of the Wilson years. When he came to the upper house in 1913, Key Pittman of Nevada wrote of his pleasure at the social recognition he received in Washington. "Door keepers bow at every hand, pages run to do my bidding. At stores my office opens credit and at the hotel they are almost servile." He reveled in the respect of his fellow members as well. "They were all cordial and easy in their manner and I soon felt at home. It is like a club rather than a legislative body." For an alcoholic such as Pittman was, the free-wheeling atmosphere of the place was a further incentive to adapt and prosper.[20]

The resurgence of the Democrats meant that their southern members were much in the public eye after 1913. Having survived the years of Republican ascendancy, the members from Dixie now took over key committees. "The South was in the saddle," wrote one journalist. Lawmakers from below the Mason-Dixon Line talked of repealing the Fourteenth and Fifteenth Amendments to undo Reconstruction. James K. Vardaman, the "white chief" of Mississippi, declared, "I expect to favor and urge the enactment of laws that will make perfect the social and political segregation of the white and colored races." Southern senators did not have the votes to achieve that goal, but they praised Woodrow Wilson's racist efforts to separate blacks and whites in the federal government.[21]

Outside the Senate, changes in the nation's population would reshape debate in the years following the era of Woodrow Wilson. "The Great Migration" of African Americans out of the South and into the cities of the North made them an electoral presence in the North during the decade that followed. Anti-lynching legislation would come to Congress within four years of Kern's retirement. Northern politicians would press for civil rights, and, in turn, the South and its politicians would defend filibusters as a means of staving off attacks on segregation. The ascendancy of southern Democrats in these years proved troubling for the party's future.

As a candidate Wilson had promised to lower the tariff, reform the banking system, and regulate corporations. Kern and his colleagues knew that their success hinged on the enactment of Wilson's New Freedom into law. "The Democrats have a task of enormous dimensions before them," wrote Henry Fountain Ashurst, a new member of the Democratic conference from Arizona. After the legislative disasters of Grover Cleveland's presidency, getting any tariff bill through Congress, not to mention the two other hot-button issues, would be a significant political victory.[22]

In dealing with the tariff, the Senate was part of an important change in executive-legislative relations. On April 8, Wilson journeyed to Congress in person to deliver his tariff message at the start of the special session. The dry and colorless custom of presidents' transmitting written messages for clerks to read went back to Thomas Jefferson in 1801. Now it had been shattered, and, Wilson noted proudly, "the town is agog about it." Senators generally liked the change. John Shafroth of Colorado said that the move was "democratic in the extreme because it brings the President in personal contact with both houses of Congress. When that occurs it should produce harmony, not discord." It was change, however, that proved in the long run to be a major accretion of presidential power relative to Congress. Wilson and the presidents that followed him used this technique as a way to appeal to the American people and enhance their stature and clout relative to the more parochial lawmakers.[23]

Within a month, the House passed a tariff bill, named after the chairman of the Ways and Means Committee, Oscar W. Underwood of Alabama. All eyes in Washington turned to the upper house to see whether the political trauma of the Payne-Aldrich Tariff would be repeated. The Underwood measure reduced tariffs on an extensive number of consumer products and made up for revenue losses with the imposition of an income tax on those earning more than $4,000 annually. The Democrats set to work to hammer out a version of their own tariff act behind closed doors in May and June. By early July the majority had written its bill, which the caucus deemed "a party measure" that all Democrats had to support. Louisiana senators, worried about the lower tariff on sugar, their state's major product, did not go along. Kern expected to make up these votes from one or two progressive Republicans.[24]

While this scenario unfolded, Wilson exerted presidential influence to shape the tariff bill in the manner he desired. His actions, which had something of grandstanding in their motives, helped to give the public a revealing look behind the curtain of how the upper house did its business. In May he denounced lobbyists working to influence the tariff bill. "An industrious and insidious" campaign was going on, he claimed, to defeat the people's will. La Follette and other Progressives called for a probe of Wilson's charges with the recommendation that members disclose their financial holdings and properties that their tariff votes might benefit. Reluctantly, and only in the face of public pressure, the Senate agreed to do so.[25]

The hearings did not reveal any direct conflicts among senators as they trooped before the press to outline their financial holdings. Most members were comfortably off; some were wealthy with extensive lands and investments. The episode removed some of the mystery from such groups as the National Association of Manufacturers, which maintained an office in the capital for easy access to senators. The findings of the committee did not lead to effective legislation to control lobbying or any disclosure requirements for the senators. Nonetheless, the aura of privacy that surrounded the body had broken down just a little.[26]

With the Democrats in control of the tariff-writing process, the Republicans could do little to stop the bill. After seven weeks of debate in late summer, the Underwood measure cleared the Senate by a vote of 44 to 37. La Follette and Miles Poindexter voted for it. All of the other Republicans voted against it. Wilson signed the measure into law on October 3, 1913.

The triumph for the Democrats transcended the enactment of a tariff law. Under "Uncle John" Kern, the majority had proved it could govern. Republican charges that they were "incapable of positive action" now rang hollow. With the first phase of the New Freedom achieved, Democrats turned to banking reform and the trusts. In so doing they created a record of accomplishment that would not be matched until the early days of the New Deal and again in the mid-1960s, with Lyndon Johnson and the Great Society. Woodrow Wilson and John Worth Kern together produced one of the rare constructive bursts of sustained lawmaking in the Senate's modern history.[27]

With the momentum running their way, Kern and his colleagues pressed ahead with banking legislation. By December 27, 1913, the Federal Reserve Act was law. The special session had ended on December 1, 1913, and the lawmakers went right into the regular session, which lasted until late October 1914. By doing so, they were able to address the third phase of the New Freedom, which involved the issue of regulating the trusts. Kern and his colleagues provided the president with the Clayton Antitrust Act, which strengthened the authority of the federal government over corporate power. In addition, the lawmakers created the Federal Trade Commission to implement the regulatory provisions of the Clayton law and other such measures.

The Democrats had done a great deal in 1913–14 to show that they could govern. Now they faced the voters in the first electoral test of how the New Freedom had gone over at the grass roots. The 1914 congressional elections were also the first contests held under the new system where voters chose senators. The Seventeenth Amendment had been ratified in the spring of 1913. George H. Haynes, already a renowned student of the Senate and its operations, wondered in print before the voters went to the polls, "Is it an epoch-making reform? Will it work a revolution in the personnel of the Senate? Will the charge cease to be made that 'predatory wealth' finds in the Senate its strongest fortress?"[28]

As it turned out, the voters were less concerned about how the Senate worked than about pocketbook issues. A downturn in the economy helped the Republicans, as did the return to the GOP of Progressives who had followed Theodore Roosevelt out of the party in 1912. The Democrats stressed that the president had kept the country out of the European war. Still, the majority party lost sixty-three seats in the House, down to a ratio of 230–193, but in the Senate picked up five seats, in California, Colorado, Kentucky, South Dakota, and Wisconsin. But there was no new day as far as the quality of senators was concerned. Ohio voters, for example, sent the handsome but lackluster Republican Warren G. Harding to Washington.

The most symbolic race in 1914 involved Pennsylvania, where the Republican incumbent Boies Penrose was returned. A reformer in his youth, the obese, toadlike Penrose (he was six feet four inches tall and weighed 350 pounds) had become the embodiment of Republican reaction and deference to business interests. Yet he won easily with an appeal for a return of higher tariffs that would, he said, bring a return of prosperity. He defeated the moderate Democrat A. Mitchell Palmer (later Wilson's attorney general and architect of the postwar Red Scare) and Gifford Pinchot, a close friend of Theodore Roosevelt's, for the Progressives. Pinchot blamed his loss on "a frightened vote, blindly hoping to secure prosperity, and willing to use any instrument for that purpose." What mattered in the end was whether a candidate could reach the voter, and that Penrose did with more flair than his rivals. To the dismay of reformers, direct elections seemed to have more to do with effective campaigning than the character and ideas of the candidate. The judgment of voters, it seemed, was no better and sometimes worse than that of state legislatures.[29]

After the elections, senators returned for the short session that ran from December 1914 into early March 1915. Tempers had become frayed as the impact of the war on the economy intensified and both parties looked forward to the 1916 presidential contest. The atmosphere had been partisan and volatile before the elections. The mixed results from the balloting left Republicans and Democrats in an even testier mood when they reassembled for the short session in December 1914. There were also indications that the president's condescending treatment of the upper house was working against his interests. Wilson complained to a friend in January 1915, "It is the senators who break down the President, generally the senators of his own party. The Democratic senators have no idea of team work like the Republicans."[30]

The first large issue that came up in the short session laid bare the partisan tensions of the moment. The outbreak of World War I had left many European merchant ships tied up in American ports for the duration of the fighting. To help the ailing merchant marine, the Wilson administration proposed to purchase these vessels from their foreign owners, most of whom were German. Shipping interests, their profits threatened, wanted the ship-purchase idea blocked. Led by Henry Cabot Lodge, Republicans labeled the plan socialism and warned that it would irritate Great Britain and France.

Republicans filibustered the legislation from January 1915 until March of that year. Reed Smoot, a Utah Republican, set the existing record for continuous talking with eleven hours and thirty-five minutes on January 29–30. "If I did not think my country was in danger by the passage of the bill, I would never say another word upon it," he declared. Passions heightened when seven Democrats, breaking with their party's leaders, sought to return the bill to committee and thus kill it once Smoot finished his remarks. The stalemate persisted until the end of the session, when the frustrated Democrats gave up the bill.[31]

The defeat convinced many Democrats that it was time to revise the rules to curb filibusters. Cutting off debate would be done through a process called cloture, in which debate on the pending measure was brought to an end and a vote occurred. Democrat William J. Stone of Missouri said, "Debate is one thing; a defiant filibuster, without pretense of legitimate discussion intended to enlighten the Senate or the country, is quite another thing." Republicans defended unlimited debate. Neither party could claim consistency, however, since all senators were prepared to talk indefinitely when their interests were at stake. Discussions of ways to achieve cloture came up again in 1916, but the talks produced no result. Only an extraordinary and unpopular filibuster seemed likely to move the members to take any action. The tired and disgruntled members of the Senate dispersed in March and did not come back until the following December. In the meantime, the World War posed further challenges for American politicians.[32]

While Congress was in recess, on May 7, 1915, a German submarine sank the British liner *Lusitania*. More than a hundred Americans lost their lives in the disaster. To the dismay of some Republican senators, who wanted a confrontation with Germany, President Wilson said that he would not go to war because there were times when a man should be "too proud to fight." Democrats applauded and the public seemed to endorse the president's position on neutrality. Controversies over relations with Germany and the nation's position on the war dominated news for the next six months. Wilson directed American diplomacy by himself and felt no urgency about summoning lawmakers back to Washington to deal with the crisis. As a result, when Congress reconvened on December 6, 1915, the session went on until just two months before the presidential election in November 1916. The atmosphere was acerbic and partisan, and major actions from the White House sparked controversy and recriminations.[33]

The Senate became involved in a confrontation with the president when Wilson nominated Louis D. Brandeis to the Supreme Court, inaugurating the first great Senate battle of the twentieth century over a judicial nominee and his fitness to serve. The president sent Brandeis's name to Congress on January 28, 1916, causing a storm of opposition matched by equally strong support. Wilson had worked with the fifty-nine-year-old Brandeis in formulating the campaign themes of the New Freedom in 1912. Known as "the people's lawyer" for his battles with utilities, railroad companies, and insurance firms, Brandeis was also a Jew, which increased the intensity of the campaign against him. Conservatives in the Northeast who disliked the nominee's economic views also made anti-Semitic allegations in private.[34]

The Senate Judiciary Committee held public hearings, which the nominee as was the custom did not attend. Stretching from February 9 through March 15, these sessions were a new departure for confirmation proceedings. Witnesses pro and con came before the panel, and all aspects of Brandeis's public career were examined. Ex-president Taft joined six other lawyers and former presidents of the American Bar Association in saying that Brandeis was "not a fit person to be a member of the Supreme Court of the United States."

Wilson threw his political prestige into the fight with a letter to the chair of the Judiciary Committee: "I knew from direct personal knowledge of the man what I was doing when I named him for the highest and most responsible tribunal in the Nation." The Judiciary Committee endorsed the nomination by a party-line vote of 10 to 8. On June 1, 1916, Brandeis was confirmed in closed-door executive session, 47 to 22, with only one Democrat voting against him. It would be fourteen years before a similar confirmation struggle occurred over a Supreme Court nominee.[35]

The Brandeis confirmation battle was but one controversy in a contentious year for the Senate. Looming over the entire long session in 1916 was the prospect of the United States being drawn into the European War. The ever-present threat of a submarine attack on shipping and a renewed dispute with the Germans worried many lawmakers. Democrats were especially torn because of the antiwar sentiments that pervaded their states in the South and West. Restrictive trade practices by the British and French irritated many on Capitol Hill. Opponents of the war watched Woodrow Wilson to be sure that he did not start down the road to intervention. As a result, the Democrats were divided about the president's call, in the name of "preparedness," to strengthen the army and navy.

A test of Wilson's authority came late in February 1916. Oklahoma Democrat Thomas P. Gore joined a sympathetic colleague in the House, Jeff McLemore of Texas, in proposing a resolution to warn Americans not to travel on ships of the warring powers. The resolution's sponsors felt that this document would reduce the risk of war by removing Americans from belligerent ships and thus avoiding provocations. The president, for his part, bristled at what he saw as an attack on his power to conduct foreign policy without congressional interference. He consulted with John Worth

Kern and William J. Stone, chairman of the Foreign Relations Committee, to have the Gore resolution tabled. Although there was some support among the leadership and the rank and file for the resolution, the Democrats did as Wilson requested. The episode, however, strained relations between Wilson and Stone. More important, it left a residue of distrust about the president among those senators who believed that Wilson was moving in ways that increased the likelihood of war. That sense that the president could not be trusted would affect how the Senate appraised Wilson's actions on the issues of war and peace that soon arose.[36]

For the moment, however, the Wilson administration got what it wanted from Congress on both the domestic and foreign policy sides. Despite some qualms of southern and western members, the Senate endorsed the White House program to increase preparedness with appropriations for the navy and national defense. The president also pushed hard for laws to restrict the use of child labor in factories, to provide agricultural credits for farmers, and to secure workmen's compensation for employees when a government contract was involved. Faced with a possible railroad strike over union demands for an eight-hour day, Wilson and Kern collaborated to pass the Adamson Act in September 1916, two months before the election. The Democratic Senate, under Kern's direction, had played a vital part in achieving the progressive reforms that sustained the president's bid for a second term. The 1916 election would test the coalition of southern and northern Democrats that Kern had assembled to such good effect in the upper house.

The major casualty of the 1916 voting was Kern himself. After 1912, Indiana had returned to the Republican allegiance it had established in the McKinley and Roosevelt era. As a result, the Democratic leader faced a difficult contest. The death of Indiana's other Democratic senator in the spring put both seats in play. Despite failing health, Kern campaigned doggedly, but with the Democrats concentrating their scarce resources in other states, Kern had little chance against the Republicans and their "systematic teamwork." "Uncle John" was beaten, and the Grand Old Party picked up both Indiana seats.[37]

The aging Kern died of complications from tuberculosis in mid-1917. With his passing amid the distractions of World War I went also most memories of his effectiveness as a Senate leader. His deft style of handling his colleagues, his low-key approach, and the results he achieved anticipated the abilities and accomplishments of one of his successors, Mike Mansfield. In the 1920s and again in the 1950s, Joseph T. Robinson and Lyndon B. Johnson would be more dynamic directors of Democratic fortunes in the Senate. All of these men, however, built on the work of John Kern.

President Wilson won a narrow and dramatic reelection victory over Charles Evans Hughes, and their defeat left the Republicans especially angry. The GOP regarded Wilson as dishonest, and they had expected that the voters would agree. When the president turned the issue of the war to his advantage, by stressing how he had avoided entering the conflict, and won a second term, Republican frustration intensified. The Republicans were in no mood to cooperate with their partisan rivals. The Democrats lost a seat in Maine, in addition to the two seats that they dropped in Indiana, but they were still the majority with an eleven-seat margin as Wilson's second term neared. A new leader would have to be chosen once the next Congress reconvened in early March to confirm Wilson's cabinet nominations.

Unlike most lame-duck sessions, the last meeting of the Sixty-fifth Congress produced high political drama and the prospect of a significant change in how the Senate conducted its business. One striking event after another marked these months. In December 1916, Wilson offered to mediate between the combatants in Europe, an initiative that revealed just how far apart the warring nations were in their aims for victory. The Senate endorsed the president's diplomatic initiative in early January 1917 with seventeen Republicans opposing the move. On January 22, Wilson appeared at the Senate to offer his "peace without victory" address in which he proclaimed that "only a peace between equals can last." That assertion aroused Republican concern that Wilson might not favor the Allied cause if the nation went to war. The president took these steps and announced these policies without much substantive consultation with lawmakers, and the latent resentment against his tactics grew among senators of both parties.[38]

At the end of January, Germany announced a policy of unrestricted submarine warfare against neutral shipping. Wilson broke diplomatic relations with Berlin but did not go to war. Senators endorsed the decision to cut ties to Germany, and only five members dissented. Washington waited to see what would happen next. With the end of the session looming, Wilson considered what steps he could take short of war to meet the German challenge. Ten days before the Congress was to adjourn, the president decided to ask lawmakers for power to arm American merchant ships. On February 26, he went back to the Capitol to make his appeal for that authority.[39]

The Republicans had already decided to prevent appropriations bills and other needed legislation from passing before March 4, 1917—failure to enact these laws would compel Wilson to bring Congress back to Washington well before the regular session began in December 1917. "I have also come to the conclusion that we must force an extra session," wrote Henry Cabot Lodge. "Although I have not much faith in Congress we should be safer with Congress here than we should be with Wilson alone for nine months." When the controversy over arming the ships began, the Republicans stepped aside and let the small group of antiwar senators who opposed the bill launch their filibuster. The existence of the Republican threat to tie up the Senate formed the background for subsequent events.[40]

The Senate took up the Wilson plan on March 2, 1917. One day earlier the Zimmerman Telegram—containing a German scheme to bring Mexico into an alliance against the United States when war broke out—had been made public. The plan would have given to Mexico Texas and other parts of the Southwest in return for its military support of Germany. Popular anger at Germany in Washington and the Northeast was intense and growing. Within the Senate, most Republicans generally favored a strong policy toward Germany, and southern Democrats also rallied behind the president's plan to arm the ships. Opponents of the plan saw it as a step to war. Antiwar sentiment was still strong in parts of the Southwest and Middle West, especially in states with sizable German-American populations. Men such as George Norris of Nebraska, William J. Stone, and Robert La Follette rallied their forces to block the president's initiative. Debate on the armed-ships legislation continued on March 3 and extended into the morning of March 4. Both advocates and opponents of the bill spoke at length. In fact, the majority, which wanted to pass the bill, filibustered on their own to prevent the opponents from getting the floor. La Follette sat in frustration as he was denied a chance to speak against the measure. Still a loner among his colleagues, he had shown himself to be an effective legislator on occasion, especially in his fight to protect American merchant seamen, which resulted in the La Follette Seamen's Act of 1915. With his many German-American supporters and his own passionate opposition to what he saw as an unnecessary conflict, La Follette wanted to have an opportunity to state for the nation why he regarded the armed-ship bill as a milestone on the road to war. But it was not to be. The legislative session ended at noon on March 4 and the armed-ships bill died for the time being, but La Follette would have other chances to express his distaste for the war and to earn the wrath of his colleagues in the process.[41]

An infuriated Woodrow Wilson issued a statement denouncing the senators who had talked the bill to death. "A little group of willful men, representing no opinion but their own, have rendered the great government of the United States helpless and contemptible." Public anger, especially in the East, exploded at the eleven senators who opposed the bill. La Follette, Stone, Norris, and Iowa Republican Albert B. Cummins were excoriated as traitors. A newspaper editor called their action "one of the most reprehensible filibusters ever recorded in the history of any civilized country." The New York Times concluded that "the Senate of the United States is the only legislative body in the world whose powers are limited by such a paralyzing condition." Several state legislatures passed resolutions denouncing the dissenters.[42]

Congress had to reconvene on March 5, 1917, for a very short session to deal with Wilson's cabinet appointments. Those few days gave the parties the chance to name new leaders and also to change the filibuster rule. To replace the departed Kern, the Democrats chose Thomas S. Martin, a Virginia conservative who had led the party before Kern. On March 8, he offered a change to rule 22 of the Senate, which governed procedures for debate. It provided for cloture and the stopping of debate under certain precise conditions: If sixteen senators asked for an end to debate on a bill and two-thirds of those voting approved when the question was posed, then further discussion would be limited. Each senator would be able to speak for one hour more on the substantive measure. Efforts to require only a simple majority to end debate failed. Democrats and Republicans had arrived at the two-thirds figure because that was the most that could be achieved at the time. The change in the rules went into effect by a vote of 76 to 3 on March 8, 1917. The New York Times observed, "A month ago this greased slipping of cloture through the Senate would not have been possible."[43]

In the long run, the change in Senate rules was less significant than it seemed at the time. It was possible to achieve cloture in unusual circumstances, but over the long haul this reform proved less consequential than its advocates had hoped. It was still possible to filibuster on procedural motions, such as whether to take up a bill or to approve the journal of the previous day's proceedings, or to undertake a host of other delaying tactics to obstruct Senate business. Clever and determined senators—and there were always plenty of those—could thus tie down the chamber with endless motions. There was no specific spot in legislation where a resolute majority could insist on working its will. Once the issue of cloture became involved with civil rights in the 1920s and again in the 1930s, the ingenuity of those who used filibusters far outpaced the resources and the will of the senators seeking to end the practice.

The Senate under "Uncle John" Kern and the Democrats from 1913 to 1917 had accomplished a good deal in the way of constructive legislation. In the favorable circumstances of a divided Republican opposition and a reasonably united Democratic bloc, the adoption of important measures became possible. The Federal Reserve Act in particular was a notable positive step for the country. Then the political environment shifted. Even though the president squeaked back into office in 1916, the Democratic hold on the Senate was eroding. The reunion of the Republicans that began in 1914 and extended into 1916 meant that a second term for Wilson would be filled with partisan strife. Hatred for Wilson and his policies would be a dominant fact of Senate history during the years of his second term.

American entry into World War I in April 1917 and the struggle over the League of Nations that followed the war sharpened partisan differences and concentrated attention on the role of the Senate. In the personal battle between Wilson and Henry Cabot Lodge over the peace treaty in 1919 arose one of the most decisive moments in the history of the upper house.

## CHAPTER FIVE

# The Senate and the League of Nations

THE SENATE'S PART IN WORLD WAR I COMMENCED ON THE SOFT SPRING
evening of April 2, 1917, when President Woodrow Wilson came to
the Congress to ask the lawmakers to take the nation into the conflict. His
address received warm applause, and even Henry Cabot Lodge said, "Mr.
President you have expressed in the loftiest manner possible the sentiments
of the American people." For a moment, but only for a moment, the partisan bitterness of the chamber yielded to the claims of patriotism and rally-
ing behind the president. Two days later the Senate voted 82 to 6 to declare
war on Germany, and the House followed on April 6. Wilson signed the
war resolution, and the American role in the conflict had begun.[1]

The six members who had voted against war found themselves assailed
as turncoats and traitors. James Reed of Missouri accused George Norris,
who had attacked the role of organized wealth in bringing on the conflict,
of "giving aid and comfort to the enemy on the very eve of the opening of
hostilities." The greatest animus in and out of the chamber was directed at
Robert La Follette. John Sharp Williams of Mississippi called his antiwar
colleague "a pusillanimous, degenerate coward." Such sentiments, which
were amplified outside Washington, led to a serious effort to expel La Follette from the Senate.[2]

In September 1917 La Follette spoke to the convention of the Non-
Partisan League, a radical farm protest group from the upper Middle West, in

St. Paul, Minnesota. The Associated Press reported that the senator won-dered "what American rights" had Germany violated. News stories also er-roneously asserted that La Follette had said, "We had no grievance against Germany." A popular clamor arose as the news of what La Follette had sup-posedly said came out. Theodore Roosevelt proclaimed that La Follette was "the most sinister enemy of democracy in the United States." Cries arose for the senator's expulsion on the grounds that he had made false statements about the origins of the war. A cartoon showed La Follette, William J. Stone, and other dissenters dreaming of a German victory and the medals they would receive from the Kaiser. In this overheated atmosphere, the Sen-ate named a special committee, led by Atlee Pomerene of Ohio, to probe La Follette's actions.[3]

The result was more farce than sober inquiry. The Senate committee moved very slowly, and La Follette stalled their inquiry as he waited for public opinion to change. Meanwhile, the Associated Press disclosed in May 1918 that its report of what La Follette had said was incorrect. By the time of the 1918 elections, the Republicans needed La Follette's vote to organize the Senate, so in December 1918 the Senate committee voted to end the investigation. A month later the Senate itself voted to drop any charges against La Follette. That outcome was a wise result. Senators real-ized that they would be setting a dangerous precedent if one of their mem-bers could be expelled for stating his opinions.[4]

The World War brought an expansion of government authority over the economy and the lives of Americans. When it came to programs of the Wil-son administration to mold public opinion and stifle dissent, the Senate was a fragile bulwark against the repressive tactics of the Justice Department, the Post Office Department, and the White House. The Espionage Act and the Alien Acts, which limited expression of opposition to the war, were en-dorsed with large majorities in the upper house. A few members, such as Hiram Johnson, Norris, and La Follette, spoke out against these dubious in-novations. When civil liberties were violated, Norris argued, "our boasted freedom" would be in danger with the result that "our great Republic will be in serious danger of degenerating into autocracy." But most senators strove to outdo the administration in limiting the rights of citizens to speak out against government policy.[5]

During World War I, cooperation between the Senate and the presidency reached a low point because of the animus and suspicion that members felt toward Woodrow Wilson. The strident opposition of the Republicans, who believed that the president had cheated them out of victory in 1916, was to be expected. Yet Democrats, too, despite their public support of the administration, resented Wilson's failure to consult them about the hard issues on which they had to vote such as taxation, raising an army through the draft, and eventually the terms of peace. "The President is in absolute command here," wrote Hiram Johnson in April 1917. "All of the Republicans and many of the Democrats, violently hate him and detest him. I cannot find any who love him." For the moment, Wilson dominated the scene, but resentment against his tactics would grow as the war developed.[6]

The presence of dissenting Democrats in the upper house made the administration's grip on the Senate very tenuous. In many battles and the key votes that followed, the Democrats' eleven-vote margin shrank to just one or two members. When it came to Republican initiatives to regulate food prices or the controversial attempt to create a committee to oversee the conduct of the war, the White House had to move with care. For example, only the timely change of mind of a Republican senator on a conference committee blocked an effort to impose a watchdog panel on the president in 1917. During the early months of 1918, senators such as Democrat George E. Chamberlain of Oregon pushed the White House to deal with the faltering war effort. Yet Wilson acted as if he had little need to be conciliatory toward even his own party members in the upper house. The president simply thought that the merits of his arguments were self-evident and would carry the day, and he did not take time to explain his case to members individually.[7]

Making things worse for Democrats were two issues, prohibition of alcohol and woman suffrage, that struck at the heart of their uneasy coalition of western and southern members on the one side and northeastern and urban colleagues on the other and exposed fault lines that had plagued the party for two decades. The Anti-Saloon League was at the height of its influence after the 1916 election. The war gave that lobbying group new ways to implement its program of barring the sale of alcohol nationally. Because many German Americans held key positions in the brewing and liquor industries, nativist attacks against alcohol sellers became intense during the war. Congress first enacted wartime Prohibition to conserve wheat, and then moved to adopt a constitutional amendment to obtain the same result in peace. Morris Sheppard of Texas, an ardent "dry," spearheaded the effort that ended in approval of the Eighteenth Amendment that was later ratified in 1919 and went into effect a year later. Rhetorical support for Prohibition by senators did not change senatorial drinking habits. One lawmaker gave a strong speech for Prohibition and then told James Wadsworth, a New York Republican, "Jim, come over to my office, and I'll give you a drink."[8]

The drinking problems of several members remained a topic mentioned only among senators and rarely discussed in public. A prominent Democrat, John Sharp Williams of Mississippi, often came to the floor "rotten drunk," Hiram Johnson wrote to his sons. Williams told friends that he gave better speeches after he had had some drinks, and had abandoned efforts to curb his alcoholism. Missouri's William J. Stone exhibited similar behavior, and Key Pittman of Nevada wrestled with alcoholism both before and after Prohibition went into effect. Frank Brandegee of Connecticut and Charles A. Culberson of Texas were well known within the clubby confines of the Senate for their alcoholic maladies.[9]

The Senate took longer to grant women the right to vote than it did to ban alcohol. The National Woman Suffrage Association (NAWSA) saw the war as its best chance to achieve the reform it had pursued for so long. The House agreed on January 10, 1918, passing a resolution to amend the Constitution to provide for woman suffrage. Now the challenge lay across the Capitol, where many southerners feared that allowing women to vote would lead to arguments that blacks should have the ballot. NAWSA had created a powerful organization in Washington to push for adoption of the amendment. Confronted with pressure from the administration as well, the Senate scheduled a vote on October 1, 1918. Despite a personal appearance from Wilson to urge adoption, the amendment came up two votes short, and twenty-one Democrats voted no. One opposition senator complained, "We find a petticoat brigade awaits outside, and Senate leaders, like little boys, like pages, trek back and forth for orders." Despite the forces in favor of suffrage, for the moment, the advocates of women voting would have to regroup and try again in the next session.[10]

The issue of woman suffrage surfaced again after the war, in February 1919, but the Democrats again failed to approve the amendment. When the Republicans regained control of the Senate in the spring of that year, after the 1918 election, they proceeded to win Senate endorsement of the amendment in June 1919 by a tally of 56 to 25. Over the next year, state legislatures approved the constitutional change so that women were able to

"Woman Suffrage Advocates Press the Senate for Action." The Senate resisted the adoption of woman suffrage until popular pressure became too great. Clifford K. Berryman depicted the process in this 1918 cartoon. (FROM THE U.S. SENATE COLLECTION, CENTER FOR LEGISLATIVE ARCHIVES)

vote in the presidential contest that year. The pressure from their constituents, more than any intrinsic belief in equal political rights for women, animated many senators in the final decision to support woman suffrage. The Senate had implemented a progressive reform in a grudging manner.[11]

From the moment the Senate began its work in April 1917, both parties looked ahead with unusual intensity to the 1918 elections, which would determine who would control the peacemaking process. No one of course knew that the war would end when it did, but Republicans and Democrats understood that their success or failure could shape any peace treaty that might be written. With so much at stake and passions already inflamed, the work of the Senate in 1917–18 went on in as highly charged an atmosphere of partisan contention as any that had existed since the debates over free silver and imperialism during the 1890s.

In this situation where conciliation could have taken a little of the edge off the potential bitterness, Woodrow Wilson behaved as if he expected his will to be law. In public statements he avowed that partisanship would not govern his handling of the war. "Politics is adjourned," he proclaimed in the spring of 1918. "The election will go to those who think least of it."

Republicans countered that the president seemed intent on making the conflict a Democratic war. They cited the case of Theodore Roosevelt, who sought to raise a volunteer division to fight in France in 1917. Republican senators had pushed for approval of the Roosevelt initiative while the White House and the military resisted on the grounds that the division would interfere with orderly planning. Left unsaid was the president's dislike of his political rival. The Grand Old Party saw Wilson's decision as part of a general policy to deny prominent Republicans such as General Leonard Wood any opportunity for battlefield heroics.[12]

The dominance of southerners in the upper house provided another partisan flashpoint. These senators shaped agricultural and tax policies that favored their region and discriminated against other sections. The Lever Act of 1917 gave the president the power to set prices for farm products that would stimulate production but not spark inflation. When the White House fixed prices for wheat, middle western farmers, who had anticipated higher profits, protested that they had been denied their fair share. Meanwhile, the price of cotton remained unregulated, because of the clout of southern Democrats on key committees, and now Republicans alleged sectional motives and revived animosities from the Civil War era.[13]

In their approach to war taxation, Democrats wrote legislation that again tilted in favor of their core constituencies. Rates were kept low for farming regions and the poor, while higher-income Americans saw their taxes rise. The sense of discrimination against such areas as the Northeast, where Republicans were strong, fed the idea that Wilson and his party were waging a sectional war.[14]

In the years 1917 and 1918, ten senators died. Many of their colleagues blamed the stifling conditions under which they had to work in the poorly ventilated chamber for the poor health and death of some. By 1918, talk of installing a cooling system for the Senate and House began to be heard, and some preliminary steps to study the question were taken.[15]

One death proved to be crucial in shaping Wilson's relations with the Senate. In October 1917, a hunting accident claimed the life of Paul Husting, Democrat of Wisconsin. To fill his seat, a special election took place in April 1918. The Democratic candidate was Joseph E. Davies, and the Republicans nominated Irvine Lenroot, a former ally of La Follette's. The White House decided to make the contest a "test" of the war effort, and they assailed Lenroot's record "of questionable support of the dignity and the rights of the country on test occasions." Vice President Thomas Riley Marshall charged that the Republican candidate was after the "sewage" vote from German Americans and their allies. When Lenroot triumphed in the contest, it was a clear rebuke to Wilson and the Democratic leadership. The loss of the seat would prove crucial to Wilson's plans for the postwar peace.[16]

This setback did not deter Wilson from attempting to influence other races in ways that favored his party and policies. He persuaded the automaker Henry Ford to pursue a Senate seat in Michigan, even though Ford had opposed the war. With every seat likely to be crucial, Wilson turned to Ford as someone with the popularity needed to win the seat, telling him, "You are the only man in Michigan, who can be elected and help bring about the peace you so much desire." Political expedience led Wilson to overlook Ford's ignorance on national issues, his anti-Semitism, and his previous opposition to the president's policies. Wilson also tried to affect the Democratic primary process in the South, speaking out in support of candidates who were identified with the administration and chastising those who had opposed him. In the case of James K. Vardaman of Mississippi, who opposed the war, Wilson claimed that the senator was unfriendly to the president's ideals. In private Vardaman called the president "the coldest blooded, most selfish ruler beneath the stars today." Vardaman went down to defeat at the hands of Pat Harrison in the Democratic primary. These presidential involvements in primaries did not help to firm up Democratic cohesion as the election neared.[17]

By late October 1918, Wilson decided to make an appeal to the voters on behalf of a Democratic Congress. The Republicans were arguing that only they could see to it that the war was waged to a successful conclusion. The Democrats believed, in light of such partisan arguments, that asking for their party to retain control of Capitol Hill was appropriate. With signs of their likely defeat appearing in abundance, the Democrats thought that they had to use the president's prestige in the waning days of the election contest. After all, the Republicans had adopted just that strategy under William McKinley twenty years earlier, during the war with Spain.[18]

On October 25, 1918, Wilson's call for the election of Democrats was given to the press. He sought a "Democratic majority" because the Republicans, even though they had supported the war, had attacked the administration. A defeat for the Democrats would be "interpreted on the other side of the water as a repudiation of my leadership." Republicans for their part reacted with outrage to what they called an assault on their patriotism. "Truly this man is a strange man," wrote Senator James Wadsworth of New York. "He conceded the Republicans are pro-war and in the next breath says they are anti-Administration." Resentment spread among the Republicans, whom Wilson would need to gain approval of any peace treaty.[19]

On Election Day, November 5, 1918, the war-weary voters, angry with the administration's tax policies and attacks on civil liberties, gave the Republicans a sweeping victory in the House, where they now held a fifty-vote margin. The margin was much narrower in the Senate. There the Republicans gained a 49–47 advantage. Only the willingness of the once scorned La Follette to vote with the GOP prevented a deadlock and Democratic control through the deciding vote of Vice President Marshall. Other deals about committee chairmanships and future legislation cemented the Republican hold on the body.

Henry Cabot Lodge now became the leader of the majority. He had succeeded Jacob H. Gallinger as minority leader when the elderly New Hampshire senator died in August 1918. The setting was perfect for Lodge to capitalize on the dislike that his party felt for Wilson. For two years, GOP senators would submerge their usual differences in order to defeat Wilson. The animus between Lodge and Wilson helped to make that result possible. According to Lodge, whatever hatred he had for Wilson was more than reciprocated from the occupant of the White House: "With the exception of Roosevelt there is no one the President dislikes more than he dislikes me."[20]

The voters sent some new faces to Washington who would shape the political scene in the decade to come. Medill McCormick, a son-in-law of Mark Hanna, ousted Democrat J. Hamilton Lewis in Illinois. In New Hampshire, the Republican challenger, Governor Henry W. Keyes, defeated the Democratic incumbent, and Republicans picked up seats in Oregon, Delaware, Colorado, and Michigan. Henry Ford lost to Truman Newberry in a contest that was immediately labeled one of the most corrupt in the nation. The

Seven Republicans on the Foreign Relations Committee assembled for a photograph in 1919 as they prepared to consider Woodrow Wilson's plans for a League of Nations. Left to right: Medill McCormick (Illinois), George H. Moses (New Hampshire), Frank. B. Kellogg (Minnesota), Philander C. Knox (Pennsylvania), Henry Cabot Lodge (Massachusetts), Porter J. McCumber (North Dakota), and Harry S. New (Indiana). (LIBRARY OF CONGRESS)

Oregon result gave Charles L. McNary, who had been appointed to fill a vacancy in 1917, a full term and set him on his way to becoming the Republican minority leader in 1933.[21]

With the election decided, Woodrow Wilson now faced the dilemma that would shape the last two years of his presidency and his struggle to gain approval of a peace treaty. He had to find votes for his policies from a hostile Republican majority. Yet there is little evidence that the new political facts impelled Wilson to rethink his approach to Capitol Hill. For six years he had treated even his Democratic colleagues in an aloof manner, and he rarely sought their opinion about how he should approach Congress. Henry Fountain Ashurst of Arizona recorded in his diary on December 1, 1918, his doubt as to whether Wilson had "twenty friends in Congress." The Democrats were willing to go along with their president, but enthusiasm for him as a person was in short supply.[22]

The political arithmetic for Wilson was stark and clear. Assuming that he succeeded in negotiating a peace treaty, he would have to add at least sixteen Republicans to the forty-seven Democrats for any such pact to go into effect. Thus, a conciliatory attitude toward his political enemies might have seemed a wise strategy. Instead, over the next months Wilson acted in a manner that sharpened tensions with the Republicans. To be sure, some Republicans displayed little interest in working with the president, but there were openings to the other party that Wilson ignored.

Convinced that he must attend the peace conference in Paris to have any effect on the ultimate treaty, Wilson announced in November that he would break the tradition that presidents should not leave the borders of the United States during their term of office. Until Theodore Roosevelt went to the Panama Canal Zone in 1906, it had been an accepted American tradition that the chief executive remained within the continental United States. Now Wilson proposed something new. He would go to France as the leader of the American delegation. Wilson wanted the creation of an international body, the League of Nations, so as to prevent another world war, and he wanted it as part of any peace treaty. A good case can be made for the wisdom of what Wilson was doing, but the initiative did not sit well with his Senate enemies, who saw the president's move as another example of his executive arrogance.

Even more upsetting to Republican senators was the delegation that Wilson chose to accompany him to the peace deliberations. Wilson faced a political predicament. He might have selected a senator to be part of the five-man team that went with him. If he chose a Democrat, he would have to have a Republican as well. The obvious choice was Henry Cabot Lodge, now the chair of the Senate Foreign Relations Committee. But that was impossible.[23]

By 1919 Wilson and Lodge had formed one of the great political hatreds in the history of American politics. They had met by mail in the 1880s when Lodge published one of Wilson's early articles. In the years that followed they took very different paths, and by the time Wilson became president there was already latent animosity based on their partisan differences. Lodge saw Wilson as a "trimmer," who had moved toward progressivism to gain the Democratic nomination in 1912. The two men had also found themselves at odds over foreign policy before 1918. In the president's first term, Lodge became convinced that Wilson was irresolute and even cowardly in the execution of foreign policy. Wilson regarded the Massachusetts senator as a rank partisan who could not be trusted to do the right thing on great issues. Lodge said in 1915 that he "never expected to hate any one in politics with the hatred I feel towards Wilson."[24]

Convinced that he must block the president by any means at hand, Lodge wrote to his friend the British foreign secretary Arthur Balfour in November 1918 that the government there should hold out for strong terms in the peace negotiations. Going behind the president's back in this way showed how much Lodge wanted to stymie Wilson. The senator also wrote Balfour that "any agreement for a League, if such a thing can be made, should be in a separate instrument. It should not be an integral part of peace terms." Thus the new chairman of the Senate Foreign Relations Committee was undermining the president's foreign policy on his own initiative. Wilson did not know of Lodge's tactics, but he correctly suspected that the Massachusetts senator would not be a sympathetic member of any peace delegation. In the end, the president decided not to take any senators with him to Paris.[25]

The decision made sense but was an error given the political landscape in late 1918. Wilson needed votes from Republicans, and putting up with Lodge would have helped toward that end. It would have been difficult to get Lodge on his side in such circumstances, but Wilson really had no choice but to try if he wanted to get the treaty approved. By snubbing the Senate and taking with him only one nominal Republican, the diplomat Henry White, Wilson continued the partisan tactics he had pursued during the fighting. No one in the Senate, even on the Democratic side, had any reason to identify his own fortunes with those of the peace treaty, which would not have been the case had several senators gone to Paris in an official capacity.

Wilson went to Europe in December and began work on the peace settlement. He insisted that the League of Nations and its founding document, or "covenant," be included in the overall treaty that the victorious Allies were hammering out. This departure from traditional American isolationism and independence worried the president's opponents. As word came back to the United States about how much Wilson was involving the nation in world affairs, Senate Republicans became even more skeptical about Wilson's vision of an international organization.

Lodge began to consider his options against Wilson. The lame-duck session of Congress would end on March 4, 1919, and the president would have to return to deal with appropriations bills and other pressing business before adjournment. The new Republican-controlled Congress was not scheduled to convene until December 1919, and the Republicans decided that they did not wish to leave Wilson in charge without lawmakers present throughout that period. Hiram Johnson believed that Wilson did not want to create circumstances where "the Senate in the coming months, pregnant with so much of extraordinary importance to the country, shall be daily in a position to comment or criticize."[26]

Returning from Paris, the president announced on February 14 that the League of Nations would be part of the treaty and asked the Senate not to make any judgments about the document until he had a chance to explain its provisions. With only a little more than two weeks before the end of the session, Lodge acted to preempt Wilson. He and the Republicans began to filibuster legislation in order to prevent further action on needed appropriations measures. Control of the Senate would shift to the GOP after March 4 and so they had every incentive to string things out to prevent the Democrats from finishing with bills to keep the government functioning.

Then came Lodge's bombshell. On March 3, 1919, at about midnight, Lodge strode into the Senate chamber and offered a resolution that would proclaim that "the constitution of the league of nations in the form now proposed to the peace conference should not be accepted by the United States." The document suggested, further, that Wilson should work out peace terms with Germany before the League was even considered. A Democratic senator objected to the introduction of the resolution, and the chair sustained it. Lodge then did what he had planned to do all along. He gave out the names of the sitting and newly elected senators who had signed the document. The total came to thirty-seven, four more votes then were needed to defeat the treaty, which had to pass by a two-thirds vote. The press dubbed the document "the Round Robin." Lodge's move revealed the extent of Wilson's political difficulties with the Senate as he prepared to return to Paris to complete work on the peace treaty itself. By preempting what the president hoped to accomplish, Lodge had taken the initiative in the impending battle.[27]

Wilson had added to his existing problems by making some indiscreet comments about his opponents. In late February he spoke to the Democratic

National Committee and denounced "the fatuity of these gentlemen with their poor little minds." He said that the senators were "blind and little provincial people" who recalled for him "a man with a head that is not a head but just a knot providentially put there to keep him from raveling out." After the Round Robin, he promised to have the League and the peace treaty so interwoven together that they could not be untangled. Wilson's rhetoric would have been more appropriate if he had the votes to approve the treaty, but nothing he had done so far had brought him any closer to that goal.[28]

While the president went back to Paris and negotiated changes in what became the Treaty of Versailles, the political equation at home remained problematic for him. In the Senate the press had identified some fifteen members who would vote against any treaty that Wilson supported. They were called the "irreconcilables" and included William E. Borah of Idaho and Hiram Johnson of California.

A senator since 1907, Borah had championed the direct election of senators and remained a regular in 1912 when Theodore Roosevelt bolted. "The Lion of Idaho" was already an attraction for the galleries whenever he chose to speak. An observant Warren G. Harding, new to the Senate in 1916, noted of Borah "that his eyes roam to the gallery with more frequency than those of any other on the republican side of the chamber." Borah had a well-deserved reputation as a ladies' man, and he often directed his remarks to his admiring onlookers. Now the charismatic Idahoan was convinced that the League represented a threat to the nation's basic interest, and he threw his energies into the effort to defeat it, saying, "If the Savior of mankind would revisit the earth and declare for a League . . . I would be opposed to it."[29]

Hiram Johnson had been elected to the Senate in 1916 after service as governor of California. He had been the running mate with Theodore Roosevelt on the Progressive ticket in 1912 and a determined foe of railroad power in his home state. Liberal in his domestic views, he was deeply suspicious of foreign countries, especially Great Britain. He saw Wilson as having yielded too much to the Allies in the peace negotiations. Johnson called the League "a base betrayal of the Republic," and he told his family, "I can't stomach and I will not vote for it, if every elector in California demands it." Johnson's view on foreign policy, like those of senators on the other side of the League fight, grew out of sincere conviction about the proper direction for the nation to follow. All but three or four of the irreconcilables were Republicans, which meant that Wilson would have to find the needed votes from among the thirty-odd Republicans who remained outside the camp of the inveterate foes of the League.[30]

Among the Republican members in the middle were those who wished to see some changes in the treaty but accepted the principle that there should be a League of Nations. The willingness of this group of ten or twelve senators to vote for an amended treaty with "reservations," meaning changes in the document itself to clarify American compliance with the document, led them to be dubbed "mild reservationists." Some of the most thoughtful and sophisticated discussions of the issues the League raised came from Irvine Lenroot and others in this faction. Those who wanted more stringent changes or had strong reservations were closer to the irreconcilables in their general outlook. For his part, Henry Cabot Lodge was most concerned about keeping the Republicans together. If he could defeat Wilson in the bargain, so much the better. He probably tended more toward the strong-reservationist camp on the merits of the treaty. In his speeches, Lodge did not descend to bringing in personalities, and he contributed to the elevated tone of the Senate debate on the League, which largely focused on the serious issues at stake.[31]

Lodge used his power as majority leader to arrange the membership of the Foreign Relations Committee so as to provide an anti-League majority on the panel. Up to that point, Foreign Relations, while prestigious, had stood behind other committees, such as Interstate Commerce and Finance, in relative importance. As Robert La Follette put it, "While Foreign Relations is a big committee at any time and the center of interest just now—in ordinary times either of the other committees out-ranks it in public interest." Lodge increased the number of majority seats on the committee from nine to ten and decreased the minority allotment to seven seats. He then added two reliable opponents of the League to the panel. He also ensured that conservative Republicans controlled the Finance and Appropriations Committees. Republican cohesion contrasted with the divided councils and faltering leadership among the Democrats.[32]

Wilson came back to the United States in July 1919 with the Treaty of Versailles, including the League of Nations at its heart. The sticking point for advocates and opponents of the League was Article X of the covenant, which pledged member nations to go to the aid of a country that was the victim of aggression. Wilson's critics objected that such language could take the United States into a war without the consent of Congress. Senators who felt this way sought wording that would preserve a role for the

Senate. Wilson for his part feared that once he began to accept amendments, the enemies of the treaty would ask for more and more concessions in a process that would water down his plan. The president's view was that the treaty should be accepted as it was. The problem that Wilson confronted was that he could not find a two-thirds majority for his position within the Senate as it existed in 1919.[33]

During the remainder of the summer, Wilson did his best to sway the Senate. On July 10 he gave a speech explaining the treaty to lawmakers, but he was ill and not in his best form, and the oration fell flat. One senator remarked that Wilson's "audience wanted raw meat, he fed them cold turnips." To bring wavering senators along, the president agreed to meet with the Senate Foreign Relations Committee at the White House on August 19. The lawmakers and Wilson sat down for three hours with stenographers present to listen to what the two sides had to say. The session, one of the few times that a president has appeared before a congressional committee in such circumstances, did not alter the political balance on the treaty fight. The two sides made familiar arguments. Wilson committed some errors in answering questions but for the most part held his own against his legislative critics. Even the unfriendly Hiram Johnson believed that the president had been tolerant and long-suffering. Johnson would have been less so: "I would have seen the Foreign Relations Committee in Halifax before I would have sat there for three hours or more permitting a lot of asses to question me."[34]

This meeting suggests that in August there might have been a chance for a compromise had the president been willing to accept some alterations. Convinced that his enemies were not honest in promising to consider "reservations" that the White House could endorse, Wilson decided not to waver on that issue. Instead, he proposed to take his case directly to the American people in a cross-country speaking tour designed to pressure the Senate to act. Once his fellow citizens knew the facts, he was sure they would respond with such intense pressure that the Senate would have to yield its reservations and approve the treaty as negotiated. In reaching that judgment Wilson moved down a path that took him into battle with the Senate and away from the realization of his dream for the League of Nations. Though it is now common for presidents to go over the head of Congress to appeal to the sentiments of the nation, for Wilson to do so was a major political gamble.

The president's tour began on September 3 and continued through September 25, when his health broke down. The political strategy of the junket was not clear. Wilson did not seek to win over Republican senators. Instead he denounced "absolute, contemptible quitters" who now opposed his views. Wilson secured some public backing for the treaty, but the irreconcilables went out on the stump too. They attracted good crowds and so the contest for public opinion seemed to be a draw. The presidential tour did not accomplish what Wilson had hoped. Senators' six-year terms buffered them from the effects of swings in public opinion, so it was not immediately clear how the president expected popular backing for the Versailles pact to show itself. Even those members up for election in 1920 had little to fear from Wilson's wrath. The speaking tour revealed how little Wilson understood the situation that the treaty faced in the Senate and how poorly he grasped the workings of the Senate itself. He would have been better served to sit across the table from his foes and seriously negotiate a compromise on the treaty.[35]

Wilson was already ill when he began his tour, and the physical strain of his determined efforts caught up with him after three weeks. On September 25, he collapsed in Pueblo, Colorado, and was hurried back to Washington. A week later he suffered a stroke that left him paralyzed on his left side with double vision and weakness in his eyes. For the rest of his term, Wilson would be an invalid and his presidency became a caretaker operation. Nonetheless, the president and his wife, Edith, imposing a press blackout on his illness, ruled out any possibility that he would resign or allocate any of his responsibilities to the vice president, Thomas Riley Marshall. The first lady screened the information her husband received and decided whether visitors got to see him. Most senators were left in the dark about the state of Wilson's health.[36]

While Wilson remained in his sickroom, the debate over the League reached a climax in mid-November. The members had been voting on amendments and then reservations to the treaty since early October. Lodge was offering his own reservations that would have watered down Article X. A month later senators on both sides of the debate realized that cloture offered a means to bring their deliberations to an end in an orderly manner. During the war there had been suggestions of ways to limit debate further, but these attempts had gone nowhere. Now, in November 1919, the Senate, on procedural grounds, imposed cloture on itself for the first time by a vote of 78 to 16. The moment was of modest significance. Since most senators wanted to close down discussion and move on to votes on the treaty, there was no real controversy. Genuine tests of the effectiveness of cloture had yet to be held.[37]

With debate limited, the Senate proceeded to decide the foregone fate of the treaty on November 19. President Wilson by that time had recovered enough to tell the acting leader of the Democrats, Gilbert M. Hitchcock of Nebraska, in a letter of his hope "that all true friends of the treaty will refuse to support the Lodge reservation" that reflected the Republican leader's views. The letter was read to the Senate before the last debates occurred. It outraged the proponents of mild reservations and indicated Wilson's intransigence about his position. Then the voting took place. The Lodge reservations went down 55 against to 35 for, and a vote on the treaty without any reservations also failed, 53 against to 38 for. For the moment, the treaty was beaten, but efforts would soon be made to revive it.[38]

During the next four months, senators discussed how they might put together a coalition that would approve the Versailles pact. Meanwhile, rumors circulated about the president's illness, including one that he had gone insane. Using a pretext about problems in relations with Mexico, the Foreign Relations Committee voted along partisan lines to have Hitchcock and Albert B. Fall, a New Mexico Republican who was avowedly anti-Wilson, visit the White House to talk to him about Mexico. The real point was to determine how sick the president really was.

When the "smelling committee" was admitted to the president's bedroom on December 5, 1919, they encountered a carefully staged tableau. Wilson's paralyzed left hand was tucked under the bed covers, and he shook hands with Fall using his right hand. Later accounts had the Republican senator saying, "I have been praying for you sir." Mrs. Wilson's memoir, published two decades later with many exaggerations, had Wilson quipping, "Which way, Senator?" In any case, the interview went off well for Wilson. Fall and Hitchcock told the press that the president had been responsive and alert. The attempt to embarrass Wilson had backfired.[39]

On the treaty, Wilson was no more amenable to any compromise. After his stroke, he became more determined to have the Senate accept the treaty as he had made it or not at all. "Let Lodge compromise," he told Hitchcock a few days later, and he made a public statement to that effect as well.[40]

In January 1920, Wilson called for a "great and solemn referendum" on the treaty in the upcoming presidential contest. There was no way to produce such a single-issue campaign within the American system, however, and the Senate remained the place where the dilemma that the Versailles pact posed had to be resolved. Responding to the public desire, expressed in newspaper editorials and some surveys of voter attitudes, that the treaty, even in an amended form, be looked at again, the senators took it up in February and extended their debate into March. On the eighth Wilson released another letter to Hitchcock in which he commented that a reservation about Article X, the pledge that member nations go to the aid of a country that was the victim of aggression, "cuts at the very heart and life of the Covenant itself." The president's refusal to compromise and his influence with Democratic senators doomed any efforts to find a means of endorsing the document. On March 19, 1920, senators voted 49 for to 35 against approving the treaty with reservations, seven votes fewer than needed to adopt the treaty. Democrats cast twenty-three votes for ratification, but enough followed Wilson's lead to ensure its defeat. After the votes were recorded, the Senate agreed to send the treaty back to the White House, from which it never emerged again. When Wilson heard what had happened, he said to his doctor, "I feel like going to bed and staying there."[41]

In later years the League fight was depicted as a moment when the Senate turned its back on a world role for the United States in favor of isolationism, but this verdict oversimplifies what happened in 1919–20. From July 1919 until the following March, the upper house conducted a high-level debate about what kind of foreign policy the nation should pursue. The majority of senators approached the complex issues in a serious way and engaged in substantive exchanges about genuine problems. Because Wilson also regarded the treaty in such philosophical terms, he did not play hardball with his opponents. Arm twisting, monetary pressure, and political deals had little role in shaping the ultimate outcome. Instead, the Senate staged as elevated a debate as was possible amid the rancor of postwar Washington. There was not a two-thirds majority in the Senate or in the country for a greater American role in the world.

Having defeated the president over the Versailles Treaty, the Senate saw its prestige rise in 1920, and in the early years of the new decade it seemed more powerful than presidents. But that heightened position could not last. The identification of Woodrow Wilson, whom most senators disliked, with the treaty had imparted a focus for debate and cloakroom action that soon dissipated once the issue of the treaty was resolved. With the treaty issue fading, it was time to elect a president to succeed the unpopular and repudiated incumbent.

The Senate contributed one of its own to the race to succeed Woodrow Wilson. When the Republicans nominated Warren Gamaliel Harding of Ohio, they picked a man who was coming to the end of his first term in the upper house. In retrospect, the disasters of Harding's presidency would make him seem a bad choice, but in the context of Republican politics he had much going for him. He was handsome, the very picture of a presidential aspirant, and coming from Ohio he had the perceived ability to carry that important state. In his rise in Ohio politics and in his five years in Washington, his affable personality, love for golf, and conservative views made him many friends. Few of his colleagues thought that Harding had the intellectual equipment needed for the presidency, but he looked like a president, and that was enough for the Republicans in 1920.

One persistent legend in Senate history is that Harding won the Republican nod as the result of the workings of a cabal, led by Boies Penrose of Pennsylvania and others from the upper house, who foisted the unqualified Ohioan on the GOP convention. The story went that in the famous "smoke-filled" room at the Blackstone Hotel, the solons vetted Harding, decided that he was a proper nonentity, and put him over. According to this tale, they shrugged aside Harding's well-known limitations and even accepted his word that there was nothing in his past that would prevent him from being president. Although this narrative persists in popular accounts of the 1920 campaign, it does not accord with the facts. The key to Harding's candidacy was always his availability and chances of being elected as a popular Republican from the key state of Ohio, not his senatorial supporters.

Even after the supposed endorsement from the Senate insiders, at the Republican National Convention, several ballots passed before the nomination was secured for Harding. Then the party leadership wanted to add another senator to run with Harding in the person of Irvine Lenroot, the sometime Progressive from Wisconsin. But Lenroot had associations, long since broken, with Robert La Follette, and the sullen convention, anxious to leave town, was in no mood to accept a vice-presidential nominee forced on them by the party hierarchy. They defeated Lenroot, the choice of the insiders, and stampeded the convention for Calvin Coolidge, the governor of Massachusetts. The alleged kingmakers among the Senate Republicans thus could not even secure the nomination of one of their own colleagues as Harding's running mate.[42]

The election itself was no contest. Harding won a landslide victory over Governor James M. Cox, also of Ohio, and the Democratic vice presidential candidate, Franklin Delano Roosevelt of New York. The Republicans picked up ten Senate seats and saw their margin increase to fifty-nine to thirty-seven. The party had even more secure control of the House of Representatives. The president-elect rejoined his colleagues on December 5, 1920, when the lame-duck session of the Senate convened. As he left the chamber, Harding joked to La Follette, "Now, Bob, be good!" The irrepressible Wisconsin senator shot back, "I'll be busy making you be good." The progressivism that La Follette had brought to the Senate was now receding into the past, and the jovial conservatism that Harding represented would dominate the next decade of Senate life.[43]

The record of the Senate in the first two decades of the twentieth century mixed constructive achievement and dogged opposition to a faster pace for reform. In the days of John Worth Kern, the upper house had demonstrated that it could govern well. For the most part, however, the senators acted as a brake on progress. At a time when the nation needed political innovation to address the problems of industrial growth and world power, the Senate contented itself with a reiteration of past policies and rebuff to new ones. Thus, on balance the Senate of these two decades did not serve the American people well.

## CHAPTER SIX

# Spearless Leaders in the 1920s

T HE SWEEPING REPUBLICAN SUCCESS IN THE 1920 ELECTIONS AND THE twenty-two-seat majority in the Senate that resulted caused the new GOP members to spill over from their side of the Senate chamber into the seats that Democrats usually occupied. These places became known as the "Cherokee Strip" after the Indian lands in Oklahoma that eager white settlers took over when the area was opened to purchase in 1891. The depleted Democrats, most of them from the South, still had enough cohesion to harry the majority and delay action on subjects where they had strong feeling such as racial segregation and anti-lynching measures.

Two Republican presidents dealt with the Senate for most of the 1920s. Warren G. Harding proved to be an ineffective executive during his two years in office. By the time of his death from a heart problem in August 1923, clouds of scandal had gathered around his administration. His successor was the dour, conservative Calvin Coolidge, who found the Senate difficult to manage from 1923 to 1929 because of Republican factionalism. The upper house rejected one of his cabinet appointments in 1925 and otherwise viewed the White House legislative programs with skepticism.

The official leader of the Republicans remained Henry Cabot Lodge, who had proved so skillful in the League of Nations battle. Now in his early seventies, the chain-smoking Lodge was preoccupied with writing his memoirs, editing his correspondence with Theodore Roosevelt, and winning his difficult 1922 reelection bid. Meanwhile, his substantial majority was divided and restless; midwestern and western Republicans, pushing aid for farmers, were often in rebellion against him in 1921. Conservative Republicans outside Washington complained that "political guerrillas like La Follette and Borah" had seized effective leadership "out of Lodge's hands and they do so at intervals in ways that are most distressing."[1]

Lodge remained in office until his death in November 1924. As his successor the Republicans chose Charles Curtis of Kansas, who made much of his Native American ancestors on his mother's side and his flexibility as a leader. His credo was, "You boys tell me what you want, and I'll get it through." Ever a publicity seeker, he lent his name and face to an ad for Lucky Strike cigarettes and proclaimed that many of his colleagues smoked the same brand. From a seat in the back row he made the deals that kept his party together. Borah called him "one of the best political poker players in America." Curtis was eager to be president, opposed Herbert Hoover in 1928, and then went on the ticket as vice president.[2]

The last Republican leader in the period was a genially corrupt conservative from Indiana, James E. Watson, who was chosen in 1929. "Expediency is the keynote of his existence," wrote the journalist Frank R. Kent of Watson in 1931. In his home state, they said, "Jim loves a majority." He and Hoover did not get along, and Watson's erratic health also limited his effectiveness. By 1932, it was evident that Watson would be defeated for reelection. His second-in-command, Charles L. McNary of Oregon, who was as moderate as Watson was reactionary, seemed the probable choice to lead the Republicans in 1933. The legislative record of Lodge, Curtis, and Watson during these twelve years showed little in the way of positive direction or effective programs for the Republicans.[3]

The Democrats started the decade under the authority of Oscar W. Underwood of Alabama. A former member of the House, Underwood became the Democratic leader in 1920. He never really adapted to the upper chamber and its individualistic ways. During World War I, he attacked the filibuster and urged its reform through effective cloture procedures. Once he became the head of the senatorial party, he dismayed his colleagues when he continued his friendship with President Harding and went on diplomatic missions for the White House. By the end of 1922, Underwood looked toward a race for the Democratic presidential nomination in 1924. He resigned as majority leader effective March 3, 1923. Few of his colleagues were sad to see him depart.[4]

The Senate was becoming more attuned to the mass media during the 1920s. One example was the willingness of the Republican leader, Charles Curtis of Kansas, to lend his name to this cigarette advertisement in 1927. Several of his colleagues joined in this campaign. (*THE AMERICAN MAGAZINE, 1927*)

In Underwood's place, the Democrats opted for Joseph Taylor Robinson of Arkansas. At fifty, the burly, feisty Robinson was a young man by the standards of the chamber. On several occasions he got into fisticuffs with citizens who did not treat him with the respect due a senator. He promised his colleagues that "a constant effort will be made to foster a policy of unity and harmony among Democrats in the Senate, and to this end frequent conferences will be held." Like most such assurances, these pledges were soon forgotten once Robinson had been named leader. He brushed aside the ineffectual opposition of Furnifold M. Simmons of North Carolina and won a unanimous vote when the Democrats caucused on March 3, 1923.[5]

Robinson would remain the Democratic leader for the next fourteen years, a record that only Mike Mansfield would exceed during the twentieth century. In his self-confidence and arrogance, Robinson resembled Lyndon Johnson, and he also possessed Johnson's capacity to work with a Republican president. Whether that translated into effective leadership before the onset of the New Deal is another matter. Many Democrats believed that Robinson was too close to Herbert Hoover and too willing to sacrifice the interest of the party for the intangible gains of going along with the White House. Al Smith said that Robinson had given "more aid to Herbert Hoover than any other Democrat." To his critics, Robinson "always mistakes force for fury and energy for emphasis."[6]

With a strong Republican majority after the 1920 elections, a period of legislative ascendancy and accomplishment seemed likely to follow. Instead, the Senate spent eight years in eclipse, more concerned with its own procedures and privileges than with the pressing needs of the country. As a result, it sank in popular repute during the 1920s. When Franklin D. Roosevelt was approached about the possibility of being a vice-presidential candidate for his party in 1924, he demurred: "To have to preside over the United States Senate, as at present constituted, for four whole years would be a thankless, disagreeable and perfectly futile task." A year later the editors of the Minneapolis *Tribune* said, "The Senate has not of late been acquitting itself worthy of the traditions of that body. It has not been performing well its job of acting as a check or as a competent shaper and polisher of legislation."[7]

The Senate was as much concerned in these years with its own comfort and perquisites as it was with passing laws. During the eight years when the Democrats were in charge of the chamber, they had made gestures toward a more economical lifestyle for the members. When the Republicans returned to power in 1919 and then increased their majority after 1920, their inclination was to bring back the amenities that made senatorial life more tolerable. The swimming pool and baths in the office building, shuttered since 1913, were reopened. There, as the editors of The Nation noted, members might "have baths as sumptuous as the toils of their office require."[8]

One persistent source of discomfort continued. The Senate chamber was not air-conditioned, and the rigors of the summer tested the stamina of members. The deaths of the ten senators during World War I led to efforts to install better ventilating systems in both houses in 1918 and 1919. These initiatives ran into resistance to the expense of the proposed changes. As a result, the upgrading did not occur for another decade.

The Senate still operated at a leisurely pace. A new arrival, Hiram Johnson, learned that "generally only ten or fifteen are present. Many of the Senators lounge in the cloak room where they are inaccessible and only Senators are permitted." The conditions of senators' offices had improved since the turn of the century. Even incoming senators could now look forward to reasonable accommodations. The annual pay had risen to $7,500 in 1907 and would go up again in 1925, to $10,000. The expense of living in Washington remained high, and members still did outside work to make ends meet.[9]

A culture of deference pervaded the work of the upper house. Young pages, still all male in their membership, were available to run errands on and off the floor. During a single week in February 1919, Richard Riedel, then an unusually young nine-year-old page, counted 310 chores on which senators had dispatched him. When it was time for senators to eat, they repaired to private dining rooms with food served at low prices. Republicans and Democrats did not mingle in these settings but generally sat along partisan lines to form their own clubs within the larger club.[10]

In 1919, Congress had adopted and the states had ratified the Eighteenth Amendment, to prohibit the manufacture and sale of alcoholic beverages in the nation. Despite this new law, which went into effect on January 29, 1920, in the Senate the old, loose approach to liquor continued. Alcoholism permeated the institution. An exact count of those members with "drinking problems" is not possible, but some lawmakers showed up on the floor in various stages of drunkenness. The most notorious was the sharp-minded senator from Mississippi, John Sharp Williams, who was a formidable debater even when he was in his cups. Charles Culberson ran for a fifth term in 1922 but could not campaign because of his alcohol-related infirmities. The picture he sent to the voters showed him so ravaged by the effects of his drinking that he was ousted from office.[11]

When Joe Robinson became Democratic leader in 1924, he set up an inner office where his aides kept bottles so that senators could drink after a hard day. Senators enjoyed the services of their own private bootlegger, "the man in the green hat," until he was arrested at the end of the 1920s. Fears that his list of customers might be made public abated when the police agreed to keep everything quiet. The personal toll on the Senate increased. Frank Brandegee, another alcoholic, committed suicide in 1924, as did Medill McCormick, despondent after the loss of his seat that same year.[12]

With so many distractions such as golf and drinking, some senators found it boring to have to show up for their duties on or off the floor. The problem of absenteeism that had bothered John Worth Kern remained a drag on the institution. Golf, the racetrack, and professional baseball games tempted members away for many afternoons of the lengthy sessions dealing with arid subjects like the tariffs or during a protracted filibuster. In 1922, the *Washington Post* complained that "the Senate Republicans habitually absent themselves from Washington, neglecting not only tariff-making but all other public business."[13]

Because of an illness that befell Ben Tillman, in 1914 the members had adopted a rule banning smoking in the chamber "at any time." Then, in one of those rhetorical tricks that characterized the body, the rule was interpreted not to apply to executive sessions. Accordingly, the majority leaders of both parties often called for such sessions, where the public was excluded, so that members addicted to nicotine could smoke.[14]

The masculine atmosphere of the Senate was little changed by the advent of woman suffrage in 1920. During the war the wives of members had formed a "ladies of the Senate" group, which continued on into the 1920s. The women met to fold bandages, exchange information, and listen to speakers. But the idea of a woman senator seemed a distant prospect. In 1922, however, an incumbent senator from Georgia, Thomas E. Watson, died while the Senate was out of session; it would not meet until after the election to choose a successor. As a public relations gesture the governor, Thomas Hardwick, appointed a woman, Rebecca Felton, to fill out the unexpired term, expecting that he himself would be the new senator. The voters selected Walter George instead, but Hardwick said that he would allow Felton to occupy the seat for two days so that she could become the first female senator.[15]

Felton, eighty-seven, arrived in Washington on November 21, 1922, posed for photographers while surrounded by happy women, and gave one brief speech on the floor about the future of women in the Senate. No one mentioned that Felton, three decades earlier, had been an advocate of lynching blacks. She then returned home, and the chamber reverted to its usual all-male condition. The second woman senator would not arrive until

Founded during World War I, the Senate Ladies Club provided a means for wives of members to do good works and to
socialize. Left to right: Mrs. William N. Butler, Mrs. Frederick
Gillett, and Mrs. Oscar W. Underwood during one of their
weekly luncheons in 1922. (LIBRARY OF CONGRESS)

Hattie Caraway of Arkansas was named to succeed her deceased husband
in 1931. During the 1930s and '40s four other women were appointed
briefly to serve out their dead husbands' terms. Women senators elected in
their own right would not appear until 1948.

In the 1920s, the nominal leaders of the Senate were merely shadows
compared with the institution's dominant personality, William E. Borah,
"the Lion of Idaho." He was fifty-five in 1920 and after thirteen years in
Washington had established himself as the preeminent orator and most
charismatic lawmaker of his time. When Borah rose to speak, the galleries
filled and excitement ran through the chamber. With his long hair, sharply
chiseled features, and ringing voice, the senator was formidable in debate.
Should Borah leave Washington, said the humorist Will Rogers, "they
might as well make stove wood of the seats in the Senate gallery."[16]

Rebecca Felton of Georgia, eighty-seven, was appointed
to the Senate to fill a vacancy and served for two days.
On November 22, 1922, Mrs. Felton (seated) heard the
cheers of well-wishers. (LIBRARY OF CONGRESS)

The press loved Borah, and he fed their needs with inside tips, regular
conferences, and the capacity to dominate the front page of their papers.
The Idahoan was well known in Europe, where his frequent pronounce-
ments about foreign policy and American isolationism attracted extensive
coverage and critical comment. Borah relished the spotlight in an age
when most politicians seemed bland. There had been celebrity senators before him, but he was the best of his time in using his position to achieve
personal fame.[17]

Borah had shown his ability to sway public opinion as one of the irreconcilables in the League of Nations battle. The popular thinking was that he
could, if he wished, win the White House. Borah wanted to be president, and
there were times when he made gestures about running either as a Republican or a third-party candidate in the 1924 election and again in 1928. The
sense that Borah was a bigger man than any of the three chief executives of
the 1920s permeated Washington. The story went that in 1924 Coolidge

called Borah to the White House and told him that he had to be on the Republican ticket that year. Borah replied, "Which place, Mr. President?"[18]

In practice, Borah turned out to be unwilling to commit himself to the hard road of actually running for president. He was always more potential than accomplishment. He did not push for the enactment of laws, and he was identified with no great policies. Eloquent about free speech and the rights of the common person, Borah was ever on the verge of a crusade for justice. A future senator, Richard L. Neuberger, caught the essence of Borah in the 1930s. For all of the gifts he possessed, Borah's "record is largely one of dissent. Constructive achievement is almost totally absent." Quick to fix on injustice or social ills, Borah drew back from enacting laws or using the power of government to address problems. He opposed child labor laws, preferred to defend the filibuster rather than to support the rights of African Americans, and saw no constitutional means to restrict lynching.[19]

His colleagues were often frustrated at Borah's lack of resolve and wavering course in the handling of legislation. If William Jennings Bryan had once been known as the "peerless leader" of the Democrats, a fellow senator dubbed Borah "our spearless leader." He would promise support on an issue and then fade away. The Idaho lawmaker was at his best in pursuit of such dreams as the campaign to outlaw war in the mid-1920s. That noble vision could be pursued for its own sake without worrying about the practicalities of implementing utopia. In many respects, Borah embodied the nature of the Senate in the 1920s—grandiloquent, windy, and irrelevant.[20]

Yet he was also an important influence on what presidents could accomplish. He helped to launch the Washington Naval Conference when he sponsored a resolution in December 1920 that asked the president-elect to summon Great Britain and Japan to a meeting about limits on the building of warships. Out of the positive popular reaction that ensued came a November 1921 conference in Washington that produced a group of treaties seeking to change the naval balance in the Pacific.[21]

Borah approved of the Naval Limitation Pact and the Nine-Power Treaty, which addressed the territorial integrity of China, as constructive results of the conference. Like Hiram Johnson, Borah rejected the Four-Power Treaty, which ended the alliance between Great Britain and Japan and bound the United States to observe the rights of France, Britain, and Japan in the Pacific. This arrangement, the two isolationist senators argued, was tantamount to an alliance to preserve the existing international order. Sensitive to these concerns, Majority Leader Lodge accepted reservations reaffirming the power of Congress to decide on war and peace. The Four-Power Pact passed 67 to 27, with La Follette, Borah, and Johnson among those voting no. Borah had started the process of naval limitation but had then backed away from the results of his legislative venture into foreign policy.[22]

Because of the presence of Borah, Hiram Johnson, and others who had defeated Wilson and the League of Nations in 1919–20, the after-effects of that controversy echoed in the chamber throughout the 1920s. The United States stayed aloof from the international organization with one key exception. In December 1924, President Coolidge urged in his annual message that his country join the World Court, which the League had established. The Senate took up the issue a year later after enemies and friends of the idea had waged a public battle in the press over the merits of the proposal.

Coolidge's commitment to his proposal was guarded. He would accept changes in language to the enabling legislation even if these reservations, as they were called, might be unpalatable to other countries. Coolidge could thus be for the court in public but willing to see it defeated if Senate backing was not evident. The lawmakers duly laid down a series of reservations that nations that had already joined the court would find difficult to endorse. The most crucial reservation had to do with whether the court could issue "advisory opinions" on matters relating to the United States. To opponents of the international body such as Borah, allowing the court to tell Washington what it could do in this way seemed to be a return to the dangers of the League of Nations.[23]

In January 1926, opponents of the court used a filibuster to block proceedings. The manager for the administration, Irvine Lenroot, invoked cloture to restrict debate, which passed on January 25 by 68 to 26. The Senate then adopted the amended resolution with the reservations two days later by a final tally of 76 to 17. The apparent success for the court was illusory, however. Other nations found the advisory-opinion reservation unacceptable and asked Coolidge to invite the Senate to make the necessary changes. That move the president would not make, and his advocacy of the World Court simply died away. Borah and his allies had succeeded in heading off another American commitment to international institutions.[24]

As an opponent of the League of Nations, Borah thought he had the answer to world turmoil in a treaty to outlaw war itself. The campaign to ban war as an instrument of national affairs gathered momentum during this period first as a way of reducing tension between the United States and France over issues of reparations after World War I and also trade relations. Peace advocates also wanted to see a general affirmation of the virtues of a warless world. Borah declared in 1927, "This is too important to confine only to this country and France."[25]

Once a treaty had been worked out between Secretary of State Frank B. Kellogg and his French counterpart, Aristide Briand, Borah labored to gain approval from his colleagues on the Foreign Relations Committee. This time the chairman fought against accepting any reservations, and to that end he included a report from his committee that would give senators who wanted to express reservations an opportunity to state their reasons without actually including them in the treaty. On January 15, 1929, the treaty was passed in the Senate 85 to 1. A cynical Hiram Johnson wrote, "The explanations and interpretations by the proponents of the treaty have made its nothingness complete." The Californian had a point. Outlawing war was a rhetorical exercise that allowed senators to feel virtuous but that did little to put the brakes on what was already a deteriorating world situation.[26]

Borah was not the only senator with his eye on the White House during these years. The early 1920s saw Robert M. La Follette resume his presidential ambitions. In his late sixties and in uncertain health, the Wisconsin senator won reelection in 1922 and turned his attention to a third-party candidacy in 1924. The discontent that gripped farmers in the Middle West in 1921–22 seemed to create conditions that gave La Follette and a third party hope of making an impact on national politics, but a return of prosperity by 1924 eroded his base of support. The Progressive ticket of La Follette and Burton K. Wheeler of Montana carried Wisconsin and ran second in some states of the West and Middle West, but with about 17 percent of the popular vote, La Follette trailed the victorious Republicans and the soundly beaten Democratic nominee, John W. Davis.[27]

Rejected and repudiated in and out of the Senate after the 1924 balloting, La Follette died on June 18, 1925. His son, Robert M. La Follette, Jr., was elected to succeed him. In 1959, a Senate committee headed by John F. Kennedy named the elder La Follette as one of the five greatest members of the Senate in its history (along with John C. Calhoun, Henry Clay, Robert A. Taft, and Daniel Webster). It was a gesture born more of politics than historical accuracy. Robert M. La Follette was more distinguished as governor of his home state than as a senator. Beyond the La Follette Seaman's

Act of 1915, a measure to protect American merchant sailors, few laws are associated with his name. The campaign to expel him during World War I was not justified, but martyrdom is not a substitute for legislative skill. In many ways, his contemporary, George W. Norris, had more impact in the Senate. La Follette's greatest influence came with his innovative political strategy of reading the roll calls and his instinct for self-publicity as a means of running for president.

Almost as famous as Borah was the group of western and southern senators who made up the so-called Farm Bloc. The leaders included George Norris, Charles McNary, Claude Swanson of Virginia, and Arthur Capper, a Kansas Republican. As a pressure group, their motives were self-interested, but their identification with agriculture made them seem attractive as an alternative to the conservative leadership of the chamber. After World War I ended and world agriculture revived in Europe and Asia, the expansion of production drove down commodity prices in the United States. From 1919 to 1923 American farmers experienced a depression, the effects of which rippled through the decade and into the New Deal era. As prices fell and farmers saw their homes and livelihoods being lost, they pleaded with their congressional delegations for government relief.[28]

In the Senate the first sign of concerted action came on May 9, 1921, when western and southern senators met at the office of the lobbying Farm Bureau in Washington. Among the most prominent figures in attendance were Williams S. Kenyon of Iowa and McNary, both Republicans.[29]

The accomplishments of the Farm Bloc in 1921 were modest and did not come to grips with the problem of overproduction, which bedeviled farmers for the next two decades. The ability of these dissident members to pass legislation and to sway the Senate leadership and the Harding administration seemed more significant at the time than it proved to be in the long run. During the remainder of the decade, the remnants of the Farm Bloc pushed for a plan to subsidize farm products and dump surplus American products on world markets. This scheme, which was both costly and impractical, received several presidential vetoes from Calvin Coolidge and never went into effect.[30]

The Farm Bloc did offer a model to other senators of how to create a regional coalition to advance sectional aims. In the 1930s, senators interested in inflation and higher prices for American silver miners would operate a "Silver Bloc" to press their priorities. Farm state senators would also prove effective during the New Deal of the 1930s and beyond in obtaining federal appropriations for their states. Whether all this Washington largesse really advanced the national interest was rarely discussed in the Senate, where clout and appropriations were measures of success.

Overlapping with the members of the Farm Bloc in the 1920s was another informal grouping of Senate Progressives, including Robert M. La Follette, Jr., Burton K. Wheeler of Montana, Smith Brookhart of Iowa, Hiram Johnson of California, and Clarence Dill of Washington. The coalition's driving spirit was the Progressive maverick and nominal Republican George W. Norris of Nebraska. Norris was most interested in a bill to provide publicly owned electric power through the Muscle Shoals dam project on the Tennessee River instead of ceding the project to private industry. He also favored an amendment to the Constitution to change the date of presidential inaugurations from March 4 to mid-January, which would change the dates of yearly congressional sessions and end the short sessions that encouraged filibusters.[31]

Other Senate reformers supported measures to restrict the use of judicial injunctions in strikes, limits on American foreign policy adventures in Latin America, and a more active role for the government in dealing with unemployment and the electric utility industry. Most of the time the Progressives were fighting rearguard actions against conservative programs. Nonetheless, they acted as a check on pro-business initiatives by the Harding and Coolidge administrations.

One way that Democrats and Progressives counterattacked the Republican administrations was through the investigative power of the Senate. The most important investigation was of the Teapot Dome scandal, which involved the leasing of federal oil reserves in California and Wyoming (Teapot Dome is a rock formation in Wyoming that from a distance resembled a teapot). In 1921 and 1922 reports circulated that leases to the reserves, after they had been moved from the control of the Navy Department to the Department of the Interior, had been illegally sold by the secretary of the interior, Albert B. Fall, to private oil companies. Spurred by such public charges, the Committee on Public Lands and Surveys launched a probe in late 1923. A potential scandal for the Harding administration, the Teapot Dome affair was now the responsibility of the new presidency of Calvin Coolidge.[32]

The driving force in the Teapot Dome inquiry was the mustachioed, determined Thomas J. Walsh, Democrat of Montana. The information Walsh elicited about bribes and corruption within Harding's cabinet led to the resignations of two holdover members of Coolidge's official family, Secretary of the Navy Edwin Denby and Attorney General Harry M. Daugherty. During this period the journalists covering the hearings awaited the latest sensational revelation about administration wrongdoing, and the sessions became a media event with day-to-day story lines. Harding's death, however, meant that his personal actions could not be investigated. In any case, much of what took place in Teapot Dome happened without the president's knowledge. In the parlance of a later time, there was no smoking gun linking the deceased president to the crimes his associates had committed.[33]

Democrats thought that Teapot Dome would help them in the 1924 elections, but when it turned out that the key private citizen in the probe, the oilman Edward L. Doheny, had made donations to both parties, the scandal's damage to Republicans decreased. Although some of the participants in Teapot Dome faced criminal trials and the Coolidge administration dealt with some short-term embarrassment, the Senate's inquiry fizzled out, and Teapot Dome was a dead issue by the time the voters elected Coolidge to a full term.

Between 1921 and 1923, the problem of making the Senate work, even with a large Republican majority, remained unsolved. When combined with the sensitive issue of race, filibusters took on a more explosive character. The rules change in 1917 enabled a majority to end debate on a specific piece of legislation, yet the framers of the change had not addressed a crucial point: their language left open the right to filibuster motions to proceed to consider a piece of legislation. So it was still possible to have extended debate on peripheral procedural issues, such as the reading of the daily journal, before the substance of a proposed law was even taken up. The Democrats used this tactic against the Fordney-McCumber Tariff bill in 1922, and the Republicans even filed a cloture petition, which was defeated. In the end, the Democrats backed off and the bill became law.[34]

When, starting in 1922, filibusters and race issues became entangled, the Senate embarked on more than forty years of frustration and torment about this most contentious of national issues. The rise in lynchings during and after World War I had persuaded Leonidas C. Dyer, a Missouri Republican with African-American voters in his district, to introduce a House bill giving the federal government the power to prosecute those in a mob of three or more citizens that put someone to death. To its critics the bill was unconstitutional because it accorded too much power to the national government. Southerners saw the measure as the first step in an all-out attack on the structure of segregation.[35]

The "great migration" of southern blacks out of Dixie between 1913 and 1921 had increased the number of African-American voters in the North. The changed political dynamic of the nation meant that northern politicians were now a little more sympathetic to the concerns of black citizens, even if the reasons had some evidence of expediency. Pressure from the National Association for the Advancement of Colored People and its leader, Walter White, impelled some GOP members to take up the cause. Following the elections of 1922, when the Republicans suffered severe losses in the Senate, the leadership decided to bring up the Dyer bill in the special session that President Harding summoned in November to address a shipping bill that the administration wanted. With a limited amount of time to deal with the lynching proposal, the situation was ideal for a southern filibuster.

The Dyer bill faced other hurdles. Not wishing to devote much political capital to the rights of African Americans, the Republican leadership assigned the task of managing the bill to an obscure, inexperienced California senator, Samuel M. Shortridge, who was clearly outmatched by the southern bloc. These senators made it clear that they would use all the parliamentary tools available to them to keep the bill from even getting to the floor. They prolonged the reading of the journal, a formality that was usually waived. They offered and then debated corrections to change trivial errors in the wording of the journal. The retiring Democratic leader, Oscar W. Underwood, made clear what was happening: "The South is absolutely opposed to [the substance of the Dyer bill], and always has been; but it goes farther than the South." Underwood added, "You have no right to rape the constitution of your country because you think somebody has violated the rights of some citizens in a particular state." Many erstwhile Progressives, including William E. Borah, believed that constitutional questions over the power of the federal government to impose laws on the states were more significant than the issue of racial justice, and their support helped sustain the southern bloc's position.[36]

There had been fifty-one lynchings in 1922, but that tragic statistic did not move the upper house to action. After four days of the southern filibuster, the Republicans gave in and agreed that the Dyer bill would be dropped, and it was not discussed in the regular short session that began on December 4, 1922. While the Republicans were aware of the black vote in northern states, at bottom they did not believe that lynching was a salient issue. They saw race as a side matter that could be finessed. As a result, the filibuster became more entrenched as a weapon in American race relations, and the processes of the Senate were accordingly distorted by the presence of this antidemocratic instrument.

The outcome of the anti-lynching controversy in 1922 convinced southern senators that seniority, the committee system, and mastery of the rules were their sure defense against further efforts to change their society's racial arrangements. The cohesion and solidarity of the southerners in the Senate in the 1920s and 1930s attested to their effectiveness in bolstering their political position in the nation at large. The modern incarnation of the "Senate Club" had its roots in the defense of racial inequality that crystallized after World War I. In the 1930s southern Democrats and conservative Republicans made common cause in a manner that established their dominance in the upper house.

Southern senators could rely on the financial support of a single benefactor, Bernard M. Baruch. A wealthy financier who had a lavish estate in South Carolina, Baruch bankrolled the Democratic Senatorial Campaign Committee and made generous campaign contributions to many individual lawmakers as well. He entertained senators at his spacious Hobcaw Barony mansion, where he presented them with his views on policy issues. There was no direct quid pro quo between Baruch and his beneficiaries. His opposition to government regulation, his support for a balanced budget, and his commitment to lower taxes tracked what his beneficiaries also believed about these subjects. At the same time, Baruch wielded great influence in shaping the agenda that Democrats such as Joseph Robinson, James Byrnes of South Carolina, Alben Barkley of Kentucky, and Pat Harrison of Mississippi followed in the upper house. The relative timidity of the Senate Democrats before the New Deal owed a great deal to their reliance on Baruch's wallet and his attitudes, which permeated the upper house.[37]

After the anti-lynching bill episode, the filibuster became ever more entrenched as a matter of Senate procedure. Wesley L. Jones, a Washington Republican, called for changes in the cloture rule in 1923, but that initiative went nowhere. Following the 1924 election and the sweeping victory of Calvin Coolidge and his running mate, Charles G. Dawes of Illinois, the filibuster faced a new assault. Ultimately, the Senate proved deft at changing the subject to protect its prerogatives and manner of doing business.[38]

No one expected fireworks when Dawes was sworn in as vice president on March 4, 1925. The swearing-in was usually a perfunctory occasion before the real business of inaugurating the president, but Dawes tried to make the moment a serious one. A former head of the Bureau of the Budget, the Illinois politician had a well-deserved reputation for plain speaking. He launched into an attack on rule 22, concerning filibusters and cloture, and asked, if the rule did not exist, "who would dare maintain that in the last analysis the right of the Senate itself to act should ever be subordinated to the right of a Senator to make a speech?"[39]

The Dawes speech angered senators. They did not appreciate having their rules criticized in such a public way. Hiram Johnson called Dawes's delivery "a disgusting and unworthy exhibition" and found that his words themselves were in "bad taste." George H. Moses of New Hampshire replied, "Our rules . . . have never kept any desirable or desired legislation off the statute books. A lot of bad legislation has been kept off the statute books by them." The Democratic majority leader, Joseph Robinson, did concede that the Dyer bill would have been passed had it not been for the filibuster rule.[40]

Dawes wanted to make the filibuster a national issue in 1925 and delivered a series of speeches on the subject, but he lost credibility a few days after he made his inaugural speech. President Coolidge nominated Charles Beecher Warren of Michigan as attorney general. Democrats alleged that the nominee's connections with the sugar industry made him a poor choice, and the Federal Trade Commission was investigating his firm. When the confirmation came to a vote on March 10, it became clear that there was going to be a tie, and Dawes's vote would be needed to break the tie and confirm Warren. Thinking that his vote would not be needed, Dawes retired to his hotel to take a nap. When he was summoned to cast the deciding ballot, he rushed to the Senate, only to find when he arrived that a Democrat had changed his vote to defeat the nomination. The faux pas produced derision of the vice president and his tardiness. The *Chicago Tribune* said that Dawes was "asleep at the switch when the Administration was going off the rails, and he may be advised hereafter to take coffee in the morning, even if it keeps him awake all day."[41] The Warren nomination came up again a few days later and again was turned down by a 46–39 vote.

Dawes continued to make the case for changing the filibuster rule and saw the Senate invoke cloture on three occasions. One vote had to do with debate on the World Court, and two others related to banking and the organization of the Treasury Department. Though Dawes's actions attracted newspaper comment at the time, they failed to move the Senate to change its filibuster rules. That body, as it usually did, looked to its immediate parochial concerns rather than to broader questions of the national interest.[42]

One overriding concern for all senators was their reelection and the campaign funds that they needed to sway voters. By the 1920s the Seventeenth Amendment, which inaugurated direct election of senators, had produced a dilemma for them. The costs of running statewide campaigns, both in primaries and general elections, mounted. Candidates regularly circumvented even the lax rules that Congress had devised during the Progressive Era to regulate such activities. Three celebrated cases placed the issue of honesty in elections before the upper house in a direct way.

The most notorious episode arose from the race between Henry Ford, then a nominal Democrat, and Truman H. Newberry, a Republican, for the Michigan Senate seat in 1918. Reports of vast expenditures for both candidates circulated freely during the contest, in which the Republican prevailed. Soon after Newberry was seated, in May 1919, Ford filed a petition challenging his election. Meanwhile, in a criminal case against Newberry he was found guilty of spending several hundred thousand dollars on his campaign, far more than the $3,750 that Michigan law allowed. The case went to the United States Supreme Court, which overturned the conviction and also declared the Federal Corrupt Practices Act of 1911 unconstitutional. Meanwhile, a Senate committee found that Newberry had been fairly elected.[43]

What Newberry had spent on his campaign shocked political Washington, perhaps because it suggested the demands of future campaigns. George Norris of Nebraska told the Senate with ample sarcasm that the Newberry-Ford contest represented a way in which, if seats in the upper house were sold, the chamber would have "a high class membership." In early 1922 the members voted 46 to 41 to declare Newberry duly elected. That year, however, enough anti-Newberry senators were elected to tip the balance against the incumbent. Knowing he would probably be ousted, he resigned in November 1922. The editors of the *Boston Herald* took note of what the Senate had failed to do: "We have made no provision for financing our political campaigns, at a time when the direct primary—the most effective device ever conceived by the mind of man for giving wealth an advantage over poverty, has doubled the inevitable cost and when woman suffrage has doubled it again."[44]

In the wake of the Newberry affair, the Senate and House approved in February 1925 the Federal Corrupt Practices Act, designed to regulate spending in Senate and House campaigns. The measure set very tight limits on what incumbent senators—but not their challengers—could expend in a general election campaign: $10,000 to $25,000 depending on the size of the state and its population. But there were exceptions that made these restrictions worthless. A committee established to support the candidate could spend without any limit at all. The law did not apply to primary campaigns, which meant that the then Democratic South was hardly affected at all, because in that region, victory in the party primary meant that success in the general election was certain. So many loopholes existed in the law that it soon became a mere formality to which few politicians paid more than appropriate lip service. Concerned more about their own status than the integrity of the election process, senators dodged the hot topic of campaign finance and would soon do so again.[45]

Within two years the weakness of the Senate's efforts to control spending on campaigns became plain. In Pennsylvania and Illinois, two Republican senatorial candidates set new records for lavish expenditures. In 1926, more than $800,000 was spent on the primary campaign of William S. Vare, the leading Republican candidate in the party's Pennsylvania primary, and his GOP opponents spent more than $2.6 million on their efforts. The same year, in Illinois, the incumbent, William B. McKinley, spent $350,000 on his losing primary campaign, while the winner, Frank L. Smith, laid out between $253,000 and $458,000. Both Vare and Smith went on to win their seats in November and expected to become members when the Senate reconvened in December 1927.[46]

Embarrassed by the furor over the money spent on these two elections, the Senate decided, after much wrangling, that Smith and Vare would not be seated. The chamber had the right to judge the qualifications of its members, and senators decided that Vare and Smith had simply gone too far. The taint of money led senators to conclude that the two men should not be allowed to take their seats. These victories for honest government proved to be largely symbolic ones. Although the Senate continued to investigate campaign fund-raising practices for the next several years, no meaningful legislation emerged from these probes. The members sought to do just enough to placate public opinion and newspaper editorial writers without disturbing the procedures that ensured their own reelection.[47]

Few sectors of American government performed well during the 1920s in meeting the economic and social problems that the nation confronted, and the Senate's record in that regard was uninspiring. During eight years when the Republicans controlled the chamber and the Democrats offered lack-luster opposition to the programs of the Grand Old Party, the Senate mirrored the conservative sentiments that dominated political affairs. The Progressives in the upper house did achieve modest results in some areas, but the majority of those accomplishments, like George Norris and Muscle Shoals, came in blocking ill-considered initiatives. For the most part, the Senate proved to be less an agent of needed change and more of an obstruction to it.

The state of affairs in the Senate seemed likely to continue following the election of 1928. The victory of Herbert Hoover over the Democratic candidate, Al Smith with Joe Robinson as his running mate, brought in eight new Republican senators. The majority had a seventeen-seat margin over the opposition and the single independent lawmaker in the chamber. With continuing economic prosperity and the popular Hoover in charge of the nation's affairs, a continuation of Republican dominance of the government seemed likely to most observers as 1929 got under way. Within a year, of course, the political landscape would be transformed. The Great Depression of the 1930s would sweep the Republicans out of power and usher in the era of the New Deal. During the six years that followed Hoover's accession to the presidency, the Senate grappled with the consequences of the Depression and the dramatic changes that Franklin Delano Roosevelt proposed to fight the economic downturn.

## CHAPTER SEVEN

# The Senate
# in the Depression

D URING THE YEARS OF THE GREAT DEPRESSION, FROM 1929 UNTIL THE
beginning of World War II, the United States Senate, like the rest of
the American government, faced challenges that defied the conventional
political wisdom of the time. Mass unemployment that sometimes exceeded 25 percent, disastrous business conditions, and outright poverty for
millions of people presented leaders with problems not seen since the
1890s. From the stock market crash in October 1929 through the early
years of the New Deal, the Senate struggled to keep pace with the onrush
of somber events.

Few politicians anticipated such a disaster at the beginning of the presidency of Herbert Hoover. The Republicans had firm control of the Senate,
and the new chief executive seemed to be the kind of administrator whose
expertise in business and knowledge of engineering would guide the country
to ever higher levels of prosperity. With president and Capitol Hill working
in harmony, the future seemed bright for the Grand Old Party. Peter Norbeck of South Dakota concluded in April 1929, "The President is so im-
mensely popular over the country that the Republicans here are on their
knees and the Democrats have their hats off."[1]

Yet, by the fall of 1929, even before the full impact of the stock market
crash was clear, Hoover's relations with Capitol Hill had deteriorated. The
president, who had never run for elective office before 1928, looked on

Congress as an annoyance and impediment to his programs. He refused to make the deals for patronage and favors that kept legislation moving, and he publicly displayed his disdain for lawmakers collectively and individually. Once the Depression hit, he showed even more impatience with the congressional politicians who stood in his way. He complained that "this job is nothing but a twenty-ring circus—with a whole lot of bad actors." He suggested that the nation would be better off if Congress simply went home. After the Republicans suffered election defeats in 1930 that narrowed their majority, he argued that senators should give up their committee chairmanships in favor of the Democrats. That would put the onus for political disasters on the opposition. Few presidents have been more inept in handling Capitol Hill than Hoover was.[2]

For their part, the Senate leaders of the day often lived down to Hoover's expectations. The main figures in the upper house were not up to the task they would soon face of dealing with a nation in an economic crisis. In keeping with their tradition of rewarding seniority and faithful service to the party, the Republicans selected James E. Watson of Indiana to succeed Charles Curtis, who had become vice president. Watson was popular with the members of both parties but was also renowned for his instinctive conservatism—pushing outdated Republican policies of small government and the protective tariff as the answer to all social problems. Hoover regarded him with barely concealed contempt as someone of "spasmodic loyalties and abilities."[3]

The president had little respect either for the other major Republican figure at the time, George H. Moses of New Hampshire, the president pro tempore. Moses had a sharp tongue and a gift for phrasemaking, dubbing the western senators of the Farm Bloc the "sons of the wild jackass." He also questioned whether direct election of senators was working to the public's advantage. "I look upon the performance of some of my colleagues and listen to their ravings, and I am led to wonder why my country should have been visited with such an awful affliction." Moses had opposed Hoover for the presidential nomination in 1920, and the two men never trusted each other after that.[4]

Hoover had more luck persuading the minority leader, Joseph T. Robinson, to go along with administration programs for budget cutting and favors to big business. Indeed, the criticism of Robinson among his colleagues was that he was too close to the White House and too willing to do whatever Hoover asked of him. Robinson had been Alfred E. Smith's running mate

The Republican leadership (left to right)—George H. Moses (New Hampshire), president pro tempore; Charles Curtis (Kansas), the outgoing majority leader; Charles McNary (Oregon), a future party leader; and James E. Watson, the new majority leader—posed for the camera on February 28, 1929. The Senate cloakrooms were the places where senators could meet informally to work out strategy and exchange political information. (LIBRARY OF CONGRESS)

in 1928, and he harbored presidential ambitions of his own. Keeping control of the fractious Democrats was not an easy assignment, even for the burly, feisty Arkansan. The sectional tensions between northern and southern Democrats continued to flare, as they had for years. Robinson's willingness to serve as a delegate to the London Naval Conference in 1930 and his support for the Hoover administration on such issues as the balanced budget and government economy attested to his innate conservatism. Because there was no alternative to him, Robinson held the Democratic reins.[5]

Serving as Democratic whip was Key Pittman of Nevada, a troubled man with a dysfunctional marriage and a history of alcoholic binges. His main legislative interest was protecting his state's silver mine owners and securing more appropriations for his tiny constituency. Seniority had made him the ranking Democrat on the Foreign Relations Committee by 1929, but he had little to contribute on foreign policy beyond silver. George Moses had him right. Pittman, said the Republican, showed "no continuity of interest in anything which cannot be turned to his personal advantage."[6]

On the margins of both parties were several senators who still wore the now aging label "Progressive" with a capital P. Journalists never tired of pointing out that these members lacked cohesion and common purpose. In April 1929, the *American Mercury* called them "a sorry bunch of weaklings and time-servers. . . . The principle of attack, of aggressive leadership, of purposeful endeavor, is completely lacking among them." They numbered about a dozen, and had they cooperated they could have been a significant swing bloc, even in the face of a large Republican majority. Although they could unite in opposition to administration nominees and policies, when they tried to put together positive programs to deal with the Depression, their members split between urban reformers and senators from rural states who distrusted cities and bigger government.[7]

William E. Borah, Hiram Johnson, and George W. Norris were among the most prominent of these dissidents. Borah was still a formidable presence, but a somewhat fading one, because of his advancing years and the continuing evidence of his tendency to vacillate in a crisis. Hiram Johnson had been reelected to a third term in 1928, but his political hatred for Hoover placed him on the outskirts of real influence with the new president. Reluctant to cooperate with men he often disdained in his private letters, Johnson was an isolationist gadfly. He could obstruct but rarely could he lead.

The most interesting of the Progressives was Norris. By now his Republican allegiance was purely nominal, and he functioned apart from both parties. He was still committed to the Muscle Shoals dam being under federal control and his effort to end the lame-duck sessions that had dogged Congress for so long. Other procedural changes, such as ending the Electoral College, also engaged his interest. Norris had many admirers for his integrity as a legislator. Few, however, envisioned him as a leader of a cohesive cadre of reform-minded lawmakers because of his stubborn independence.[8]

Younger Progressives showed traces of original thinking. Robert M. La Follette, Jr., had demonstrated a flair for the details of congressional business that had eluded his father. "Young Bob" developed expertise in tax policy and displayed an early concern about the plight of the unemployed. The dapper, handsome La Follette impressed some critics in Washington as affecting "the hirsute adornment of a drug store yahoo" and practicing "the political disin-genuousness of a Jim Watson." That was unfair to a talented lawmaker who would play a larger role in the Senate as the economy collapsed.[9]

Another complex progressive Republican was Bronson Cutting of New Mexico. Appointed to the Senate when the incumbent died in December 1927, he took his seat the following month. The sophisticated, refined Cutting was not yet forty. Educated at Harvard and independently wealthy, he had moved to New Mexico for his health in his twenties. He proved an adept player in the state's rough Republican politics and laid the ground-work for the political organization that ultimately took him to Washington.

Cutting was not your usual senator. He criticized the use of customs laws to ban "obscene" books such as D. H. Lawrence's *Lady Chatterley's Lover*. A "confirmed bachelor," in the argot of the period, he had a number of intense friendships with younger men. A sometime correspondent of the poet Ezra Pound, Cutting brought a refined sensibility to the cause of reform. The jour-nalist and literary critic Edmund Wilson wrote that Cutting was "rather like an English liberal—like some of the men in the Labor government—we've never, so far as I know, had that type in the Senate before."[10]

The inability of the Progressive senators to work together was only a mi-nor irritant before the onset of the economic hard times in the autumn of 1929. The decline in the stock market that occurred in September and Oc-tober 1929 of course marked the onset of the Great Depression. To senators at the time, the downturn in securities was not an event with ominous meaning. Like other informed Americans, they expected Wall Street to right itself and resume its upward climb. Only the failure to see a turn-around and the worsening business situation indicated that something had gone wrong with the economy itself.

No faction in the Senate had a workable answer to the business slowdown. The inability of the upper house to find a constructive role contributed to the political shocks of the Depression. In their secret hearts, Republican senators were happy to see President Hoover stumble. The Democrats had little to of-fer in response to the crisis except budget cutting and strict economy in ex-penditures in accordance with their commitment to small government. If they had been enacted, these measures would only have worsened the defla-tionary pressures that the nation faced. Progressives developed some helpful

The stifling atmosphere of the Senate chamber, especially during the humid Washington summers, was notorious and sometimes deadly for the members. Air-conditioning came in 1929 thanks in part to the efforts of Royal Copeland of New York. A doctor himself, Copeland (on the right) is shown inspecting one of the existing ventilating fans with R. H. Gay, the Senate engineer, on February 16, 1928. (LIBRARY OF CONGRESS)

ideas about unemployment relief and government spending but lacked the votes and the guile to put their solutions into effect.

The regular session of Congress convened in December 1929 as business conditions began to deteriorate. With the administration's political fortunes in decline, Hoover's enemies found opportunities for payback in two judicial nominations early in 1930. In the winter, Chief Justice William

Howard Taft resigned because of failing health. The president nominated Charles Evans Hughes to replace him. As a former Republican presidential candidate in 1916, secretary of state under Warren G. Harding, and a distinguished attorney, Hughes seemed certain to be confirmed without great difficulty. The Judiciary Committee approved the nomination, though George Norris filed a minority protest. Still, the prospects for an easy Senate endorsement seemed good.

Once the nomination reached the floor, however, the Progressive critics of Hughes launched an attack on his judicial philosophy and public record. "No man in public life," said George Norris, "so exemplifies the influence of powerful combinations in the political and financial world as does Mr. Hughes." The aloof and icy Hughes had made few friends in politics, and his condescending personality made him easy for members to dislike. To their surprise and political pleasure, the Hughes opponents found that their criticisms were gaining converts. As Hiram Johnson wrote, "When it started there was nobody literally to vote against the bewhiskered individual. Two days later if the men had been left to their own devices, they would have beaten him." A message of support for Hughes from majority leader Joe Robinson in London, however, helped keep Democrats in line for the nomination. Hughes won out by a vote of 62 to 26 that did not reflect the amount of real dissent that his selection had aroused. Within a few weeks another Supreme Court nomination roiled the Senate again.[11]

A few days after Justice Terry Sanford died, Hoover selected a circuit court jurist, John J. Parker of North Carolina, to fill the vacancy. A Republican politician and gubernatorial candidate in 1920, Parker had gone to the bench in the Fourth Circuit in 1925 without any controversy. Once he was named for the Supreme Court, however, two issues emerged to rouse opposition to his selection. In ruling on cases concerning organized labor, Parker had upheld the legality of the "yellow-dog" contract, which required prospective workers to state that they were not a member of a labor union and would not join one if given a job. And as a candidate for governor in 1920, Parker had told white North Carolina voters that "the Negro as a class does not desire to enter politics. The Republican party of North Carolina does not desire him to do so. We recognize the fact that he has not yet reached the stage in his development when he can share the burdens and responsibilities of government." Parker's status as a "lily-white" Republican made him attractive to Hoover as a way of expanding the party's gains among southern voters from the 1928 election.[12]

The announcement of Parker's nomination on March 21, 1930, caused the American Federation of Labor and the National Association for the Advancement of Colored People to oppose Parker's confirmation. Not since the fight over Louis D. Brandeis in 1916 had a Senate action on a judicial nominee sparked such controversy. Southern Democrats, seeing their political base among white voters under attack, came out against Parker. At a hearing of a three-member subcommittee of the Judiciary Committee on April 5, both the NAACP and the AFL led the attacks on the jurist. The NAACP mounted letter-writing campaigns against the nominee. Parker himself did backstage lobbying on his own behalf. Nine days after the hearing, the subcommittee voted 2 to 1 to send Parker's name to the full committee with a favorable endorsement. By that time black protest in the North had influenced Republican senators from that region to oppose the nomination. On April 21, 1930, the Judiciary Committee decided not to have Parker testify and then voted 10 to 6 to report adversely on the nomination.[13]

The Senate debate on Parker's fate opened on April 28 to great popular interest and crowded galleries, and more than a week of discussion followed. Currents of racism ran through the chamber as some senators denounced the efforts of the NAACP. Rumors of ransacked offices among anti-Parker senators and patronage deals for supporters of the judge added to the tense atmosphere. When the roll was called, Parker was defeated by a vote of 41 to 39, not counting senators whose vote had been paired with that of a colleague (an arrangement in which absent senators in opposite parties indicated how they would have voted if they had been there; their votes, of course, canceled each other out or were "paired"). If all the pairs were tallied, the vote was 49 against Parker and 47 for. The nomination failed because of Parker's conservatism, his anti-black racial views, and the labor issue. This confirmation battle was one more step toward the great struggle over the nature of the Supreme Court that lay seven years ahead for the Senate.

The collapsing economy in 1930 left Republicans anxious about their ability to hold onto the Senate in the fall elections. They pressed ahead to enact the Smoot-Hawley Tariff, which raised customs duties to even higher levels. Protectionism would, so GOP thinking went, enable American industries to recover. The law became a symbol of how little the Senate understood the economic crisis the nation was facing. Passage of the protectionist law came to seem like a capitulation to special interests and American parochialism as economic disaster loomed.[14]

Meanwhile, in early March, President Hoover assured the public that "the worst effects of the crash upon unemployment will have been passed away during the next sixty days." Other positive statements followed from the White House and the Senate leaders. But the portents all indicated that the party in power was in trouble. With more and more people out of work as the economy contracted, the Republican Party, said one insider, "is going to get the damnedest licking it has had for a long time."[15]

Amid the gloom, there appeared the chance that the upper house might gain its first elected female member. Ruth Hanna McCormick, the daughter of Mark Hanna, wife of Medill McCormick, and a congresswoman-at-large (elected from the whole state) from Illinois, won the Republican senatorial nomination in the spring. Such success in what had been a strongly Republican state presaged victory in November for many observers. The prospect did not please the sometime Progressive Hiram Johnson, however. "It is quite true," he wrote his family, "that the Senate may not have lived up to its tradition of late years, but its thorough breakdown and demoralization, in my opinion, will come with the admission of the other sex." Happily for Johnson, though not for the cause of a more diverse Senate, McCormick went down to a substantial defeat in the fall contest at the hands of the Democrat J. Hamilton Lewis.[16]

So concerned were the Republicans about holding onto the Senate in 1930 that they resorted to some dubious tactics. Angry at the popular maverick in Nebraska, George W. Norris, the state party enlisted a young grocer with the exact same name and tried to have him run in the Republican primary. The ploy did not work, and "Grocer Norris" was not allowed to make his phony run against the incumbent. Senator Norris easily won the primary and the general election. The episode further embarrassed the already beleaguered national Republican cause.[17]

The day after Election Day, 1930, it was clear that voter anger had stung the Republicans at the polls. With as many as five million people unemployed, banks failing, and the White House seemingly oblivious to their plight, the electorate registered their discontent. In the House, the GOP lost fifty-two seats, but the outcome hung in the balance until the deaths of several Republicans following the elections allowed the Democrats to establish a slim majority. In the Senate Democrats gained nine seats, but the GOP clung to a one-vote majority. Republicans lost where they had been thought to be strong, for example, in Ohio, Kansas, Colorado, and Illinois.

The Depression was changing the composition of the upper house, and the full impact of the hard times had yet to be felt. If the economic indicators did not turn around, the outlook for Hoover and his party was grim.

An important new arrival in the Senate after the 1930 election was Josiah W. Bailey of North Carolina, who had challenged the sitting senator, Furnifold M. Simmons, then seeking his sixth term. Simmons had come out against Alfred E. Smith for president in 1928 and was vulnerable on the issue of age. Bailey was a loyal Democrat with a strong streak of conservatism that would lead him to emerge as a staunch opponent of the New Deal. Though he was not personally popular with his colleagues, he quickly established a rapport with fellow conservatives in the upper house. Creating his own organization in North Carolina, he soon had a secure political base. For the moment, with Hoover in the White House, Bailey seemed just another southern Democrat, but his impact would expand once the New Deal began.[18]

The last session of the Seventy-first Congress reassembled in December 1930 in the shadow of the worsening economic crisis. The dismal results for the Republicans in the recent elections suggested that the public wanted solutions, not political posturing. Outside the Senate there were abundant calls for action to address the ever-mounting number of unemployed Americans. Senator La Follette argued that "if any government entity is responsible or has had any share of responsibility in producing the economic crisis, then surely it is the Federal government." That was not the language that President Hoover or the Senate hierarchy wanted to hear in early 1931. At the same time Progressive senators such as La Follette could not organize themselves into a cohesive unit and agree on a coherent program. The White House accepted, because it had to, some modest measures that Robert F. Wagner, Democrat of New York, proposed to have the government gather information about the dimensions of the unemployment issue and the economic situation. With the exception of La Follette, among senators there was little support for direct relief to those out of work. The short session produced little but futility.[19]

Once Congress left Washington on March 4, 1931, President Hoover sighed with relief that lawmakers would be out of his way until December. The president enjoyed himself making cutting remarks about the people's elected representatives. He rebuffed calls for a special session on the grounds that it would do no good for the economy. "We cannot legislate ourselves out of a world economic depression; we can and will work ourselves out." Hoover even floated the nonsensical notion that the Republicans should give up their narrow majority control of the Senate. In that way, he contended, the Democrats would have to make the hard decisions and bear more of the onus of the economic troubles. Of course, such a move would have also meant relinquishing committee chairmanships, something that no sane senator would contemplate. Hoover's initiative had no chance of implementation. All that it accomplished was to alienate the president further from his own party.[20]

When Congress convened in December 1931, the human toll of the Depression was rising and the presidential election of 1932 loomed. Senate Democrats were determined not to give Hoover any political advantages in the run-up to the voting, but their own answers to the immediate economic needs of the country remained as conservative and cautious as ever. Like most politicians of the day, they saw a balanced budget and reduced spending as the keys to restoring business confidence, but the progressive Republicans and reform-minded Democrats in the upper house did not plan to be so patient. They wanted the government to take direct steps to relieve the situation of the unemployed. These constructive impulses soon ran into the inherent reluctance of the administration and the Senate leadership to move beyond the limits of economic orthodoxy.

The most pressing business before the Seventy-second Congress was the Depression, and the lawmakers actually gave President Hoover much of what he asked for in the months that followed, including the Reconstruction Finance Corporation (RFC), whose purpose was to supply loans and credit to insurance companies and banks. These powerful institutions in turn were supposed to encourage business expansion, an idea that did not work that well in practice. The Glass-Stegall Act was supposed to broaden credit through the Federal Reserve Board, but it too failed to spur investment. The Home Loan Bank Act was aimed at making the ownership of a home more available. Designed to stop bank failures and promote business confidence, these laws were worthy accomplishments in a general sense. They did little, however, to provide immediate relief to those out of work or to boost the economy out of the slide that had begun in 1930.

Efforts to address the relief problem, led by La Follette, Edward P. Costigan of Colorado, and Wagner, ran up against several crippling obstacles—the conservatism of Republican senators, fears on the part of southern Democrats that a more powerful federal government would intervene in the southern racial regime, and the opposition of Hoover to anything that smacked of the dole. The most that the White House would accept was a system of loans to the states through the RFC as a way of providing indirect relief. The Senate went along when the House defeated an attempt to impose a sales tax during the spring of 1932 to help balance the federal budget. Instead, the lawmakers passed the Revenue Act of 1932, which raised rates on higher-income Americans, increased estate taxes, and imposed excise duties on a number of products. These policies reflected the fiscal orthodoxy of the day against deficit spending.

By the time the session adjourned in July 1932 Congress had cooperated with the White House in passing some modest initiatives. That agenda represented about as much as the Senate would do to defeat the Depression if left to its own devices. Democrats in the upper house were as conservative and hidebound in their thinking as their GOP counterparts. The constructive thinking of the progressive bloc never commanded the support of more than a fraction of the Senate. Had the attack on the Depression been left to members of Congress after 1932, little would have been done to accelerate recovery.

Other important pieces of legislation did come out of this session. The Norris–La Guardia Act limited the use of judicial injunctions in strikes and other labor disputes. Senator Norris, who had long campaigned for the change, also saw his colleagues approve and send to the states the constitutional amendment to move the inauguration of the president to January 20. Once ratified, that reform would do away with the lame-duck sessions that had been such a feature of Senate life for so many years. Worthy initiatives in a general sense, these measures had scant impact on the overriding problem of hard times. The men in the Senate were coming up short at a time of national crisis.

In the midst of the economic tumult, the Senate gained its first elected female member, thanks to Senator Huey Long, Democrat of Louisiana. Following the death of Senator Thaddeus Caraway of Arkansas in November 1931, the governor appointed his widow, Hattie, as an interim successor, and she took her seat on December 9. She was also a candidate to fill out the remaining year of her husband's term in the special election that was held on January 12, 1932, which she won easily. So far it was largely a ceremonial victory, since male politicians in the state expected to beat her in the Democratic primary in August to choose a candidate for the full term. As that contest approached, Senator Caraway announced her candidacy, but few observers anticipated that she would be more than an also-ran against the six men who had filed to run for the seat. To all appearances, it looked as if Caraway would become just another of the women who sat in the Senate briefly after the deaths of their husbands.[21]

Long had other ideas. He had come to the Senate in January 1932, after defeating the incumbent. The fiery, vulgar Long had already created a personal political machine that made him virtually the dictator of Louisiana. Once he took the oath of office, he showed his colleagues that he was not going to be an average senator. Long served no apprenticeship of silence and displayed no respect for the traditions of the institution. He launched attacks on Joseph T. Robinson that exposed the ties that the Democratic leader and his law firm in Arkansas had with corporations in that state. His goal was nothing less than the presidency, and he was laying the foundation for a White House run in the years ahead.[22]

Long had struck up a friendship with Hattie Caraway—neither of them had much respect for the elders of the chamber, who dictated how the place worked. Long had by now crossed swords with Joe Robinson on several occasions and was looking for a chance to embarrass the Democratic leader. On May 21, 1932, Caraway wrote in her journal, "Huey called me [and] offered to donate to my [primary] campaign and work for me." After she obtained Long's promise that he would not attack Robinson in a personal manner, Caraway agreed to accept his assistance. Long's motives had more than a tinge of self-interest. "I can elect her and it will help my prestige."[23]

The early August campaign was vintage Huey Long. He took a caravan of cars and supporters across the border into Arkansas and began speaking. He railed at big financiers and the leadership of Congress without naming names. "They've got a set of Republican waiters on one side and a set of Democratic waiters on the other side, but no matter which set of waiters bring you the dish, the legislative grub is all prepared in the same Wall Street kitchen." Captivated crowds gathered at country crossroads to hear Long in full flight. In what one Arkansan called "a circus hitched to a tornado," Long, with some help from Caraway herself, turned the tide toward the incumbent. She beat the six male candidates for the nomination and went on to become the first woman to win a Senate election on her own terms. Caraway would go on to win another term in 1938, over John McClellan, and then lost to J. William Fulbright in 1944. She was never an important element in Senate deliberations during her Washington tenure. Allen Drury, the novelist, would describe her in the year of her defeat as "a nice little old lady, very unassuming and quiet, thrust by the whim of the electorate into a job far beyond her capacities." Considering some of her male colleagues, Caraway stacked up better than that, but she failed to make a strong impression on the Senate.[24]

Huey "The Kingfish" Long's intervention in the Caraway race enhanced his reputation as the biggest tourist attraction in the Senate during the early 1930s. Long jousting on the floor of the Senate with his colleagues was a sight to behold. By 1934 he had evolved a program that he hoped would take him to the presidency. He called his organization the Share Our Wealth Society and promised that it would make "Every Man a King." By taxing fortunes worth more than $5 million and annual income in excess of $1 million (worth far more then than now), the federal government, Long claimed, could fund an annual income for poorer citizens of $2,000 to $3,000. The workweek would be only thirty hours and everyone would have a month's vacation. In economic terms the scheme was a disaster, but for needy Americans the promise was alluring. The mail that poured in and the attention he attracted fueled Long's dream of becoming president. In 1932, however, he knew that the Democrats would look elsewhere, and they did.

Franklin Delano Roosevelt, the governor of New York, and Alfred E. Smith (Roosevelt's predecessor as governor) vied for the Democratic nod to take on the weakened Hoover, and by the time Roosevelt won the nomination, prospects for a Democratic victory looked better than they had at any time in the previous sixteen years. A united party rallied behind Roosevelt, who promised "a New Deal for the American people." So good were Democratic chances that Tennessee Senator Kenneth McKellar told the nominee, "It looks as if it is all over but the counting and the shouting."[25]

The 1932 presidential election put the progressive-bloc senators on the spot in the race between Hoover and Roosevelt. Most of these members were Republicans, and they disliked Hoover and his policies. After a heavy dose of soul-searching and an ample amount of courting from the Democrats, the group splintered into three sections. Two liberal Republicans, Charles McNary of Oregon and Arthur Capper of Kansas, stuck with Hoover and formally endorsed him. Four western and midwestern GOP stalwarts stayed neutral—the ever-cautious William E. Borah, plus Gerald Nye of North Dakota, James Couzens of Michigan, and Henrik Shipstead of Minnesota. Roosevelt received outright backing from La Follette, Hiram

Johnson, Bronson Cutting, and George Norris. "What this country needs is another Roosevelt," Norris proclaimed when he introduced the candidate at McCook, Nebraska, in late September 1932.[26]

In November 1932, Roosevelt swamped Hoover in a landslide victory that swept the Democrats back into decisive control of the Senate for the first time since 1918. They gained twelve seats to open up a 59-to-36-seat edge over their rivals. Such GOP stalwarts as Jim Watson went down before the Roosevelt tide. Other longtime symbols of Republican conservatism such as Reed Smoot and George H. Moses joined Watson on the list of defeated incumbents. Hiram Johnson noted happily, "The old line Republicans have been knocked into a cocked hat."[27]

The outcome impelled the Republicans to pick their most popular figure to lead them on the eve of the New Deal. When the next session of the Senate assembled after Roosevelt's inauguration, the GOP minority opted for a fresh face. During the lame-duck session from December 1932 to March 1933, Jim Watson gave way to Charles McNary of Oregon as the presumptive head of the Republicans. During the next eleven years, the moderate, affable McNary would prove to be an effective spokesman for his party and a master of the personal politics of the chamber. Forty-nine in 1933, McNary had been in the Senate since 1917. "He seldom asks for a vote," noted one reporter. "He merely paints the picture and lays it before the prospective voter. Senators usually elect to follow his uncanny judgment." McNary was not a strong partisan, and his Oregon farm held more attractions for him than did controversies in the Senate.[28]

The shift from Hoover to Roosevelt was the focus of public attention, but in early 1933, for the history of the Senate, two new arrivals were more significant. Both men, Richard B. Russell of Georgia and Harry Flood Byrd of Virginia, appeared in Washington as a result of unexpected vacancies that politics and death had caused in the Senate roster. In Georgia, Senator William J. Harris died in April 1932. Governor Richard B. Russell appointed an interim successor and then in September announced that he himself was a candidate for the remainder of Harris's term. Russell then won a landslide triumph and arrived in Washington in January 1933 to claim his seat. At thirty-five, he was the youngest member of the Senate.

Russell would be reelected to six terms and become the incarnation of courtliness and Senate tradition. For many of his colleagues, Dick Russell embodied the best traits of the upper house. Courtly and quiet, a master of the rules, he exuded authority and commanded respect. A lifelong bachelor, he devoted his life to his work and spent countless hours reading the *Congressional Record* and committee reports. A pledge from Dick Russell could be relied upon by friend and enemy alike. On the subjects of his expertise, his mastery of the facts was undisputed. If the Senate "Club" of the 1930s, 1940s, and 1950s had a leader, he was that man. Mark Hatfield, a Republican who came to the Senate in the 1960s, recalled that even at the end of his career, Russell, suffering from emphysema, had the courtesy to listen to a freshman deliver his maiden speech. To Hatfield, the incident revealed Russell's "respect for the binding, catalytic force of civility."[29]

Russell was also a virulent segregationist. That bigotry flawed his career was a point that his colleagues ignored. He masked his views with soft phrases and disclaimers of any prejudice, but behind that facade was a man obsessed with the prospect of sexual relations between black and white. In 1944, he told a friend that the Fair Employment Practices Commission was "the most sickening manifestation of the trend that is now in effect to bring social equality and miscegenation of the white and black races in the South." He argued in the Senate that an anti-lynching bill would imperil "the white civilization" of the South and bring back Reconstruction and black rule. For his region to endure "social equality and the commingling of the races in the South" would be intolerable. Russell expressed these cramped views for three decades on the floor and in the cloakroom. Even so, his personal reputation swelled as "the Senate's senator."[30]

Russell's private life revealed a more complex picture. He had a drinking problem that he kept well hidden, stowing a bottle of Jack Daniels bourbon in his desk drawer. Toward the end of his life his alcoholism spilled over into thoughts of suicide. He was also something of a womanizer, though careful never to be led to the altar. His most intense relationship ended because of the Catholicism of his bride-to-be. There was a loneliness in Russell's life that impelled him to make the Senate his real family.[31]

Harry Flood Byrd of Virginia brought the mind of a skinflint to the upper house. A former governor, Byrd dominated politics in the Old Dominion for four decades. When Franklin D. Roosevelt appointed Senator Claude A. Swanson of Virginia secretary of the navy, Byrd moved up to fill out Swanson's unexpired term. Byrd believed in small government and strict economy and brought these ideas to Washington. He was a friend and supporter of Roosevelt in 1932 and as a candidate for reelection to the Senate in 1936 grudgingly endorsed the president for reelection that year. After that point his loyalty to the national Democratic Party vanished.[32]

Byrd was an avid and prosperous apple grower in a risky business that depended on cheap labor. He kept his wages low and resisted any attempt on the part of his workers to unionize. Much of the New Deal—its labor policies, regulation of agriculture, and expansion of government spending—had no appeal for him. On race too, Byrd, like Russell, found little to applaud in the modest efforts of the Roosevelt administration to broaden the opportunities of African Americans. He was not the vehement racist that Russell was. Instead, Byrd was a fanatic on economy in government, and he poured his energies into his Joint Committee on Reduction of Nonessential Federal Expenditures. For Byrd, every dollar that the government spent represented a suspicious act. One reporter said that friends of the president looked upon Byrd "as a humorless dusty scrooge able to skin a flint and likely to hoist a civil servant into stir for joy-riding in a government motor car."[33]

The skinflint Byrd found kindred spirits among the southern Democrats he met in March 1933. In the crisis of the Depression when Roosevelt took office, these members went along with the leader of their party for a few years. Apart from those transient pressures, however, these senators loathed government activism. Russell and Byrd created personal alliances with such conservatives as Georgia's Walter George, North Carolina's Josiah Bailey, and Maryland's Millard Tydings. For the moment, their complaints were only for the cloakroom and private consumption. A shared sense of devotion to segregation also underlay their bond of fellowship. Even before the New Deal was launched, the senators whose convictions included devotion to white supremacy and doubts about big government were in place, ready to coalesce into the powerful conservative Club, which dominated the Senate during the forties and fifties. If Roosevelt faltered or the New Deal went too far, these men were ready to bring the Democrats back to their state rights and segregationist roots.

In March 1933 the Senate reverberated with the clamor and excitement of Franklin Roosevelt's inauguration and the special session that produced the celebrated "One Hundred Days" of the early New Deal. The nation stood in the midst of an imminent economic collapse. Banks were failing, unemployment was soaring toward record levels, and confidence in the national leadership had slipped badly. The first impulse in Congress was to give the new president the powers that he needed to save the banking system and restore a sense of social stability. As a result, the Senate acted at the outset of Roosevelt's administration to approve almost everything the White

House sought to accomplish. That period of deference was short-lived, as the natural tendency of the upper house to assert its role soon reappeared.

In the special session that began on March 9, both houses of Congress adopted an emergency banking bill within an eight-hour span. Members shouted down efforts to amend the measure in the Senate. Carter Glass of Virginia told his colleagues, "I appeal to you, Senators, not to load it down with amendments." When Huey Long persisted with comments against the bill, Glass gave him a tongue-lashing on the floor and told the Louisiana senator to "be more civil." The members agreed with Glass, and the bill sailed through by a vote of 73 to 7.[34]

In the first two weeks of the session Congress passed the Emergency Banking Relief Act; the Economy Act, which cut back on federal expenditures; and the Beer-Wine Revenue Act, which amended the Volstead Act (which enforced Prohibition) to allow the sale of 3.2 percent beer and levy a tax on alcohol. These steps offered a dramatic testament to Roosevelt's executive energy, but the Economy Act was also deflationary in its impact, for lower government expenditures meant fewer government jobs and more people out of work. More legislation was needed to deal with the problems of agriculture and industry. As these issues moved to the front of the national agenda, the Senate's role became more crucial in the development of the New Deal.

The depressed agricultural sector came first on Roosevelt's agenda. In mid-March the president proposed what became the Agricultural Adjustment Act. Farm-state senators and those with silver-mining constituents, most notably in Nevada, pressed the White House to include inflationary remedies in the legislation. An amendment to mandate the free coinage of silver into money fell only ten votes short of adoption in April 1933. As his soundings on Capitol Hill emphasized that such legislation would soon be passed, the president bowed to the inevitable. Looking for ways to inflate the currency to stop the slide in prices, Roosevelt took the nation off the gold standard within a few days. Senatorial pressure to do more to subsidize the use of silver eased somewhat but did not disappear.[35]

With rural issues at the forefront, George Norris saw his chance to help the Tennessee Valley. Throughout the 1920s Norris had fought attempts to turn over the Muscle Shoals power facilities on the Tennessee River to private utility interests. He favored making the Tennessee Valley a demonstration project to show what public power might accomplish to develop a whole region. Coolidge and Hoover had vetoed bills to make Muscle Shoals government property. Roosevelt agreed with Norris's vision and even extended the senator's ideas in shaping what became the Tennessee Valley Authority to give the proposal a broader focus for the entire region. Norris pushed the bill through the Senate in May and made sure his version emerged from the conference committee. After a twelve-year struggle, the Nebraska lawmaker achieved his dream that an entire river could be developed for public use. At that time no one foresaw the environmental damage that would accrue along with the benefits of the TVA.[36]

As the issue of the struggling industrial economy gained in importance, Hugo Black of Alabama proved to be another senatorial prod to Roosevelt. Black stood out among the southern delegation for his economic liberalism and public loyalty to Roosevelt. Yet at the same time he would not wait for the president to act in the economic crisis. To spread a limited volume of work among the many unemployed who needed it, Black offered a proposal to bar from interstate commerce goods made by employees who worked more than thirty hours a week. Spreading work out in this way, so its proponents contended, would raise wages. The upper house was forcing the president's hand about reviving the dormant economy. Black's campaign, though unsuccessful, helped push the White House toward the creation of the National Recovery Act.[37]

Robert F. Wagner of New York had been wrestling with the employment issue since his arrival in the Senate in March 1927. The senator most interested in urban and labor problems, Wagner conducted a running seminar on these concerns out of his office in suite 125 of the Senate Office Building. A shy, sensitive widower, Wagner was fifty-four in 1933 and had already earned a reputation for thoroughness and hard work. One journalist remarked that Wagner "relies on his persuasiveness in the cloak room more than debate on the floor to win support for his measures." Though his more conservative colleagues often disagreed with his policy views, they respected his dedication to his job.[38]

Wagner managed the passage of the National Industrial Recovery Act on the Senate floor. He worked to have the measure include a provision allowing unions to engage in collective bargaining in what became Section 7(a) of the final law. The proposed legislation encountered tough opposition and finally passed by a margin of seven votes on June 13. The minority worried about the provisions that allowed businesses to write codes for their industry even if these actions violated antitrust laws. Progressive senators such as Borah, fearing an erosion of trust enforcement, voted no for that reason. The momentum of the early New Deal still carried the day for the administration in the Senate, but there were signs of emerging resistance to Roosevelt's executive authority.[39]

The Hundred Days ended on June 16. Congress had engaged in a frenzy of lawmaking the likes of which did not occur again for three decades, until Lyndon Johnson's presidency. Senators needed a rest after their unaccustomed exertions. "President Roosevelt, during the special session, sent Congress so many messages that we grew dizzy," wrote Henry Ashurst in his diary. "We ground out laws so fast that we had no time to offer even a respectful gesture toward grammar, syntax, and philology. We counted deuces as aces, reasoned from non-existent premises and, at times, we seemed to accept chimeras, phantasies and exploded social and economic theories as our authentic guides."[40]

To make them act, Roosevelt had withheld patronage from Democratic lawmakers until after the special session was over. One commentator on Congress concluded that "his relations with Congress were to the very end of the session tinged with a shade of expectancy which is the best part of young love." In the early days of his presidency, with popular opinion behind him, Roosevelt established the practices that would affect his handling of the Senate. He was engaging, affable, and conciliatory to his congressional visitors, who appreciated his warmth after Hoover's coldness.[41]

Over time, however, it became clear to many in the upper house that Roosevelt had a ruthless and vengeful streak that surfaced when he was crossed. For example, after Bronson Cutting opposed him on the Economy Act of 1933, their political relationship never recovered. The president held grudges and worked out his revenge, in some cases taking months and years to do so. More important for politicians who believed that their word was their bond in dealing with colleagues, Roosevelt often issued promises—to men such as James F. Byrnes, Pat Harrison, and Joe Robinson—that proved only temporary in their operation. Particularly among southern senators, Roosevelt would act as a conservative when they were in his office, and then move in a more liberal direction when advisers raised protests against what he had promised. Naturally, such shifts of ground gained for Roosevelt a reputation as a trimmer who could not be trusted. As Alben Barkley of Kentucky once told Roosevelt, "Mr. President, you play with men like a cat plays with a mouse."[42]

These grievances did not matter much in 1933 and 1934, when Roosevelt was following policies that most Democrats were either comfortable with or accepted as politically necessary. But there were rumblings of discontent among such conservative Democrats as Josiah Bailey, Carter Glass, Millard Tydings, Thomas P. Gore of Oklahoma, and Harry Byrd. In the face of the president's popularity, these dissenters did not have a large impact on legislative events. At the moment, with the Republicans an embattled minority, Roosevelt did not have to fret about Democratic defectors.

The Republicans, still shocked from their drubbing in 1932, sought to regroup under the leadership of McNary. The GOP leader decided not to pick fights he could not win with the White House. "To oppose the President now in a purely partisan spirit would be rocking the boat at a particularly unfortunate time," he said in August 1933. At the start of 1934 he commented, "The majority of the Republican members of the Congress will continue warmly to support those measures fashioned materially to improve the economic conditions of the country." With McNary ill during much of the spring of 1934, the Republicans remained only a token opposition to Roosevelt's agenda.[43]

The 1934 elections produced one of the major political surprises of the century. Instead of losing seats as usually happened to the president's party, the Democrats actually picked up ten seats in the Senate and almost as many in the House. In the formerly Republican stronghold of Pennsylvania, a bitter dispute within the GOP even allowed a staunch New Dealer named Joseph Guffey to win a seat. Almost everywhere the Democrats picked up the doubtful seats and the Republicans fell into further disarray.

In New Mexico, the senatorial contest in 1934 had implications that went beyond its result in the state. Bronson Cutting, who had attacked Roosevelt over the Economy Act, was running against the Democratic challenger, Dennis Chavez. Although the president and Cutting had been personally friendly, Roosevelt was angered by Cutting's opposition on this one bill and intervened to help the Democratic candidate in ways both open and clandestine. It was an example of the president's penchant for the tricky side of politics. Cutting won a narrow victory at the polls, despite the help that his opponent received from the White House. Chavez then challenged the result before the Senate. Hiram Johnson called Roosevelt's animus against Cutting "small, ungrateful, and cruel," and many of the progressive Republicans in the Senate felt the same way about the president's callous attitude.[44]

The episode had a tragic ending. In the course of fighting the Chavez challenge, Cutting had to fly back and forth to New Mexico. On May 6, 1935, his plane crashed and Cutting was killed. The governor appointed Chavez to succeed him and become the Senate's first Hispanic member. Some of his colleagues blamed Roosevelt for Cutting's death in the sense that dealing with the Chavez challenge put the senator in a plane when he should have been safe in Washington in his Senate seat. For these friends, Cutting's passing symbolized the degree to which the president allowed personal grievances and political revenge to steer his actions. The animosities that grew out of the Cutting tragedy helped undermine support for Roosevelt in the upper house in ways that anticipated the later alliance of conservative Republicans and like-minded southern Democrats.

From the outside, the election of 1934 seemed to ratify the hold that Roosevelt had established on the Senate. With sixty-nine Democrats to twenty-five Republicans (plus two independents), the president could, if he mobilized his party, achieve almost any legislation that he wanted. Yet the sense of dominance was illusory. There were enough conservative Democrats remaining in the Senate to provide a roadblock to Roosevelt's initiatives. For example, Byrd was grumbling about Roosevelt in public statements that invoked Adolf Hitler and the Nazi regime and accused the New Deal of introducing "regimentation." Between 1934 and 1941, the emergence of the coalition of southern Democrats and northern Republicans in response to the New Deal opened a fresh chapter in the history of the Senate. In the process, the Senate gained another legendary institution that shaped its history and perceptions of it: a group of insiders, most of them resolute conservatives, who controlled the upper house in the 1940s and 1950s and came to be known as the Club. That Club-dominated Senate would stand as a roadblock to legislation to implement racial justice and social reform for more than a generation.[45]

## CHAPTER EIGHT

# The New Deal and the Conservative Club

With the arrival of the New Deal and the quickened pace of legislation during the Depression, the Senate by 1935 was a busier place than had been the case thirty years before. Working well into the humid summer was now more common with the advent of air-conditioning, and the long recesses had faded in the memory of all but the older hands. Modern communications and press coverage of the Senate also heightened public interest in the upper house. The amount of mail that poured in each day, especially during times of peak controversy, often overwhelmed even the most capable staff. During the Supreme Court fight of 1937, Hiram Johnson noted, "There's a tremendous amount of mail comes here on the subject, most of it approving my stand, but neither I nor the office has time to pay attention to it." A senator with a national following, such as George Norris, kept three or four secretaries busy just dealing with letters from two dozen states beyond his own Nebraska. Since the rest of Washington outside the Capitol was as yet not air-conditioned, the rigors of summer sessions taxed the stamina of older members.[1]

The victory of the Democrats in the 1934 elections seemed to ensure that Franklin Roosevelt could have almost whatever he desired from Congress. That assumption was deceiving. The Democrats in the Senate reflected the older party that still adhered to state rights, economy in government, a limited role for Washington, and, in the South, a commitment to racial segregation.

With the seniority they had acquired, these members dominated the committee chairmanships during the New Deal era. Pat Harrison of Mississippi held the chair of the Finance Committee, Ellison D. Smith of South Carolina oversaw the Agriculture Committee, and Duncan U. Fletcher of Florida headed the Banking and Currency Committee. The power of the conservatives in the Democratic Party gave the emerging Club in the Senate its growing influence.

During his first two years in office, the president had deferred to the sentiments of the upper house in many of these areas. Relief for the unemployed had been sporadic and short in its duration. Roosevelt himself believed in balanced budgets and frugality in expenditures. The deficits the government ran were modest and not at all designed to stimulate the economy. Yet two dozen or so senators from his own party found even the modest steps that the White House had taken to be too aggressive. Spending government money on relief projects for the poor, manipulating the currency to spur inflation and raise prices and wages, and even providing aid for black Americans—all these steps raised hackles among the southern wing of the party, so even loyal Democrats in the upper house had their restive moments. In the depth of the economic crisis of 1933–34, Democratic senators went along because they knew that Roosevelt was popular and they wanted the Democrats to prevail. But their tolerance for New Deal initiatives had its limits. The tension between party loyalty and the desire of Democratic legislators to pull the White House back toward more conservative policies played a large part in events after 1935.

The year 1935 started out for Roosevelt on a negative note. In January he proposed that the United States should take part in the World Court at The Hague, which reawakened isolationist sentiments that harked back to the fight over the League of Nations. Feelings about the World Court were influenced by other events that reminded Americans of the Great War. During 1934, Americans had followed the deliberations of a Senate committee whose task was to probe the arms industry and its role during World War I. The seven-man panel had taken the unusual step of electing a Republican, Gerald P. Nye, as their chairman. [2]

Out of the Nye committee's hearings came the conviction that "merchants of death" had lured the nation into a needless war with Germany in 1917. Midwestern and western senators knew that their voters believed what the Nye committee was finding. These Americans wanted no part of any further involvement in European quarrels. Even the spread of fascism in Italy and Germany did not change minds among senatorial advocates of isolationism. Borah, for example, had more to say about the perceived inequities of the Treaty of Versailles than about Adolf Hitler's persecution of Jews from 1933 onward.[3]

When it came to Roosevelt's World Court initiative, the conventional wisdom was that the president would attain his two-thirds majority after a tough struggle against Hiram Johnson, William E. Borah, and their supporters outside the chamber. By the end of the month, when Majority Leader Robinson scheduled a vote for the following Tuesday, January 28, it seemed as if the administration had prevailed. Over the weekend, however, the combined efforts of the newspaper magnate William Randolph Hearst, the homespun humorist and political columnist Will Rogers, and the right-wing radio commentator Father Charles E. Coughlin produced a deluge of messages and letters from constituents to wavering lawmakers, which changed the outcome. When the votes were cast, the pro–World Court coalition fell seven votes short of the needed two thirds. Hiram Johnson said he had "won the toughest and the biggest and most far-reaching contest legislatively in which ever I have been engaged."[4]

In 1935 the desire to remain out of European and colonial conflicts expressed itself in the adoption of the Neutrality Act. Senator Nye offered legislation that would prevent the United States from selling war materials to warring nations and also bar Americans from traveling on ships flying the flag of a belligerent. Feeling the pressure from a public anxious to avoid entanglements overseas, senators made it clear to the White House that the Neutrality Act was going to pass. Roosevelt's efforts to maintain the option to take action against an aggressor, as designated by the League of Nations, swayed few votes in the upper house. Key Pittman, now chair of the Foreign Relations Committee, informed the president's aides that Roosevelt "is riding for a fall if he insists on designating the aggressor in accordance with the wishes of the League of Nations." The lawmakers insisted on language that restricted Roosevelt's options, and he had no choice but to go along. The Neutrality Act of 1935 sailed through at the end of the session in August. Johnson, Borah, and Nye put severe restraints on Roosevelt's freedom of movement in foreign policy right down to 1939. The Senate had achieved a kind of parity in foreign policy at the expense of the national interest.[5]

Along with the opposition to his foreign policy from the isolationists, Roosevelt faced challenges on domestic policy from the left. The appeal of Huey Long was catching fire with those who had yet to benefit from the relief and recovery programs of the New Deal. Long's "Share Our Wealth" program might be economic nonsense, but there was little doubt of its political appeal to those with low or no incomes. On May 15, as Congress proceeded to fail to take much action on pressing issues, Long told his colleagues, "Congress is going to adjourn with nothing whatever done to increase the purchasing power of the masses." On a personal level, the Louisiana senator was spoiling for a fight against the man in the White House. "I can take him," Long assured Arthur Krock of the *New York Times*. "He's a phony. I can take this Roosevelt. He's scared of me. I can out-promise him, and he knows it."[6]

Long had the capacity to become the leader for the forces of discontent. He could look for help to Father Coughlin; to Dr. Francis Townsend, who promised old-age pensions; and to unhappy farmers to expand his Louisiana power base. Roosevelt responded by unleashing the Federal Bureau of Investigation and the Internal Revenue Service against the Long machine. Wrongdoing among Long's lackeys came to light, but no clear criminal case emerged against the senator himself. The sense of persecution that Long felt only made him more determined to confront Roosevelt. The White House, for its part, treated the senator as a potential rival for 1936.

By mid-1935, the New Deal and Roosevelt seemed to be in political trouble for the first time in his presidency. Frank Knox, a prominent Republican, wrote to his wife that his party's leadership in the Senate was "much encouraged over the way Roosevelt is slipping, and the improved prospects for Republican victory next year." The New Deal received another political rebuff when the Supreme Court declared the National Industrial Recovery Act unconstitutional at the end of May. The president denounced the decision as an example of "horse and buggy thinking." Instead of yielding to political adversity and the general sentiment of lawmakers for an adjournment, Roosevelt counterattacked.[7]

During the rest of the summer, in what became known as the Second Hundred Days, Roosevelt drove lawmakers to pass the Social Security Act and the National Labor Relations Act (generally called the Wagner Act for its sponsor, the New York senator) and establish a system of permanent relief, adopt a banking reform bill, and regulate public utilities. The Roosevelt agenda also included tax legislation to punish big business for its speculative excesses in the 1920s and its opposition to the administration. The most liberal phase of the New Deal occurred during these hectic weeks as the president accepted nothing less from Congress than enactment of his priorities. In one of the most productive sessions in the history of Congress, Roosevelt attained reforms that few would have thought possible when the year began.[8]

The result came at some cost to the president's future relations with the Senate. The events of 1935 showed Roosevelt at his best and at his worst in handling the legislative branch. By setting bold priorities and by aggressively pushing his programs through, Roosevelt demonstrated how a national leader could govern. The accomplishments of the Second Hundred Days were a bravura performance. Roosevelt and his team, especially "Tommy the Cork" Corcoran, and Corcoran's sidekick, Benjamin V. Cohen, wrote legislation on the fly that impressed seasoned lawmakers such as Sam Rayburn of Texas and Wagner.[9]

The process revealed Roosevelt's drawbacks as well. In the case of the Revenue Act, or Wealth Tax Act, to raise revenues from business and the upper classes, for example, he set unworkable deadlines and sought definitive action from Congress within a scant six days. Those importunate demands left Pat Harrison, chairman of the Finance Committee, and Majority Leader Robinson scrambling. Then the president implied that Harrison and Robinson had not acted at his behest. Furious at his ingratitude, the two suppressed their ire for the sake of party unity, but suspicion and animosity lingered. Roosevelt drew the wrong conclusion from his string of successes: that he could surprise senators and then bend them to his will. He did not understand how much of his political capital with Congress he had expended in 1935.[10]

Had Roosevelt comprehended the limitations he faced with Congress, he might have restrained the harm to his standing on Capitol Hill. Instead, he decided that in the end he would always prevail. For someone whose faith in his own destiny was the basis of his personality, the president concluded that Congress would invariably come out on the losing end of their battles. If anything, the events of 1935, when so much went Roosevelt's way, made him resolve not to change his methods toward senators in any fundamental manner.

Then in early September 1935, shortly after Congress adjourned, Carl Weiss, a young doctor outraged at Long's stranglehold on Louisiana, shot and killed him at the state capitol. By the time of his assassination, Long had become less effective in his role as a Senate maverick, but he remained a box office draw for the galleries in the filibuster he had run for a record nineteen hours on June 12, 1935. Like Robert La Follette, Sr., a generation earlier, Long saw the Senate as his springboard to national office. Whether he could have brought it off is questionable, but in his brief career in the upper house he showed what a demagogic senator could do to make himself a national figure. Two decades later, Joseph R. McCarthy would build on Long's example.[11]

Without the charismatic Long to torment Roosevelt and with the election in the offing, the 1936 session of Congress lacked the fireworks that characterized the preceding year. Even some of the more conservative members such as Josiah W. Bailey tempered their animus against Roosevelt until they were safely reelected. Nevertheless, amid the Democratic harmony, future problems emerged. At the 1936 Democratic National Convention in Philadelphia, the party, at the behest of the White House, dropped the rule that presidential nominees had to receive a two-thirds majority to win. That provision had deadlocked the Democrats in 1924 and nearly frustrated Roosevelt's candidacy in 1932. The change was designed to erode the influence of southern lawmakers by breaking their veto power in selecting candidates. The resulting sense of alienation that these senators felt from their party subsequently reinforced their inclination to oppose Roosevelt's policies during his second term.

The race issue, never far below the surface for the Democrats, surfaced when the convention assembled. Senator Ellison D. "Cotton Ed" Smith of South Carolina arrived at the hall just as an African-American clergyman was delivering a prayer to the delegates. Smith, a racist who had gotten his nickname when he proclaimed, "Cotton is king and white is supreme," said in a loud voice, "By God, he's as black as melted midnight." The senator then stomped out of the convention, with a loud blast to his home-state newspapers. The defection was unimportant in itself—Smith's lack of brains caused some in South Carolina to call him "Cotton Head"—but Smith's instinctive bigotry commanded wide support among his constituents, who saw the Democrats as too friendly with black voters in the North. Carter Glass restrained himself only because of the exigencies of the presidential campaign. In private he said that he was "incensed . . . beyond expression" at the presence of the black clergyman. The use of federal money in the South to provide relief payments for African Americans threatened the political structure of segregation. As a result, weakening the power of the president and the New Deal seemed a matter of survival to a majority of the southern Senate Democrats.[12]

For the moment, the results in the 1936 election appeared to reinforce Roosevelt's ascendancy in national politics and leave the conservatives without good options. In addition to his landslide victory over Republican Alfred M. Landon, the president saw the Democratic total in the Senate rise to seventy-six seats. However, the voters also returned some conservative Democrats to the upper house, an indication that members of the upper house had public support that did not derive from Roosevelt's popularity. Sixteen Republicans plus four independents rounded out the Senate membership. The potential strength of conservative Democrats and Republicans stood at just twenty-eight members. With his political enemies defeated and his hold on the Senate and House seemingly secure, Franklin D. Roosevelt prepared to tackle the only remaining threat to his dominance of the government, the Supreme Court.

The president had long chafed at the decisions of the Court in 1935 and 1936 that declared some major New Deal legislation unconstitutional. The "nine old men," as they were called, had ruled against the White House on the National Recovery Act, the Agricultural Adjustment Act, and the Guffey Coal Act, among others. Roosevelt believed that he faced a Court determined to throttle his reform programs, and he decided that after the election he would take steps to transform the Supreme Court into a branch of government more sympathetic to the administration. First he would increase the number of judges on the Court. The number nine was not set in concrete; the number of justices had been higher in the nineteenth century, but the clear purpose of what Roosevelt proposed was to shift the high court to the left. Consulting no one besides his attorney general and a small group of advisers, Roosevelt worked out his scheme in late 1936 and early 1937. On February 5, 1937, he submitted to Congress a plan to reorganize the judiciary, which included among numerous other measures the proposal to increase the number of justices to fifteen.

Roosevelt's plan came as a political bombshell, especially to lawmakers who had no idea what he had been contemplating. From the outset of the controversy, commentators recognized that the president had failed to take legislative leaders into his confidence. Whether Roosevelt thought that lawmakers would have to go along or he feared that they might reject his program is not clear. In any case, he decided to fall back on the technique of the sudden disclosure of his intentions, the methods he had used with his prior legislative successes in 1933 and 1935. The strategy had worked well for him at that time, but there was a crucial difference in 1937: He misjudged the mood of the American people, and his bold move fell flat with them. Roosevelt assumed that his fellow citizens shared his impatience with the Court and its decisions striking down some New Deal legislation. In fact, Americans did not want dramatic changes in the Court, as the White House soon learned.[13]

Roosevelt's miscalculations about the Senate doomed his court plan from the outset. He secured the support of Joe Robinson through the implied promise of the first Supreme Court vacancy, a pledge that the president knew would be difficult to keep in light of the majority leader's conservatism. Roosevelt did not take such liberal allies as George W. Norris into his confidence, and his sly tactics alienated the volatile Burton K. Wheeler of Montana, who proceeded to become the liberal leader of the anti–Court packing forces in the Senate. Roosevelt simply thought that in the end he would bulldoze his way past the opposition. Instead, he made himself the target for plausible charges of dictatorship and a grasp for absolute power.[14]

With only sixteen members in his coalition, Charles McNary recognized that outright Republican opposition to the Roosevelt scheme would solidify the Democrats, so he had his troops keep silent and make no public response to the proposals, and he persuaded national GOP leaders to do the same. Circumstances played into McNary's hands. In the House, the chairman of the Judiciary Committee, Hatton Sumners of Texas, would not let the White House proposal go through his panel. That situation meant that the Senate would deal with the legislative proposal first. Having the fight focus on the upper house made the anti-Roosevelt members the central players in the drama that enthralled Washington for the first six months of 1937. The Republican strategy of staying out of the spotlight contributed to the press emphasis on the splits within the president's party.[15]

From the start of the struggle, Senate opponents of the Court proposal went at the battle in a systematic manner. They kept accurate counts of sentiment and arranged for their members to watch out for political defectors to ensure their loyalty to the coalition. The White House, on the other hand, did sloppy vote tracking and displayed an abundance of self-delusion. Roosevelt did not want to hear bad news, and he scoffed at reports that his idea was a flop. The people were with him, he told friends—which was not true, but even if it had been true, making the impact of such popular sentiment felt in the Senate would have been a problem. Like Woodrow Wilson in 1919, Roosevelt misread the Senate.[16]

Stored-up grievances against executive power and the way Roosevelt had wielded his authority since 1933 animated his adversaries beyond their dislike of the Court plan itself. When it suited him Roosevelt had treated the Senate with cavalier disdain, and he made the fatal error of underestimating the political power of the upper house. At first he offered the disingenuous argument that the Supreme Court was inefficient and behind in its work. When Burton Wheeler arranged for Chief Justice Charles Evans Hughes to demolish that case in a public letter, the president then revealed his genuine grievance with the Court over its policy positions. By the time the White House made the argument that the Court was wrong on substance, the public had already decided that Roosevelt's plan was not the right solution for the nation's ills.[17]

If the president had been willing to compromise and accept the enlargement of the Court by two justices, as some senators suggested, the Senate would have been ready to swallow that answer as a face-saving settlement of the dispute. But Roosevelt was so adamant about the correctness of his position that he held out for acceptance of his whole plan until it was too late to obtain anything. Events transpired that gave credence to the Senate's position: The Judiciary Committee reported unfavorably on the bill to implement Roosevelt's plan in mid-May. Justice Willis Van Devanter resigned at the same time and the president had a vacancy to fill with a successor to the conservative Van Devanter. Six days later, on May 24, the Court ruled that the Social Security Act was constitutional. The Court shifted away from its unyielding position on other issues as well. The policy rationale for Roosevelt's urgent need to reshape the Court was collapsing.[18]

Van Devanter's departure meant that Roosevelt would now have to make good on his promise to offer Robinson a seat on the Court. With characteristic duplicity, as far as the Senate was concerned, the president stalled in hopes that Robinson might let him out of his pledge. But Robinson was intent on getting on the Court, and during the weeks that followed, he pushed his colleagues to provide Roosevelt a face-saving solution that would not change the court in a radical way. A bitter battle ensued in which Robinson worked himself to exhaustion. Long burdened with a weak heart, he died on July 14; he was found amid his documents on the floor of his apartment. With his passing went Roosevelt's last, faint chance at any compromise. Burton Wheeler told his colleagues, "I beseech the President to drop the fight lest he appear to fight against God."[19]

Official Washington paused while Joe Robinson's body was taken back to Arkansas for burial. Then Roosevelt compounded his difficulties with the Senate by another executive interference in the chamber's private business: supporting a new majority leader to fill the vacancy caused by Robinson's death. The Democrats had two candidates: Pat Harrison of Mississippi, the chairman of the Finance Committee, and Alben Barkley of Kentucky. Harrison was well liked for his genial personality and hard-hitting debating style against Republicans, but the White House considered him too conservative. Moreover, if he became majority leader, the Finance Committee chairmanship would fall to Utah's William H. King, whose strident opposition to the New Deal made him anathema to the president. As a result, Roosevelt concluded that he could not simply leave the choice to the Democrats but must indicate a preference for Barkley.

Roosevelt blundered. He wrote the Kentucky senator a letter, soon released to the press, addressed to "My Dear Alben" in which he chided the Senate for playing politics while Robinson lay dead and professed a determination to press ahead with his Court plan. Soon released to the press, the letter was taken, as the president hoped it would be, as an indication of his preference for Barkley as majority leader. Of course, Roosevelt denied any such intention in public. The phrase "My Dear Alben," which marked Barkley unfairly as a stooge of the White House, became a weight that he carried around for the rest of his public career. Roosevelt now had his candidate, but winning the election for the Kentuckian would not be easy. The smart money in Washington was on Harrison as the date for the balloting neared.[20]

During the train journey from Arkansas after Robinson's funeral, the Court plan died. Recognizing that the president's package no longer had a chance and mindful of the splits in the party the issue was fomenting, eight freshman Democrats announced to Vice President John Nance Garner that upon their return to Washington from Arkansas they would not vote on the proposal but instead would vote to recommit the Court-packing plan to the Judiciary Committee. That procedural move would doom the proposal, since the Judiciary Committee would not consider it again. Roosevelt was beaten, as Garner duly informed him. On July 22, 1937, the Senate voted 70 to 20 to return the bill to the Judiciary Committee. When he heard the news, Hiram Johnson exclaimed, "Glory be to God!"[21]

A day earlier the Harrison-Barkley leadership contest had also been decided. As the voting neared, the White House put pressure on wavering

In a bitter leadership struggle, Alben Barkley of Kentucky (left) emerged victorious by one vote over Pat Harrison of Mississippi (right) in the summer of 1937. Key Pittman of Nevada (middle) looks like his usual inebriated self in this moment of Democratic crisis. (University of Kentucky Library)

Democrats. In Illinois, William Dieterich was counted as being in the Harrison camp. Behind the scenes, intense pressure on the senator from the Democratic machine in the state changed his mind. Tommy Corcoran was making deals to assemble enough votes for Barkley, though the attempt to have Harry S. Truman of Missouri switch his vote failed. When the Democratic senators voted, the result was a tie until the last, the seventy-fifth ballot, was revealed. Barkley won by 38 to 37. The new majority leader later recalled, "When the teller reached in and pull out the last folded slip, it looked as big as a bed quilt." Harrison moved to make the vote unanimous, and on the surface, harmony prevailed.[22]

Because of his single term as Harry Truman's vice president from 1949 to 1953 and his reputation as an amiable raconteur, Alben Barkley has become a minor figure in American political history. He was a few months short of his sixtieth birthday when he became majority leader. He had been elected to the House of Representatives in 1913 and then moved on to the Senate in 1927. Coming from the border state of Kentucky, Barkley was more flexible and enlightened than many of his contemporaries from the Deep South. He said in February 1937 that the Constitution "is a living, moving, vital instrument of government not to be preserved in a museum but to be preserved by a fair and liberal interpretation of its powers as well as a progressive and sane interpretation of its implied powers." That kind of rhetoric pleased the White House at a time when it badly needed sympathetic senators. Private opinions of Barkley were less kind. Recognizing the leader's oratorical skill, one Democratic Senate aide concluded, "I think he became something of a show horse on the Senate floor." The press fastened on a few early slips in his performance as majority leader and dubbed him "Bumbling Barkley."[23]

The heavy-handed tactics of the White House in the leadership vote compounded the damage that the Supreme Court fight had already inflicted on Senate Democrats. Barkley lacked real legitimacy as the party leader, and resentments surrounding his elevation irked the conservatives. Once again, Franklin Roosevelt had said one thing to senators and done another—assured neutrality in the leadership contest while fighting hard for Barkley in the back alleys of national politics. The result was that the administration would be left without an effective advocate in the upper chamber for the rest of the president's tenure.

To restore some appearance of unity after the traumas of the first half of 1937, Barkley held a dinner on August 10 to commemorate his selection as the Democratic leader. His colleagues ate well and sang festive songs, and Barkley's rendition of "Wagon Wheels" was the hit of the evening. A friendly note from Roosevelt, who wisely stayed away, added to the lighthearted mood of the moment.[24]

Reality intruded the next day on the Senate floor. In the midst of what seemed to be routine debate, Robert F. Wagner of New York took advantage of a lull in the proceedings when no one else was on the floor to obtain recognition from Vice President Garner and moved that the Senate take up a bill "to assure to persons within the jurisdiction of every state the equal protection of the laws and to punish the crime of lynching." Barkley had other scenarios in mind for the day and protested against what was happening. Garner told him and other senators that "when only one Senator is standing and demanding recognition the chair has no choice" but to recognize him.[25]

Wagner had brought up race, the issue that ran as a fault line through the Democratic Party in the upper chamber in the 1930s and underlay the power of the Club. An increasing number of African-American voters in the North, activated by the New Deal, wanted to see lynching ended. The National Association for the Advancement of Colored People made such a law one of its priorities in the 1930s and pressed northern Democrats for help. In 1934 Wagner had joined with Edward P. Costigan of Colorado to sponsor legislation to address these crimes.[26]

For southern senators any hint that their racial system might be subjected to federal regulation was intolerable. As in 1922, they were ready with a filibuster if the issue should come to the floor. Faced with that prospect and a White House reluctant to confront the South, the bill languished. Then, in the spring of 1937, on the day a horrible lynching took place in Mississippi, an anti-lynching bill cleared the House and was sent to the Senate. The Senate Judiciary Committee approved the bill, but it was stuck at the bottom of the calendar and in the regular order of things had little chance of coming to the floor before the now-imminent adjournment on August 21.

Wagner's timely procedural coup on August 11 changed the situation. If the bill was taken up for debate the southerners would filibuster and block all the legislation that the White House needed before Congress left town. Yet if the bill was forestalled, Wagner himself could also tie up Senate business with a filibuster of his own. To get Wagner to back down, Barkley had to agree with the New York senator to consider the anti-lynching bill in January 1938. The Democrats would now confront their most volatile problem early in an election year. The president did not wish racial issues to disrupt the Democratic coalition and his congressional majority, but there was little he could do about this move in the Senate.

In the meantime Roosevelt took his revenge against the Senate for opposing his Court-packing plan, in mid-August nominating Senator Hugo L. Black of Alabama to replace Willis Van Devanter. Black had been in the upper house since 1926 and had gained a reputation as a zealous investigator who was tough with unfriendly witnesses. He was also a southern liberal with few ties to the rest of the regional delegation. In fact, Black was not at all popular with his colleagues. One of the few genuine advocates of Roosevelt's

Court plan, he was a choice who would grate on the sensibilities of his fellow senators, but they could do little to block him, as the conservatives could not be seen as standing in the way of one of their Senate colleagues. For Roosevelt all these considerations made Black an ideal nominee. Donald Richberg, a former Roosevelt aide, told a newsman that Roosevelt was angry and had decided to give the Senate a nominee who would be "most disagreeable to it yet which it could not reject."[27]

Despite their resentment at what Roosevelt had done to spite them, the Senate confirmed Black overwhelmingly on August 17. Then the situation took an unexpected, and for Roosevelt an unwelcome, turn. Black had been selected despite reports that the new appointee had long-standing ties to the Ku Klux Klan in Alabama. The whispers now turned into newspaper disclosures about Black's past that embarrassed the administration and put the new justice under intense pressure to clear up his personal history. Black made a radio broadcast on October 1 in which he tried to explain away his links to the hooded order. The controversy and the speech attracted a good deal of national attention. One employee in Senator Tom Connally's office said that "it stirred up things here more than any incident I can recall in recent years." Although Black did well enough to still the clamor for his resignation, his selection was one more reason for the conservatives in the Club to be convinced that Franklin D. Roosevelt could not be trusted.[28]

Democratic factionalism intensified as the economic situation turned sour in the second half of 1937; cutbacks in government spending and a rise in unemployment were stirring up talk of a Roosevelt recession. Conservatives clamored for a balanced budget; liberals wanted to press ahead with more relief programs. In the Senate the mood shifted toward more opposition to the president and his initiatives. Since the senators assumed that Roosevelt would leave office after 1940, they did not believe that taking him on involved the kind of political risk that it had before the Court fight. On a number of bills a coalition of rural Democrats joined Republicans in opposing measures that favored cities and labor unions. The sit-down strikes of the Congress of Industrial Organizations (CIO) in auto plants and elsewhere frightened middle-class voters and emboldened Roosevelt's enemies. The Senate became the most public arena where the strains within the president's party were fought out.[29]

As the economic situation worsened, Roosevelt summoned Congress back for a special session in November. Part of his strategy was to shift the onus for the downturn and its effects onto the lawmakers. In response, some conservative Democratic senators talked about issuing a joint statement of principle in which they would publicly reject the excesses, as they saw it, of the New Deal. These discussions led to a "Conservative Manifesto" in December 1937 that reflected the suspicion of big government that animated the anti-Roosevelt bloc. The framers of the document, including Josiah Bailey, Millard Tydings, and the Republican Arthur Vandenberg, called for tax reductions, a balanced budget, and limits on the rights of organized labor. Beyond stating these principles and making their grievances known, the writers of the manifesto did not accomplish much. McNary and the Republicans, sensing a chance for a GOP victory in the 1938 elections, decided against overt collaboration with sympathetic Democrats. The manifesto was, however, a sign that the conservative members of the Democratic side were coming together to solidify the Club that would dominate the Senate into the late 1950s.[30]

The regular session of 1938 underscored how matters had changed for the Roosevelt administration since the Court fight. The first two months were consumed with a filibuster of Wagner's anti-lynching bill, which went on until it became clear that the southern enemies of the measure were not going to yield. Theodore G. Bilbo of Mississippi said that passage of the anti-lynching proposal would "open the floodgates of hell in the South," while Richard Russell alleged that communists were using the legislation to create "a soviet Negro republic." By mid-February, with other business pressing and the White House indifferent about the fate of the proposed law, the Senate dropped the Wagner bill and moved on to other business. Once again the filibuster had been used to perpetuate racial injustice.[31]

Roosevelt's troubles mounted when he advanced an ambitious initiative to reorganize the executive branch for greater efficiency. Opponents denounced the scheme as another of Roosevelt's power grabs. The Senate passed the measure in the spring, but it was defeated in the House. Similarly, the upper house, under the direction of Pat Harrison and Vice President Garner, by now an undeclared enemy of the White House, rolled back New Deal tax legislation that had placed higher levies on corporations. The White House had received two painful rebukes.

Yet the rest of the session saw Roosevelt and his allies rebound on Capitol Hill as the 1938 elections approached. Lawmakers passed a spending measure to stimulate the sluggish economy that even some conservatives, soon to face the voters, endorsed. The administration also won out on the Fair Labor Standards Act. Mindful of the impending elections and the residual power of the White House, senators were careful not to challenge the president directly. The ability of the New Deal to provide initiatives or address unmet needs was diminished as a result of the events of 1937, and the chief executive had to defer to the conservative sentiment in the Senate. The forward progress of the New Deal had been halted and a generation would pass before liberal legislation would receive congressional approval.[32]

The impending election of 1938 gave Republicans hope and worried the Democrats. The recession deepened while middle-class voters recoiled at the activism of militant labor and its tactic of sit-down strikes. After six years, the Roosevelt administration was showing its age. As a result the Democrats lacked focus and unity. Still seething from his rebuff in the Court fight, Roosevelt debated whether to reform his party by launching an attack on the enemies within it. The wisdom of such a risky strategy could well be questioned. State elections often turned on local issues that lay beyond the control of any president. Nonetheless, Roosevelt was very tempted when encouraging signs appeared at the start of the election year. In Alabama, Lister Hill, a solid New Dealer, captured the senatorial nomination over a reactionary opponent. More important, Claude Pepper, an avowed liberal serving an unexpired term, won the Florida primary after Roosevelt's son James stated publicly, "We hope that Senator Pepper will be returned to the Senate." After Pepper won, Roosevelt told him, "Claude, if you were a woman I'd kiss you." The president drew the wrong conclusion from these events. Hill and Pepper were isolated examples of relative southern liberalism, not the start of a trend.[33]

From these favorable events and continued urgings from liberal Democrats that he get involved, the president concluded that he ought to take a direct hand in some key Senate races. He endorsed Alben Barkley in Kentucky over Governor A. B. "Happy" Chandler and the majority leader came through with a victory largely on his own. Then the party reform effort went sour. Roosevelt attacked Walter F. George in Georgia and "Cotton Ed" Smith in South Carolina. These sallies did not hurt their intended targets much. Nonetheless, Roosevelt pressed on with what the press was now styling a "purge" of conservative Democrats, a word that was associated with purges by Stalin and Hitler of their enemies. The term did not help Roosevelt's cause with the voters.

The most inviting target of the president's wrath was Millard Tydings, the two-term conservative Democrat from Maryland. Senator Tydings had been an articulate and sarcastic critic of the New Deal, and he rubbed Roosevelt raw with his tactics. Throughout his first ten years in the Senate, Tydings had been one of the city's most eligible bachelors. Gossipy reporters disclosed that he was "known to offend sedate Georgetown ladies by playing 'footie' with them under the table." In 1936, he married Eleanor Davies Cheeseborough, a divorcée who was the daughter of a Democratic insider, Joseph E. Davies. Perhaps their shared sense of self-confidence and contrasting political philosophies caused Roosevelt and Tydings to clash. Tydings feuded with other New Dealers as well. His sharp tongue irritated the president and his aides. The president told his interior secretary, Harold Ickes, in March 1937, when Ickes was attacking opponents of the Court plan, including Tydings, that he hoped Ickes "would take Tydings' hide off and rub salt in." So it was with special delight that Roosevelt assailed his old rival in the summer of 1938.[34]

Alas for Roosevelt, the White House attempt at attaining party purity fizzled. The legislators that he marked out for defeat struck back with allegations of presidential meddling and thinly disguised appeals to racial resentments. Tydings said, with a nice bow to Maryland's experience in the Civil War, that he was sure that "the people of Maryland will act, and act decisively to let the Federal administration and all the people of the country know that the Maryland Free State shall remain free." On primary day, Maryland remained "liberated" as Tydings crushed his liberal opponent and became a lock for another term in the fall contest against a token Republican challenger. The primary results were similar for Walter George in Georgia and "Cotton Ed" Smith in South Carolina. Roosevelt put the best possible face on the situation, but he had been rebuked and the position of the conservatives, enhanced. [35]

The 1938 general election brought more bad news for the White House. The Republicans gained eighty-one seats in the House (the Democrats had 261 seats and the Republicans 164) and added seven new members in the Senate to make the breakdown sixty-nine Democrats, twenty-three Republicans, and four independents. The major figure among the seven new GOP senators was Robert A. Taft of Ohio, the son of the former president, who had beaten a lackluster New Deal Democrat. Taft was immediately spoken of as a future Senate leader and potential presidential aspirant. With this rebound from the 1936 disaster, the Republicans had climbed back to political respectability and were prepared to harass Roosevelt for the remainder of his term. The GOP members would work with the conservative Democrats on many issues in the years to come, though partisanship prevented full cooperation across the whole range of subjects with which the Senate had to deal. The upper house had never been dependably liberal, even during the heyday of the New Deal. Now it presented a roadblock to the aspiration of the president to extend his reform legacy.

The ascendancy of the southerners imparted a conservative tone to the Senate that lasted for twenty years. Some issues, such as segregation and racial discrimination, remained outside the scope of debate. When these topics did arise in other contexts, the southern Democrats made their determination to resist change very clear. Serious social problems simply were not discussed in a candid and open way. That race became a taboo subject during the heyday of the southern dominance was one of the lasting legacies of the ascendant Club.

Amid the resurgence of conservatism after the 1938 elections and the onset of World War II in the late summer of 1939, the Senate came under scrutiny from the world of mass entertainment. Frank Capra, a very popular Oscar-winning director, decided to make the upper house the subject of his next film. *Mr. Smith Goes to Washington* is about an idealistic young man named Jefferson Smith who is appointed to a Senate vacancy after the death of the junior senator from his state. He goes to Washington and comes under the tutelage of a female secretary and a jaded reporter, who instruct him in the ways of the capital. He then learns that the senior senator, who is his supposed mentor, is actually the tool of the political boss of his state, and a crooked land deal is about to be passed. Smith stages a filibuster to foil the plot. Jimmy Stewart played Jefferson Smith with his customary skill, and the melodramatic but fascinating narrative unfolds within Capra's reconstruction of the Senate chamber.[36]

Some elements of Senate history were incorporated into the film. The Senators' hazing of Smith by walking out during one of his speeches is based on the experience of Robert La Follette. The senior senator, played by Claude Rains, even looks a little like John Coit Spooner in modern dress. The big filibuster scene captures some of the drama of La Follette and the 1908 Aldrich-Vreeland episode. The ending, with the Rains character attempting to commit suicide, is melodramatic and improbable, but it solved Capra's need to find a happy outcome.

Capra and his studio wanted to make a large production out of a premiere in Washington in October 1939, and a gala ceremony brought much of officialdom out for the evening. To the director's dismay, however, his audience balked at the themes of the film. Senators were upset at the idea that one of their colleagues, even in fiction, might be a grafter for a political boss. Frank Capra later recalled that some members of the audience walked out; this was not the case, yet the Senate was genuinely outraged. Majority Leader Alben Barkley complained that the movie "showed the Senate as the biggest aggregation of nincompoops on record!" He said that the hazing scene "was so grotesque it was funny." Senators threatened retaliation against Capra and his studio.[37]

As time passed, however, the strengths of *Mr. Smith Goes to Washington* became evident. The affection that Capra had for American institutions and the high quality of the performances won over the critics in the end. The title of the movie became a catchphrase for real-life lawmakers heading to Washington to make their mark on the culture of the Senate. Writing in 1986 about how much the movie diverged from political life in the 1980s, Hendrik Hertzberg said that modern politics embodied an "idealism that has learned the practical way of the world so well that it has forgotten what it set out to build in the first place." Yet there remains something iconic and enduring in the image of Jimmy Stewart, his voice breaking, making his filibuster and falling unconscious from fatigue in the attempt.[38]

*Mr. Smith Goes to Washington* helped shape how a generation of Americans saw the upper house and its inner workings. Until the emergence of C-SPAN in the late 1980s, this movie and a later film, *Advise and Consent*, based on Allen Drury's novel, were the only available substitutes for actually visiting the Senate chamber to get a personal sense of the institution. The blend of idealism and cynicism that the Capra movie conveyed resonated with audiences proud of their politics and jaundiced about their leaders.

Capra's film opened as the world was descending into World War II. For its part, at this moment, the Senate was most concerned with imposing restrictions on Roosevelt and his domestic programs. The administration could not stop the effort to cripple controversial New Deal programs such as the Federal Theater Project, which ended in 1939. At the same time the conservatives could not muster the energy and votes to roll back what the New Deal had accomplished. The Senate would have to live with what Franklin D. Roosevelt had initiated. After all, as far as his enemies knew, he would be leaving office in January 1941. But the worsening international situation in 1938–39 changed these political calculations. New tensions and crosscurrents within the chamber developed as foreign policy once again shaped how the Senate and the White House struggled for ascendancy.

## CHAPTER NINE

# The Senate in Wartime

A MID ALL THE DOMESTIC RANCOR OF THE NEW DEAL, THE FOREIGN policy dilemmas of the 1930s had seemed to be of secondary importance to the Senate. The controversies about the World Court and neutrality laws in 1935 had shown that such issues could stir public opinion. Yet the immediacy of the Depression and its effects on Americans made the rumbles of diplomatic storms seem far away. Most lawmakers engaged international questions only when they had to.

By 1938, the power of an expansionist Japan was mounting in Asia. In Europe, Germany under Adolf Hitler loomed ominously. Foreign affairs demanded thought and action. Popular sentiment to stay out of overseas quarrels dominated, but the threats to national security were changing attitudes of some in the upper house. Until war was actually declared in December 1941, however, serious divisions between isolationists and internationalists provided a new fault line in the Senate for debate and acrimony.

Isolationists exerted a strong influence in the Senate. Veterans of the battle over the League of Nations such as William E. Borah and Hiram Johnson monitored Franklin Roosevelt to be sure that the president did not demonstrate any signs of Wilsonian thinking. Borah in particular dismissed the chances of war in Europe. "The United States is getting worked up over the prospect of war," he told a reporter in mid-1938. "I'm not." Borah and Johnson sought to assert American rights as a neutral nation to be sure that the nation did not go to war. Others such as Gerald Nye of North Dakota favored an isolationism by means of laws that drew the United States away from international involvement. A common animus toward Roosevelt and the State Department motivated both camps.[1]

The upshot in the Senate was that the adversaries of the White House held the upper hand until the war began, in September 1939. Because the president depended on the votes of some of these legislators on domestic issues, he appeased them on foreign policy and neutrality questions until after 1938. Once the Supreme Court fight had been lost, as isolationists and Republican conservatives came together, Roosevelt had less need to conciliate Burton K. Wheeler and others. He also found southern Democrats more willing to back him on foreign policy questions. But through much of 1939 the senatorial isolationists had the initiative.

Men who feared the consequences of overseas commitments operated from sincere motives and honest convictions. Their suspicion of executive power also came to seem prescient during the excesses of the Cold War and the Vietnam era. Yet there are limits to a realistic rehabilitation of the isolationist senators. If their hearts were often in the right place as idealists, their judgments about the dangers that Japan and especially Hitler's Germany posed were often naïve. Some of these politicians, Borah and Nye among them, displayed a good deal of indifference to the plight of Jews under Nazi rule. Many others in and out of the Senate shared these prejudices. The blinkered thinking of the isolationists on this issue did their cause no credit.

The seniority system made Key Pittman of Nevada chairman of the Foreign Relations Committee in this crisis. He took charge of the panel when Claude Swanson of Virginia joined Roosevelt's cabinet as secretary of the navy. When sober, Pittman was a capable lawmaker whose priorities were his state's silver-mining interests and his own political survival. The senator had a long struggle with alcoholism, and he was losing the battle as the 1930s unfolded. He drank all day, and kept an icebox filled with liquor in the Foreign Relations Committee's room. Pittman was often drunk on the Senate floor during debates, and his incapacity showed up during deliberations about the neutrality bill in 1935. His colleagues simply ignored Pittman's behavior.[2]

In the summer of 1939, senatorial isolationism showed its worst side. With war impending in Europe, the president wanted to have the embargo on trade with belligerents lifted through repeal of that part of the Neutrality Act. Restraints on the ability of the executive to act now seemed unwise. Given the hold of the isolationists on the Foreign Relations Committee, the White House turned first to the House of Representatives. Having carved out a narrow victory there, the next step was the Foreign Relations Committee. On July 11, 1939, the committee voted 12 to 11 to put off any further discussions of revising the Neutrality Act until the next session, scheduled for January 1940. Hiram Johnson, who had put the coalition together, called it "a beautiful fight, and if it has to be begun again, we'll go to the limit."[3]

A week later, on July 18, Roosevelt met with key senators at the White House, including Borah, to sound out opinion on trying neutrality revision once again. The president and the secretary of state, Cordell Hull, warned of the imminence of war in Europe as a rationale for repealing the embargo clause. Borah replied, "I do not believe there is going to be any war in Europe, between now and the first of January or for some time thereafter." Hull urged the Idaho senator to read State Department cables for proof of his claims. Borah replied that he did not "give a damn about your dispatches" and proclaimed that he had better sources about what was taking place in Europe than did the State Department. The senator was basing his judgment on a left-wing British magazine of dubious accuracy to which he subscribed. Such was the level of senatorial expertise that often confronted the Roosevelt White House. Borah's pomposity had always verged on self-parody. On the brink of war, he became an object lesson in the dangers of self-importance in the upper house.[4]

The consensus of the meeting was that nothing could be done about neutrality at that time. Six weeks later Germany invaded Poland, England declared war, and the Second World War had started. Borah's statement demonstrated the degree to which some senators, in their ire against Roosevelt, had allowed emotion and wishful thinking to cloud minds about the threats that the United States faced in 1939. The episode became, in the minds of some policymakers, a cautionary tale about what might happen if senators were allowed to play too large a role in foreign policy.

The onset of World War II brought a new Republican leader to the forefront in the Senate. Though he would not prevail in his efforts to keep the United States out of the war, Robert A. Taft established himself as an effective spokesman for the resurgent Republicans in these months. Charles L. McNary was the nominal voice of the GOP in the Senate, but increasingly Taft was the man his colleagues looked to for direction and guidance. Taft

A view of the Senate chamber from the press gallery during a Senate debate in 1939. The press furnished most of the information about the proceedings, since radio broadcasts of the Senate's proceedings were not allowed. (SENATE HISTORICAL OFFICE)

went on to be the dominant figure among Senate Republicans for the next twelve years. He put his stamp on a period of Senate history by the force of his intellect and private personality. When he tried to move beyond the upper house and win the presidency, Taft failed. But on his chosen ground he was a major player in the history of the institution.

Robert Alphonso Taft was fifty when he came to the Senate. His political lineage was long and impeccably Republican. His grandfather had served in the cabinet of Ulysses S. Grant, and his father was the only man to serve as both president and Supreme Court chief justice. Young Robert was an outstanding student at Yale and the Harvard Law School. During World War I he served in the Food Administration under Herbert Hoover, who along with his father proved to be one of the dominant influences in his political thought. To public affairs Taft brought a deep suspicion of government planning and skepticism about world organizations such as the League of Nations and later the United Nations. He had an instinctive distrust of the New Deal, which he regarded as a precursor of socialism.[5]

Behind Taft's steel-frame glasses and high forehead lay a powerful intelligence. The joke around Washington was that Taft had the best mind in the city until he made it up; then he was dogmatic and tenacious, even a little unfair on occasion. Never charismatic, he was at his worst when he sought to reflect a common touch he did not really possess. His tenacity won him staunch admirers who fought for him within the Republican Party through three nominating contests. He worked hard in the Senate, mastered the rules, and gained almost universal respect. Senator Taft was as well suited to the Senate as his father had been to the Supreme Court. Not satisfied with that political fate, Bob Taft stepped onto the larger stage, where his austere persona did not play well even with Republican voters.

The start of the war in Europe broke the deadlock over neutrality legislation. Roosevelt called Congress into special session on September 21, 1939, to ask it to remove the embargo on arms and allow warring nations, which meant Great Britain and France, to buy munitions. To facilitate passage of the measure the president kept a low profile and reached out to conservative Democrats. Roosevelt got what he wanted in terms of repealing the arms embargo but had to accept the retention of isolationist language from the 1937 Neutrality Act. Through the rest of 1939 and into the early months of 1940 the war paused and the international situation seemed calmer. Perhaps the isolationists in the Senate had it right.

In this moment of quiet, William E. Borah's long career ended. The "Lion of Idaho" collapsed at his Washington home on January 16, 1940, with a brain hemorrhage and died there three days later, at age seventy-four. From the perspective of over six decades, Borah's reputation seems more quixotic than substantial. Though he was often regarded as a liberal Republican, he stood against the expansion of government power and believed in a less active national state. Opposed to civil rights, regulation of child labor, supervision of large corporations, and other aspects of the New Deal, the "Lion of Idaho" was often more blather than accomplishment in the history of the institution. Once he passed from the scene, it was hard to tell just what had made Borah seem so important. When World War II exploded in the spring of 1940, the isolationist Borah seemed a relic of a vanished time.

In May 1940, the Germans unleashed their blitzkrieg on the Low Countries and France. Within weeks the Nazis were in Paris, and Great Britain stood alone against Hitler. World events had undercut the isolationists and their ideas, once so powerful in the Senate. Now to be against American involvement in World War II was no longer a political winner.

Two Republican senators felt the immediate effect of this shift in mood and circumstance as they sought their party's presidential nomination in 1940. Arthur H. Vandenberg, a former newspaper owner in Grand Rapids, Michigan, who had been in the Senate since 1926, hoped to turn his hard-line isolationism into the Republican nomination. Vandenberg's serious-ness, however, was in some doubt; as he said to one reporter, "Why should I kill myself to carry Vermont?"[6]

The more serious contender was Bob Taft, with just under two years of Senate experience and abundant self-confidence. The dour, stern Ohioan based his first run for the White House on his opposition to the New Deal and his antipathy for war. "This is no time for the people to be wholly ab-sorbed in foreign battles." Rather, he contended, it is the New Deal that may leave us "weak and unprepared for attack." As Hitler's tanks surged across western Europe in May and June, Taft's rhetoric seemed more and more out of touch with reality. To say that the New Deal was more likely to lead to "the infiltration of totalitarian ideas" than were "any activities of the Com-munists or the Nazi bund" appeared irresponsible in light of the fall of France and the danger to Great Britain. Those developments posed real dangers to the United States. Taft's candidacy began to fade.[7]

When it came time for the Republican National Convention in late June 1940, the candidacies of Taft and Vandenberg, along with that of Gov-ernor Thomas E. Dewey of New York, fell before the wave of enthusiasm that swept Wendell Willkie to the GOP nomination. For the moment the Republicans had opted for internationalism over senatorial isolationism. To balance the new ticket, Willkie turned to the Senate Republican leader, Charles L. McNary, who had made his own race for the top spot but never achieved much traction. As a westerner and advocate of public power McNary offset Willkie's New York residency and utility executive back-ground. While not thrilled with the idea of making the race, McNary agreed and was duly nominated. Even Democrats concluded that the popu-lar Oregon senator was a strong addition to the Republican ticket.[8]

In the end McNary's presence on the ticket made little difference as Willkie went down to defeat at the hands of Roosevelt. McNary returned to the Senate as the issues of war and peace became more intense and divi-sive. Once again, as had been the case since Harding's nomination and election in 1920, the Senate had not proven to be an effective base from which to seek national office.

While the presidential campaign was being fought out, the White House had been asking Congress for the tools of war in the event the United States had to confront the Germans or the Japanese. Lawmakers voted to increase defense appropriations, but the nation still faced the reality that it possessed only a skeleton army. In 1940, the army had an authorized strength of fewer than 300,000 soldiers. Advocates of the Allied cause proposed legislation to start a peacetime draft. Isolationists railed against the scheme. Senator Taft adopted a strong position against conscription because, he asserted, there was no need for coercion. "I do not think that any of these nations will attack the United States, and I believe that even if they do our present forces can defend us against an attack across 3,000 miles of water." The Senate beat back Taft's effort to limit the size of the army and passed the draft by a substantial though not overwhelming margin.[9]

By early 1941, Great Britain desperately needed money and weapons to continue fighting. The United States had already taken a long stride toward a de facto alliance with Britain in its destroyers-for-bases deal of September 1940. Several months later, however, Roosevelt announced that the British were running out of money to pay for American war materials. To keep that nation in the war and to protect American security, the president proposed a program called Lend-Lease to provide the British what they needed. The money and supplies would be lent to the British and they would return them or repay the United States once the war was won.

The announcement provoked an immediate furor, and isolationists and their main organization, America First, mobilized public opinion against it. Montana's Burton K. Wheeler, his liberal past now long forgotten, following his commitment to keeping the United States neutral, said that the Lend-Lease idea resembled the New Deal's agricultural policy (which had involved taking acreage out of cultivation by destroying crops) applied to diplomacy. "It will plough under every fourth American boy." California's Hiram Johnson predicted that if Lend-Lease were adopted, war would follow. When the Senate passed the bill by 60 to 31, the California senator bemoaned: "Last night we did the dirty deed. We assassinated liberty under the pretext of aiding a belligerent in the war."[10]

Democrats, even southerners who were skeptical on domestic policy, had rallied to the White House position. Roosevelt asked James F. "Jimmy" Byrnes of South Carolina to manage the Lend-Lease bill on the floor, and also interceded to have Byrnes and Carter Glass of Virginia added to the Foreign Relations Committee. Byrnes had long been one of the most influential southern senators, and he handled matters with such skill that he came within a single vote of predicting what the actual count would be when the bill passed two months later. As a reward, the president named Byrnes to the Supreme Court that summer—despite the qualms of civil rights groups because of Byrnes's opposition to anti-lynching legislation.[11]

The political stakes were considerable in a special election for a Senate seat during the summer of 1941, a race that brought a future majority leader and president to national attention. After the death of the Texas senator Morris Sheppard, an election was to be held to name his successor. Congressman Lyndon Baines Johnson of the Tenth District entered the contest as an avowed champion of Roosevelt and the New Deal. The White House threw its support behind the young and at the time liberal House member. The popular governor, W. Lee O'Daniel, also entered the race, saying that his platform was "one hundred percent approval of the Lord God Jehovah, widows, orphans, low taxes, and Ten Commandments, and the Golden Rule." The race was close, and Johnson lost by a mere 1,311 votes because of some late and possibly fraudulent returns from East Texas. O'Daniel won a full term in 1942 and spent it as "a man with perhaps the lowest reputation in the Senate." His opponent promised to run again. The Senate had not heard the last of Lyndon B. Johnson.[12]

Like other Americans on the East Coast, the United States senators heard the news of the Japanese attack on Pearl Harbor on December 7 in the early afternoon. The chairman of the Foreign Relations Committee, Tom Connally, was on a romantic Sunday drive in the country with Morris Sheppard's widow when news of war reached his office. An aide, Edith Parker, set about drafting the declaration of war that her boss would need when he and his future wife got back from their sojourn. The next day Roosevelt made his "day of infamy" speech, the Senate and the House voted to declare war, and the United States entered the conflict.[13]

Throughout World War II, the Senate acted in a cranky and contentious manner toward the White House. Relations between Roosevelt and Capitol Hill, which were sour before Pearl Harbor, deteriorated during the nearly four years of war. The increasing clout of the Club of conservative southerners and like-minded Republicans acted as a check on presidential options. Mindful of what had happened to Woodrow Wilson in 1919–20, Roosevelt was careful to keep the Senate informed and involved about the plans for the

United Nations and the extent of American participation in a world organization. In other areas, however, politics went on as usual with the coalition of southern Democrats and conservative Republicans anxious to roll back the New Deal wherever possible. Alben Barkley continued as a majority leader without a firm grip on his Democratic colleagues, and the divisions created by the New Deal and the war meant that the White House was very much on the defensive, since it lacked a working majority. Many senators would have had little reason to disagree with the assessment of Franklin D. Roosevelt that Isaiah Berlin, then a member of the staff of the British embassy, offered of the president's character: "He is (a) absolutely cold, (b) completely ruthless, (c) has no friends, (d) becoming a megalomaniac and is pulling our Mr. Churchill along rather than vice versa."[14]

Roosevelt could count on the support of some administration loyalists in the upper house. Lister Hill of Alabama could be relied on when race was not involved. Joseph Guffey of Pennsylvania was a staunch New Dealer but lacked influence with his colleagues. Claude Pepper of Florida, Robert F. Wagner of New York, and James Murray of Montana were others in the liberal camp. The election of 1942 removed several New Deal stalwarts and saw the departure in particular of George Norris of Nebraska. The number of votes the White House could depend on fell well short of a majority in the Senate during the Second World War.[15]

The Senate came under fire in the early part of the war as the members seemed to be taking advantage of their privileged position. A move to include lawmakers in the government's generous retirement plan aroused public outrage. Indeed, in the long run the initiative proved to be a very lucrative benefit for future legislators, for their annuities and, later, other benefits such as health insurance usually exceeded anything offered by the private sector. The ability of members of Congress to acquire X-cards, which allowed holders to purchase unlimited amounts of gasoline during a time of rationing, seemed further evidence that senators regarded themselves as apart from and a cut above their fellow citizens when it came to accepting the inconvenience of fighting World War II. In response to complaints from the public, the Senators voted 66 to 2 to maintain their gasoline privileges—just to demonstrate their independence and disdain for opinion outside Washington.[16]

An episode involving a Democratic opponent of Roosevelt's foreign policy illustrated the testy temper of the Senate in the spring of 1942. David I. Walsh of Massachusetts had been a New Deal Democrat who became an isolationist in the years before Pearl Harbor. Walsh was also gay, though the Senate took no notice of his sexual preferences. In early 1942, federal agents raided a house in Brooklyn, New York, where homosexuals gathered. Some military personnel and alleged German agents were arrested. The *New York Post*, which disliked Walsh's isolationist politics, ran a story on May 1, 1942, with the headline "Link Senator to Spy Nest" and charged that Walsh had been a frequent visitor to the building.[17]

Walsh denied all the allegations, the FBI cleared him, and Alben Barkley delivered a speech exonerating his colleague. In the course of the probe, pro-Walsh senators correctly alleged that a New York attorney, Morris Ernst, had brought the information to the White House as part of a smear campaign against isolationist senators. A kind of senatorial cover-up ensued to spare Walsh any further embarrassment. With that, the episode died away, but what happened had confirmed for Roosevelt's opponents in the Senate that he would use any means to hurt his enemies.[18]

As the Walsh case indicated, there was no political truce in the wake of Pearl Harbor. Within a few weeks Taft was proclaiming that criticism of the administration in wartime was a patriotic duty in a democratic government. In the face of such opposition, Roosevelt was petulant and passive as he grappled with the demands of fighting a global war. His secretary of the interior, Harold Ickes, complained in August 1942 that "Congress is a menace and it looks as if the President would have to sustain heavy losses on the political front. He's doing nothing about it."[19]

In fact, there was little that Roosevelt could do to stem the currents of conservatism that pervaded Congress during the war. No majorities existed to extend and expand the social programs of the New Deal. When the president announced that "Dr. Win the War" had replaced "Dr. New Deal," he was only conceding what the realities were as far as the Senate was concerned.

At the beginning of the conflict the Senate conservatives were ascendant and the power of that bloc expanded with Republican victories in the elections held in November 1942. The GOP resurgence grew out of voter unhappiness with the direction of the war, for few victories for the Allied cause came in 1942. The invasion of North Africa, the first successful Allied military action in the European theater, came several days after the balloting, too late to help the Democrats. The Grand Old Party gained ten seats as a number of Democratic stalwarts succumbed to voter disaffection and a lackluster Democratic campaign. The most notable casualty was Independent Republican George Norris, who lost to a conservative Republican, Kenneth Wherry. Norris had probably stayed too long in the Senate, and his constituents had turned against the New Deal's agricultural policies by the end of the 1930s. The increase in the Republican strength to thirty-eight members meant that the Republican–southern Democrat union had effective control of the Senate.[20]

As the war intensified, African Americans offered a direct challenge to the conservative coalition. If the United States was fighting for freedom abroad, black leaders asked, why did it deny rights to its African-American citizens? In 1942 liberals offered legislation to repeal the poll tax, on which eight southern states relied as one means of preventing blacks from voting. The legislation had passed the House, and Alben Barkley, an opponent of the poll tax, brought it up in a way that demanded immediate consideration by the whole Senate. Such a tactic, which prevented the measure from being killed in a Southern-controlled committee, outraged the conservatives. Angered at Barkley's move, Richard Russell, Tom Connally, and other conservatives decided to block the bill by simply staying away from the chamber, thus preventing a quorum. Thus, there could be no action on the bill and the leadership would be forced to move to other business. Barkley then instructed the sergeant-at-arms to "arrest" the absentees and bring them to the Senate. The southerners reacted with even more bitterness and decried the effort to secure their presence as further evidence of Barkley's subservience to the White House and his lack of respect for Senate traditions.[21]

The advocates of poll-tax repeal could not assemble even a simple majority for their position. Their attempt to impose cloture fell short in December 1942, with thirty-seven voting to end debate and forty-one opposed. The poll tax stayed in place. The press talked again of "Bumbling Barkley" and the lack of respect he faced from his Democratic colleagues. More important, the Senate once again was proving to be a barrier to even a mild change in the racial practices of the South. The consequences of the failure to expand democracy for all citizens would be played out after the war as the civil rights movement gathered power.[22]

The poll-tax battle showed just how determined southern Democrats were to resist the pressure for civil rights reforms. The leader of the bloc in this regard was Richard Russell, even though such shrill bigots as Theodore G. "That Man" Bilbo received more newspaper coverage. Russell devoted his abundant energies and parliamentary skills to opposing such administration initiatives as the Fair Employment Practices Commission (FEPC). That body, set up in 1941 as the White House's grudging response to complaints from the black community about workplace bias, was designed to correct employment discrimination but had only modest powers to do so. In the Senate and in private letters Russell railed against what he saw as the imminent danger of racial equality and miscegenation in his region and told his correspondents that there was no "greater menace to the future of the entire country, and especially to our Southland."[23]

Racial segregation could not have found a more effective champion in the Senate than Russell. He outworked and outstudied almost all of his colleagues to achieve mastery of the rules and the parliamentary context. He used a courtly approach and his gentlemanly manners to lull enemies into underestimating his talents. When racial issues were not involved, Russell's intellect made him a constructive force. Unfortunately, for Russell, as for so many southern senators during and after World War II, race affected almost every issue. The possibility of a filibuster or an eruption of lurid southern oratory on race hung over the chamber. Race was an issue that might provoke Russell and his allies to hamstring the Senate at any moment. In the genteel atmosphere of the upper house, proponents of civil rights, outnumbered as they were during World War II, shrank from provoking Russell into a battle over segregation.

Race shaped the Senate battle over the voting rights of soldiers fighting across the world. The White House and the Democrats wanted the fighting men and women to have a chance to cast their votes for the president and his party in 1944. One reason for their poor showing in the 1942 elections, Democrats contended, was that many of their loyal voters had been drafted and were away from the polls. But who should send the ballots to the fighting men and women in the field? Having the federal government provide the ballots might help voters in the military record their support for Roosevelt. Republicans wanted the states to send out ballots, and the southerners joined them in that position. If the states controlled who got ballots, then black members of the military could be excluded from the electoral process in southern states.

The battle over this issue in 1943 and 1944 was complex and protracted. In the end, the conservative coalition held the upper hand and had the votes so that the outcome left the decision about the ballots largely in the hands of the states. Some states chose to send their own ballots, and others let the federal government do so. Faced with a bill that he did not much like, Roosevelt let the legislation take effect without his signature. Only a relatively small number of military personnel could use the federal ballot option in the final result. The controversy over the soldier vote illustrated again how tenuous was the administration's hold on Congress when racial issues came into the mix.

The underlying tensions within the Democratic party erupted in December 1943 in the course of the debate about the voting legislation. Joseph Guffey, a liberal Democrat from Pennsylvania who was not widely esteemed within the chamber, charged that there was a coalition of northern Republicans and southern Democrats seeking to prevent soldiers from voting. Guffey called it "the most unpatriotic and unholy alliance that has occurred in the United States Senate since the League of Nations for the peace of the world was defeated in 1919." Harry Byrd responded with a stinging indictment of Guffey as "a pouter pigeon." Josiah Bailey of North Carolina declared, "There is a reason why the South has voted Democratic. . . . The time will come . . . when the southern people will demand that there shall be no meddling with their affairs."[24]

Though no formal alliance operated between the southern contingent and the resurgent Republicans after 1943, their de facto alliance also served the needs and ambitions of Robert A. Taft. The emerging Republican leader found common cause with Russell, Harry Byrd, and Walter George on economic issues such as taxation and the reduction of government spending. For Taft, who used the lower-case to describe "negroes" in his private correspondence during the late 1940s, the community of interest with these men was evident. Taft said of Harry Byrd that the two men agreed nine times out ten, adding "that's about as high a degree of agreement as I have with any Republican senator." In later years, Byrd and Taft would sit together as they checked off senators' names during a roll-call vote—a collaboration that emphasized their thoroughness and their power.[25]

Taft remained content to exercise power at a distance. In 1943 the Republican leader, "Charlie Mack" McNary, continued in nominal charge of the GOP, but the time for his quiet, deferential leadership was passing. By March 1943, McNary was ill with the brain tumor that killed him a year later. As he faded from the scene, Taft came forward as the guiding spirit of his party. He did not want to be the minority leader because the routine of floor management and the need for surface geniality and tolerance of fools held no attractions for the reclusive Taft. The official leadership passed to Wallace White of Maine, and Taft got what he really wanted. In January and February 1944 he was named chairman of a nine-member steering committee created by the Republican Conference whose task it was to establish policy for the Senate minority. From that strategic position, Taft moved forward to articulate an anti–New Deal agenda for his colleagues and fashion a more united opposition that could assail Roosevelt and his administration. Facing a tough reelection fight in Ohio, Taft stayed out of the race for the Republican presidential nomination in 1944.[26]

A journalist who observed the senator in the summer of 1944 told his editors that a visitor to Taft's office late in the evening would "find all of his secretaries gone, the Senator, his coat draped over a chair in his inner office, sitting at a desk piled high with books, committee hearings and reports, drudging away." In his interaction with other senators he followed "a thoroughly frank, sometimes amazingly frank—if humorless—method." He never tried to charm or please, but simply said what he thought. So evident was his dedication to his principles that few of his Republican fellows chafed at this aloof treatment. As a result, Taft rose steadily in the estimation of both Democrats and Republicans.[27]

Within the wartime environment, an otherwise obscure Democratic senator was quietly making a name for himself while attention centered on the policy debates that so engaged Robert Taft, Richard Russell, and others. Harry S. Truman first came to the Senate in 1935 after a constructive career as a county judge in the politics of Kansas City and his native western Missouri. An association with the Tom Pendergast Democratic machine gave Truman an undeserved reputation as an instrument of his unsavory patron. Truman won a second term in 1940 despite the covert opposition of the Roosevelt White House. Early in 1941, as the American war effort gathered momentum, Truman proposed that a committee be created to probe how the defense program was operating. Gaining approval from the leadership, Truman assembled a committee and a staff. During 1941 he exposed fraud and abuse in the defense procurement regime, but once war began he had to justify the panel's continuing existence. Surmounting that obstacle, Truman made his committee a constructive part of the war effort by finding ways to reduce costs and identifying abuses. *Time* put him on its cover in 1943 and called him "a personally honest courageous man." The Senate knew that Harry Truman was a comer, even if many members disliked him personally.[28]

As the 1944 presidential election approached, politicians knew that Roosevelt would run for a fourth term. Insiders also recognized that the president's health was failing. The odds were that he would not live out another term. The Democratic vice-presidential nomination thus seemed a ticket to the White House and national power. The incumbent vice president, Henry A. Wallace, was considered too liberal and was thus a potential electoral liability. Speculation turned toward someone such as Truman, who could help the ticket in the South and the border states but also was liberal enough to be acceptable to labor and big-city Democrats.[29]

Within the Senate itself, 1944 brought more evidence of worsening relations between lawmakers and Roosevelt. Alben Barkley had faced his restive colleagues on such issues as the Smith-Connally bill in 1943, a measure that aimed to cripple organized labor by barring strikes in defense plants after a thirty-day cooling-off period between management and workers. Roosevelt vetoed the legislation, but the Senate and House overrode him. Coming in as a new reporter to cover the upper house in late 1943, Allen Drury found "a growing general bitterness between the White House and the Hill." Barkley, Drury reported, "acts like a man who is working awfully hard and awfully earnestly at a job he doesn't particularly like."[30]

As the war entered its third year, Roosevelt and the Treasury Department proposed a large tax bill to meet the ever-growing costs of the world conflict. The administration was also concerned about the threat of rising prices and inflation. It sought $10.5 billion in new taxes, but Congress balked. The House came back with a bill that produced $2.1 billion. The Senate version was in the same range. In his 1944 State of the Union message Roosevelt criticized these alternatives and suggested that Congress should do more to raise revenues in a manner that further rankled on the Hill. Nonetheless, Congress passed its version of the tax bill and sent it on to the White House. Roosevelt vetoed the bill with a stinging message that indicted Capitol Hill for capitulating to special interests: "It is not a tax bill but a tax relief bill, providing relief not for the needy but for the greedy."[31]

For the patient Barkley, who had suffered with Roosevelt's tactics for six and a half years, the veto message brought him to the end of his patience. He had warned the president that Congress would not accept another tax bill, and the two men had argued about the issue in heated terms. On the way back from one of these meetings, Barkley told Vice President Wallace, "I can't get the votes in the Senate under the methods that are being followed." When the veto message came with its caustic language, Barkley thought he had no choice but to break with the White House. In his memoir he wrote, "I was not a yes-man, a me-too man" but "a liberal and a progressive long before I ever heard of Franklin D. Roosevelt."[32]

By the morning of February 23, word buzzed around the Senate that Barkley was going to resign his post. In a speech that day the majority leader derided Roosevelt's veto as wrong-headed and intemperate. The president's quip about the needy and the greedy was "a calculated and deliberate assault upon the legislative integrity of every member of the Congress of the United States." Barkley urged his colleagues to pass the tax bill over Roosevelt's veto and added that he would resign the next day. At the conclusion of his remarks, the chamber erupted with wild applause from senators and gallery. To one observer, Barkley had reasserted "his own dignity and his own self-respect and gained thereby an increased stature among the men with whom he works."[33]

The Democratic senators reelected Barkley the next day with a resolution that called him "capable and courteous, faithful to his trust, diligent and courageous in discharge of his duties, and equal to all the trying demands of his position." To the press they said that "he speaks for us to the President." Roosevelt had already sent another "Dear Alben" letter that was as close to an apology as the imperious president could muster. Barkley responded that mutual respect between Congress and the executive was important and should be restored.[34]

On February 25, the Senate overrode the veto by a vote of 72 to 14, echoing what the House had done. Barkley and the Senate had prevailed in this sudden showdown with Roosevelt. During the remainder of Roosevelt's presidency, Barkley received marginally better treatment from the White House, though signs of an underlying tension persisted. But within the Senate, the Kentucky senator's new authority brought only limited positive results for the White House.

Barkley's personal act of defiance had an important long-term impact, in that it further legitimized senatorial resistance to the programs of liberal presidents. The surge of fellow feeling that the majority leader's gesture evoked had at its core a desire to bring down Franklin D. Roosevelt after too many of his snubs, cute tricks, and lies. But it also meant that the goals for which the president stood, many of them laudable, came under a cloud as well. Opposing the president on principle gave the wartime Senate an excuse to stand against his measures of social reform, which it was already disposed to do.

In one key area of foreign policy, Roosevelt and the Senate interacted in a more productive manner. The president wanted to create an international peacekeeping organization after the war, and he was determined not to duplicate Woodrow Wilson's errors in handling the Versailles Treaty and the League of Nations. Roosevelt had political advantages that Wilson had not enjoyed. The Democrats had control of the Senate throughout the war and thus could determine when foreign policy issues were debated. Although the president's relations with many senators were strained, there was no animosity of the Lodge-Wilson kind with any of the key players during World War II. The Republicans, fearful of being tagged as isolationists, had an incentive to go some distance toward the administration's position on peace and the creation of an international organization to maintain it. So in many respects the years from 1942 to 1945 presented a very different picture from what had been the case a generation earlier.

The main Senate participants also wanted to avoid a replay of the Wilson experience. The chairman of the Foreign Relations Committee, Tom Connally of Texas, looked like the stereotypical southern solon of the old school. Some observers, such as Henry Wallace, believed that he was "essentially a demagogue with no depth of perception, no sense of the general welfare, and no interest in it." An assistant secretary of state, Dean Acheson, was kinder about the Texan in his later assessment. "Behind the black clothes, the black bow string tie, the white curls under the collar, were irony and sarcasm. Under the irony and sarcasm were perceptions of the great issues to be decided in the war and postwar years, and strong unfailing support for the measures to deal with them."[35]

Connally reached out to his Republican counterpart, Arthur H. Vandenberg of Michigan, to achieve bipartisan unity on the issue of a postwar organization of nations and a presumed peace treaty that would resolve the whole conflict. Until the start of World War II, Vandenberg was a Republican conservative and isolationist more renowned for writing adoring biographies of Alexander Hamilton than for any tangible achievements in office. His speeches were cliché-ridden and his views conventionally Republican. It is unclear why Vandenberg moved toward an acceptance of internationalism—whether he succumbed to the flattery of the Democrats or reached a new position out of genuine conviction after Pearl Harbor. He now told his friends that the GOP could not repeat its rejection of a peace settlement and retreat inside the nation's borders. Some Republican cooperation with the State Department and the administration on these issues would have to occur and better to do it in a constructive way. Working with Secretary of State Cordell Hull, Vandenberg moved into a constructive stance with the administration. The Michigan senator became a symbol of a new attitude that went by the name of bipartisanship in foreign policy. It was a fragile concept that never claimed the full allegiance of Vandenberg's Republican colleagues, but it was an important moment in Senate history nonetheless.[36]

The significant developments in this process of bipartisan activity began in March 1943 with the introduction of a resolution by Joseph Ball of Minnesota, Harold Burton of Ohio, Carl Hatch of New Mexico, and Lister Hill of Alabama (a group soon known as B2H2) calling for, among other things, a United Nations army to repel future aggressive acts. Vandenberg produced his own resolution, which was closer to Republican thinking, and these ideas were blended in what became the Connally Resolution calling for American participation in a world organization. The resolution was adopted in October 1943 by a vote of 85 to 5 after prolonged debate. The outcome on the resolution indicated that the Senate would not be the roadblock to a potential peace settlement that it had been in 1919–20.[37]

Vandenberg continued down his new path when he negotiated a Republican statement of principle about the proposed international organization at the Mackinac Island (Michigan) conference of GOP leaders in September 1943. The Republicans were able to endorse the idea of something like the United Nations, as long as the Senate ratified a treaty to take the United States into the proposed international organization. Vandenberg also worked during the 1944 election to see that the Republican candidate, Thomas E. Dewey, did not emphasize foreign policy issues in a manner that interfered with bipartisanship. Republicans waged the election primarily on domestic issues and attacked Roosevelt for some softness toward Communism.

The presidential contest brought another victory for Roosevelt and continued dominance of the Democrats in the Senate, where they had fifty-seven seats to the Republicans' thirty-eight and one independent. The senatorial class included J. William Fulbright of Arkansas, who ousted Hattie Caraway after two terms. Fulbright would soon assume a leading role in the Senate on foreign policy questions while placating his constituents with opposition to civil rights. On the Republican side Indiana sent the dependably conservative Homer Capehart, and the more mercurial Wayne Morse won a seat for the GOP from Oregon. Morse would soon demonstrate that as a political maverick and irritant to other senators he had few equals in the history of the chamber.[38]

Some other famous and infamous senators went down in the 1944 election. Gerald P. Nye found that his isolationist views no longer appealed to North Dakota voters. Bennett Champ Clark of Missouri, long one of the most notable alcoholics in the chamber, also was rejected at the polls. Prewar isolationism had receded, but the Republicans would have new critics of Democratic foreign policy in the Senate throughout the remainder of the 1940s.

Arthur Vandenberg was naturally disappointed with Dewey's loss, but he continued to evolve as an elder statesman. On January 10, 1945, he delivered a famous oration that Allen Drury believed reached "a high level of nonpartisanship and constructive suggestion." In his speech, much of which was drafted for him by *New York Times* columnist James Reston and *New York Herald-Tribune* columnist Walter Lippman, Vandenberg said that he was prepared, "by effective international cooperation, to do our full part in charting happier and safer tomorrows." He wanted "maximum American cooperation, consistent with legitimate American self interest, with constitutional process and with collateral events which warrant it" to make the ideal of collective security and international cooperation a reality. The speech, demonstrating in such a public way that he had moved away from his isolationist heritage, cemented Vandenberg's reputation as a statesman.[39]

By January 1945 Franklin D. Roosevelt was on the verge of taking the oath of office for a fourth term. The atmosphere between the executive and the Senate, despite the constructive signs on foreign policy issues, remained poisonous. The White House encountered stiff resistance when Roosevelt named Henry A. Wallace to be secretary of commerce, and a bitter confirmation battle ensued before Wallace was approved. Southerners also stripped funding for the Fair Employment Practices Commission and, in a direct rebuke to the president, defeated the nomination of the liberal Aubrey Williams to be head of the Rural Electrification Commission. As far as the Senate was concerned, the president's fourth term would have been played out in the context of an abiding distrust on both sides about each other's motives and good faith.

The death of Roosevelt on April 12, 1945, made the issue moot. When Harry S. Truman became president, one of the Senate's own attained the White House. An initial mood of good feeling soon yielded to partisan rancor. Yet, the period of the New Deal and the war represented a crucial junction in the evolution of the upper house. In many ways, the Senate did act to make the social reforms of the Roosevelt era possible and to collaborate in the successful war effort. On the large issue of race, however, the chamber proved hostile and regressive. Repeal of the poll tax, the efforts to end lynching, the modest initiative of the Fair Employment Practices Commission—all these salutary changes were blocked or limited because of the power of the southerners and their Republican allies, under the leadership of Taft, to filibuster and delay. In that sense, the record of the Senate on race between 1935 and 1945 represented one of the enduring moral failures in the history of the institution.

## CHAPTER TEN

# The Senate at Mid-century

T HE SENATE DURING THE TWO DECADES AFTER THE END OF WORLD
War II looked from the outside to be little changed from the upper
house as it had operated since the beginning of the century. The familiar
contests that pitted Republicans versus Democrats or legislative branch
against the executive went on in the customary manner. But the political
and social world outside of the chamber felt the effects of a powerful new
means of communication. In the postwar era the influence of television and
the expansion of a media culture began to reshape how congressional politics functioned. At mid-century, the Senate was at a turning point in its
history.

During this era just before the full advent of television, the Senate operated in a semi-public way. Visitors filled the galleries for important speeches
or moved in and out of the chamber on routine days while a few members
droned through their remarks. Constituents came to the offices of the lawmakers to lobby for their cause or interest. Meanwhile, as one of the pages
wrote in his diary during the 1956 session, "notoriously senators consider
themselves august and distinguished and that larger personification of
themselves, the Senate, the world's greatest deliberative body. This attitude
entails great hauteur in public, for which they compensate in private."[1]

The sense of aloofness from the rest of society did not disappear all at
once, but the presence of television intruded in ways large and small, beginning in the late 1940s. From its starting point in the cities of the Northeast, television spread out across the country to encompass ever-larger

segments of the population. Politicians, said one television critic of the day, now confronted "the most fundamental task of any impresario—to attract and hold the attention of millions." At first both the House and the Senate adopted rules barring television from their chambers. Speaker of the House Sam Rayburn went so far as to forbid the showing of committee hearings, though the Senate instituted no such ban. Gradually, however, both houses of Congress opened themselves to the media—no longer simply the "press." The members of the upper house authorized the presence of broadcast booths in the press gallery, where live and recorded interviews could be prepared. Senators made increasing use of a studio with a backdrop of the Capitol to prepare televised "reports" for their constituents.[2]

The dramatic realization of the potential for televised hearings to make a national career arrived with the Kefauver hearings into organized crime in 1950–1951. In fact, television coverage of Senate hearings began in 1947 with sessions about the Marshall Plan. Discussions of aid for war-torn Europe, however, lacked the box office appeal of mobsters on the witness stand. Estes Kefauver was a Tennessee Democrat, first elected to the upper house in 1948. Ambitious and shrewd, he had long been interested in the problem of organized crime. He also saw the subject as a means to seize the Democratic presidential nomination in 1952. A womanizer and a heavy drinker, Kefauver regarded himself as a candidate who might be the party's choice if President Harry S. Truman did not run again. Getting on television nationally was a key to his personal scenario for the White House.[3]

The Special Committee on Organized Crime in Interstate Commerce, which came to be known as the Kefauver Committee, consisted of its chairman, two Democrats, and two Republicans. Established in 1950, the panel conducted hearings around the country at which law enforcement officials and mob figures appeared. Kefauver's moment before the cameras came as the number of home television sets grew—Americans bought as many as 20,000 sets each day in 1950. Viewers now had a morality play in their homes. Gangsters faced tough questions and in many cases declined to testify on grounds of self-incrimination. The camera made a media star of Kefauver. In the New York City hearings, the mob boss Frank Costello asked that his face not be shown. Instead, the coverage focused on his hands as they clenched and gestured under the intense questioning of Committee Counsel Rudolph Halley. Suddenly the Senate and its committee had grabbed the media spotlight.[4]

Not much in the way of legislation stemmed from the Kefauver hearings. Crime was too diffuse and diverse to frame a single solution. For the Senate Democrats, the probe was one more electoral blow. Crime personalities figured in the big-city politics that the party dominated. Kefauver used the process and the publicity to mount a strong run at the 1952 Democratic nomination. He was eight years too early since the Democratic Party insiders were still powerful enough to deny him the prize and select Adlai Stevenson. By 1960, another Democratic senator, the charismatic, telegenic John Fitzgerald Kennedy, would ride television to the White House.[5]

In the public's mind, the televised hearings made the Mafia a reality with which law enforcement would have to reckon in the future. Indelible images from the Kefauver inquiry show up in motion pictures such as *The Godfather II*. While many senators fretted at Kefauver's skill as a publicity seeker, they also noted what the hearings did for his career. From the end of the 1940s onward, lawmakers calibrated the extent to which television would advance or retard their fortunes. An important step had been taken toward exploiting the allure of show business as an integral part of the upper house.

Television fame came at a price. Televised campaign ads first appeared in presidential elections in 1952 and their power to affect races soon made them a standard feature of senatorial contests. The advent of television advertising meant that the cost of running a contested campaign in even a medium-sized state much exceeded what politicians had previously been required to spend in an election or reelection effort. The growing necessity of serious fund-raising sent both challengers and incumbents out to ask friendly donors for ever-larger sums of money. The influence and role of contributors thus expanded throughout this period. Both parties embarked on a money chase that escalated throughout the remainder of the century. To gain and hold a seat in the postwar Senate meant that lawmakers had to be more versed in the ways of this new, seductive medium.

By 1946 some members of Congress also thought that Capitol Hill needed substantive changes to bring their procedures into the contemporary world. Criticisms of lawmakers were familiar ones—high pay for little result in terms of good laws, aloofness from the needs of the average American, a privileged lifestyle—but they resonated more powerfully in the postwar atmosphere than previously. Writing in the *Washington Post*, the columnist Merlo Pusey indicted Congress "for its failure to replace its outworn legislative machinery which reduces law-making to a hit-or-miss process." There were too many committees, too much irrelevant busy work, and not enough focus on the larger issues that should engage lawmakers. One academic critic said that the "inefficiency of Congress is a national scandal."[6]

The Legislative Reorganization Act of 1946 was intended to deal with such concerns and also sought to reclaim for Congress some of the power that had been lost to the presidency during the New Deal. The law pared the number of Senate standing committees from thirty-three to fifteen. The Military Affairs Committee and the Naval Affairs Committee were combined to create the Senate Armed Services Committee. Lawmakers received more staff for their committees, and the legislation placed limits on the number of committee assignments. Sponsors of the law also established a budgetary process for Congress to follow.[7]

The Senate was modernizing in other ways. A 1938 inspection of the Capitol had revealed that the ninety tons of ceiling and roof could fall in at any time. During the war, unsightly steel beams held the ceiling up. The inadequacies of the room with its stained glass ceiling, poor acoustics, and stifling air prompted a full-scale review of what needed to be done to make the chamber more habitable for those who used it. Plans were developed for modern air-conditioning, a new ceiling, better lights, and adequate acoustics. The chamber underwent extensive renovation in the late 1940s to eliminate the continuing risk that the roof might collapse and to upgrade other features. From July 1949 to January 1951, the Senate met in its old cramped chamber down the corridor while work went forward on the renovation. The more tolerable structure that is the contemporary Senate chamber was finished and the members went back to their duties on January 3, 1951.[8]

Male dominance of the Senate did not waver during World War II. With the defeat of Hattie Caraway by J. William Fulbright in 1944, the upper house reverted to its usual all-male status for four years. In January 1949, Margaret Chase Smith, a Maine Republican, took her seat after winning the party primary over three male rivals. Victory in the general election was assured in a state that was then a solid bastion of the Grand Old Party. After the death of her congressman husband, Smith had spent eight years in the House of Representatives as his successor. On the day she was sworn in as a senator, the gallery, filled with women, applauded as she took the oath of office. Ten days later the new senator introduced an equal rights amendment for women but offset that feminist gesture with pictures in the

During the 1950s Margaret Chase Smith of Maine was the only woman member of the Senate. Her "Declaration of Conscience" speech against Joseph McCarthy in 1950 did not receive much support from her more cautious male colleagues. (MARGARET CHASE SMITH LIBRARY)

*Saturday Evening Post* showing her in the kitchen, wearing an apron, in the act of stirring batter.[9]

Margaret Chase Smith would soon stir the chamber with her "Declaration of Conscience" speech against Joe McCarthy in 1950. Over the span of her four terms in the Senate, in which she was the only woman for eighteen of the twenty-four years, she accommodated to the masculine folkways of the place by not pushing for female pages or seeking better treatment of women in general. She operated on the margins of the institution and suffered repeated slights. When she displayed independence by voting against the confirmation of Lewis Strauss as secretary of commerce in 1959, she felt the sting of President Dwight D. Eisenhower's displeasure—he refused to appear with her in a campaign photo. "Ike said," reported Everett Dirksen, "he would be happy to have his picture taken with every Republican senator but that Smith woman." But getting along by going along was not Smith's way. When she exercised her independence, the men in the Senate responded with their usual chauvinism.[10]

Women figured in the life of the post–World War II Senate either as wives of the members or in the expanding staffs of individual senators or the committees. There had been women staff members for senators in the 1930s. Edith Parker had worked with other women in the office of Tom Connally, and Hiram Johnson had grappled with the problem of having an alcoholic woman among his employees in the late 1930s. Within the Senate, the pages remained an all-male contingent. When young women asked Senator Smith in 1956 "about the possibility of her sponsoring a female page," she declined. The first female page would not be named until 1971, when Jacob Javits, a New York Republican, broke the barrier.[11]

In 1946, the Senate took a small step toward acknowledging the existence of women in their role as secretaries on Capitol Hill. Informal tradition dictated that only male secretaries could come on the Senate floor to consult with their bosses. After the war there were twenty-two women secretaries working for senators, and they could not gain access to the floor. Ralph Owen Brewster, a Republican from Maine, responded to the urgings of his secretary, Frances Dustin, that the situation should change. On July 22, 1946, Brewster obtained a ruling from the chair that women should be granted equal status with men in this area. Mrs. Dustin entered, had her conference with Brewster, and departed, promising that she and other women secretaries would not "abuse the privilege" they had been granted. Coverage of this event in *Newsweek* attested to the slow pace of change in the Senate on matters of gender access.[12]

Senate wives have not attracted the attention that has been devoted to first ladies or female members of Congress. A few wives of senators, such as Lady Bird Johnson and Elizabeth Dole, have gained fame in their own right. Most senatorial spouses, however, have remained obscure or achieved unwanted notoriety when their personal difficulties appeared in the media. Joan Kennedy received tabloid coverage for her periodic bouts with alcoholism and Marvella Bayh's tragic losing fight with breast cancer attracted media attention.

The catchphrase in Washington, originally attributed to Fannie Holmes, wife of Supreme Court Justice Oliver Wendell Holmes, is that the city is filled with distinguished men and the women they married when they were very young. It might also be said that Washington is inhabited by capable women and the ambitious men they married when they were equally young. Senate wives existed in a kind of connubial limbo where they were expected to be available for campaign appearances, maintain a home and take care of the children, and interact with other spouses in the various feminine institutions that dominated the Washington scene. "It was taken for granted," wrote Abigail McCarthy, the wife of Eugene McCarthy of Minnesota, "that to be the wife of a man in politics and the mother of his children was not only a full-time occupation but a worthy calling in itself."[13]

For the Senate wives, there was the Senate Ladies Club, which had continued since its origins in World War I. Upon the convening of Congress each year, the club gave a luncheon to honor the first lady and the wives of cabinet members. "These have become very fine affairs," recalled Eleanor Tydings, wife of Millard Tydings of Maryland, "with palms, flowers, music, and speeches, and, oftentimes, gifts for the First Lady." Through classes offered by the Ladies Club and the Capital Speakers Club Mrs. Tydings and Lady Bird Johnson learned Spanish in the 1940s and 1950s.[14]

Other wives spent their time working in their husbands' offices or threw themselves into the perpetual campaigning that was becoming an accepted aspect of Senate life. Ellen Proxmire, wife of the Wisconsin Democrat William Proxmire, was an unpaid employee for her husband during the 1950s and 1960s, getting out the newsletter, welcoming constituents, and "overseeing the operation of the office while Bill was in Wisconsin." The pressures of juggling home, family, and senatorial obligations put a continuing strain on relationships and tested marital bonds.[15]

Men in the Senate were ambivalent about infidelity. In public everyone paid lip service to the idea of domestic fidelity and the strength of marriages. At the same time, in an era before sexual harassment was even a concept in most men's minds, a certain amount of senatorial privilege toward the opposite sex was expected. Reporters would write of members who were "fun-loving" and "enjoyed a good time." These were code words for aggressive philandering and pursuit of the young women who flocked to Capitol Hill for jobs. Senators behaved as if their job was so difficult that they deserved feminine companionship for relaxation even out of wedlock.

Any reckoning of which senators excelled in these extramarital pursuits has to be impressionistic. For example, John F. Kennedy and his sidekick, George Smathers of Florida, were renowned for their active and incessant pursuit of women in and out of Congress. Richard Russell was an improbable swain, but one whose power and pleasing personality made him more successful with the ladies than an outside observer might have expected. Even Hubert Humphrey reportedly had a mistress tucked away in a discreet apartment near the Senate for trysts when needed. Estes Kefauver had a succession of affairs, none of which ever competed with his marriage. There were even credible allegations that aides procured women for him, though the stories that he traded legislative favors for sex seem less credible.[16]

The minority leader in the 1950s, William F. Knowland of California, carried on a long-running affair with the wife of Blair Moody, a reporter and, briefly, a senator himself. So ardent was the vigorous Knowland that he underwent a circumcision to please his mistress. His wife, seeking revenge, had an affair with Moody, and also composed and published a mystery novel in which her husband was a thinly disguised character.[17]

Because he has been the most studied of the senators in this period, Lyndon Johnson's tangled sex life has come under the closest scrutiny. His crude claims that he "had more women by accident than Kennedy had on purpose" seem mere Johnsonian braggadocio. If Johnson sometimes failed in his quests, however, it was not for lack of trying. Heedless of the feelings of Lady Bird Johnson, he endeavored to show the world just how virile he was with passes at staffers, wives of newspaper reporters, and women he casually encountered. Issues of good taste and appropriate behavior did not constrain the importunate Johnson when his lust was up. Sorting out what is true and what is false in Johnson's marital and extramarital history is a task that has yet to be completed. By any standard he set an example for his colleagues that impelled few of them to curb their desires for sexual favors.[18]

The most sensational sex scandal of this period formed the basis for a bestselling novel about the Senate, Allen Drury's novel *Advise and Consent*. The book's hero was a senator tormented by a homosexual encounter in his youth, and the plot drew on the real incident of Lester C. Hunt, Jr., son of the Wyoming senator, who committed suicide when his son's sexual orientation became public. The Hunt episode arose in the context of campaigns, led by Senate members, to force "perverts" and "pansies" out of government service. Driven by conservatives such as Kenneth Wherry of Nebraska, the investigators sought to show that Communism and homosexuality were intertwined. Wherry was probing "the infiltration of subversives and moral perverts into the executive branch of the United States Government." On the grounds that Communists would exploit the proclivities of gays and lesbians for blackmail purposes, homosexuals should be rooted out of government employment. A "lavender scare" began that drove lawmakers to see Washington, D.C., as a den of corruption and sexual deviance. A Senate committee concluded in 1950 that homosexuals should be barred from government employment.[19]

The Hunt affair began when Senator Lester C. Hunt's son was arrested in 1953 for soliciting gay sex from an undercover policeman in a city park. Since the incident was young Hunt's first offense, the police decided not to prosecute, but two Republican senators, Herman Welker of Idaho and Styles Bridges of New Hampshire, learned of the case. They went to Senator Hunt and told him to drop out of his reelection race. When Hunt refused, Welker and Bridges pressed the police to prosecute. The younger Hunt was tried and convicted of soliciting sex.[20]

With the Senate closely divided in 1954, Hunt's reelection was crucial for the Democrats. His shame at what had happened to his son caused him to withdraw from the race. Republicans pressed him to resign at once so the Republican governor could appoint a successor. Under intense personal pressure, Senator Hunt shot himself in his Senate office on June 19, 1954. The press called the senator's death a "blackmail suicide." The Democrats retained the seat when Joseph C. O'Mahoney won the fall election. Nevertheless, the Hunt case disclosed how sexual politics in the 1950s reached even into the Senate itself.[21]

Placed as it was in Washington, D.C., a very segregated city, the Senate observed without much thought the customs of separate and unequal. Black Washingtonians might work in the Senate dining room or occupy menial positions within the Capitol, but any hint of equal status with whites was taboo at least until after the end of World War II. In 1946, the Senate still barred African-American reporters from the press gallery. Louis Lautier of the National Negro Publishers' Association asked to be granted press privileges but was denied on the grounds that he worked for a weekly and not a daily newspaper. Since Lautier had access to White House press conferences, the Senate was obviously on shaky ground. Nonetheless, Lautier did not get press privileges until the Republicans gained control of Congress in 1946 and only then after complaints from his colleagues in the press. The House and Senate press galleries were then integrated. Thus, like the rest of society in those years, the Senate slowly shifted toward a more enlightened posture.[22]

Blacks worked in many menial jobs in the Senate, sometimes for little pay but what members sent their way at the end of the year as a bonus. The staff of the Senate dining room was particularly exploited under the segregationist regime of the Club. Meanwhile, African-American citizens could not eat in the dining room, which was for whites only. In 1949, newly elected senator Hubert Humphrey took a black staff member to the dining room. "We were stopped by the embarrassed head waiter, a Negro himself, and told that we could not be served." Humphrey insisted, and for his staff members the segregationist precedent was broken.[23]

A low-wage, intensive labor system provided indispensable support for the comfortable lifestyle of members in the postwar years. Hidden subsidies permeated the institution. There was a barbershop, a gymnasium, and a smallish swimming pool. The dining room offered very inexpensive if often not well-cooked meals. On September 10, 1949, for example, a luncheon plate of chicken a la king casserole with melba toast, vegetable, and salad bowl cost 85 cents. Other small perquisites went with the job. Leverett Saltonstall of Massachusetts, who arrived in early 1945, found that his office received each day "six bottles of White Rock and two of Poland Water, together with ice." The unstated assumption was that a senator would need a mixer for an alcoholic beverage later in the day.[24]

The salary for Senate members had been raised to $12,500 in January 1947, plus an expense allowance of $2,500, which was nontaxable. In 1953, the senators raised the salary to $15,000 and eliminated the allowance. Two years later, in the midst of 1950s prosperity, the salary went up to $22,500 and it rose again in 1965 to $30,000. At a time when the average annual earnings for citizens were between $3,000 and $4,000 per year, senators were far from underpaid.[25]

For those members without an outside income or personal wealth, there were the expenses of maintaining two homes, plus the burdens of commuting. Those who went home every weekend, such as the conscientious William Proxmire of Wisconsin, needed a strong constitution to withstand the exacting schedule. Other senators stayed in Washington until the recesses and then took the train or drove home to the West and South. For Lady Bird Johnson, those annual trips to their Texas home alerted her to the spread of visual pollution and billboards; this awareness later culminated in the Highway Beautification Act of 1965. The senators received one paid round-trip home each year, which meant that most of the cost of travel came from their own pockets.[26]

In some cases, the personal resources of the senators were substantial. Lyndon Johnson is perhaps the most famous example of a senator who built a large personal fortune from his leadership position. The radio station in which he and Mrs. Johnson had invested in the 1940s blossomed into a media empire by the late 1950s. Careful to avoid formal intervention with the Federal Communications Commission, which might have given ammunition to his political enemies, Johnson used indirect influence and a cluster of powerful friends in television to obtain advertising and programming for his stations. As one observer told the television critic of the *New York Times*, the Senate majority leader could make a success of a television station in the Gobi Desert. By the time he became vice president, Johnson's net worth was well over $10 million.[27]

On the Republican side, Styles Bridges of New Hampshire was less subtle than Johnson. According to columnist Jack Anderson, Bridges "took money under the table." Following his death in 1961 his wife received six large envelopes that, rumor had it, contained unreported cash contributions from lobbyists and corporations. She said at the time of her husband's funeral that the senator had "left her a million dollars in cash, money that was never accounted for." Bridges did legal work for the United Mine Workers to the tune of $35,000 per year and had other well-heeled friends such as industrialist Armand Hammer and members of the influential China Lobby. Having accepted the cash, Bridges did favors for his friends that tipped the balance for bills not connected with his Republican ideologies. The contributors of this clandestine cash seem to have gotten their money's worth from the New Hampshire solon.[28]

In the 1950s there was virtually no regulation of campaign contributions. The Corrupt Practices Act, dating back to the mid-1920s, was hardly ever enforced, and so senators ignored its strictures. The most celebrated fundraising scandal occurred in 1956, when the members were debating whether to remove the authority of the Federal Power Commission to regulate the sale of natural gas. In effect the law allowed gas producers in the Southwest to charge more for their product, and so billions of dollars were at stake in the fate of the legislation. The measure had the support of such heavyweights as Johnson and Robert Kerr of Oklahoma and seemed headed for approval. The administration of Dwight D. Eisenhower also endorsed the bill. Then, on February 3, 1956, a little-known senator named Francis Case, a South Dakota Republican, addressed his colleagues. He reported that he had received a campaign contribution of $2,500 in cash, "the largest single contribution

I could remember for any campaign of mine," from a person who favored the natural gas proposal. There was nothing illegal in what the donor had done, but Case felt he had to report the episode. Up for reelection in 1956, he may have seen the incident as an opportunity to establish his reputation for honesty.[29]

Suddenly, the smooth passage of the bill was in jeopardy because of the public outcry against the apparent effort of corporate power to sway votes on the floor. Consumer groups contended that powerful lobbying interests were spreading cash around to grease the passage of the deregulation measure. Case was near the end of his first term, and he had been most noted for serving on the special committee that recommended the censure of Joseph R. McCarthy of Wisconsin in 1954. Otherwise, Case, "a mousy little man," in the words of one observer, was not a major figure in the body.[30]

Case's allegations caused a brief sensation in the press, and Lyndon Johnson named a select committee of two Republicans and two Democrats, chaired by Walter George of Georgia, to look into the matter. They found that Case had not been bribed, but that the purpose of the donation was to sway his vote on the natural gas measure. Meanwhile, nothing daunted, the Senate continued to write the legislation, which they passed and sent to Eisenhower. The president vetoed the bill because of the Case incident.

The Senate also constituted another special committee to consider whether lobbying practices in the body should be more closely scrutinized. Under the direction of John McClellan of Arkansas that panel made a desultory attempt to probe the problem but never came up with much specific information about lobbyists and their abuses. During its fourteen-month tenure the committee could not discover a single case of lobbying involving a senator. The Senate had had enough delving into the most sensitive issue that members faced, the source of their campaign contributions. Rather than engage the problems, the institution simply turned away any opportunity for genuine reform of the process.[31]

Opinions diverged about how hard senators worked during these years. The freshman senator Richard L. Neuberger of Oregon wrote an article that outlined his average weekly schedule, persuasively describing long hours and pressing demands from constituents and committee work. For a workaholic like Lyndon Johnson who arrived early in the morning and kept his staff at work into the evening, there were not enough hours in the day to fulfill his desire to be at the Senate. His employees became accustomed to getting phone calls in the middle of the night with instructions from their boss. During long sessions of the Senate or the periodic filibuster, it would be customary to see weary members appearing exhausted on the floor or grabbing a few hours' rest in the cloakrooms.[32]

The members of the Club who kept the Senate moving imparted an ethos of responsibility and hard work to those of their colleagues who wanted to advance in the institution. A five-day workweek was more common than it would be half a century later, when senators often left Washington to campaign from Thursday to Monday. So, too, was socializing across ideological and party lines. Committee chairs exercised large powers and younger senators had to serve an apprenticeship by carrying out mundane duties and displaying deference. Despite the biases and limitations of the Senate system, especially in the area of race, in the 1950s there were fewer of the media-driven, self-promoting members so common at the end of the twentieth century. Without the constant attention from the press and television, members had fewer occasions to grandstand for the cameras.

Of course, there were senators who did not work hard. Jack Kennedy, for example, was regarded as a poor senator because of his indifference to committee meetings and roll-call votes and his love for partying. Lyndon Johnson often distinguished between senatorial work horses and show horses, a formulation that had been around for years, and he scorned those who did not put in the time that he did. But there were senators who slept through the proceedings on the floor or read mysteries while the debates continued, and there were one or two alcoholics who got drunk during the days when the chamber was in session. Others simply relied on their staffs to do most of the day-to-day chores that a senator faced.

After World War II, as a consequence of the increasing volume of business of the Senate, the size of the staffs expanded. No longer did lawmakers have to make do with a single secretary and two or three typists. By 1960 the average size of a senator's staff was eleven, and some individual senators hired many more. World War II had brought a surge of people to Washington, many of them young women, and after 1945 they found work in the expanding bureaucracies of the Senate and its committees. Insecurity was the key element in the life of these employees. "The job leads nowhere," said one staffer. "We all view our jobs as temporary interruptions in some other career." Of course, many of them stayed for years and became powerful in their own right as surrogates for their bosses.[33]

Senators became political celebrities during the 1950s and 1960s. The increasing press coverage of their activities, the televising of committee hearings, and the institution of the Sunday-morning talk shows gave the public greater exposure to lawmakers. Although they remained in the shadow of presidents, they attained a higher degree of recognition than ever before. As this process gathered momentum, their staffs acted as a kind of entourage that moved the lawmaker from place to place each day, dealt with the ever-increasing flow of mail, and prepared the politician's public statements, handed out news releases, and drafted legislation. Some of the wealthier members could hire even more staff. Those with less private income enlisted family members to help. Some put their wives and adult children on the payroll, as Truman had with his wife, Bess. In other cases relatives worked on a voluntary basis. There was a possibility of nepotism, but since so many senators followed these practices there was a tacit understanding that they would not blow the whistle on each other.[34]

Socializing was a large element in the busy Washington scene. Senators were prime catches for Washington hostesses, and they could indulge as much as they wanted to in the round of dinners, dances, and conversational gatherings. The heady mixture of power and sex produced its own kind of intoxication. "Take an ordinary unassuming small businessman and put him into this atmosphere and he'll be a prima donna in no time," said one staff member in the 1950s. Once politicians became accustomed to the delights of Washington, they proved reluctant to return to their hometowns, even after an electoral defeat. Richard Neuberger caught the atmosphere in his pithy aphorism, "They never go back to Pocatello."[35]

But the rounds of party-going and entertainment came at a price. As had been true since the turn of the century, alcoholism was the hidden element in the Senate's daily life. Prohibition, never really enforced in the upper house, was now a distant memory, and hard drinking was the order of most days. There were some senatorial abstainers, such as Robert Kerr of Oklahoma, but generally liquor flowed through the Senate without much restraint. The prevailing ethos was that real men, as were most senators in their own minds, played hard and drank even harder. Cocktails for lunch, martinis in the late afternoon, and then the ever present social circuit meant that alcohol was the most available drug. The Senate Democratic Cloak Room, said Bobby Baker, was the place, late in the day, where "flasks were nipped."[36]

Joseph McCarthy came to the Senate in 1947 with major drinking problems, and he continued his bibulous habits throughout his controversial tenure. Estes Kefauver chased women and drinks with equal ardor. He drank with the pages at parties, covered his breath with gum and other products, and went on periodic benders. Other notable examples of senators with alcoholic tendencies included John McClellan of Arkansas, Russell Long of Louisiana, Everett Dirksen, Thomas C. Hennings of Missouri, and Harley Kilgore of West Virginia. A culture of denial flourished in the chamber as ample excuses were made for colleagues who could not "handle their liquor" as others did.[37]

The problem of drunken behavior on the floor thus festered throughout this period. Meg Greenfield of the *Washington Post* recalled being in the press gallery in the mid-1960s "and observing the raving drunk Senate floor manager of the bill under consideration having to be helped out of the chamber by another senator and an aide." A page in the 1950s recorded in his journal occasions when members fell into a stupor in the chamber or reeled out drunkenly. For the most part, however, a tolerant ethic prevailed, and senators did not inform on one another about their alcoholic lapses. The press, itself composed of hard-drinkers, kept the senatorial secrets too. Leaving the Senate in 2004, Ernest F. Hollings of South Carolina reported that when he arrived in 1966, "We had five or six drunks."

The downside of such indulgence, of course, was that the senators who needed help with their drinking problems did not get any relief. An aide to Mike Mansfield of Montana remembered, "Excessive drinking under the Capitol dome had been one of the not-very-well-hidden sins of the Senate." That would change when Mansfield became majority leader in the 1960s, but in the days of Lyndon Johnson, no mean drinker himself, an atmosphere of indulgence for alcohol flourished in the upper house.[38]

One incident underscored how excessive drinking spilled over into serious issues. Early in 1954 backers of the Bricker amendment to limit the force of treaties and executive agreements in a rebuke to the White House brought their idea to the floor for a vote. Needing sixty-one votes to adopt a constitutional amendment, they fell one tally short at sixty to thirty-one. The key senator was Harley Kilgore, a Democrat who voted no. According to the story, Kilgore had been drinking in a Washington tavern when the leadership found him, brought him back for the balloting, and a voice blared out "no" when Kilgore's name was called. On such considerations, key votes in the Senate sometimes turned.[39]

Senators with drinking issues and other personality troubles had one resource available to them in the institution of the chaplain of the Senate. In addition to starting legislative days and then every meeting of the chamber with a prayer, the chaplain could act as a spiritual guide for members. The chaplain was a man and always Protestant for a Senate with a few Jews, some Catholics, and a vast majority of Protestant members. The duties of the chaplain involved a prayer at the start of the daily session, ministering to members in the hospital or during illness, and private counseling.

During the postwar era, the office of chaplain, which had not been much noted outside of the Senate, briefly gained a media star. Peter Marshall was a Presbyterian minister of impressive oratorical skills. A native of Scotland, he had worked his way to the United States and begun his religious studies at Columbia Seminary. Ordained in 1931, he was pastor at churches in Atlanta and then at the New York Avenue Presbyterian Church in Washington. One of the members of his congregation was Kenneth Wherry of Nebraska. When the Republicans gained control of the Senate in 1946, Wherry and Styles Bridges used their clout to interrupt the tenure of the incumbent chaplain and have Marshall selected in his place. Peter Marshall proved to be a compelling pulpit orator and a favorite with the members. He was retained after the Democrats took power again in 1949. However, his tenure was brief. Afflicted with a heart condition, Marshall died of a sudden seizure on January 15, 1949.[40]

Marshall's widow, Catherine, then wrote a biography of her husband, *A Man Called Peter*, which became a best-seller in the early 1950s. That led in turn to a movie with the British actor Richard Todd in the title role. The film traced in Hollywood fashion Marshall's career and his romance with his wife. Senators with ethical and emotional problems received counsel and wisdom from the star of the movie. The chamber served as the backdrop for the film as Marshall/Todd moved toward his early passing. As a result of his biography and the film, Peter Marshall is the most famous and influential of all the individuals who have served in the chaplain post. The popular interest in Marshall's life attested to the way the Senate was becoming part of popular culture during the 1950s.[41]

Yet the biopic about Peter Marshall did not make the Senate a sensation in the 1950s. That feat was left to Allen Drury's novel *Advise and Consent*, which appeared in 1959 and quickly found a place on the best-seller list. Forty-one years old in 1959, the Stanford-educated Drury had first started covering the upper house in 1943 for United Press International. Later he worked for the *Washington Star* and the *New York Times*. In his spare time

Drury began writing a novel about the Senate, which he completed in 1958. He gave it to his *Times* colleague Russell Baker to read in manuscript. Preparing to be bored, Baker found himself engrossed in Drury's story: "You couldn't put the thing down."[42]

Published the next year, *Advise and Consent* stayed on the best-seller list for almost two years. His story was involving. At the center is the nomination of a secretary of state interested in arms control but with Communist associations in his background, an amalgam of Dean Acheson and Alger Hiss. As the confirmation fight develops, the focus shifts to an up-and-coming senator named Brigham Anderson, from Utah, who has a secret in his past. During World War II, Anderson had a brief affair with a man before marrying and embarking on a political career. A bachelor himself, Drury wrote with striking sensitivity about the feelings of his conflicted senator, who, under intense pressure because of his secret, finally commits suicide. In his tale Drury blended elements of the Lester Hunt story, the Alger Hiss–Whitaker Chambers case, the censure of Joseph R. McCarthy, and other episodes from Senate history. His writing was an indictment of the "lavender scare" against homosexuals, which had gripped Washington earlier in the decade. A political conservative, Drury also turned the plot by making the senatorial villain a dovish senator who used McCarthy-like methods to pursue an unwise peace with the Soviet Union. What made the book work at bottom was not Drury's narrative, which rested heavily on melodrama, but his knowledge of how the Capitol worked and how people behaved in Washington society high and low.[43]

Drury won the Pulitzer Prize for fiction in 1960, and his book became a Broadway play and in 1962 an Otto Preminger film with Henry Fonda, Charles Laughton, and Don Murray as Brigham Anderson. To even mention homosexuality in films was very bold for the early 1960s, and the film scored at the box office. Drury went on to write other Washington novels, lots of them, but although they sold well, none ever quite recaptured the excitement of *Advise and Consent*. Drury and his magnum opus are not in the same league as Robert Penn Warren and his 1946 political novel *All the King's Men*, a thinly disguised portrait of Huey Long. But for the Senate at that time he gives an indelible portrait of how the institution looked to an informed outsider.

One of Drury's journalistic counterparts was William S. White, also covering the Senate for the *New York Times*. A friend of Lyndon Johnson's, whom he had known since 1933, White was widely believed to be the conduit for the majority leader about Senate strategy. In 1954 White won the Pulitzer Prize for his biography *The Taft Story*, and three years later he turned his attention to the Senate itself. Close to the members of the Club, White had internalized their view of the Senate. He shared the attitude of Johnson and the southerners toward northern liberals, and was willing to tolerate a certain degree of racism in exchange for the alleged gentility and restraint that the inner circle of the institution displayed. The result was *Citadel*, a book that praised the Senate as it was almost without qualification.[44]

White spoke of the ideal "Senate man" who would act in a way that pleased the institution's elders, adopt the folkways of the Club, and wait patiently for the right time to gain power and influence. In contrast were the liberals, who stressed ideas, would not compromise, and pursued the elusive goal of social change. In this context, Lyndon Johnson and Richard Russell were paragons for White; liberals such as Paul Douglas or Herbert Lehman seemed posturing showboaters. He characterized the Senate as "the South's unending revenge upon the North for Gettysburg" through the Dixie members' knowledge of the rules, their reliance on the filibuster, and their more perfect sense of how the Senate operated than that of their critics.[45]

White was a talented reporter and his description of how the Senate worked in the 1950s had a good deal of truth to it. His analysis of the Club and its mores proved enduring Senate scholarship. As his book proceeded, however, his discussion of how the institution functioned slid into approbation for how the body conducted its affairs. To be sure, he was critical of the excesses of the Kefauver investigation and Joe McCarthy as examples of the Senate gone wrong. But of the civil rights revolution that was gathering in the country when White wrote he had words only for how senators reacted to the protest movement. That the Senate was standing against a democratic campaign for greater social justice aroused less of his ire than the spectacle of men violating the code of the institution.

White's analysis proved to be very influential, and his description of the inner workings of the Club became a classic treatment of that secretive Senate within the Senate. The later success of Lyndon Johnson as majority leader and then as president gave credibility to what White had written. Fifty years after its first publication, *Citadel* is a valuable text both for what it reveals about the Senate in the 1950s and for its place in the history of the chamber.

Five years after White's book appeared, an academic named Donald R. Matthews brought out a more scholarly version of what White had tried to do. *U.S. Senators and Their World* rested on the extensive interviews that Matthews had conducted on Capitol Hill from the start of his study in 1947 through the end of 1957, and he approached the upper house with the eye of a social scientist. "Few Americans," he wrote, "could live with the job's tensions, moral dilemmas, intrigue, and insecurity." Matthews traced the occupations of senators, their behavior on the floor, their reaction to party leadership, and their relations with press and lobbyists. The result was a book that was not entertaining to read as William S. White's was, but it contained an abundance of information about the public performance of the men (and Margaret Chase Smith) whom Matthews studied with such care. From his work flowed a generation of social science research based on a combination of interviewing and analysis of roll-call voting.[46]

In later years, after 1960, the Senate of the postwar era would be seen through a nostalgic haze as a time when the institution was less partisan, less obsessed with fund-raising and continuous campaigning, less devoted to the interests of publicity-seeking members than would be the case in the last four decades of the twentieth century. Like much human experience that becomes infused with nostalgia, that verdict had many elements of truth to it. In the age before jet travel facilitated regular trips even to the West Coast, senators spent much of the time during the sessions in Washington. Thrown together by circumstance, they formed friendships outside of partisan alignments. Such notable relationships as the daily breakfast of George D. Aiken, the Vermont Republican, with Mike Mansfield, the Montana Democrat, were examples of this bipartisan socializing process.

Partisan warfare, which was one of the purposes of the Senate, existed in abundance during these years. However, it was not the all-consuming pursuit that it became by the end of the century. There were not the majority and minority staff members who stoke the passions of the members in the modern Senate. On issues of national defense and in areas of domestic policy, it was possible to find elements of consensus beyond partisanship. Had senators been told that their chamber would in time evolve in the direction of the House of Representatives, where partisan majorities ruled and minorities had little voice, they would have been shocked and dismayed. The Senate, they would have said, was set apart from the hurly burly of the lower chamber. They believed that the Senate was timeless in its place in the government. Even as they expressed that point of view, technological and social changes were making the Senate very different from the lawmaking body of the prewar era. With the new medium of television and the pressures of the Cold War, the late 1940s and early 1950s would become renowned as the age of Joe McCarthy and the Red Scare that is still associated with his name.

## CHAPTER ELEVEN

# The Senate Club in the Age of Joe McCarthy

THE SUDDEN ACCESSION OF HARRY TRUMAN TO THE PRESIDENCY ON April 12, 1945, and the ensuing end of World War II opened a turbulent eight years in senatorial politics. The power of the conservative coalition reached a peak of influence and importance. The Republicans looked more and more to Robert Taft as their intellectual leader and partisan guide. The divided Democrats found that their southern wing had the power to prevent civil rights legislation and indeed most other social reform programs. The Club, two decades in the making, set the pattern for how the upper chamber behaved. Truman and his new administration had to adapt to that inescapable legislative reality.

The volatile issue of civil rights thrust itself forward as African-American veterans and advocates of racial equality pressed for justice and change in the segregated South. Since any legislative remedies had to run the Senate obstacle course, the filibuster and the power of the southerners to wield that device reappeared throughout the postwar era. Conservatives linked civil rights and Communism as twin threats to their supremacy and used the stigma of internal subversion to assail the goals of those clamoring for attention to racial injustice.

With the advent of the Cold War and the threat from first the Soviet Union and then Communist China, the intertwined issues of anti-Communism and internal subversion moved to the front of the Senate's

concerns. By 1950, with the rise of Joseph R. McCarthy to national prominence, the Senate commenced a long struggle with that gentleman who
stretched the rules of the chamber in new and unexpected ways. Eventually
McCarthy was tamed, but the techniques that he employed became after-
ward one more weapon for lawmakers who were intent on using the Senate
for their own purposes.

Senator Joseph R. McCarthy of Wisconsin came to the Senate as part of a
Republican surge in the 1946 elections. He had ousted the incumbent,
"Young Bob" La Follette, in the Republican primary and then gone on to
victory in the fall voting. All over the country, Republicans duplicated
McCarthy's success. The first year of Truman's presidency had brought economic and political turmoil in the aftermath of war. High prices, labor unrest, and apprehension about the mounting rivalry with the Soviet Union
made voters uneasy and ready for change after fourteen years of Democratic
rule. Lawmakers had passed some important legislation, including the Employment Act of 1946, which set prosperity as a national goal and committed Congress to measures designed to maintain the country's economic
health. None of it registered with the restless electorate in the postwar era.
The Republican question was "Had Enough?" and it struck home with a
testy nation.[1]

The opposition gained thirteen seats to bring their numbers to fifty-one
in the upper house. For the first time since 1930, they had control of the
committees and issues. In addition to McCarthy, whose fame lay three years
in the future, the GOP added such men as John W. Bricker of Ohio, John J.
Williams of Delaware, and William E. Jenner of Ohio. Jenner had unseated
a Republican incumbent in his state's primary by promising "a final blasting
of the New Deal." That was the spirit that the freshmen senators brought to
Washington in January 1947, and they rallied behind Taft as their leader.
With control of Congress, they expected the Republicans to oust Truman
in 1948 and see the return of their party to the White House in 1949.[2]

Because the Republicans believed that they were entitled to regain power
after what they thought of as a generation of Democratic misdeeds, they saw
the issue of anti-Communism and subversion as a legitimate weapon against
their political foes. Recent scholarship has shown that Russian espionage
was a serious problem with larger dimensions than was perceived at the
time. But the difficult process of uncovering spies became conflated with allegations of disloyalty against liberals, Democrats, and homosexuals in and

out of Washington. The Truman administration helped prepare the ground for McCarthy through the creation of various boards to review the loyalty of government employees. Republicans in the Senate pushed the White House for the dismissal of even more suspected subversives and complained loudly when in their minds Truman fell short. In those years, few Republicans warned about potential excesses in the search for Communist influences.[3]

The other great pressure on the Senate was civil rights. African Americans had decided, in the wake of a war for democracy and after generations of oppression, to seek their long-denied political rights. In the cities of the North and in the more rural South, protests against segregation and disenfranchisement gathered momentum in the late 1940s and early 1950s. Notorious lynchings added to popular outrage and impelled the Truman White House to take action against racial violence. For the advocates of civil rights, the Senate, with its powerful Club, committees in the hands of segregationists, and ever-present filibuster threat, loomed as the great barrier to laws that would promote more rights throughout society.[4]

Southerners, led by their most ardent racist spokesman, Richard Russell, did not plan to yield on their exclusionary creed without a determined battle. They had their arguments that they so often articulated on the floor and in the cloakroom. Most of all they had their tactics, their knowledge of the rules, and their collective stamina. For Russell and his allies, the civil rights issue was not one among many that the Senate faced. It was the sine qua non of their political existence. Their cohesion, control of chairmanships, and willingness to respond to any legislative threat made them more resolute than their potential adversaries throughout the 1940s and 1950s.[5]

After 1945, an important change took place. During the 1930s, racism pervaded many minds in the United States. In the wake of Hitler and the Nazis, however, overt and institutionalized racial discrimination had become discredited as a way of viewing the world. Racism itself of course persisted, but the social consensus was moving toward a belief in equality. As that happened, the South in the Senate seemed for opinion-makers in such cities as New York, Washington, and Los Angeles to be guarding an outmoded creed. The result was to call into question the legitimacy of the southern-dominated upper house and its methods as the segregationist lawmakers practiced them. Slowly but perceptibly history turned against the southern position and made their ideology more difficult to defend during debate.

The southern bloc, behind the leadership of Russell, displayed its power with the defeat of the nomination of the New Dealer Aubrey Williams as head of the Rural Electrification Administration and attacks on the Fair Employment Practices Commission in 1945. Harry Truman recommended that FEPC be made permanent in September 1945 as part of the administration's agenda for Congress. Early in the new year, Dennis Chavez, a New Mexico Democrat, proposed a measure to put the commission on a permanent basis. A southern filibuster ensued. After several weeks of debate, a cloture motion failed by a vote of 48 in favor of cloture to 36 against (two-thirds of those voting being needed to invoke cloture). This event foreshadowed other civil rights battles to come in the upper house. For the moment, the South, with its conservative Republican allies, had its defenses intact.[6]

The first two years of the Truman era saw the foreign policy differences with the Soviet Union harden into the alignments of the Cold War. In March 1947, the president declared the Truman Doctrine to support anti-Communist governments in Greece and Turkey against the threat of subversion or conquest from Moscow. The policy became known as "containment" of Soviet expansion. Soon the White House and the secretary of state, General George C. Marshall, announced the European Recovery Program, which became known as the Marshall Plan, to rebuild the war-torn economies of Western Europe to make them less vulnerable to pressure from Moscow. The early years of this policy recast Senate allegiances and produced new divisions within the chamber.

The Truman Doctrine was embodied in a $400 million aid bill for Greece and Turkey that senators debated in April 1947. Arthur Vandenberg guided the legislation through the upper house over the objections of some of his fellow Republicans, who saw the bill as a step toward excessive American involvement overseas and a waste of taxpayers' money. Proponents contended that stopping the Russians at that time would avoid a repetition of the mistakes of Munich in 1938. Robert Taft was persuaded that the measure was necessary but worried that the nation might be drawn into more such trouble spots. "I do not regard this as a commitment to any similar policy in any other section of the world," the Republican leader warned. He was dubious about Vandenberg's ideal of bipartisanship in foreign policy. For the moment the administration and the internationalists prevailed by a vote of 67 to 23.[7]

The Eightieth Congress enacted more elements of the Truman Doctrine once the Marshall Plan came to Congress in December 1947. Republican critics denounced the scheme as socialism. Accordingly, Vandenberg made concessions about the size of the package and limited its initial duration to only one year. Suitably amended, the plan went through the Senate easily. The coalition of Democrats and internationalist Republicans held up through 1948.

On the domestic front, the Eightieth Congress passed, over Truman's veto, the Taft-Hartley Act on labor relations, designed, in the mind of Taft, to undo the perceived errors of the Wagner Act of 1935 that had made unions too powerful and politically effective. The Senate, like the House, took little account of the president's objections. On other subjects, the Republicans proceeded as though the 1946 elections had given them a mandate to overturn the New Deal. Their misreading of the nation's political sentiment gave Harry Truman the opening he needed in the 1948 presidential race.

The election of 1948 turned out to be one of the most interesting and controversial in the Senate's history. Taft made a run at his party's nomination but came up short against the man presumed to be the certain winner for the GOP: Thomas E. Dewey. To run with President Truman, the Democratic convention named the minority leader, Alben Barkley, to the national ticket. That selection shuffled the Democratic leadership in the Senate in a way that would produce large consequences for the party down the line. Truman ran against the "do-nothing" Eightieth Congress in his successful race against Dewey. It was a winning tactic with the voters but not one that endeared him to lawmakers. In fact, for a president who had been lightly regarded by his colleagues when he was in the Senate, Truman's attack on Congress exacerbated his problems in his second term.

Some fascinating new members entered the upper house in January 1949. The electorate sent Robert S. Kerr of Oklahoma, Estes Kefauver of Tennessee, Clinton Anderson of New Mexico, and Paul Douglas of Illinois to Washington. The liberal star of the class of 1949 was Hubert Humphrey, who galvanized the Democratic National Convention when he called for the party "to get out of the shadow of states' rights and walk forthrightly into the bright sunshine of human rights." Humphrey had then gone on to defeat the incumbent Republican, Joseph H. Ball, in the Minnesota senatorial contest. Humphrey came to the Senate eager to promote change and soon found himself at odds with the Club and its southern advocates. The Minnesota senator faced a long and taxing apprenticeship before his legislative skills won him acceptance.[8]

The most sensational state election of that pivotal year involved Lyndon Johnson in a Democratic primary runoff with Coke Stevenson in Texas. In the first round of the primary, Johnson, then a congressman from the Tenth District, barely made it into the runoff with Stevenson, a popular former governor whose racist views played well with his constituents. Johnson had a scant four weeks to close the gap. In a whirlwind effort that featured campaigning by helicopter, abundant cash, and attacks on the conservative Stevenson for being soft on the Taft-Hartley law, Johnson made the final result very close. Stevenson was overconfident and did not campaign with vigor during those climactic days.

So close was the contest when the ballots came in that Johnson, mindful of what had happened to him in 1941, had to find extra ballots from the boss-ridden counties of South Texas where votes often appeared after the election was over to help the favored candidate. In Jim Wells County, one controversial ballot box recorded a decisive margin for Johnson, providing an eighty-seven-vote lead over Stevenson. Credible allegations of fraud have surrounded this contest ever since. Johnson prevailed thanks to support from the courts in a long series of court battles, the Truman administration, and key Texas Democrats. He entered the Senate with the derisive nickname "Landslide Lyndon," but he did gain the seat.

Had Stevenson won, the southern bloc would have added a new and very regressive member. For all his manifold personal flaws, Johnson represented as much progress as the Texas electorate could stand in 1948. The next eleven years would demonstrate just how crucial this single election was to the history of the Senate.[9]

With Truman's upset victory over Dewey, the Democrats won back control of Congress after two years of Republican dominance. In the South, four states defected to the States' Rights ("Dixiecrat") ticket that Strom Thurmond headed, but most of the region remained in the Democratic column. Senators from Dixie made up a core part of Democratic strength on Capitol Hill. The Democrats held a twelve-seat advantage over their rivals, fifty-four to forty-two.

Democrats did not have much time to revel in their success. Truman offered an ambitious program that he called the Fair Deal. It expanded liberalism and pursued programs such as national health insurance that went beyond what Roosevelt had been able to enact during the 1930s. In doing so the new president outran his base of support in both houses. Like the Republicans in 1946 who wrongly thought they had a mandate to scale back the New Deal, the Democrats assumed that the voters wanted more federal programs. Instead, Americans had voted to leave what the 1930s and 1940s had brought in place without expanding the role and size of government.

For Truman's program to pass, the filibuster rule had to change or the conservative coalition would bury anything that the White House wanted. The defects of rule 22 on filibusters, adopted in 1917 at the time of the armed-ship controversy, persisted. A cloture motion could be filed on the substance of a pending bill, but cloture could not be applied to motions to take up a bill, to amend it, or to other procedural issues. So the capacity of opponents of a civil rights bill, for example, to talk it to death with endless debate on even the most trivial motions remained intact.

To change the rule, the new majority leader, Scott Lucas of Illinois, proposed that a simple majority would be enough to end debate on a motion or a bill. Lucas was an uncertain champion of procedural change and was not a strong leader. He was the consensus choice among the Democrats, divided as they were between northern and western liberals and conservative southerners. Liberals were now arguing that the Senate was not a continuing body with rules that carried over from session to session. Therefore a majority of senators had a right to propose new rules when Congress convened at the start of a session.

The Republicans in 1948 had proposed changes to rule 22 but deferred bringing them up until the following year when they expected to once again be in control. As the minority in January 1949, they now urged in public that the filibuster be reformed. Yet the proposed wording that they put forward contained a gift to the conservatives that undercut their ostensible purposes. Senator Kenneth Wherry of Nebraska offered language that mandated a two-thirds vote of all the members of the body instead of the senators present and voting. In a ninety-six-seat Senate, that would raise the total necessary to end a filibuster to sixty-four. The Wherry proposal let the Republicans have it both ways. They were against filibusters when they appealed to black voters in the North but were in favor of procedures that strengthened the power of the conservative coalition.[10]

To make a change in the filibuster rule, the liberals first needed a favorable ruling from Vice President Alben Barkley. He had to assert that rule 22 did not apply to all matters involving a pending bill. In March 1949, when a cloture motion was filed, a senator raised a point of order on that question. Barkley had to decide on the issue. Never a fan of the filibuster and mindful of his own experiences as majority leader, Barkley said that in 1917, when the filibuster rule was first adopted, the Senate had not intended to prevent senators from taking action or "to freeze its own rules in perpetuity." The vice president therefore rejected the point of order.[11]

Richard Russell at once asked the Senate to overturn Barkley's ruling. With the votes of conservative Republicans and southern Democrats working together, the opinion of the chair was rejected by forty-six in favor and forty-one against. That outcome meant that the southern filibuster, whenever started, against a rules change could not be stopped by the 1949 Senate. Kenneth Wherry's requirement of a two-thirds vote of the entire Senate to end a filibuster also went into effect. One advocate of civil rights said of this disappointing turn of events, "It is hard to recall a more discouraging, more complicated or more fantastic legislative picture." As *The New Republic* put it, the Senate had voted "to put states wrongs ahead of civil rights."[12]

The Southern Democrats as inner members of the Club made it plain to unruly newcomers that the Senate frowned on civil rights agitation. Hubert Humphrey received the brunt of such criticism. Shortly after he arrived in the upper chamber, he passed a group of southerners engaged in conversation. Richard Russell said for all to hear, "Can you imagine the people of Minnesota sending that damn fool down here to represent them?" Humphrey's natural talents as a legislator eventually won over his critics, as did the Minnesota senator's ties with Lyndon Johnson, but the episode illustrated the tensions that the civil rights issue imparted to the Senate in the postwar years.[13]

With the conservatives dominant, the Fair Deal stalled in Congress in 1949. Lawmakers either rejected or watered down the president's ideas about medical insurance, federal housing, and aid to education. A sign of the Senate's lack of interest in reform and change came when the White House reappointed Leland Olds to be chair of the Federal Power Commission. An outspoken liberal, Olds's support for government regulation of oil and gas won him the enmity of Robert S. Kerr of Oklahoma, a new force in the chamber, and other southwestern lawmakers. Seeing an opportunity to burnish his credentials with conservatives, Lyndon Johnson led the attack on Olds as being soft on Communism and too liberal. It was a squalid performance, since Olds was probably doomed anyway, as the 53–13 vote to reject his nomination showed. The upper house in 1949 was not about to cede further regulatory authority over oil and gas to the Truman White House and its agencies.[14]

As Truman's domestic program faltered in 1949, the issue of Communism pressed for attention. In a dismaying sequence of events during that year, the Soviet Union exploded an atomic bomb, China became a Communist nation, and the perjury trial of Alger Hiss, a former State Department official who had been accused of lying about his Communist and espionage role, raised the specter of domestic subversion. In Washington, the political mood fostered probes of gays in government jobs. Four years after World War II, the people of the United States seemed even less secure than they had been when the 1940s began. The Republicans believed that the Democrats were "soft" on Communism. The issue appeared to be a political winner for a party that felt cheated out of victory in 1948. They denounced the Truman administration as socialist, even Communist, in its basic values and guilty, in the words of Homer Capehart of Indiana, "of laxity, negligence, and disloyalty."[15]

The Republican senator who became most identified with anti-Communism and charges of subversion against the Democrats was Joseph R. McCarthy of Wisconsin. McCarthy has become one of the most famous and controversial senators in the nation's history with a tag "McCarthyism" that has passed into the language. In just eleven years in the upper house, McCarthy was obscure for three, world-famous for five, and disgraced for the last three and a half years of his life. He does not rank in legislative accomplishments with any of the greats of the Senate, but in terms of impact and influence, McCarthy has few equals.

Fifty years after he died he remains controversial. His supporters on the right now claim that he did in fact uncover Soviet spies or at least was right about the extent of their espionage in the country. Critics contend that the Wisconsin senator was an unprincipled demagogue, and that indictment remains valid. In the history of the Senate, McCarthy was a kind of legislative freelancer who played the Senate and its traditions for his own purposes. When McCarthy went too far in attacking individual senators themselves, he provoked a reaction that ended his career as a national figure. A creature of the worst aspects of the Senate, he was done in when he crossed the invisible boundaries of proper decorum that were the essence of the Club.[16]

McCarthy became famous in February 1950 with a speech in Wheeling, West Virginia, to a Republican audience in what was expected to be a routine example of partisan oratory in the winter months of an election year. The speaker told his listeners that he had "in my hand" a list of the names

Joseph R. McCarthy of Wisconsin became famous for his anti-Communist crusades during the early 1950s. For this picture from March 24, 1950, he sat at his desk surrounded by the mail that came in when he assailed alleged subversives in the government. (LIBRARY OF CONGRESS)

of known Communists and spies (the exact number soon became a source of disagreement) who were employed in the State Department. Prior to this speech, McCarthy had been a little-known lawmaker. Born in 1908, he had studied law, won election as a judge in Wisconsin in the 1930s, and then went off to war in the Marines. His military record in the South Pacific was respectable but routine. He embarked on some milk-run missions that featured use of machine guns on Japanese targets. That enabled McCarthy to style himself "Tail-Gunner Joe."[17]

Once in Washington, McCarthy settled toward the bottom of the Senate. He sought publicity, jousted with members of his own party, and became enmeshed in some shady deals with a soft drink company that led to the title "the Senator from Pepsi-Cola." His reelection in 1952 was by no means assured. A genuine opponent of Communism who shared the Republican dislike of the Democrats, Secretary of State Dean Acheson, and the New Deal, McCarthy also sensed that the subversion issue could take him toward the notoriety he craved. An alcoholic with a vicious streak, McCarthy hungered for approval. He found that he had a talent for demagogy in the Senate setting. The response to his Wheeling charges indicated what a rich vein he could tap because of public fears of Communism and the belief in some right-wing circles that the Truman administration had been penetrated by Soviet agents.

Aware that what a senator said made news, McCarthy realized that the more sensational the charges the more extensive the coverage. An allegation of his would land on the front page; the response from the person attacked appeared, if at all, in the back pages. He also exploited the credulity of the press and public. If a United States senator said something, it must have a modicum of truth to it. Careful to time his releases for maximum effect and always ready with another revelation for the waiting scribes, McCarthy made great copy. If his charges did not pan out or he exaggerated, that was too bad. In the Senate, meanwhile, the Republicans encouraged him to lash out at the Democrats. Few of his colleagues, whatever their private feelings, tried to rein him in.

One Republican did take on McCarthy only to find herself with no support. Margaret Chase Smith believed that the Wisconsin senator's charges about subversive influences were insubstantial, and she eventually decided to say that to the Senate. She asked other Republican moderates to join her in a statement that expressed doubts about McCarthy's methods. Six agreed to do so. On June 1, 1950, she delivered her "Declaration of Conscience" address, in which she contended that the Senate "has too often been debased to the level of a forum of hate and character assassination sheltered by the shield of congressional immunity." She criticized the Truman administration but her main target was McCarthy. The Senate, she concluded, should not become "a publicity platform for irresponsible sensationalism."[18]

Unfortunately for Smith, five of her moderate associates soon bolted and sought political cover when McCarthy and his supporters assailed Smith. Only Wayne Morse, then a Republican, stayed loyal. Smith suffered in her committee assignments and was further marginalized for her apostasy. The larger lesson was not to challenge the junior senator from Wisconsin. Courage in that regard would be in short supply for the upper house over the next four years.[19]

Joe McCarthy was not the only practitioner of the politics of anti-Communism in the Senate. Pat McCarran, a Nevada Democrat, did as much as and in some respects more than his Wisconsin colleague to exploit the fears about alleged subversion in the government. McCarran was instrumental in passing the Internal Security Act of 1950 and the McCarran-Walter Act of 1952. These measures provided a legal basis for the assaults on suspected subversives and foreigners that shaped the anti-Communist ethos in the chamber. But McCarran never became a household name and the symbol of an era in the way Joe McCarthy did.[20]

McCarthy's political clout grew when the Democrats tried to make him prove his allegations. They created a subcommittee of the Foreign Relations Committee to look into his charges in February 1950, headed by the conservative Democrat Millard Tydings of Maryland, the onetime adversary of Franklin Roosevelt. Scott Lucas and the Democrats hoped that the tough-minded Tydings would put the upstart Republican in his place. In that way the Senate through its own internal discipline would tame McCarthy before his sensational charges gained further traction.

The strategy backfired. McCarthy turned the Tydings hearings into a media circus that put the chairman and the Democrats on the defensive. In the aftermath of the Alger Hiss case, the Communist victory in China, and the Russian atomic bomb, McCarthy's charges seemed plausible. The start of the Korean War in June 1950 added to the urgency of McCarthy's appeal. Republicans saw him as a large asset in the upcoming election. Tydings found himself under assault for being too lax about Communists. Already vulnerable in a bad year for Democrats, Tydings endured a vicious campaign that impugned his loyalty. A doctored photograph, created by McCarthy's staff, showed Tydings with his arm around a Communist Party official he had never met and had never been anywhere near. The overheated atmosphere of the time made the image a devastating one and Tydings went under.[21]

One primary contest in 1950 between incumbent senator Claude Pepper and his challenger, George Smathers, in Florida, has passed into American folklore. Smathers, a conservative Democrat, attacked Pepper on issues of race and Communism in what became a tough and bitter campaign. According to political legend, Smathers impressed backwoods Florida voters by saying that Pepper was known in Washington as a "shameless extrovert" who practiced "nepotism with his sister-in-law." Moreover his own sister was "a thespian in wicked New York" and Pepper had "habitually practiced" celibacy before his marriage. Smathers denied he ever used those words and phrases, and in fact they seem to have been made up by a puckish journalist. The contest ended with Smathers defeating Pepper by a sizable margin in another demonstration of how anti-Communism and race reinforced each other in 1950.[22]

The 1950 election also brought Richard Nixon to the Senate after he bested Helen Gahagan Douglas in California amid charges that her left-wing sympathies made her the "pink lady." In all, the Democrats lost five seats. Another casualty was Majority Leader Lucas, who fell to the conservative Everett Dirksen in Illinois. That left the majority leadership position open, and the Democrats selected Ernest W. McFarland of Arizona as their new spokesman. In a contest that insiders watched but the public ignored, the Democrats also chose Lyndon Johnson to serve as majority whip. Just two years after arriving in the Senate, the intense and driven Johnson had worked his way into the Democratic hierarchy. The incumbent whip, Lister Hill of Alabama, wanted to leave the job because of fears that his constituents would regard him as too liberal on civil rights. Otherwise, the position did not seem important enough for any Democratic members of the Club to take the trouble to forestall Johnson. Richard Russell threw his weight behind the Texan as someone who would supply the energy that McFarland lacked. Johnson had taken another step toward Senate power.[23]

The election of 1950 was a severe blow to the Truman administration. The intervention of China in the Korean War had inflicted a defeat on American and United Nations forces. Tensions between the White House and the commander in the Pacific, Douglas MacArthur, added to the troubles of the president. The nation struggled to understand why the war had produced such dismaying results. Charges of Communist influence in the government explained for many Americans why Korea was such a mess. McCarthy's reputation blossomed in such an atmosphere.

A major confrontation between Truman and Congress loomed in mid-April 1951, when the president relieved General MacArthur of his command of American troops in the Far East. MacArthur wanted a more aggressive approach to the stalemated war in Korea, including attacks on Communist Chinese bases in Manchuria. The general carried his argument with the White House into the press, and Truman fired him for insubordination. The public reaction to this unpopular move was a political uprising on Capitol Hill. McCarthy told reporters, "The son of a bitch should be impeached." Secretary of State Acheson and George C. Marshall, both of whom had advised that MacArthur be fired, also became targets of senatorial wrath.[24]

As the debate heated up, Republicans called for a probe into the MacArthur dismissal and the underlying quarrel over American strategy. Democrats recognized that some sort of inquiry would have to occur. Washington braced for a public confrontation about these divisive issues of war and peace. At its heart, the MacArthur controversy raised the perennial issue of whether civilian control of the military could be safeguarded by means first of the presidency and then of the United States Senate.

The natural locations for hearings would be in the Senate—either the Foreign Relations Committee or the Armed Services Committee. Democrats proposed that both panels, under the chairmanship of Richard Russell, look into MacArthur's case and any proposed changes in national strategy. It was an ideal situation for a senator of Russell's ability. Race would not be an issue in the inquiry and so he could look at the problems on their merits. From the first moment that he started thinking about hearings, Russell decided that the proceedings would be conducted in executive session. With television still in its infancy, it was possible, as it would not be just a few years later, to persuade the public that the Senate could do its job in closed hearing. The title for the inquiry was "Military Situation in the Far East," but of course MacArthur was the central figure under review.[25]

Russell faced some Republican sniping over closing the hearings and the related issue of whether administration witnesses could invoke some form of executive privilege about what they had told the president. Yet over seven weeks of hearings MacArthur and his critics received ample time to make their case. Detailed briefings kept the press informed about what happened each day with the documents suitably edited to remove potential revelations about intelligence or military secrets. As the Joint Chiefs of Staff testified about the weaknesses in MacArthur's argument for a more aggressive policy toward Communist China, the energy and passion drained out of the general's support and his appeal faded as a potential Republican candidate in 1952. The Russell hearings of 1951 became an object lesson in how the Senate should deal with a highly charged national security issue. Closed sessions, control of what the press received, and a disdain for sensationalism were the ingredients for a sober assessment of a national problem. The difficulty in the future would be that the special circumstances of the Russell probe could not be re-created. As television coverage became more common, high-profile Senate hearings could not retreat behind closed doors. That the Russell inquiry happened a year before a presidential election also helped to make the proceedings more restrained than if they had been held during an election year.

As the 1952 election year approached, Robert Taft intended to use the Senate one more time to achieve the Republican presidential nomination he wanted so much. Beset with domestic scandals and mired in an unpopular war, the Truman administration and the Democrats were in desperate shape with the electorate. If he could secure the nomination, Taft had every hope of national victory. McCarthy and anti-Communism had prepared the ground for Taft to tap into such sentiment without having to become involved himself in the ugly side of politics. By late 1951 the Ohio senator was accumulating numbers of committed delegates and seemed to be the front-runner.[26]

In foreign policy, however, Taft was vulnerable. Skeptical about the value of European alliances and the focus on that part of the world as a top national priority, Taft worried about the extent of American commitments around the world and the wisdom of such an expansive and expensive approach to the challenge from Moscow. For internationalist Republicans, Taft seemed a danger to the bipartisan approach to foreign affairs and the use of containment in handling the Soviets. Their thoughts turned to Dwight D. Eisenhower and his military reputation as the architect of victory in World War II. A conservative Republican on domestic policy, he might be the alternative to Taft that the party needed. By the spring of 1952, Eisenhower was in the race and overtook Taft at the Republican National Convention to claim the party's nomination. Once again, Taft, who was Mr. Republican to a generation of party loyalists, had come up short on the national stage. His thoughts turned back to how he might operate in the Senate as the recognized leader of the party.

Other senators in 1952 eyed the presidency too. Estes Kefauver announced for the Democratic nomination. Using the celebrity he had gained through the crime hearings and his folksy campaign style (complete with Tennessee coonskin cap), he won several primaries, including a defeat of Truman in New Hampshire that persuaded the president to announce he would not run again. Kefauver won in Wisconsin and Nebraska, and did well in other states where primary contests did not decide delegates. The senator proved that he was popular nationally, but he failed to address the issue of securing delegates. As a result, he could not stop the alliance of party insiders who turned the nomination to Governor Adlai Stevenson of Illinois. Fame could make a senator a viable candidate, but by itself it was not enough to win a nomination.[27]

Richard Russell also learned that power in the Senate and a strong base in the South were not enough to make him a credible national hopeful. From the outset, Russell's candidacy was improbable. His denunciations of civil rights made him unpalatable to black voters in the North and liberals. He lacked support from organized labor and never established a plausible electoral presence outside of his Dixie base. (Adlai Stevenson was tepid about African-American rights, but that could be overlooked because he was a northerner from Illinois.) Russell was unable to convince most Democrats that he would not bring his racial prejudices to the presidency. Southern votes enabled Russell to do well on the first ballot at the convention but then he fell back as Stevenson surged to the nomination. The message was clear to Lyndon Johnson and other aspiring southern senators. Too much identification with the South was fatal for a national Democrat.[28]

On the Republican side, one young senator emerged from the 1952 sweepstakes with a bright future. Richard Nixon had been in the upper house for only two years. Nonetheless, his ability to win a statewide race in California impressed Republican elders, who saw that state as crucial to their hopes. Nixon's youth would also be a good counterweight to Eisenhower's age. Once the general had been nominated, the choice of Nixon, who had been talked about before the convention as a possible vice presidential nominee, was logical. In the campaign that followed, the California senator underscored the emerging power of television. After he was accused of having a personal fund for political expenses from wealthy donors, Nixon went on television in September 1952 in what became known as the Checkers speech (mentioning the dog Checkers, which his daughters had been given). In a half-hour address to a nationwide audience, Nixon laid to rest doubts about his honesty and evoked a national response that cast aside any thought that he might be dumped from the ticket. Politicians took note of how use of the new medium might benefit their careers.[29]

While Eisenhower was beating Stevenson in the national race in 1952, other senatorial careers were being launched. John F. Kennedy from Massachusetts had served three terms in the House when he decided to challenge the incumbent senator, Henry Cabot Lodge, Jr., grandson of Woodrow Wilson's antagonist. At first, the odds looked long for Kennedy against a popular senator who was identified with Eisenhower and who would have the benefit of the Republican candidate's lengthy coattails. With his family's money to draw on, his own skill as a campaigner, and Lodge's preoccupation with the presidential contest, Kennedy proved to be a more formidable opponent than the Republicans had anticipated. The large Kennedy family campaigned for their relative across the state, and in a heavy turnout of voters the Democrat gained a narrow but important victory. On the morning when the results were official, Kennedy received a phone call from Lyndon Johnson, who was already looking for votes to become the Democratic leader. A tired and bemused Kennedy concluded, "The guy must never sleep."[30]

Johnson was on the phone because in Arizona, Ernest McFarland, the Democratic leader who had succeeded Scott Lucas, had been defeated by another senatorial newcomer, Barry Goldwater. McFarland was a tired, stale, and ineffectual politician by 1952, and the Republicans tied him to Harry Truman. The handsome Goldwater, a World War II pilot, caught the conservative wave that was growing in the Southwest and rode it to a narrow 6,700-vote victory over the incumbent. Goldwater's success, along with other Republican victories, gave the party a 48–47 edge over the Democrats in the new Congress. Wayne Morse of Oregon, formerly a Republican, called himself an independent after bolting the Eisenhower ticket. Even if Morse had voted with the Democrats, the new vice president, Richard Nixon, would have broken the tie to give the Republicans control of the chamber.[31]

Both parties shuffled their leadership in the wake of the election. The Republicans decided to make Robert Taft their official leader and did so unanimously. Taft said, "You can't have a lot of fellows running down to the White House and then coming back to the Senate to speak for the President. That voice has got to be one voice." If Taft and Eisenhower could work in harmony, they would make a powerful team, and in the few months that Taft functioned as majority leader, there was a high degree of cooperation. Then Taft fell ill with cancer and died on July 31, 1953. The Senate mourned the passing of what everyone agreed was one of its great figures. In retrospect, however, Taft seems less of a giant than he did five decades ago. Except for the Taft-Hartley Act, he was not adept at enacting legislation. His foreign policy views have not proved credible in light of the history of the Cold War, and his pandering to McCarthy was a sad spectacle. Bob Taft was an excellent senator in his day, but not an enduring force in the history of the chamber.[32]

On the Democratic side, Lyndon Johnson seized the opportunity after McFarland's defeat to claim the post of minority leader for himself. Richard Russell did not want the responsibility that went with the position of staying on the floor and rounding up Democratic votes. Moreover, he sought to husband his energies to lead the southern bloc against any prospective civil rights legislation. Seeing Johnson as the best hope for a southerner to become president in the future, Russell threw his support behind the Texan. For the fractured Democrats, jolted by their national defeat at the hands of Eisenhower, Johnson was the closest thing to a consensus candidate available in late 1952. Hubert Humphrey and the liberals had their own alternative to Johnson in James Murray of Montana, but that effort soon collapsed before the Texan's superior organizing skills. Russell placed Johnson's name in nomination on January 2, 1953. After one ballot showed Johnson's insurmountable lead, his rival withdrew to avoid embarrassment. The Democrats unanimously elected Johnson as their new leader.[33]

The end of the Truman presidency and the arrival of Eisenhower opened a new chapter in the history of the Senate. In those years, Lyndon Johnson would be the dominant figure. In early 1953, however, the shadow of Joe McCarthy still hung over the chamber. Nothing had yet curbed the power of the Wisconsin senator to shatter reputations and make politicians defer to his popularity. Even Eisenhower, campaigning for McCarthy in Wisconsin, had removed favorable references to George C. Marshall lest they offend the senator and his followers. With McCarthy's party in the majority and a chairmanship likely to be at his disposal, observers wondered how a Republican administration would deal with this controversial member. The Senate had largely quaked before McCarthy from 1950 onward and had lowered the tone of public life in the process. It remained to be seen whether the members would continue down that road or do something to restore the dignity of the institution. So much was at stake for the Senate when Eisenhower took the oath of office on January 20, 1953.

## CHAPTER TWELVE

# Pawed All Over:
# Lyndon Johnson and the Senate

L YNDON JOHNSON'S EIGHT-YEAR TENURE AS LEADER OF THE DEMOCRATS in the Senate has become a legend in the history of the chamber. After two years as head of the minority, from 1953 to 1954, he came into his own when his party regained control of the upper house with a slim margin in 1955. For the next three years, Johnson dominated the chamber with his overbearing personality and his driven method of intense, hands-on leadership. He had no interests or diversions outside of the Senate, and he was consumed with the issues large and small that animated the chamber. After big Democratic gains in the 1958 elections, Johnson's approach palled on his colleagues and his influence waned by 1960.

Accounts of Johnson's mastery in these years are numberless. George Smathers of Florida recalled that Johnson was, on occasion, "a real tyrannical, tough, disagreeable dictatorial fellow," but he also noted that "when it came to getting things done, there was nobody that was equal to Lyndon, before or since as far as I could see." Colleagues remembered "the Johnson treatment": the tall majority leader would place his face inches from theirs and let loose his persuasive powers. After one such encounter, the object of Johnson's attention observed, "You really felt as if a St. Bernard had licked your face for an hour, had pawed you all over." A master of psychology in these one-on-one moments, Johnson knew how to cajole, persuade, bully, harass, and implore to get his way. And for a season, the Senate responded to his importunate will.[1]

In the history of the institution, however, Lyndon Johnson did not change the Senate or create an enduring new role for the majority leader. Johnson enjoyed a brief period when an evenly divided upper house and a fractured Democratic Party allowed his special abilities to flourish. Once these circumstances shifted, after 1958, the chamber reverted to a more individualistic style, and Johnson's methods lost their power. After he became vice president, in 1961, Mike Mansfield, his successor as leader, returned to the more collegial approach of Alben Barkley. The leaders, Republican and Democrat, who have followed Mansfield have not sought a return to the Johnson technique of governing the Senate. Had any of them done so, they would have faced open revolt.

Lyndon Baines Johnson was forty-four when he was chosen as minority leader in early 1953. For the senators who knew him then, his personal narrative was of a Central Texas boy, raised in poverty, who had clawed his way up from Johnson City to Southwest Texas State College to a stint as a congressional secretary. After directing the National Youth Administration in Texas for eighteen months, he won a House seat in 1937. He lost his Senate race in 1941 and then prevailed against Coke Stevenson seven years later as "Landslide Lyndon."

The broad outlines of this life history were familiar to all in and around the Senate. The ways in which Johnson exaggerated his father's poverty and overstated his humble origins escaped most observers then and since. Larger than life, as everyone said, Johnson was a frontier tall-tale artist creating and reshaping his personal story as he went. While senators realize that he was often economical with the truth, only with the presidency would it become clear how much of a liar Johnson was. Realizing that his colleagues, like most Americans, tended to take an individual at face value, Johnson created his own image as a masterful, decisive legislator and then lived up to it, and more. As with his presidency, however, Johnson's tenure as majority leader started well and then faltered as the defects of his style became more evident.

In the evenly balanced situation of 1953–54, Johnson saw the best role for the Democrats to be one of assisting President Dwight D. Eisenhower and avoiding direct confrontations with the White House or the Senate Republicans wherever possible. Johnson had little taste for partisan warfare himself, and he preferred backroom consensus to acrimonious public debate. In that manner he could hold the fractious Democrats together and avoid going up against the very popular Eisenhower.[2]

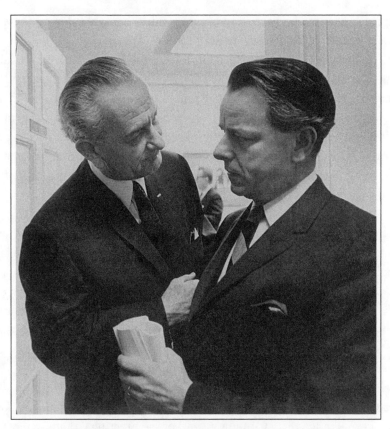

Lyndon Johnson as majority leader spent many
hours talking with his colleagues in what became
known as the "Johnson treatment." In 1959 or 1960
he spoke with then freshman senator Robert Byrd
of West Virginia, who would later became majority
leader himself. (SENATE HISTORICAL OFFICE)

To make his plans work, Johnson had to create a system of monitoring
opinion in the chamber, finding out the needs and wants of the members,
and cataloguing their personal failings. Johnson's assistant in this endeavor
was Robert "Bobby" Gene Baker. The young South Carolinian was the chief
page among the Democrats when Johnson tapped him to be assistant secretary to the minority leader. Baker had a courtier's eye for snatches of gossip
and hints of scandal that could feed Johnson's insatiable need to know every
foible of his colleagues. In time, Baker's lust for money and influence

tempted him into shady motel ventures and bribery, but during the early 1950s he was a valuable instrument of Johnson's purposes.[3]

As he gained his footing as leader, Johnson did not challenge the clout of the Club. He deferred to Russell, Harry Byrd, Walter George, and the other powerful southern committee chairs. At the same time, he created his own version of the Club with those senators who shared his way of doing business and his vision of politics. Earle Clements of Kentucky became minority whip, and his ties to liberal Democrats made him an asset in broadening Johnson's reach. George Smathers, Robert S. Kerr, and Stuart Symington were other members of the inner circle of senators on whom Johnson relied for votes.[4]

The more liberal senators were in Johnson's mind "bomb throwers" who could not be relied on in a crisis. Yet he needed the votes of Paul Douglas of Illinois and Herbert Lehman of New York. So he enlisted Hubert Humphrey as the link to the reformers and gradually pulled the Minnesota liberal over to his side. On issues other than race in the mid-1950s, Johnson could afford to cast votes for progressive causes and preserve his credentials as a sometime southern liberal. In general, however, he was impatient with those to his left, considering them unrealistic and impractical.[5]

Johnson changed how the Democratic Party operated in the upper house to add to his power and placate potential opposition. He enhanced the power of the Democratic Policy Committee and of the Steering Committee, which assigned members to the key committees. To offset this accretion of authority, he also pushed through a rules change to give younger senators at least one seat on a major committee. That shift reconciled some of the potential opponents to Johnson's rule. As a Johnson aide put it in 1957, this policy showed that the Democratic leadership "tries to make the most out of what it has to work with in terms of national—rather than sectional—problems."[6]

Johnson's counterpart on the Republican side was William F. Knowland of California, who had been elected in 1953 to succeed Robert A. Taft. During his illness with cancer, the ailing Taft had indicated that Knowland, who had been appointed to succeed Hiram Johnson in 1945, should be the Republican leader. The passing of Taft and the death of another Republican left the GOP with forty-six seats to forty-seven for the Democrats, and one independent, Wayne Morse of Oregon. Morse voted with the GOP, and the vote of Vice President Richard Nixon made Knowland the majority leader for the next two years.

Not known for his intelligence, Knowland believed that he represented the members of his party in the upper house, not the administration. He thus reserved to himself the right to oppose administration measures when it suited him, much to the disgust of Eisenhower, who had expected Republican senators to cooperate with the White House. As a result, Eisenhower often had to look to Lyndon Johnson and House Speaker Sam Rayburn to get important legislation through Congress. Johnson found this the ideal situation for his consensus-building talents. Soon he was overwhelming the outmatched Knowland. As reporter William S. White put it, "He really just sort of overwhelmed Knowland with his brilliance as a leader."[7]

Johnson, Knowland, and the Senate faced a continuing problem in the person of Joe McCarthy, whose investigating zeal had not at all diminished with the arrival of a Republican administration. With the GOP in power, the White House and his colleagues in the chamber expected McCarthy to fall into line and avoid his excesses during the Truman period, but McCarthy was incapable of stopping his probes and behaving like a regular senator. His celebrity and his influence depended on a continuing series of revelations about Communist subversion. So he pressed ahead with inquiries into various aspects of the government until he hit upon the United States Army as a potential target. During an inquiry into subversion with the military, McCarthy focused on an obscure dentist at an army laboratory in New Jersey. That probe in turn soon expanded into a larger investigation of whether McCarthy's aides Roy Cohn and G. David Schine had pressured the army for special treatment for Schine as a soldier.

To examine this tangled set of events, televised hearings occurred during the spring of 1954. The daily proceedings of the Senate panel riveted the nation as viewers saw McCarthy in action, badgering his colleagues and frequently shouting "Point of order!" Under the hard light of the cameras, the image of the Wisconsin senator suffered. An anti-McCarthy documentary by Edward R. Murrow on his *See It Now* program also tilted public opinion away from the senator.[8]

What the Senate should now do about its reckless member remained a dilemma for both parties. Democrats outside the chamber clamored for disciplinary action against McCarthy, but he remained the darling of many on the Republican right. Lyndon Johnson had no stomach for McCarthy's tactics, but neither did he want the Democrats to be seen as coddling Communists. "At this juncture," William S. White recalled Johnson saying, "I'm not about to commit the Democratic Party to a high school debate on the subject, resolved that Communism is good for the United States, with my party taking the affirmative." Johnson intended to wait until McCarthy made a fatal blunder that rendered him vulnerable to Senate discipline. To the disappointment of liberals, that meant silence from the minority leader well into 1954.[9]

Johnson had been tracking McCarthy's relations with other senators. He noted how McCarthy's attacks on such elders as Carl Hayden of Arizona had stored up potential ill will against him. But Johnson knew that until Republicans themselves criticized the Wisconsin lawmaker, any attack on McCarthy coming from Democrats would simply energize Republicans and backfire on the Democrats. This strategy did not sit well with the liberals in Johnson's party, but they acquiesced in what he was trying to do.

The process of rebuking McCarthy began when Ralph Flanders, a Vermont Republican, criticized him on March 9, 1954, and said that he was preparing a resolution of censure. That document was introduced on July 30, and charged that McCarthy had attacked members of the Senate. He had also, Flanders went on, abused an army general, Ralph Zwicker, during one of his investigations. The door was now open for Johnson to act.[10]

Working with Knowland, Johnson moved to name a special committee to air the charges against McCarthy. The Senate agreed by a vote of 75 to 12 on August 2 to follow that course. Johnson then outwitted Knowland in deciding which senators would serve on the committee. The minority leader wanted members who were not known as anti-McCarthy partisans, were respected in the Senate, and were not candidates for reelection in the 1954 races. That is precisely what he got with the three Republicans and three Democrats who were chosen. The chairman, Arthur V. Watkins, a Utah Republican, insisted that there be no television cameras. He and his colleagues also restricted McCarthy's ability to interrupt the proceedings and generally sought as little publicity for their work as possible. Such an approach took the sting out of McCarthy's tactics and gave him little leeway to operate as he had in the past.[11]

The Watkins Committee recommended that McCarthy be censured for his denigrating actions toward the Senate Committee on Privileges and Elections that had looked into McCarthy's tactics in the 1950 election and for the verbal abuse of General Ralph Zwicker in which he had engaged during the Army hearings. To avoid a partisan wrangle, the panel stayed away from the issue of McCarthy's charges about Communism and the merits of his overall career on that issue. His treatment of senators and the military became the focus of the report. Still, the report evoked passion from voters divided about McCarthy and his methods. When Francis Case of South Dakota, a conservative Republican, took a position favorable to the Wisconsin senator in the course of the Senate deliberations, one of his correspondents wrote: "It looks like McCarthy has a dossier on you."[12]

The Senate leadership decided to let the debate on the McCarthy resolution take place after the 1954 congressional elections. The issue of McCarthyism did not figure directly in the off-year contest, but anti-Communism still seemed a vote getter. Vice President Richard Nixon and other Republican speakers contended that the Eisenhower administration was cleaning out Communists from the Truman administration. The Democrats countered with a bill outlawing the Communist Party itself, and they insisted in public that they would, in the words of Johnson and Sam Rayburn, "continue to protect the rights of the President against the Republican old guard."[13]

After a hard-fought campaign, the result of the 1954 elections, to the disappointment of the Eisenhower White House, left the Senate alignment unchanged. The Democrats had forty-eight seats, the Republicans forty-seven, and Wayne Morse was an independent. Morse sought a seat on the Foreign Relations Committee, which Johnson was delighted to provide, and the Oregon senator voted with the Democrats to organize the upper chamber. By a vote of forty-nine to forty-seven, Lyndon Johnson was now the majority leader. He was just forty-six years old, and he had risen in a dramatic way since his arrival in the Senate under an electoral cloud six years earlier. He stressed again his willingness to work with Eisenhower in the same manner as when he was the minority leader.

McCarthy and the censure remained the unfinished business of that session of Congress. The debate on the Watkins Committee report took place in November, and Johnson made sure that the Democrats allowed the Republicans to stress McCarthy and his record. He also saw to it that all the Democrats, with the exception of the ailing and conflicted John F. Kennedy, would vote to condemn McCarthy. (With many pro-McCarthy constituents in Massachusetts, Kennedy preferred not to take a stand.) By the time the vote took place in early December, the charges against the Wisconsin senator had been reduced to a single question. Had he brought the Senate into disrepute by his charges against the Watkins committee itself during debate over the censure resolution? Had he, in effect, broken the rules, written and unwritten, of the Senate itself? The answer, for two-thirds of the chamber, was that he had in fact done so. The episode ended McCarthy's power and his influence. Over the next two and a half years, drinking heavily and a shadow of his former bullying self, he haunted the Senate until he died in the spring of 1957.[14]

Lyndon Johnson had waited McCarthy out and allowed the demagogic senator to bring himself down. McCarthy had not been an effective foe of Communist spying. The job of counterespionage was not one that the Senate was supposed to do or had the tools to accomplish with any degree of efficiency. McCarthy at the end was what he had been at the beginning of his rise to fame: an opportunist. He exploited popular fears of Communism in a shameless manner. The Senators tolerated his excesses until he turned on their institution. Then and only then did they discipline him. Lyndon Johnson deserves credit for McCarthy's political demise, but he was also an enabler himself of the dark impulses that the Wisconsin senator embodied for too long on the American political scene.

While the McCarthy controversy was on the front pages, the perennial issue of race arose for Lyndon Johnson and the Senate when the Supreme Court struck down segregation in the public schools in *Brown v. Board of Education* on May 17, 1954. Johnson did not attack the Court's decision, as some southern senators did, and he hoped that the chamber might avoid a debate that was certain to divide the Democrats. The race question hovered in the background for most of the rest of 1954, and the majority leader drove the Senate to consider other matters during the first six months of 1955. Such topics as reciprocal trade legislation, a hike in the minimum wage, and public housing were the kind of issues that Johnson was comfortable seeing the Democrats advocate. As a result of his constructive record, there was even some discussion of running Johnson for president in 1956 or 1960. Johnson played down the talk, but he hoped that, if the race issue could be managed, his national ambitions might prosper.

Meanwhile, Johnson was putting his personal imprint on the post of majority leader. He spent hours each day on the telephone, in the cloakroom rounding up votes, testing sentiment, and making deals. His obsession was political intelligence, which he craved from every source. Bobby Baker brought such news to him and also doled out cash from his office to grease the wheels of politics and lawmaking. In the intimate setting of the Senate, Johnson was a master of personal negotiations and backstage arrangements.

He also knew the rules and practices of the Senate better than almost anyone there save Richard Russell. More than previous majority leaders, Johnson relied on the unanimous-consent agreement to push laws through the process and keep the Senate in line. That device allowed Senate business to go forward if no senator objected when the leader said, "I ask unanimous consent" to take a proposed course of action. Usually negotiated with the Republican leader and key committee chairs, unanimous consent prevented obstruction by a few members but also reduced the opportunities for debate. Despite being a member of a deliberative body, Johnson was not one for actual discourse in public. When he invoked the Bible about "reasoning together," he meant that senators should retreat to a backroom, cut their deals, and then present a united face to the public. At some basic level, Johnson trusted the democratic process only when he had set it up to produce the result he wanted in advance. For him, the Senate functioned best as a participatory autocracy.[15]

Relentless in his desire to get things done, Johnson often pushed the limits of Senate propriety in his zeal to get his way. With Democratic control of the upper house so tenuous, the majority senators went along because they had to. Liberals might chafe about their leader's methods, but they applauded his results. As time passed, however, Johnson became less solicitous of the feelings of others. As a result, he stored up grievances that would resurface in years to come.

In the summer of 1955, Lyndon Johnson's years of late hours, overeating, excessive smoking and drinking, and constant stress caught up with him. On July 2 he had a serious heart attack that took him out of national politics for the remainder of the year. Rest and recuperation did not mute his ambition. He took better care of his health, but his zeal for power still burned. Now he wanted the presidency and the chance to realize his vision first for the Senate and then for the nation.[16]

While Johnson convalesced in enforced idleness at his Texas ranch, the civil rights movement, which had been gathering strength for years since World War II, pressed for national attention. The boycott of segregated buses in Montgomery, Alabama; the lynching of a black teenager, Emmett Till; and the hard work of countless African Americans who made their views known with their personal defiance of segregation—all these were signs to the country that race could not be left as a secondary issue. Black protest confronted intense white opposition in the South. Southern senators knew that their constituents wanted more than token outrage at the prospect of racial equality. White citizens councils and other organizations threatened violent action to block the march of civil rights. Harry Byrd of Virginia proclaimed, "If we can organize the Southern States for massive resistance to this order [by the Supreme Court in *Brown*], I think that in time the rest of the country will realize that racial integration is not going to be accepted in the South."[17]

Russell, Byrd, and Strom Thurmond created the "Southern Manifesto," or "Declaration of Constitutional Principles." Issued in a speech by Walter George of Georgia on March 12, 1956, the document praised the actions of "those States which have declared the intention to resist forced integration by any lawful means." Their goal was to force southern legislators in Washington to line up against civil rights. Failure to sign the manifesto would be regarded as an act of treason to their region and a signal to voters that dissenters should be turned out at the polls.[18]

Three southern members did not. Estes Kefauver of Tennessee had long made clear his distaste for such tactics. As a presidential candidate in 1956, he could not sign the document and remain a credible national hopeful. Albert Gore, Sr., also of Tennessee, refused to sign the document when Senator Thurmond thrust it at him on the Senate floor. Gore noted that southern reporters were stationed in the press gallery to watch Thurmond's gesture. Nonetheless, he still refused. The third member not to sign the manifesto was Lyndon Johnson. The drafters of the manifesto did not ask him to sign on the grounds that as majority leader he should not be confronted with such a difficult choice. Since he distanced himself from the controversy, Johnson was able to tell northern liberals that he would not have signed under any circumstances, while letting the southerners know that he understood their predicament. At the same time, he let his constituents understand that "I am not a civil rights advocate." In any event, the challenge that the Southern Manifesto posed for the Senate was not about to disappear.[19]

For the presidential election of 1956, Estes Kefauver once again donned his coonskin cap and headed for the hustings. Lyndon Johnson was hoping that lightning might strike his long-shot candidacy, and John F. Kennedy was hoping that the vice presidential nomination might come his way. With Adlai Stevenson likely to get a second nomination, these senatorial hopes all proved illusory. Kefauver and Kennedy fought a floor battle at the Democratic convention for the vice presidency with the Tennessean coming out the winner. The close defeat lifted Kennedy's prospects as a candidate for 1960 should Stevenson lose, as it seemed likely he would do to the popular Eisenhower.[20]

The incumbent president did win a landslide victory over Stevenson in November 1956, but the Democrats retained control of the Senate by the same two-vote margin that had existed before the voters went to the polls. Johnson was again majority leader with the benefit of two years of experience in the job and a battle-hardened organization at his disposal. The Republicans stayed with William Knowland as their leader, despite his lackluster performance against Johnson. The election results reflected the enduring strength of the Democrats in the Senate, based on the alliance of southerners and northerners who otherwise diverged on civil rights. With Eisenhower having run well among black voters in the North, both Republicans and Democrats discussed what should be done in light of that development. The prospects of legislation to deal with civil rights was actually being examined as a serious option.

For Lyndon Johnson, his hopes for 1960 and national leadership of the Democrats rested on his ability to rise above the southern label that he had carried for so long. A civil rights bill of some kind would help him toward that end. But achieving such a goal would not be easy. Russell and the southerners would like to have seen Johnson become president but they were not going to give up any advantages for segregation in the process. So the leader would have to find a way through the conflicting demands of the civil rights movement and the stubbornness of the southern bloc in the upper house.

The Civil Rights Law of 1957 was the major achievement of Lyndon Johnson's Senate career. Because he followed it up with another civil rights law in 1960 and even more sweeping measures as president in 1964 and 1965, the 1957 measure takes on an added significance as Johnson's first break with his anti–civil rights past in the Senate. The law itself was a very modest enactment compared to what came after it, but, Johnson later said, a first step was necessary to break down eighty-two years of opposition to anything that smacked of civil rights in the Senate.[21]

The progress of the 1957 bill in the upper house was anything but easy. The interplay among the Eisenhower administration, liberals, civil rights groups, Johnson, and the southerners was so complex that monographs and lengthy narratives in Johnson biographies have been crafted about this single episode. The Civil Rights Bill began in the House and that chamber passed it 286 to 126 on June 18, 1957. With that kind of support and with the endorsement of Eisenhower, the measure seemed headed for passage in some form. In its original version the legislation set up a civil rights division within the Department of Justice, established a commission to monitor civil rights enforcement, and gave federal district attorneys more authority to punish violations of civil rights especially as it affected school desegregation. Richard Russell decided that even an all-out filibuster could not stop enactment of the bill. He did not want cloture to be voted on this kind of mild civil rights bill lest he open the way for the breaking of filibusters on stronger legislation in the future. His best approach was to amend the bill to make it less onerous to southern opinion. In the bargain, he would assist Lyndon Johnson's chances to become president.[22]

For Johnson the civil rights issue posed a major test. He wanted to free the South from racial divisions that held back its economic development. He sought to show that the Democratic Party could govern, and he believed that the Senate should not get bogged down in a sterile filibuster that would bring public criticism on the institution. So he negotiated with Russell to find out what the southerners would accept and to convey what civil rights advocates might insist upon having. These parleys worked to erode an already tame piece of lawmaking. Johnson so believed in the symbolic power of enacting a civil rights bill into law that concessions to Russell seemed a reasonable price to pay. Of course, the weaker the bill the more it kept Johnson's southern base quiet for a race in 1960.[23]

The two and a half months of Senate consideration that ensued showed Johnson at his most creative (or devious) as a legislative leader. He allowed but did not support a move to bring the House bill directly to the floor and bypass the Judiciary Committee. That panel's chair, James O. Eastland of Mississippi, would have buried this bill. For this vote, Johnson did some sectional trading with western senators. He gave them passage of the Hells Canyon Dam in Idaho in return for their votes not to refer the measure to Judiciary as well as other modifications in the civil rights bill. Working again with westerners who had few black constituents, as well as the tacit endorsement of the White House, Johnson succeeded in stripping out a section to enforce school desegregation.[24]

The majority leader was equally deft in handling what became a key point of contention in the final stages of the debate. If a federal judge held an accused person in contempt for a civil rights violation, should that defendant receive a jury trial? Presumably, white juries would be less likely to convict in those circumstances. So Johnson found language that provided for trials but otherwise left the bill with some power. In this effort, Johnson brought into his camp such newcomers as Frank Church of Idaho, elected in 1956, who gave a key speech in defense of an amendment about the form of jury trials. Johnson outworked and outthought Knowland and Richard Nixon on the Republican side. The bill passed the Senate, went to a conference with the House, and returned with some changes that strengthened the jury trial provision.[25]

On balance, Johnson had prevailed as the civil rights law neared passage. There were grumbles from African Americans about the measure's weaknesses, but Johnson remained steadfast that the key to the process was a final bill. Southerners in the Russell camp believed that they had watered down the bill as much as they could have and had rendered it as innocuous as possible under the circumstances.

One southern lawmaker did not share this opinion. J. Strom Thurmond of South Carolina had come to the chamber in January 1955 as a nominal Democrat. An ardent segregationist, Thurmond had run as an avowed racist on the States' Rights, or Dixiecrat, ticket for president in 1948. In the 1957 debate, he said that "traditions, customs, and mores cannot be resolved by political agitation, by court fiat, or by force of law." (Apart from a few insiders in his home state, no one in the Senate knew that Thurmond, for all his talk of preserving white racial values, had fathered a daughter with a sixteen-year-old African American in the 1920s.) Personal hypocrisy aside, Thurmond was the embodiment of regional resistance to civil rights. He was not going to go along with Russell and his insider approach to the bill. Thurmond resolved to make a final filibuster against the bill, even though it was certain to pass. He spoke for twenty-four hours and eighteen minutes, a Senate record, and then the bill went through. Russell had fought a skillful rearguard action; Thurmond had grabbed the headlines.[26]

The position of Senate Democrats further strengthened in 1957. The death of Joe McCarthy in May led to a special election in Wisconsin, which was won by a liberal Democrat, William Proxmire. The Democrats rushed Proxmire to Washington to be sworn in even as Strom Thurmond was in the midst of his filibuster. Proxmire would prove to be an irritant to Johnson in the near future, but for the moment he was another omen of impending Democratic success.[27]

Then came the school integration crisis in Little Rock, Arkansas, when President Eisenhower sent in troops to enforce federal court orders, outraging southern senators. Richard Russell denounced what he called tactics drawn from "the officers of Hitler's storm troopers." This episode drove southern lawmakers back toward their Democratic allegiance. The launching of the *Sputnik* satellite in October 1957 seemed to put the United States behind the Soviet Union in space, and the development gave Johnson and his party a chance to emphasize their toughness on national defense.[28]

A severe recession further enhanced Democratic prospects in the 1958 elections. An influence-peddling scandal in the White House involving the chief of staff, Sherman Adams, and a wealthy businessman gave the opposition more ammunition with the voters. Lyndon Johnson had no problems holding his troops together as victory seemed ever more probable. With Eisenhower threatening to veto any antirecession legislation, the White House and the Republicans seemed out of step with public opinion. The GOP had twenty seats to defend, against only twelve for the Democrats. After six years, Eisenhower and his team were running out of political energy and new ideas.[29]

For the Senate Republicans 1958 was a calamitous year. Their difficulties started when the minority leader, William F. Knowland, announced that he would not seek reelection in 1958. Anxious to run for governor of California, in part to save his faltering marriage, Knowland also had presidential ambitions. With the economy souring, the Republicans picked 1958 to make a concerted attack on labor unions across the country, which only energized their opponents. Add in some weak candidates, and the makings of an electoral rout were in place.[30]

The Democrats gained fifteen seats in 1958 and now had sixty-five seats to the Republicans' thirty-four. More important, the election began a twenty-two-year period when the Democrats enjoyed substantial majorities in the upper house. Although the Senate did not become a liberal bastion, it moved away from the conservatism of the past. Democratic senators from northern states became committee chairs in the 1960s and 1970s, and the institutional power of the southern bloc dissipated.[31]

The incoming class of 1958 contained lawmakers of impressive talents. Philip A. Hart of Michigan, Edmund S. Muskie of Maine, and Eugene J. McCarthy of Minnesota would all go on to make a mark in the Senate and in American politics. Another six liberals of the second rank would be useful additions within the chamber. These incumbents would benefit six years later from the Johnson landslide of 1964. It turned out that 1958 was one of those fortunate years to have been elected to the Senate.

The Republicans' most immediate concern, amid their now diminished numbers, was to select a new leader. Knowland lost his bid for the California governorship and left the Senate. Other conservative stalwarts such as John Bricker of Ohio had gone down in the Democratic tide. Barry Goldwater, first elected in 1952, survived in Arizona, and some conservatives saw him as a potential architect of a Republican revival in the nation. The leading candidate for the post of minority leader was a midwestern conservative, Everett McKinley Dirksen of Illinois. For the next decade, he would be the public face of the GOP in the upper house.[32]

Sixty-three in January 1959, the grandiloquent, curly-headed Dirksen had been in the Senate for nine years, since defeating Democratic leader Scott Lucas in 1950. In that time he evidenced striking talents as a crowd-pleasing orator; he was sometimes called the "wizard of ooze." He probably never said the words with which he is most identified: "A billion here, a billion there, sooner or later you're talking about real money." The sentiment, however, was authentic Dirksen. He was a hard-drinking, tough-fighting Republican who battled in the Senate all day and relaxed with Lyndon Johnson over a bourbon once the battle was done. His GOP colleagues saw the combative Dirksen as someone who could take on the majority leader on the floor and survive the experience intact.[33]

Dirksen's opposition within the Republican Party caucus was John Sherman Cooper of Kentucky. An urbane progressive who exuded the sophistication that came from an education at Yale and Harvard Law School, Cooper was respected for his intellect. John Kennedy regarded him as the senator to watch when complex issues appeared. Yet Cooper was seen as not partisan or hard-edged enough to stand up to Johnson. Dirksen, on the other hand, proclaimed, "I am a Republican, period—no tags, no labels, no qualitative adjectives."[34]

When the vote was taken on January 7, 1959, Dirksen beat Cooper 20 to 14. A relative moderate, Thomas Kuchel of California, became the whip. Dirksen soon created a constructive working relationship with Eisenhower, a big change after the tensions of the Knowland era. Within weeks the Republican minority, armed with the threat of a presidential veto, was battling the Democrats on even terms. The result, said one moderate GOP member, was that "the Republican side of the aisle has functioned with more harmony this year than I have ever known it to do."[35]

For Lyndon Johnson, on the other hand, Democratic success in 1958 meant that he could no longer insist on party unity because of the narrowness of their majority. With more liberals in the chamber, anger about the majority leader's peremptory style, long pent up, came out. A friend called it "this undercurrent of emotion against your leadership in the last six years." Johnson's sense of grandeur and need for personal monuments led him to take over and then renovate a suite of seven offices across from the Senate floor at a cost of more than $100,000. Members with lesser accommodations naturally chafed at this display. With the White House in 1960 on his mind, Johnson needed to keep the Senate tame. Nonetheless, resentment against his heavy-handed tactics was increasing.[36]

The filibuster issue came up early in 1959 when Johnson, making a gesture to the liberals, proposed to change Rule 22 to allow two-thirds of senators present and voting to end debate. A return to the original 1917 rule, the change did not make much practical difference, as the southerners recognized. However, Johnson wanted consensus with his usual zeal. During a meeting with a new senator, Edmund Muskie, Johnson told him, according to the Maine senator's later memory, in deciding how to cast a vote: "Many times, Ed, you won't know how you're going to vote until the clerk calling the roll gets to the M's." Johnson, on the issue of the filibuster rule change, later asked Muskie how he intended to vote. The implication of the question was that the Maine senator should do what Johnson wanted. "The clerk hasn't gotten to the M's yet," Muskie replied. For that apparent act of independence and defiance of the Leader, Muskie was tagged as "chickenshit" by the majority leader and relegated to less favorable committee assignments.[37]

William Proxmire, in February 1959, assailed the majority leader's tactics and approach to his position. Proxmire wanted to participate in the workings of the Senate and not simply be a reliable vote for the Johnson operation. Moreover, Johnson had denied him a seat on the Senate Finance Committee because of Proxmire's opposition to the oil depletion allowance that was so crucial to the Southwest. "Initiative and responsibility appear to begin and end with the Majority leader. There is no place for senators outside his inner circle," Proxmire said. Ever sensitive to slights, Johnson reacted with anger to Proxmire's charges, but did not change his ways. Always at his best when he dominated a situation, Johnson performed less well when he had to deal with individual personalities who were not dependent on his power and authority.[38]

Democratic control of the chamber led to a nasty confirmation fight over an Eisenhower cabinet appointment that pitted the Senate against the executive branch. Eisenhower wanted Lewis Strauss to serve as secretary of commerce. In his role as chair of the Atomic Energy Commission, the domineering and haughty Strauss had aroused resentment among several key lawmakers, most notably Clinton Anderson of New Mexico, who headed the Joint Atomic Energy Committee. When the nomination reached the Senate, opposition flared among the Democrats and a few Republicans. Anderson was a particularly effective critic of the nomination and helped to build support for rejecting Strauss. In mid-June the members voted 49 to 46 to turn down the nominee, with two Republicans, Margaret Chase Smith and William Langer of North Dakota, providing key votes against the Republican president. Eisenhower was livid at the outcome, saying, "This was the most shameful thing that had happened to the U.S. Senate since the attempt to impeach a President many, many years ago."[39]

By mid-1959 the preliminaries for the presidential election contest were under way with the Senate providing the major contenders for the Democratic nomination. Four senators were announced or would-be candidates. Stuart Symington of Missouri hoped that circumstances might shape themselves so that his border-state residence, identification with national defense, and moderate record could lead to a victory. Symington was not an exciting figure, and his hopes always rested on an improbable deadlock.[40]

A more serious aspirant was Hubert Humphrey. Since coming to the Senate in 1949, he had surmounted the early dislike from the southerners about his civil rights views to gain entry to the chamber's inner circle. Members might joke that he uttered a hundred words a minute with gusts up to two hundred, but Humphrey's hard work, expertise, and pleasant demeanor had won over some of his early critics. He saw himself as the liberal candidate in the race on the basis of his support for civil rights, his record in the Senate, and his contacts within the party.[41]

Many senators viewed John F. Kennedy's candidacy with skepticism. During his seven years in the chamber, Kennedy had struck many of his colleagues as a less than serious figure who never really committed himself to the hard work of the Senate. Of course, Kennedy's goal lay elsewhere, in the White House, and he used the upper house as a means of reaching it. After winning reelection in 1958 with a huge majority, he embarked on a campaign to obtain the nomination. His youth, Roman Catholic religion, and uncertain reputation as a liberal at first seemed likely to work against him, but Kennedy soon demonstrated that he had a national appeal that neither Humphrey nor Lyndon Johnson could match. By early 1960, the Massachusetts senator was the well-financed front runner.[42]

Lyndon Johnson of course thought that he was better qualified than either Kennedy or Humphrey to be president. Never really comfortable with national politics, however, Johnson shrank from entering primaries where his southern background would put him at a disadvantage. Instead, he decided to make the most of the Senate, carry out his duties, and line up the support of the members who could then help him win their state delegations. He endeavored to demonstrate his legislative powers by passing another civil rights bill during the spring of 1960. The resulting measure, influenced by negotiations with Richard Russell, was very mild and did little to jump-start Johnson's candidacy.[43]

Where Johnson erred was in the assumption that power in the Senate translated to power with Democratic primary voters and caucus goers in individual states. While Johnson was talking in the cloakroom with men he thought had control of their constituencies, Kennedy and Humphrey battled it out for primary victories. Kennedy and his well-financed organization also lined up the power brokers in the Democratic Party in those states where organization was the key. Johnson's strategy depended on a convention deadlock where he would be the compromise choice. Television was already changing the nominating process to make conventions less central than they had been in the past. Master of the Senate as he was, Lyndon Johnson did not really understand the party to which he belonged once he stepped off the Senate floor or had to operate outside the boundaries of Texas.

The result was that Johnson's presidential candidacy stalled. His challenge to Kennedy at the Los Angeles convention was late and ineffectual. Once Kennedy had been nominated on the first ballot, Johnson's fortunes shifted. With his presumed ability to deliver Texas and its crucial bloc of electoral votes, the majority leader became a good complement to Kennedy on the Democratic ticket. Whether the nominee wanted Johnson to be vice president or only expected him to decline the nomination remains in dispute. From Johnson's perspective, a run for the vice presidency made sense. At age fifty-two he knew that men in his family died of heart disease in their early sixties. If Kennedy won in 1960 and Johnson was not his running mate, he would lose his best chance to gain national exposure, for he would be the majority leader under a Democratic president. If Johnson failed to join the ticket and Kennedy lost, he would be blamed for the defeat.[44]

Johnson also deluded himself into thinking that if he became vice president he could, through the force of his example and the legacy of his leadership of the Senate, retain some or all of the power he had built up as majority leader. He campaigned hard for the ticket and was instrumental in the narrow victory that Kennedy secured. Had Johnson not been the running mate, the South might have experienced more defections to the Republican ticket of Richard Nixon and Henry Cabot Lodge with the outcome a defeat for the Democrats. So after helping his nominee secure victory, Johnson expected a role in the new administration along with a maintenance of the power he had enjoyed since 1953 in the Senate.

The election left the alignment of the Senate unchanged—with sixty-four Democrats to thirty-six Republicans—and thus at the start of the Kennedy administration, Democratic dominance of the upper house was assured. Lyndon Johnson proposed to his allies that he should preside over the caucus of the sixty-four Democratic senators. When Alben Barkley was vice president during the Truman administration, he had played a role in the Democratic Senatorial Conference, though not with the clout that Johnson wanted to have. Johnson informed Bobby Baker that if his idea went through he would make sure that everything is "gonna be just the way it was." There is little evidence that Johnson prepared the ground for this initiative before the Democratic senators met, other than discussing the proposal with those who were already committed to it.[45]

When the Senate Democrats gathered on January 3, the selection of Mike Mansfield as majority leader and Hubert Humphrey as whip went through unanimously. Then Mansfield proposed "that the Vice President-elect preside over future Conferences in the tradition of Barkley and others." Opposition surfaced at once from senators who had been subjected to the "Johnson treatment" for eight years. Albert Gore, Sr., said, "The distinguished Vice-President is no longer a Democratic senator." What Mansfield suggested was "highly irregular and entirely improper." Others made similar arguments, but the real point was that Democratic senators had had all they wanted of Lyndon Johnson. Mansfield's proposal went through by a vote of 46 to 17, but Lyndon Johnson knew that it was only a paper victory. The language of the resolution only allowed Mansfield to invite the vice president to be the presiding officer. The tacit understanding of all present was that such invitations to Johnson would not be forthcoming. Johnson grumbled to the press, "I know now the difference between a caucus and a cactus. In a cactus all the pricks are on the outside."[46]

Johnson had no one but himself to blame for his embarrassment. Had he been more of a gentleman and respected the feelings of others when he had power, he would not have stored up the resentments that defeated him in January 1961. In effect, he wanted to stage a senatorial coup d'état that would shift the balance of power toward the vice presidency solely for his own aggrandizement. He tried to impose the scheme without argument or debate as if it were his due to be accorded this new authority. When he was spurned, he sulked and left the Senate enraged.

This final episode of Lyndon Johnson's senatorial career summed up the strengths and drawbacks of his eleven years in the upper house. As a leader, Johnson could be a legislative virtuoso in assembling votes and working his way through the intricacies of a bill or resolution to achieve a majority. Yet at times he seemed more interested in the production of a law for its own sake rather than emphasizing the substance of an issue. The 1957 civil rights law illustrated that process.

But Johnson's larger failing as majority leader was his reluctance to use the power he had accumulated for anything other than his own personal needs. Rather than make changes in the workings of the Senate that would endure past the time he stepped down, he simply accepted the institution as it was and made it his goal to gain mastery of the existing structure. He could have transformed the office of majority leader to make the Democrats a more united and cohesive delegation. That would have made possible the enactment of progressive legislation during the Kennedy years. Instead, by his overreaching and aggressiveness, he ensured that no future majority leader would ever approach the kind of power he had seized on a temporary basis.

As a result, Lyndon Johnson, for all of his fabled skill as majority leader in the 1950s, left no permanent mark on the place. Like Nelson Aldrich, he seemed a towering figure at the time, but his essential lack of vision about the Senate limited his impact. The future of how the institution would operate lay with his mild-mannered successor, Mike Mansfield, and a series of cautious leaders in both parties who followed the Montanan. For the Senate, Lyndon Johnson was like a noisy summer storm that rattled the windows of the upper chamber and then moved on, leaving few traces of its passing.

## CHAPTER THIRTEEN

# Mike Mansfield's Senate

THE FACE OF THE SENATE IN THE 1950S WAS LYNDON JOHNSON. WITH his departure in 1961, the institution became more of an ensemble production than a vehicle for a single starring lawmaker. During the 1960s, many members at different times came forward to reflect the unsettled and changing condition of the upper house. Mike Mansfield and Everett Dirksen were the party leaders on television, but it was also the decade of Barry Goldwater, J. William Fulbright, Robert Kennedy, and Eugene McCarthy. The Democrats looked to the chamber for candidates on their national tickets, and the clash of presidential ambitions provided a background for legislation and investigations. By 1970, the more liberal Senate had become a major opposition force to Richard Nixon's presidency. Meanwhile, television expanded its effect on the institution as candidates tailored their messages for the small screen. Little by little show business spread its influence within the Senate.

The new Democratic leader, Mike Mansfield, was anything but a telegenic personality. Quiet and reserved, he did not seek press coverage, an abrupt change from Johnson's clamor. The senators, wrote Johnson aide Harry McPherson, were like "boys in a prep school when an old tyrannical headmaster who believed in the redeeming power of work was replaced by a permissive young don." Mansfield believed that all senators should be treated with equal respect and he disdained the coercive tactics on which Johnson had relied. He realized that the particular historical moment that had made Johnson's tenure as majority leader possible had passed, and that running the

Senate would have to take into account these changed circumstances. For sixteen years, until he retired in 1977, Mansfield pursued his own personal manner of leadership in a way that suited the modern Senate.[1]

Michael Joseph Mansfield was born in New York City in 1903 and after the death of his mother in 1910 moved to Montana to live with relatives. As a young man, Mansfield served in the Navy, Army, and Marine Corps. He was stationed in Asia and brought a close knowledge of that region to his political career. He returned to Montana in 1922 and worked in the cooper mines, and received his A.B. from the University of Montana, where he became a professor of political science and history. Elected to the House in 1942, he won a Senate seat ten years later despite the intervention of Joe McCarthy for his opponent and a Red-baiting campaign against Mansfield himself. Johnson picked Mansfield to be majority whip in 1957 because he was "the least objectionable to most of the Democratic senators." Mansfield's reticence hid a shrewd political intelligence. His terse, aloof public persona did not win him many headlines, but it earned for him a large measure of respect from his peers.[2]

After John F. Kennedy was elected president and Johnson, vice president, a contest began to see who would succeed Johnson as majority leader. The two most obvious contenders were Hubert Humphrey and George Smathers. Humphrey was too liberal for the southerners, and the playboy image of the handsome Smathers held him back. John Kennedy regarded Mansfield, a fellow Roman Catholic, as someone who would be loyal in the Senate and would push the White House program. Once Kennedy had made his preference known, the votes accumulated for Mansfield and he won a unanimous election on January 3, 1961. Even the stillborn effort to have Johnson be the presiding officer for the Democratic Conference did not dent Mansfield's authority. In fact, he may have allowed Johnson the latitude to damage himself in the eyes of his former colleagues.[3]

Mansfield proceeded to scale back the perquisites of the majority leader and return the post to a more modest profile within the Senate. Where Johnson had tried to be first among equals, Mansfield genuinely thought that all senators should be represented in how the institution operated. He did not see his role as lobbying for votes or dictating policy for his colleagues. After the Johnson years, the change was refreshing for many senators, but in time Mansfield came under attack himself for not being as forceful and demanding as his predecessor had been. For the most part, however, Mansfield's even-handed style proved more suited to the way the Senate worked during the 1960s.[4]

Mansfield also moved to cut back on the presence of alcohol in and around the chamber that Lyndon Johnson had actually encouraged. Mansfield issued no edicts about alcohol consumption, but he took steps to make liquor less readily available. Nonetheless, the problems persisted. Harold Hughes, himself an alcoholic, encountered a drunken colleague on the floor after he took his oath of office in 1969. The Iowa Democrat spent the night counseling Harrison Williams of New Jersey. Despite what Hughes did with other colleagues and the hearing he held on alcoholism as a social problem, the Senate in the 1960s and 1970s struggled with the untreated alcoholism of several of its members.[5]

The surge of liberal Democrats into the chamber moved the institution somewhat to the left during that decade, and a number of these lawmakers established national reputations of their own. Hubert Humphrey was the most visible of the liberals, but he had to yield some space to Wayne Morse of Oregon, Robert Kennedy of New York, Ralph Yarborough of Texas, and Philip Hart of Michigan. Other Democrats such as Henry M. "Scoop" Jackson of Washington were liberal on domestic issues but more conventional on matters of national defense.[6]

The South remained a core bastion of Democratic strength; Richard Russell and his two dozen colleagues stood prepared to defend racial segregation through filibuster and delay. In the early 1960s, the first signs of the swelling Republican tide of white voters in the South were appearing. The liberalism and racial policies of the Kennedy administration fed this groundswell of opposition to civil rights. Most southern Democrats were able to fend off challengers in this period. In Texas, however, a Republican college professor named John Tower won a special election to fill Lyndon Johnson's seat, and he turned out to be the forerunner of other Republicans from Dixie in the years to come. The liberal majority of the 1960s among the Democrats thus rested on a core of southern party members who would see their electoral base weaken over the next three decades.[7]

On the conservative Republican side, Dirksen continued to be the most prominent GOP member. His regular press conferences with House Minority Leader Charles Halleck became known in Washington as the "Ev and Charlie Show," and they helped to make the rumpled, loquacious Dirksen a political celebrity. He even had a hit record with a rendition of a patriotic recitation called "Gallant Men." Other Republicans vied with Dirksen for Senate prominence. By the early 1960s, Barry Goldwater of Arizona had become the darling of Republicans on the right, and he spent the first four years of the decade in pursuit of the presidency. The Republicans still had a contingent of more moderate voices in John Sherman Cooper, Jacob Javits, Clifford Case of New Jersey, and Hugh Scott of Pennsylvania. The Senate had not yet become as ideologically polarized as it would be three decades later.[8]

Older senators were moving into positions of influence on key committees that would shape the debates of the 1960s. J. William Fulbright took over the Foreign Relations Committee in 1959 and held the post of chairman for the next fifteen years, transforming the committee into a kind of miniature State Department in which he could develop his ideas on foreign policy. Fulbright installed Carl Marcy as chief of staff for Foreign Relations, and Marcy became an adept leaker to a cadre of friendly journalists who covered the committee. As a result, Fulbright achieved a kind of independent power base within the Senate that would, when the controversial issues of foreign policy arose during the 1960s, make him a counterweight to Lyndon Johnson and his Vietnam War.[9]

The decade began when the Senate convened for its opening day in January 1961. Watching from the gallery, Ellen Proxmire observed that the institution—"like a theater—has the quality of being a world separate and detached." During that ceremony, one telling moment came when Margaret Chase Smith escorted Maurine Neuberger, a newly elected senator from Oregon, arm in arm to the vice president's desk to take the oath of office. It was big news in that time that the chamber now had all of two female members, chosen by the voters of their states.[10]

The Senate had now reached a total of one hundred seats since Alaska and Hawaii had become states in 1959. Salaries had risen to $22,500 in 1955 and would go up again in 1965 to $30,000 per year. More than 2,700 employees worked in and around the Senate in 1961; that number would rise to 4,100 by 1971. The small, personalized chamber of the early twentieth century was a receding memory. As a key Senate aide, Richard Riedel, wrote in 1969, "The job of Senator has become as involved and fragmented as the government itself."[11]

The Senate during the Kennedy administration proved unreceptive to the legislative programs of the new president. Although there were ideological reasons, especially among conservative Republicans, for the coolness toward Kennedy's New Frontier, part of the problem was the reputation that John Kennedy had acquired during his eight years of service in the up-per house as a senatorial lightweight. He had not done the hard work of committee service and courting his colleagues. So while no one said so out loud, there was some sense of retribution from men who believed, as did Lyndon Johnson, that a presumptuous politician was now sitting in the White House.[12]

Kennedy compounded his problems with the Senate with the aloofness and occasional disdain that he brought to his relations with his former col-leagues too. He rarely consulted Republicans beyond Everett Dirksen and did not do the small things that eased the way among politicians of both parties. Lawmakers were invited to large receptions at the White House, but they were largely excluded from the smaller, exciting events that sym-bolized the dazzle of the New Frontier. There was an administration "fa-vors" file that provided boons to lawmakers, but in terms of the Senate Kennedy simply lacked the touch that would have made all the difference. Foreign policy fascinated him; domestic politics and courting lawmakers was a necessary bore. It did not take long for the Senate to figure out where Kennedy stood.[13]

In the early 1960s, Congress came under renewed scrutiny from the press and its own members for its failures to engage the nation's problems with urgency. Members of the Senate such as Joseph Clark of Pennsylvania in-dicted the body for failing to address such glaring social problems as the race issue. Perhaps the most famous outside critique came from a political scientist, James MacGregor Burns, who wrote in 1963 of *The Deadlock of Democracy*, in which he charged that stalemate had rendered Capitol Hill incapable of positive action. While the investigative journalism of the Wa-tergate period was still a decade in the future, such reporters as Drew Pear-son and Jack Anderson investigated the lapses of lawmakers about favors from lobbyists, nepotism, and deals for constituents. Congress had become accustomed to the lax procedures of the Johnson era, and there were scan-dals simmering that would first appear in the Kennedy years.[14]

The legislative accomplishments of the New Frontier were modest, and that added to the sense of malaise that pervaded Congress in the first three years of the 1960s. As the presidential election year of 1964 approached, there were critics who believed that the administration had little to show for itself on the domestic side. A civil rights bill was bottled up in the House. So too was the Kennedy initiative for substantial tax cuts. Mike Mansfield re-ceived some of the blame for the slow pace of work in the Senate, and the majority leader prepared a rebuttal of his critics that he planned to deliver on November 22, 1963.[15]

To be sure, the Kennedy White House did have some achievements in foreign policy. In the summer of 1963 the upper house took up the Nuclear Test Ban Treaty, which the president had negotiated with the Soviet Union. The modest pact restricted testing in the atmosphere. Conservatives regarded these tentative steps as a sellout of American security to the Soviet Union, and the White House knew that achieving Senate approval would require an intense lobbying effort with the upper house. For one of the few times in his presidency, Kennedy actually became engaged with a legislative question and saw that the treaty was approved. He made sure that his remarks when he signed the treaty had the maximum public relations effect. "We got to hit the country while the country's hot," he told Secretary of State Dean Rusk. "That's the only thing that makes an impression" on these "goddamned senators." Republicans assailed the White House as soft on Moscow and its threat. The president also faced opposition from some Democratic members such as Henry M. Jackson of Washington, who argued that Moscow could not be trusted to keep its agreements.[16]

To gather the needed votes for approval, Kennedy had to look to Everett Dirksen to disarm Republican opposition. The hope was that Dirksen would bring with him key Republican votes. The White House flattered the vain Republican leader. Kennedy also called in some political debts with Dirksen and former president Eisenhower to ensure that they provide public endorsement of the test ban treaty. With that kind of backing, the pact received strong approval on September 24, 1963, by a vote of 80 to 19.[17] The test ban treaty episode saw the Senate fulfill one of its explicit constitutional duties in relatively high-minded fashion.

During this same period, Senate insiders cooperated to hush up a potential scandal for President Kennedy, Vice President Johnson, and the institution itself. Inside the Club, political expediency still held sway. The source of the problem was Bobby Baker, the Johnson aide, whom Mansfield had kept on as the secretary of the Senate. Baker had Johnson's lust for personal wealth but lacked his patron's deft touch about hiding his business affairs. Anxious to succeed as a power broker, Baker had invested in a Maryland hotel that opened with a gaudy and celebrity-studded party in July 1962. But the venture ran into construction problems, which led to shady loans and eventually a lawsuit from one of Baker's associates. The news of the affair attracted the attention of John J. Williams of Delaware, a Republican with what amounted to an obsession against wrongdoing by government officials.[18]

Williams's probe led to Baker's resignation under fire on October 7, 1963, and an inquiry by the Senate Rules Committee. Out of that investigation and the digging of reporters came revelations about a woman, originally from Germany, named Ellen Rometsch, who had had sex with John Kennedy and a number of unnamed senators. So dangerous was the prospect of her testimony that Attorney General Robert Kennedy had had her deported in August. Yet there was still the danger that her professional services to Senate members might become public. Accordingly, Mansfield and Dirksen cooperated with the Kennedy and Johnson administrations in preventing the investigation of Bobby Baker from looking into any sex scandal involving senators. Baker went to jail for his financial crimes, and the stories of sex capers never came to light. Once again, the informal masculine ethos led to suppression of any knowledge of the seamy side of the upper house and the presidency itself.[19]

These events, and the sparse nature of Kennedy's legislative record, produced a sense that the Senate was not doing the nation's business in the fall of 1963. Restiveness about Mansfield's leadership style had increased. Senators who had chafed under Lyndon Johnson now complained about Mansfield's failure to push measures through and act as more of a director for the Senate. There was no overt challenge to Mansfield's dominance but unease could become outright rebellion. These qualms about Mansfield became so prevalent that the majority leader planned to deliver a major address about the matter that rebutted the case for his alleged passivity. Before he could do so on November 22, 1963, news came to the shocked Senate of the murder of John F. Kennedy in Dallas. After the Kennedy funeral, Mansfield put his speech into the *Congressional Record*, where it remained as a relic of Senate history that events had overtaken.

Lyndon Johnson had been gone from the chamber for three years. Now he was back as president, as demanding and forceful as ever. Much as in the early days of his leadership role in the 1950s, Johnson began with a burst of constructive energy to which the Senate responded. Soon, however, signs of a backlash and suspicions about Johnson among his former colleagues also appeared. The strong presidency that Johnson embodied encountered institutional resistance from the Senate he had once dominated.[20]

For the members of the chamber, Lyndon Johnson was everywhere in December 1963 and into the early months of 1964. He was on the phone cajoling, browbeating, and finally convincing a reluctant Richard Russell to serve on the commission, headed by Chief Justice Earl Warren, to investigate the Kennedy assassination. "We've got to get a states' rights man in there," said the new president, "and somebody that the country has confidence in." Anxious to help his friend, Russell gave in. To get the tax-cut bill that Kennedy had sponsored through the Senate, Johnson trimmed the budget to under $100 billion to impress the ever-frugal Harry Byrd as chair of the Finance Committee. "If Congress is to function at all and can't pass a tax bill between January and January," Johnson told Dirksen, "why we're in a hell of a shape." With Johnson's patented arm-twisting, plus the political and economic appeal of tax cuts, Byrd helped get the tax bill adopted in the upper chamber.[21]

When Johnson addressed Congress on November 27, 1963, he told the lawmakers of his intention to continue the initiatives that John Kennedy had begun. The most controversial and difficult of these items was the civil rights bill that had been stalled when Kennedy was killed. Johnson knew that his presidential hopes for 1964 depended on his ability to get a civil rights bill through the Senate. The measure would ensure that African Americans had equal access to public accommodations, equal opportunity in employment, and other long-denied rights. Only by passing such a sweeping and powerful bill could he demonstrate an ability to rise above his southern roots and govern as a true national leader. Instead of the caution he had shown during the 1957 struggle over a much milder piece of legislation, the president realized that he could not show weakness on this issue or be seen as the architect of a face-saving compromise. If that meant facing down his old friend and mentor Richard Russell, Johnson knew that he had to do so.[22]

There was never any doubt that the Civil Rights Bill in 1964 commanded a majority in the Senate. The problem was how to break the inevitable southern filibuster and achieve cloture. The White House and the Senate leadership needed sixty-seven votes to end debate. To accomplish that result required Republicans from the party's conservative wing to agree to vote for cloture. In turn, that dictated an approach to Everett Dirksen as the minority leader that would enlist him on the side of civil rights. Only in that way could the administration find the fifteen or twenty Republican votes for cloture that would in turn achieve the sixty-seven senators needed to shut off debate. Suspicious of expanded government power and aware of his party's

Mike Mansfield's leadership style included intense consultation with Everett Dirksen (right), the minority leader.
During the process of enacting the Civil Rights Law of
1964, the two men worked out the details of the proposed
legislation. Mansfield's patience helped the measure become law. (SENATE HISTORICAL OFFICE)

reliance on southern votes to block other legislation from Johnson, Dirksen
was also mindful of Republican identification with civil rights in the past
and the oft-invoked memories of Abraham Lincoln.[23]

Out of these considerations emerged an administration strategy to win the
parliamentary battle. Mike Mansfield decided that the Senate would have to
go through an extended debate on civil rights without trying to coerce members into accepting cloture. In previous contests, there had been all-night, or
"pajama," sessions to wear out the southerners with round-the-clock debates.
That tactic was showy and impressed journalists, but it usually backfired on
its advocates. As it turned out, in these protracted filibuster battles it was easy
for Russell and his allies to have one or two members wage the filibuster with
occasional quorum calls that roused pro–civil rights senators from sleep to
come to the floor. Mansfield would have none of these tactics. He informed
Russell that debate would continue on a regular basis without extraordinary
devices to wear down the opposition. Mansfield thought that there were the

makings of a coalition to vote for cloture. He had seen it happen a year earlier when the Senate did so to end debate on a bill about commercial satellites. Patience, believed the leader, would lead to passage of the bill.[24]

To direct the pro–civil rights forces, the president and Mansfield decided that Hubert Humphrey was the clear choice. His credentials as a proponent of reform were unquestioned. He could speak with the civil rights groups that were pressing the Congress to act. At the same time, Humphrey had gained enough respect from southerners for his legislative skills that he could negotiate with them and with Dirksen in good faith. The Minnesota senator proved to be a masterful manager of the bill. He did what was necessary to achieve passage and was an eloquent advocate of the principles for which he was fighting. "I would have kissed Dirksen's ass on the Capitol steps" to get the bill through was how Humphrey later described his attitude toward the Republican leader. The Minnesota Democrat organized his forces well to cover all aspects of the bill and engage the southerners in the extended debate. The civil rights forces proved as cohesive as the southerners in this contest.[25]

The impending legislative battle attracted national attention. CBS News assigned correspondent Roger Mudd to cover the debate over the civil rights bill. Although no television record of the proceedings was possible at a time when cameras were excluded from the chamber, Mudd's nightly bulletins from the Capitol enhanced the suspense about the outcome and riveted public attention on what was taking place. The intricacies of the legislative strategy, while not revealed in all their complexity, were laid out in sufficient detail to provide for striking political theater. The Senate was slowly moving into the media age.

Richard Russell and his allies used the time-tested techniques of race baiting and delay to argue that enacting civil rights would ruin the nation. After all, the southerners had defeated all eleven attempts to impose cloture on civil rights–related proposals since 1938. They knew how to make the fight. Strom Thurmond said on a television program that the bill was not "public accommodation. It's invasion of private property. This will lead to the integration of private life." Russell had his forces well organized. The eighteen southerners were divided into three groups of six to contest numerically superior proponents of the bill. What had worked for Russell in the past, however, did not operate with the same effectiveness in 1964. The southern bloc had older men in it now, which made them less able to sustain a filibuster. But the main problem for Russell and the men he led was the transformation in the historical circumstances. In the early 1960s, equal rights in law for African Americans seemed to the nation the right thing to do. Within a few years, a white backlash would erode that consensus. But in 1964 civil rights was a cause with the power of American opinion behind it. For one of the few times in the annals of the Senate, the body was inclined to do something for the disadvantaged and excluded in American society.[26]

With Lyndon Johnson urging him on to court Everett Dirksen, Humphrey drank with the minority leader, pampered him, and fed his ample vanity. Dirksen knew what was happening and went along with the process because it painted him as a national leader. He intoned that the civil rights bill was, paraphrasing Victor Hugo, "an idea whose time has come." On June 10, 1964, the Senate voted on the cloture motion. One fatally ill senator, Clair Engel of California, was wheeled in on a stretcher and pointed at his eye ("Aye") when the roll was called. The final vote was 71 to 29 in favor of ending the debate. Barry Goldwater, the presumptive presidential candidate for the Republicans, voted no as part of the emerging GOP strategy of courting southern white voters. For the first time in its history, the Senate had voted to make it possible for a strong civil rights bill to be passed.[27]

The Civil Rights Act of 1964 is justly celebrated as one of the triumphant moments in the Senate's long history. Cloture could be invoked, the chamber could act, the national interest was advanced. However, the long-range problem was that the confluence of events that led to the dramatic step forward in 1964 would not always be developed in future controversies. In fact, this unusual legislative event may have helped sustain filibusters in the future. Proponents of unlimited debate could always cite the achievement of cloture in 1964 as a reason not to make further changes in the system. In addition, the senators were able to congratulate themselves for finally doing something that in fact should have happened a generation earlier.

If the passage of the Civil Rights Act of 1964 represented one of the constructive moments in Senate history, one of the more embarrassing episodes followed in its wake. Facing the candidacy of Barry Goldwater in the fall election, Johnson wanted to shore up his national security credentials as an effective war leader. Goldwater had charged that Johnson was not being tough enough on the perceived Communist threat in Vietnam. In early August 1964 reports reached the White House that American ships in the Gulf of Tonkin had been attacked by North Vietnamese vessels. Whether the shelling of the Navy vessels had actually occurred or not was unclear at the time, but Johnson seized the opportunity to obtain congressional authorization both for an immediate retaliation against North Vietnam and for what amounted to a blank check in Southeast Asia to wage war as he deemed best. The White House had prepared a congressional resolution for just such an eventuality. Now Johnson could show Goldwater and the nation that he could be tough in a crisis with North Vietnam. The problem was that some of the supposed attacks on American forces had never happened. For the moment, the president wanted a political victory and did not care about the evidence that he used to support his tough measures against the enemy in Southeast Asia.[28]

Johnson had put Democratic senators in a box. Few of them wanted to see Barry Goldwater, a man whose intellect and views were not much respected on Capitol Hill, become president. The impulse was still strong to rally behind the chief executive during a time of foreign crisis. Putting aside the qualms that some of them had about Lyndon Johnson's veracity, they accepted what the White House had said about the incident and prepared to adopt what was being called the Tonkin Gulf Resolution. That document gave Johnson wide authority to respond to what was believed to be North Vietnamese aggression.[29]

Johnson's senatorial point man became J. William Fulbright of Arkansas, the chair of the Foreign Relations Committee. Although the president and the senator were apparently friendly at that time, Johnson had not briefed Fulbright on the extent of American military activity in the Tonkin Gulf that could have provoked a North Vietnamese response. Nor did the president tell Fulbright that the resolution he would be pushing was designed as a rationale for a wider conflict during a second Johnson term. Instead of exploring the subject with care, Fulbright, at the behest of the White House, was ready to press ahead with consideration of the resolution.[30]

Most senators concluded that the United States Navy had been the victim of aggression from a Communist country. Republicans thought Johnson's resolution and retaliatory military action were much overdue. Democrats did not wish to be seen as standing in the way of their president acting in a forceful manner. Public sentiment seemed to be in favor of what Johnson was proposing and in that highly charged political environment the majority of the Senate was ready to go along with the president.

The debate on August 6–7 in the upper house went according to Johnson's plan. Fulbright managed the measure through the ten-hour session in ways that limited any potential dissent from skeptical members. Just two opposing voices were heard. Wayne Morse of Oregon, a perennial and unpopular maverick voice, spoke up, and so too did Ernest Gruening, Democrat of Alaska. Morse had learned from a source in the Pentagon that the Navy ships were in the Gulf to support South Vietnamese raids there. When he asked Secretary of Defense Robert McNamara about the matter, the Pentagon official covered up what had really happened. Morse's colleagues did not explore the episode in any depth. The sentiment of the time was to stand behind the president and the administration. As a result, the White House got its resolution by 88 to 2. Morse and his criticisms seemed at the time a sideshow to the main debate. In the years ahead, the Oregon senator would become an antiwar prophet who had exposed the reality behind the administration's deceptions.[31]

The incident proved to be a very hollow victory for Johnson and his presidency. As the Vietnam War escalated in 1965 and 1966, the factual basis for the Tonkin Gulf Resolution collapsed. Participants in the Gulf of Tonkin incident leaked information to the press about the tenuous basis for Johnson's initiatives in August 1964. The official account of what had happened could not withstand sustained scrutiny. The complexity of events in that region, and the American role in bringing on the attacks, revealed that senators had not done their constitutional duty in August 1964. They had relied on Fulbright, and he had depended on what Lyndon Johnson had told him about the facts. The president secured only a short-term victory with this deceitful strategy. Within a year, the lies that Johnson had told came back to hurt him as antiwar sentiment appeared and then grew within the ranks of Senate Democrats. Lyndon Johnson sacrificed credibility that he never recovered. In addition, he fostered suspicion of the presidency as an institution that shaped how the Senate reacted in future foreign policy crises.

In the 1964 election, the Senate furnished parts of both national tickets. Barry Goldwater swept aside the opposition of Governor Nelson Rockefeller of New York to win the Republican nomination and oppose Johnson with all the fervor of the right wing of his party. For his vice-presidential running mate, Johnson dangled the prize before Eugene J. McCarthy of Minnesota before settling on Hubert Humphrey. Humphrey's liberalism balanced the ticket with Johnson's southwestern roots and moderate voting record. Like

Johnson before him, Humphrey deluded himself into believing he would have a meaningful role as vice president. Johnson soon showed the former senator the error of his assumptions.[32]

Johnson won the 1964 election in a landslide over Goldwater. In the Senate races, Robert F. Kennedy gained a seat in New York that raised the Democratic advantage to sixty-eight seats compared with thirty-two for the Republicans. The Democrats also made gains in the House as the GOP suffered the effects of the Goldwater debacle on congressional candidates.

With that advantage, Lyndon Johnson moved in 1965 to enact the domestic programs of his Great Society. In a whirlwind burst of lawmaking, Congress enacted the Voting Rights Act of 1965, landmark education legislation, Medicare, highway beautification, and other environmental legislation. The Senate was a strong partner in this activism, which rivaled Woodrow Wilson's record in 1913–14 and the heady early days of the New Deal.[33]

While Congress was making these headlines, the war in South Vietnam was worsening for the Americans. The ability to sustain a government in Saigon was eroding, and senators began hearing from their constituents about the escalation of the conflict. Meanwhile, American intervention in the Dominican Republic during the spring of 1965 to put down what the White House called a Communist coup also alienated key senators, including J. William Fulbright. The president and the State Department hyped the danger of a left-wing government on the Caribbean island. The president had been caught playing tricks with the truth in foreign policy.

The crisis in the Caribbean soon passed, but the episode renewed doubts within the Senate about Johnson's honesty and emotional stability. The real running sore was Vietnam, which seemed to worsen by the month during 1965 and 1966. The optimistic scenarios that the administration put forward about imminent victory in Southeast Asia seemed in conflict with events on the ground. As the weeks and months passed, more and more senators asked themselves if Wayne Morse and Ernest Gruening had not been right about the Tonkin Gulf Resolution after all.[34]

In early 1966 the Senate Foreign Relations Committee decided to hold public hearings on the course of the conflict in Southeast Asia. With a shrewd sense of public relations, the staff of the committee briefed the television networks on the potential spectacle of senators interrogating key government officials. To counter that possibility, the president refused to let his men appear. Fulbright and his aides then received the cooperation of the head of CBS News, Fred Friendly, in having live coverage of anti-administration witnesses. The hearings became a compelling attraction for daytime television audiences until Johnson pressured TV news executives to have the proceedings taken off the air. CBS complied but NBC did not.

Eventually, the White House saw no alternative but to let major policy makers such as Secretary of State Dean Rusk appear. The witnesses for the White House came under intense grilling from uneasy senators, and the ensuing discussion about the rationales for the war fed doubts about the wisdom of the conflict itself. The Fulbright hearings did not make Americans turn against the war, but they did undercut the rationale for the conflict. They did not quite attain the star power of the Kefauver hearings or the excitement of the Army-McCarthy proceedings, but the Foreign Relations Committee sessions were further evidence of how the Senate could impact popular opinion when the right moment came.[35]

Like the rest of the people of the United States in the mid-1960s, the Senate was of many minds about the war in Vietnam. Some senators remained committed to Lyndon Johnson and the administration's policy of containing Communism. The desire to stand behind the chief executive during a time of war gave this faction a powerful means of countering growing dissent in the chamber. Among Democrats, however, there were more doves to offset the presence of hawks. Even within the ranks of the Republican minority, divisions existed about the wisdom of the Vietnam commitment. One GOP elder, George D. Aiken of Vermont, said, in what became his most famous phrase, "Just say we won and get out!" Within the Senate in the mid-1960s, there was as yet no clear majority for either escalation of the war or an American pullout.[36]

As a result of Vietnam and growing racial tensions at home, the dramatic Democratic landslide of 1964 had already begun to unravel within two years. The enactment of the legislation for the Great Society, the war in Vietnam, and racial unrest that commenced with the Watts Riots in Los Angeles in 1965 ate away at support for the party in power. The broad electoral base of the Republicans also showed itself in the 1966 elections. Paul H. Douglas, a three-term senator from Illinois, faced a challenge from the millionaire executive and GOP moderate Charles H. "Chuck" Percy. The retirement of Maurine Neuberger of Oregon, one of the two women senators, enabled Governor Mark Hatfield, another middle-of-the-road Republican, to make a strong run at a Democratic seat. The death of a Democratic

Senators from minority backgrounds did not appear
in any numbers until the end of the twentieth century. Edward Brooke, a Massachusetts Republican,
won a Senate seat in 1966 and spent two terms in
the chamber as the only African-American member.
(LIBRARY OF CONGRESS)

incumbent in Michigan produced a vacancy that Robert P. Griffin filled for
the Republicans. In Tennessee, Howard H. Baker, Jr., won the seat held a
few years earlier by Estes Kefauver, and soon became a rising figure in the
party leadership.[37]

In what proved to be only a temporary step toward a more diverse Senate,
Edward Brooke of Massachusetts won the race to succeed Leverett Saltonstall; his victory added an African American to the Senate. Brooke was
the first black to sit in the Senate during the twentieth century and only the
third African-American senator since Reconstruction. Brooke did not, however, become a major Senate figure during his two terms in the chamber.

Though outright GOP control of the upper house still lay in the future, the Republicans and Everett Dirksen now had a large enough presence to make life more difficult for Mansfield and Lyndon Johnson. The 1966 result foreshadowed the erosion of Democratic strength in the Senate that occurred in the 1970s and 1980s.

During what proved to be the final two years of Lyndon Johnson's presidency, the Senate provided a pair of presidential candidates for the Democrats. As the war in Vietnam dragged on without prospect of victory, discontent with the leadership of President Johnson mounted. Few senators believed that Johnson could be denied another nomination in 1968. Still, Democrats looked for an alternative. The most charismatic name was that of Robert F. Kennedy of New York. As the brother of the slain president, Kennedy embodied the hopes of the New Frontier and the intense anti-Johnson sentiment now burgeoning among Democrats. That Kennedy and Johnson loathed each other added to the personal dynamic at work. But Kennedy, who liked being a senator, saw no value in taking on Johnson in what seemed likely to be a hopeless cause. He rebuffed efforts of Democratic liberals such as Allard Lowenstein to get him to declare against the president.[38]

Eugene J. McCarthy of Minnesota was more receptive to these pleas from the Democratic left. Elected in the 1958 landslide after a decade in the House, McCarthy made a promising start in the upper chamber. He was conciliatory toward the South on the oil depletion allowance and achieved a coveted seat on the Finance Committee as a result. By the mid-1960s, he was losing interest in the Senate and was alert for other political opportunities. One of his friends recalled that by September 1967 he seemed "really sick of politics, sick of being in the Senate, bored, and we'd had the distinct feeling he was looking for another career, out of politics."[39]

McCarthy was also outraged with the administration and its Vietnam policy. During a Foreign Relations Committee hearing in August 1967, McCarthy bridled when an undersecretary of state defended the Tonkin Gulf Resolution as a virtual grant to the president of the right to make war in Vietnam. An outraged McCarthy told a reporter, "This is the wildest testimony I've ever heard. There is no limit to what he says the President can do. There is only one thing to do—take it to the country." Suddenly, McCarthy was putting himself forward as a senator who could challenge a sitting president for the nomination.[40]

The Tet Offensive by the Viet Cong and the North Vietnamese in February 1968 shocked the American public into realizing that the war might not be won. McCarthy's campaign seemed quixotic until he ran a strong second to Johnson in the New Hampshire primary in March 1968. That media success for McCarthy's long-shot challenge suggested that Johnson might be vulnerable. The result brought Robert Kennedy into the race, and the two senators vied for the Democratic nomination during the spring—until Kennedy's assassination in June. Meanwhile Johnson withdrew from the race on March 31. In the Senate, the effect of the Tet Offensive was to strengthen the growing skepticism about the war in both parties. Everett Dirksen, a staunch supporter of the president's foreign policy, found his members less inclined to follow his leadership on that issue and others. The heated presidential race between Richard Nixon and Hubert Humphrey added to the political tension.[41]

In that turbulent year, political assassinations transformed the political environment. The murder of Dr. Martin Luther King, Jr., on April 4 led to the passage of one more civil rights law. During the winter and spring of 1968 the White House had pressed for a civil rights bill to provide fair housing for African Americans. By now the backlash against the civil rights movement had made passing such measures much more difficult than it had been four years earlier. A series of cloture votes occurred with the Republicans evenly divided on the decision to shut off debate. Then King's death made passing the bill seem a tribute to his memory. On the fourth try for cloture and after staunch lobbying by Dirksen and other Republicans, the Senate voted to close off debate by 65 to 32, the precise tally needed to achieve victory. As before, the threat of a filibuster shaped the way the upper house approached civil rights legislation.[42]

Just as King's death affected the upper house, the Senate became the focus for another judicial confirmation struggle that foreshadowed the battles to come in the 1980s. Chief Justice Earl Warren, fearing a Richard Nixon victory in the presidential election, decided to retire while Lyndon Johnson could still name his potential successor. The president wanted to select his close friend and political ally, Justice Abe Fortas, whom he had appointed to the Supreme Court in 1965. With Fortas thus elevated, Johnson would name a Texas friend, Homer Thornberry, from his seat on the Circuit Court to fill the remaining place on the Court. If Johnson had thought about the Senate carefully, he would have realized that such a scheme was designed to alienate members. Even though Johnson got the support of Dirksen for this move, he reckoned without the other Senate Republicans who believed that they would win the presidency in the fall and be able to secure their own choice to be Chief Justice. The result was the first Senate rejection of a Supreme Court nominee since John J. Parker in 1930.[43]

Years of ill treatment of the Senate and a misreading of the body's mood now came back to haunt Lyndon Johnson. The Republican conference rebelled against any deal that Dirksen had made. The dissidents issued a statement promising a negative vote and a filibuster against Johnson's nominees. Their leader, Robert Griffin of Michigan, argued that Johnson was abusing his powers and had to be defeated. Conservative Democrats, suspicious of Fortas, made it likely that the opposition would prevail. Richard Russell and Johnson saw their long friendship end over the episode. In fact, the administration had to struggle to get the Judiciary Committee to report the Fortas selection for a vote. When the nomination got to the floor, a filibuster ensued and the administration failed, by a vote of 45 to 43, to close off debate. In the end, Dirksen turned against Fortas when it became clear that his nomination was doomed to failure.[44]

The Fortas opponents advanced ideological arguments against the nomination. His liberal decisions on free speech, his critics charged, had made pornography more available and corrupted the nation's values. Though the jurist was qualified for his seat on the high court, his decisions on a number of sensitive areas such as crime in the streets had alienated conservatives in the Senate. They took their opportunity to exact political revenge. Fortas had also advised Johnson about policy matters while on the bench, and there were revelations that he had profited from his links with wealthy contributors. Nonetheless, the episode represented a prelude to other contested judicial confirmations that would occur within a year in the Nixon administration and then recur under Ronald Reagan.

The presidential election in 1968 produced a Republican victory for Richard M. Nixon over Hubert Humphrey and George Wallace. The outcome left the Senate and the House in Democratic hands though several key antiwar senators, such as Wayne Morse and Ernest Gruening, saw their careers ended at the polls. Nixon was the first president in the twentieth century to take office with a Congress that his opposition controlled. Still, with some finesse on the president's part, he could have managed the situation. Both Mansfield and Fulbright were ready to give Nixon some latitude to bring the Vietnam conflict to an end as he had signaled during the campaign that he would do.[45]

When the new administration attempted to both withdraw American troops and use air power to help South Vietnam gain victory in the conflict, the Senate mood turned to opposition in short order. Though he had served in the Senate for two years and been vice president for eight more, Nixon had scant respect for the institution or its members. He saw the upper house as filled with his political enemies, particularly Edward M. Kennedy of Massachusetts, and he intended to provide them with little respect or opportunities for capitalizing on his mistakes. Such liberal senators as Gaylord Nelson of Wisconsin, who promoted the idea of Earth Day, seemed to the White House to be using environmental issues to bash the president. In a moment of pique in 1973, Nixon revealed his inner feelings about the upper house when he told Hugh Scott of Pennsylvania, "You can vote any way you want. No one gives a shit what the Senate does or how the Senate does."[46]

Both parties saw leadership changes during 1969. Mansfield remained the majority leader. When the party conference met in January 1969, however, Edward Kennedy had the votes to be named majority whip over Russell Long, 31 to 26. Long, the son of Huey Long, had neglected the duties of the whip post and his drinking further undermined his standing with his colleagues. The move was seen as further evidence of Kennedy's presidential ambitions for 1972 or beyond. Whether Kennedy would prove proficient in the day-to-day duties of the whip was another matter. For the talented Long, the defeat led him to control his alcoholism and further his rise to power on the Senate Finance Committee.[47]

On the Republican side, Everett Dirksen was in failing health for much of 1969. He died later in the year. The GOP members elected Hugh Scott of Pennsylvania, a moderate who had been chosen minority whip in January. With his mustache and glasses, Scott looked like a mild-mannered lawmaker. In fact, he was a tough partisan who led his members effectively for the next seven years. Yet the affable Pennsylvanian, who was polite to his opponents, did not suit the Nixon White House. The president's aides, always impressed by those who acted tough, did not deem him partisan enough for the job. They labeled him a "machine politician" and a "hack." Nixon and Scott coexisted uneasily, and the minority leader would prove to be a skillful defender of the prerogatives of his institution against incursions from the men around the president.[48]

An initial confrontation between the upper house and the Nixon administration occurred over the president's proposal for an antiballistic missile system. First contemplated under the Johnson administration, the nation's missile defense would, so the White House argued, protect American deterrent capacity from a Soviet first strike. Opponents, led by Edward Kennedy and John Sherman Cooper, responded that the system would not work, was too expensive, and would intensify the arms race. The White House regarded the contest as the "first battle of 72, vs. Teddy Kennedy, and we *must* win." As a result, the administration mounted a maximum political effort to win the struggle. With the help of such sympathetic Democrats as Henry M. Jackson, the president's forces created a 50–50 tie on August 6, 1969, which Vice President Spiro Agnew broke in favor of the ABM system. The White House prevailed, but other contests with the Senate lay ahead.[49]

Richard Nixon also wanted to reshape the judiciary in a more conservative direction to counter the effects of what he believed to be judicial activism under Chief Justice Earl Warren. Nixon appointed Warren Burger to succeed Warren, a nomination that the Senate easily confirmed. Then investigative reporting disclosed that Justice Fortas had committed even greater ethical lapses that called into question his fitness to remain on the Court. The Justice had accepted money directly from a foundation established by a convicted stock swindler. Once Fortas resigned in 1969, the president nominated Judge Clement Haynesworth from an appeals court to fill the place. Since Haynesworth was from South Carolina and had showed skepticism about civil rights in some of his rulings, the appointment indicated Nixon's desire to reshape the high court in a manner that assisted the overall "southern strategy" of the new administration.[50]

Haynesworth had ethical problems of his own. Some of the companies in which he held stock had been litigants before his court. Organized labor and civil rights groups also announced their opposition to the nominee. That coalition proved more powerful and effective than the White House lobbying effort, and Haynesworth's confirmation was defeated when fifty-five senators, including seventeen Republicans, voted against him on November 21, 1969. An irritated Nixon promised to nominate another southerner. Meanwhile, Nixon excluded Minority Leader Scott and another Republican leader, Robert Griffin, from a White House meeting in retaliation for their votes against Haynesworth. Nixon, wrote his aide H. R. Haldeman, "is determined to hold to his line of the cold shoulder for those who don't stick with us."[51]

To show his contempt for the Senate, Nixon now selected a barely qual-ified jurist, G. Harold Carswell of Florida, as justice. Newspaper probes and other research revealed that Carswell was a mediocre judge and an overt racist. In one of the more bizarre moments in the history of the upper house, Roman Hruska, a Nebraska conservative, asserted that Carswell should be confirmed because "there are a lot of mediocre judges and people and lawyers. They are entitled to a little representation, aren't they, and a little chance?" As the White House aide Bryce Harlow told Nixon, sena-tors thought that Carswell was "a boob, a dummy," and, Harlow added, "What counter is there to that? He is." Carswell's nomination was defeated as well, with fifty-one votes against him. Nixon finally named Harry Black-mun, who was then easily confirmed.[52]

While the Senate feuded with Nixon over judicial appointments, other legislation reshaped how the chamber conducted its own affairs. The Legisla-tive Reorganization Act of 1970 provided for some opening up to the public of the proceedings of the two houses and modest limitations on the power of seniority that foreshadowed more intense changes in the rest of the decade. The legislation codified and expanded the role of partisanship in the staffing of committees. As the Senate became more ideological during the next two decades, the staff members, eager to impress their bosses, became a source of greater partisanship for the chamber as a whole.[53]

As the role of television increased with the expansion of the nightly net-work newscasts from fifteen minutes to half an hour in 1963, senators with presidential goals did as much public posturing as they did legislating. Indi-viduality flourished while the power of the Club waned. Southern Demo-crats such as Richard Russell, who was ill with emphysema, saw their power decrease. The retirement of Harry Byrd in November 1965 had taken away another key member of the southern contingent. As senatorial schedules became more hectic and constituent demands expanded, members found less time for interaction with their colleagues or participation in floor de-bate. Complaints about the frantic pace of Senate life grew more common. Reliance on staff also spread and senators interacted more with aides than with their colleagues.

Some of these shifts resulted from the escalating costs of running for office and seeking reelection. Winning an election in the television age put a pre-mium on personal attractiveness and image, rather than on a mastery of is-sues and policy. A perceptive look at how the Senate was being transformed in electoral terms came in a 1972 film, *The Candidate*. Robert Redford portrayed Bill McKay, an idealistic Democrat running for the Senate from California. The interplay of television and celebrity was observed in satirical fashion as McKay developed a winning public persona only to be left with the pointed question after his victory: "What do we do now?" The handsome, photogenic Redford became a cultural surrogate for the many empty suits who arrived in the chamber during the 1970s and 1980s.[54]

Hollywood and the media believed that the upper house was becoming emptier and less ideological. In the Senate as it existed, the real change was in the direction of greater partisanship as both Republicans and Democrats turned to harsher methods to achieve their ends. The Democrats, certain that their control would last, stressed reform and openness in the way the Senate worked. Republicans, more interested in policy outcomes and eventual majority status, pushed for ideological purity and the implementation of a conservative agenda. The outcome was a Senate that moved away from the older style of the Club and more in the direction of the contentious and highly partisan House of Representatives. What followed was a decade of contention and polarization in the upper house during the 1970s that laid the foundation for more partisanship and contention during the remainder of the century.

## CHAPTER FOURTEEN

# "Juggling Too Many Balls"

THE MOST ENDURING IMAGE OF THE SENATE DURING THE 1970S IS OF
Howard Baker of Tennessee at the Senate Watergate hearings. Sitting
in the hearing room with the committee chairman, Sam Ervin of North
Carolina, he framed the key question about Richard Nixon's involvement
in the political scandal: "What did the President know and when did he
know it?" That was the upper house during the decade—probing, questioning, and confronting chief executives and White House policies. In addition to the Watergate problem, senators sought to curb the war in Vietnam
through the Cooper-Church Amendment of 1970 and the War Powers Act
of 1973. Committees led by senators such as Frank Church of Idaho looked
into the performance of the American intelligence community and turned
up significant abuses in the way that clandestine information was acquired
and used in foreign policy. Richard Nixon, Gerald Ford, and Jimmy Carter
all felt the sting of Senate opposition to their initiatives. The perennial
question of the balance of power between the legislative and executive
branches was very much alive during this turbulent decade.[1]

During these years, members sensed that the Senate of the Club was giving
way to a new kind of political institution. Edmund Muskie of Maine said in
1975, "Days can go by when you don't run into more than one or two senators." Jacob Javits, a New York Republican, had a similar complaint four years
later: "There are just too many balls that we have to juggle at one time." The
importance of staff grew accordingly, and there emerged a bureaucracy beneath the actual members that conducted most of the day-to-day negotiations

about what was taking place in the institution itself. The Senate had more than 4,100 employees in 1971 and more than 6,900 a decade later. At the same time, the need to raise large sums of money for the next election resulted in senators' devoting more and more energy to accumulating funds rather than discussing the issues that involved substantive policy matters. The increasing efficiency of air travel facilitated regular trips back home to even distant states on weekends. Slowly the working week of the Senate shrank as members left on Fridays and returned on Mondays to get in a weekend of campaigning at home.[2]

These developments occurred while the tension with the Senate over Vietnam that had marked the first year of the Nixon presidency intensified in 1970. The White House sought both to extricate the nation from the conflict and to achieve some sort of military success. When the United States invaded Cambodia on April 30, 1970, nationwide protests erupted over this escalation of the conflict. Two senators, Frank Church of Idaho and John Sherman Cooper of Kentucky, stepped up efforts they had already begun to ban the use of funds for further military actions in the war. The two men made an unlikely pair. Church was the eloquent, ambitious Democrat who saw himself as the heir of William E. Borah and his tradition of involvement with foreign policy issues. Like "the Lion of Idaho," Church also had his eye on the White House. Cooper was a chain-smoking, inarticulate liberal Republican. They were convinced that the Vietnam War could not be won. In 1969 they proposed cutting off some aspects of funding for the conflict.[3]

The two senators then offered an amendment to the Foreign Military Sales Act in mid-May 1970 that would have ended the use of funds to support a ground or air war in Cambodia. Church said to the Foreign Relations Committee, "Too much blood has been lost, too much patience gone unrewarded, while the war continues to poison our society. If the Executive Branch will not take the initiative, then the Congress and the people must." The Foreign Relations Committee endorsed what was known as the Cooper-Church Amendment, and the measure went to the floor, where a prolonged debate ensued about presidential war power and the proper role of Congress.[4]

Nixon and his aides disliked the amendment, which they saw as a curb on the president's executive authority. A bitter battle raged in May and June to water down or kill the offending language. Efforts to modify the wording of the amendment failed on the floor, and on June 30, the full Senate endorsed Cooper-Church by 58 to 37. The House then tied up the bill in conference for six months before the amendment was added to a foreign aid bill and dropped from the original military assistance bill. Nixon signed the legislation in early January 1971. The battle over Cooper-Church represented an attempt to reassert congressional war power after the presidential excesses of the 1960s. More efforts to rein in the White House would follow as the 1970s progressed.[5]

The clamor that erupted after the Cambodian invasion in the spring of 1970, along with the persistence of the Vietnam War, formed the backdrop for the elections in the fall of that year. The Nixon administration hoped to use popular discontent with the antiwar protests as a means of forging a Republican Senate majority. Nixon's priority was to oust such southern liberals as Ralph Yarborough of Texas and Albert Gore, Sr., of Tennessee, who represented states moving in a conservative direction. Other endangered incumbents were Gale McGee in Wyoming and Thomas Dodd in Connecticut. The Senate had rebuked Dodd in 1967 for financial improprieties, and the voters in the Nutmeg State had cooled on him. Ready to use social issues such as a fear of crime, along with some thinly veiled racist appeals, the Nixon forces felt confident about their chances during the spring.[6]

The slowing economy and Democratic resilience, however, limited Republican gains in the fall. One of Nixon's speeches on a campaign tour was aired just before the election. It had a heavy emphasis on protesters and violence, and even Republicans concluded that it went too far. In contrast, Edmund Muskie, who provided the Democratic response, came across as judicious and responsible. The episode gave the Democrats a much-needed lift. Some other phases of the GOP scenario did not work out as the Nixon operatives had planned. Yarborough fell to Lloyd M. Bentsen, Jr., in the Texas Democratic primary, but Bentsen then outpaced George H. W. Bush in the fall election. Albert Gore went down at the hands of William Brock in Tennessee, but McGee survived in Wyoming. Lowell Weicker won the Connecticut seat for the Republicans in a three-way race with Dodd and another Democrat. Overall the GOP picked up only two seats, for forty-five, leaving the Democrats with fifty-five. The Democratic ascendancy that had begun after the 1958 election was slowly ebbing away, but it would not disappear for another decade.[7]

The Democrats had to choose their leadership once again in early 1971. Mansfield faced no challenge as majority leader, but Edward Kennedy was not so fortunate in his role as majority whip. Ever since becoming the whip in 1969 Kennedy had been lax in discharging the duties of that position, as far as his fellow senators were concerned. Kennedy was most interested in issues. He had little time for the routine of favors, listening to opinions of his colleagues, and cultivating senators that the job demanded. As well, his involvement in the automobile accident in July 1969 that took the life of his passenger, Mary Jo Kopechne, had made him vulnerable. Robert Byrd of West Virginia saw his opening and quietly began rounding up support to replace Kennedy when the caucus met in January 1971.[8]

While Byrd did the work of assisting his fellow senators with their personal needs, Kennedy had been losing some potential allies. He had alienated J. William Fulbright and the Foreign Relations Committee when he intruded on their turf. He had also opposed spending programs that benefited such senators as the hawkish Henry M. Jackson of Washington. When the voting took place on January 21, 1971, Byrd won by 31 to 24, putting him on the path to be the majority leader whenever Mansfield retired.

The ambitious and resourceful Byrd was fifty-three when he took over as whip. Orphaned as a child, he worked in shipyards during World War II, ran for the West Virginia legislature in 1946, and moved on to the U.S. House six years later. He won a Senate seat in the Democratic sweep of 1958. Byrd had been a member of the Ku Klux Klan as a youth, and he voted against the 1964 Civil Rights Act. Like Lyndon Johnson before him, Byrd labored with tireless zeal to ingratiate himself with the Senate elders and create an independent power base. He could be folksy, and his country-style violin playing became a trademark. Devoted to Senate traditions, he defended filibusters while ensuring that his state was showered with federal appropriations. As he showed against the far more famous Kennedy, Byrd was an effective tactician, and his impact on the institution and its history would prove significant.[9]

During the Kennedy-Byrd contest, Richard Russell died after a long illness from the emphysema that his lifelong smoking had exacerbated. Eulogists spoke of his reputation for integrity and his special standing in the Senate as an elder statesman. His virulent and unrelenting racism went largely unmentioned in the summaries of his career and contributions. On that issue, he allowed race and his hatred for black Americans to guide his decisions. The qualities for which his colleagues admired him were ones that he extended to them as fellow white Americans. Had Russell had his way, African Americans would always have been excluded from full equality. That such a cramped spirit attained "greatness" in the Senate says more about the institution than about Russell himself.

The onset of the presidential election of 1972 overshadowed Russell's passing. The contest brought Democratic senators into the race for the nomination in a crowded field of aspirants. Edmund Muskie, Hubert Humphrey, Henry M. Jackson, and George McGovern all sought their party's prize. To foil them and stymie the potential of Edward Kennedy, Richard Nixon embarked on a campaign of political dirty tricks and crimes that led to the Watergate scandal.

In the short run, Nixon achieved his goals. First, his operatives drove Edmund Muskie, generally considered the strongest candidate, from the race with false stories attacking his wife. The White House and the Committee to Reelect the President (CREEP) also did what they could to have George McGovern, a liberal from South Dakota who seemed the weakest contender, win the Democratic nomination. When McGovern capitalized on the antiwar sentiment in his party to defeat his colleagues and gain the prize, that result served Nixon's purposes too.

After a tumultuous and badly managed convention, the Democratic nominee was tabbed as a sure loser. And so it proved in November 1972. But although the Democratic national ticket went down before the Nixon tide, the Democrats gained two seats in the Senate and thus retained the ability to investigate the administration and stymie Nixon's initiatives. That alignment would lead to a confrontation with Nixon as the Watergate scandal unfolded in 1973.[10]

The 1972 election saw an end to the career of Margaret Chase Smith, now the only woman in the upper house since Maurine Neuberger's departure in 1967. The aloof and imperious Smith was now seventy-five, and her connections with her Maine constituents had frayed during her fourth term. She faced a tough opponent in forty-eight-year-old Bill Hathaway, and she campaigned with something less than the vigor she had shown in previous years. Smith lost the race by thirty thousand votes even as Nixon was carrying the state. As she said of her defeat, "They wanted someone younger."[11]

Despite Richard Nixon's landslide victory, Congress persisted in its efforts to assert itself on such issues as war and peace. In 1970 Jacob Javits had introduced a resolution on war powers designed to put limits on presidents' power to commit troops overseas. Now, Javits found support from those who opposed the Vietnam conflict and from conservatives such as Democrat John

Stennis of Mississippi, chair of the Armed Services Committee, who, even though he supported the war, thought that the executive had gained too much power in foreign policy. The War Powers Resolution was adopted in 1973 by a strong majority in the Senate and a narrower total in the House. The resolution said that the president had sixty days to gain congressional endorsement of a combat involvement overseas. Otherwise, he would have to withdraw the units. Richard Nixon vetoed the resolution, but Congress overrode the veto on November 7, 1973. In the years that followed, presidents ignored the War Powers Resolution, and it proved impossible to enforce. It remained significant only as a sign of congressional unease with executive power during the Nixon years.[12]

Mike Mansfield was determined that the Senate should investigate the reports of illegal campaign practices during the 1972 election. He decided that Edward M. Kennedy should not be involved because of his possible presidential candidacy in 1976. At the same time, the Judiciary Committee, chaired by James O. Eastland of Mississippi, was not a suitable venue because of the closeness of Eastland and the president. Mansfield opted for a select committee, with no 1976 hopefuls on the panel, to probe what had occurred. Sam Ervin of North Carolina became the chair of that group with Howard Baker of Tennessee as the ranking member on the Republican side.[13]

By the time the Ervin committee opened televised hearings in the spring of 1973, the Nixon administration was already in deep political difficulty. The break-in at the Democratic National Committee headquarters in the Watergate building in June 1972 had led to criminal trials and newspaper coverage of the interlocking crimes of the Nixon White House. The probe into campaign excesses gripped the nation as White House insiders like former presidential counsel John W. Dean told of the president's efforts to cover up the burgeoning scandal. The key moment of the senatorial inquiry came when Alexander Butterfield, a White House aide, revealed that the president had installed a taping system in his office. This disclosure meant that Congress and the legal system could obtain evidence to help them decide the extent of Nixon's personal and criminal involvement in the Watergate scandal. The Ervin committee made an important contribution to the chain of events that eventually drove Nixon from office.[14]

In the process, the hearings elevated the public image of the members of the Ervin panel. The chairman came across as a folksy defender of the Constitution (though he would not extend many of its guarantees to African

The Watergate inquiry was one of the most famous and controversial Senate investigations in history. Howard Baker's (left)
question "What did the president know and when did he know
it?" made the Tennessee Republican a national figure. (Senator
Sam Ervin, center) (SENATE HISTORICAL OFFICE)

Americans) against the depredations of Nixon's White House. The key
question from Howard Baker about the president's knowledge of Watergate
events probably arose from a desire to protect the incumbent, but it ended
up as an implicit assault on Nixon's shaky integrity. A Connecticut Republican, Lowell Weicker, defied his party to push for a full accounting of the
misdeeds of Watergate, a tactic that did not endear him to his colleagues.
Overall, the prestige of the Senate increased during the constitutional confrontation with the presidency.[15]

Another consequence of the unfolding Watergate imbroglio was an assertion of congressional authority over the budget process. In order to control
spending, Nixon had sought to impound appropriated funds, leaving Congress without real control of the money. Congress decided that lawmakers

needed to make clear their intention to remain on an equal footing with the president. A budget law would also enable legislators to address the rising problem of budget deficits. Passed in July 1974, the Congressional Budget and Impoundment Act set up a Congressional Budget Office and created budget committees in both houses. As Edmund Muskie remarked, "Congress has seen its control over the federal purse strings ebb away over the past fifty years because of its inability to get a grip on the over-all budget." The 1974 law represented a step to redress the imbalance that Muskie had noted.[16]

Out of the revelations during the Watergate inquiries about illegal campaign contributions and other excesses came an effort, led by Edward Kennedy, to reform the system of financing elections. In 1973 Kennedy had worked with the Republican leader, Hugh Scott, a supporter of public financing, to craft such a measure, but their proposal ran into conservative opposition, led by Democrat James Allen of Alabama. "If a man seeks the Presidential nomination," Allen contended, "it is not up to the American public to pay his way." The campaign finance proposals were attached to a bill to raise the limit on the national debt, legislation that had to be passed for the government to keep functioning. Coming up near the end of the session, the debt law was vulnerable to a filibuster that Allen started on November 30, 1973. Mansfield and the Democrats could not achieve cloture, the election language was dropped, and the issue rolled over until 1974.[17]

Kennedy, Scott, and the reformers then had better results. They overcame another Allen filibuster in April and then passed the bill. The House was less enthusiastic, and rejected federal funding for congressional elections (a move that did not displease the Senate). After a conference between the two houses, the final bill applied federal funding only to presidential races. The power of incumbency in Congress had been safeguarded.[18]

The 1974 elections came after the resignation of Richard Nixon and the accession of Gerald Ford. Voter discontent with the Republicans over Watergate and an economic downturn made it a tough year for the Grand Old Party, and the Democrats added three seats. The Democratic tide helped such potentially endangered liberals as Frank Church, George McGovern, and Gaylord Nelson to win additional terms. For the moment the Democratic hold on the Senate seemed to have a new chance of continued dominance.[19]

A notable casualty of the 1974 elections was the chairman of the Senate Foreign Relations Committee, J. William Fulbright. After thirty years in Washington, aristocratic, haughty Fulbright had lost touch with his constituents. His challenger, Dale Bumpers, was the governor and an adept campaigner. By the time the Democratic primary occurred, it was evident that Bumpers was going to win, and he administered a decisive defeat to Fulbright.[20]

In New Hampshire, the contest for an open seat between the Republican, Louis Wyman, and the Democrat, John A. Durkin, resulted in a virtual tie. The Democratic leadership referred the contest to the Senate Rules Committee, where a partisan vote would decide which of the two men should be seated. Republicans complained that Robert Byrd and the Democrats were trying to steal a seat that the GOP had won. "It's just as dirty and rotten as was Watergate a year ago," said Barry Goldwater, back in the Senate since winning an election in 1968.[21]

The Durkin-Wyman issue dragged on for months in 1975, until the Senate decided to have another election. In that contest, the Democrat, Durkin, emerged victorious. What made the episode important, however, was its effect on Republican unity. The minority believed that the Democrats, led by Byrd, were using unscrupulous tactics to capture a seat from the Republicans. According to a key GOP aide, the Democrats thus "solidified the Republican side of the aisle" in 1975 and the years that followed. From this newfound cohesion came more effective challenges to Democratic supremacy at the end of the Gerald Ford administration and into the presidency of Jimmy Carter.[22]

Democratic success in 1974 in the wake of Watergate produced lasting changes in how Congress operated. The House felt the effects more than the Senate did with committee chairs ousted from their longtime positions by the new liberal members elected in the reaction against Watergate. The consequences on the Senate, where each member acted individually, proved more subtle. During the second half of the 1970s, for example, the authority of a dominant conservative chairman such as John C. Stennis of Armed Services was slowly whittled down through the efforts of his more liberal Democratic colleagues on the committee. Resurgent Republicans on Stennis's committee, led by their ranking member, John Tower, capitalized on this opportunity to increase their influence over the panel.[23]

Conservative Republicans felt disadvantaged during the long spell of Democratic dominance, and in 1974 they took steps to organize themselves through the creation of what they called a Senate Steering Committee. The goal was to promote determined resistance to the Democratic leadership and to pressure their own party leaders to be more conservative. Founded by

Carl T. Curtis of Nebraska and James McClure of Idaho in May 1974, the group sought to infuse discipline into the minority. "I got tired of being defeated on the floor," Curtis said later. "I was disappointed that one of my colleagues would have a good amendment that was defeated because nobody knew anything about it. I decided what we needed was a little organization."[24]

Organizations outside the Senate also contributed to a resurgence of conservatism. During the mid-1970s, the impact of right-wing pressure groups, based on effective direct-mail campaigns from many small donors, began to be felt in the Senate. These organizations could rouse their membership to flood Capitol Hill with messages about a single-issue controversy such as abortion or the Equal Rights Amendment. Because of their increasing clout within the Republican Party, the political action committees and direct-mail campaigns soon moved the center of gravity of the Grand Old Party further to the right. Senators were not seen as representatives of a state who had the autonomy to vote as they deemed best on peripheral issues. Now every recorded tally could be used as ammunition to launch a mail campaign to exert pressure on lawmakers much in the fashion of Robert La Follette and his roll calls. Campaigning and fund-raising were transformed into round-the-clock enterprises. Incumbents complained of the pressures of intense efforts to seek money for the next campaign, and then the next.[25]

During early 1975 the perennial unresolved issue of the filibuster once again appeared to bedevil the Senate. Despite the successes in closing off debate over the civil rights laws of the 1960s, the use of extended debate became more prevalent. Ten cloture votes occurred each year from 1971 to 1973. Efforts took place in 1969 and 1971 to change the cloture rule to make sixty votes the threshold needed to cut off debate, but these initiatives failed to win Senate approval. The question then came up again in January 1975.[26]

The persistence of the filibuster into the 1970s owed a great deal to the efforts of James Browning Allen of Alabama. Schooled in the rules of the legislature of his home state, the determined and resourceful Allen spent much of the decade before his death in June 1978 devising ways to use the procedures of the upper house against the liberal legislation he so much disliked. Largely forgotten now, Allen did as much as any single individual to shape the workings of the modern Senate.

Before coming to Washington in 1969 at the age of fifty-six, Allen had been the lieutenant governor of Alabama during the early 1950s and then again, under Governor George Wallace, from 1963 to 1967. When the

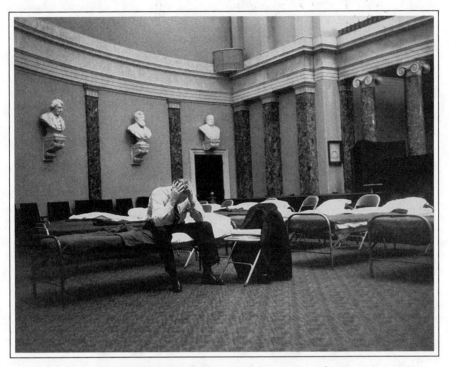

Some filibusters led to all-night sessions when senators had to rely on cots to get some rest. In this photograph, a tired lawmaker fights the effects of exhaustion. (SENATE HISTORICAL OFFICE)

longtime incumbent, Senator Lister Hill, announced that he would not be a candidate for reelection, Allen entered the primary and won the runoff to take the seat. His goal, he proclaimed, was "to put more Alabama beliefs into our nation's capital." His own credo included an ample supply of racism, conservatism on economic issues, and a disdain for the mainstream convictions of national Democrats. He brought with him to Washington the expertise on legislative rules he had gained as the presiding officer of the state senate.[27]

Allen took on the often boring chore of presiding over the Senate, which few of his colleagues wished to discharge. He capitalized on the experience to learn the rules thoroughly and to find ways they could be employed to advance his agenda. As one observer of Allen later wrote, "He trained himself in what has become his favorite form of combat[:] cool, quiet, paralyzing tactics of parliamentary guerrilla warfare." Polite, affable, and determined, Allen proved to be a master of the subtle arts of legislative obstruction.[28]

Allen's most significant innovation became known as the post-cloture filibuster. Usually, when a cloture vote had ended debate, each senator had only one hour for further comments on the pending bill. Allen realized that if he held onto his time carefully, he could use his opportunities for any number of delaying motions. He would be allowed, for example, to bring up a single amendment, ask for the language of the amendment to be read, insist on quorum calls, and otherwise stretch out the process to slow down the Senate. The time that was spent to remove these procedural obstacles did not count against Allen's allocated one hour of debate. The prospects for protracted stalling were almost limitless. Once Allen had shown the potential of such an approach, other senators opposed to him ideologically could use his methods to their own advantage. The filibuster had achieved a revived, more efficient form, and the means by which the Senate could be ensnared in procedural tangles had reached a new sophistication. By 1975, it seemed that something had to be done to change the cloture rule again.[29]

Walter Mondale, a Minnesota Democrat, and James Pearson, a Kansas Republican, sponsored a cloture change. To succeed, they needed a parliamentary ruling from the presiding officer, Vice President Nelson A. Rockefeller, that the Senate was not a continuing body that carried over from session to session. If such a ruling was adopted, then a simple majority of the Senate could change the rules at the beginning of a congressional session. If Rockefeller decided the other way, the reformers would need two-thirds to prevail.

When Pearson offered his motion, Mike Mansfield raised a point of order that the Pearson-Mondale proposal violated the Senate rules. In a break with precedent and rules, Vice President Rockefeller did not rule on the point of order, as was customary, but instead submitted the question to the body for a vote. This departure from usual Senate procedure confused the cloture issue. A parliamentary battle ensued in which Rockefeller came under attack from James B. Allen and others. In the end, the senators voted 51 to 42 to table Mansfield's point of order. The Senate had apparently agreed that a simple majority could change the rules.

Over the next two weeks, the leadership of both parties decided to overturn what Rockefeller had done because it went against Senate precedents. The members reconsidered the vote by which the Mansfield point of order had been tabled and affirmed that Mansfield's position was the correct one. At the same time, the reformers won something of what they wanted. From then on, according to a compromise devised by Senator Byrd, sixty votes would be the standard for approving a motion on cloture during debate on a bill. A two-thirds majority would be needed for any change in the rules. This compromise remained in effect for the rest of the twentieth century. The problem of the post-cloture filibuster, however, had not been solved. That would have to be addressed in the years to come.[30]

Changes in the filibuster procedures, while important for the institution itself, did not attract much public attention in 1975. A controversial probe of the Central Intelligence Agency, on the other hand, aroused widespread interest at the time and produced effects that resonate into the present. In January 1975 the upper house created the Senate Select Committee on Intelligence Activities, popularly known as the Church Committee after its chairman, Frank Church of Idaho. Although it existed for only a little more than a year, the panel has become famous in Senate history. According to one interpretation from conservatives, the Church Committee had a long-lasting negative effect on the American intelligence community. Following the terrorist attacks on September 11, 2001, for example, the *Wall Street Journal* labeled the Church hearings "the moment that our nation moved from an intelligence to anti-intelligence footing."[31]

The Church inquiry grew out of sensational press revelations regarding CIA excesses that appeared in the wake of the Watergate scandals. In late December 1974 reporter Seymour Hersh disclosed that the agency had spied on Americans inside the country in violation of its charter, which forbade such activities. There were also reports of assassination plots run by the CIA as well as the use of drugs against dissidents and enemies of the country. The Ford administration sought to dampen the public outcry with its own commissions, but pressure grew for Congress to act. Democrats decided to conduct such an investigation in January 1975 along with a similar probe in the House. The select committee of six Democrats and five Republicans was duly established.[32]

Frank Church had an abiding interest in intelligence matters, and he was also contemplating a run for the presidency in 1976. He lobbied hard with Mansfield to be the chairman of the select committee, and the majority leader acquiesced. Critics on the left at the time thought that the Idaho senator was too accommodating to the agency and its needs. At the same time friends of the CIA resisted any disclosures about its performance.

Church tried to find a middle ground by cooperating with the two major Republicans on the committee, John Tower of Texas, the vice chairman, and Barry Goldwater. The committee became embroiled in controversies over political assassinations, particularly those that took place during the Kennedy administration. It did not reveal the identity of any active agents, and there is little evidence that national security was ever compromised. The CIA had gotten out of control, and further congressional oversight was an appropriate response.[33]

Some halting steps toward oversight occurred as a result of the Church hearings and the information that they disclosed. In the end, little changed as far as the intelligence agency was concerned. In light of the events surrounding September 11, 2001, it would probably have been better for the country if more sustained legislative supervision of the CIA had taken place. The 1980s and 1990s did not see such excellent performance by the agency in measuring the threat from the Soviet Union or in anticipating the dangers of terrorism as to justify criticism of what Frank Church and his colleagues had sought to accomplish. To a large degree, their efforts revealed what had been done in the past and did not look forward to making the CIA a better instrument of American foreign policy. The problem with the Church probe was not that it was too hard on the spying arm of the American government but that it did not do enough to make the CIA an asset to the American people.

Church conducted his hearings with the 1976 presidential race in mind. Many other Democratic lawmakers saw that year as a chance to move up to the White House; Lloyd Bentsen of Texas and Henry M. Jackson of Washington also tried to gain the nod to oppose Gerald Ford. The inability to campaign full-time and discharge duties in the chamber, however, worked against these aspirants. To the surprise of most observers, Jimmy Carter, the former governor of Georgia, emerged from the crowded field to gain the prize and in the end the presidency itself. Church did the best of the three senators, but his late entry into the race meant that he had no chance of overtaking Carter.[34]

Mike Mansfield's Senate career ended in 1976. On March 4, he told his colleagues that he would not seek reelection. There was, he said, "a time to stay and a time to go. Thirty-four years is not a long time, but it is time enough." The tributes poured in to a man whom most members of the body on both sides of the aisle liked and respected for his honesty and candor. If he had the guile of Lyndon Johnson, he kept it well hidden and relied instead on openness and equity in the way he treated fellow lawmakers. Yet Mansfield sensed that the Senate he had first known was changing, and not for the better. Civility and a sense of fair play were giving way to more partisan considerations. Mansfield himself in part allowed these developments to occur on his watch because of his indulgence of the whims of individual senators. As one assessment of his tenure as majority leader notes, "He was less creative than he might have been, more permissive than he should have been, and not as attentive to the Senate's day-to-day business [as] many thought he needed to be." Mansfield will always stand in the shadow of the more sensational and controversial Lyndon Johnson, but his record in the position, in terms of laws passed and programs adopted, will bear comparison with the accomplishments of his predecessor.[35]

The 1976 election brought Jimmy Carter to the White House and a resurgence of Democratic dominance on Capitol Hill. The majorities in the House and Senate equaled those of the Democratic heyday in the 1960s, but this ascendancy would prove to be very short-lived. During the Carter years, the Democratic majorities vanished. For the moment, however, the two parties in the Senate turned to the selection of their leaders in January 1977.

For the Democrats the leading contender was Robert Byrd. Through his ability to anticipate the needs of the members and his endless service of their desires, he had established an unassailable position. Long gone were the memories, as one cynical journalist wrote, of the days when he ran around "in the woods wearing a sheet and calling for the rebirth of the Ku Klux Klan." He faced a halfhearted challenge from Hubert Humphrey, who was ill with the cancer that would kill him a year later. Humphrey received word from his supporters that "You don't have the troops and we think the best thing to do is to withdraw from the race." Byrd was partially magnanimous in victory. He would not give Humphrey a meaningful role in the leadership but did agree to have the Minnesota senator and former vice president named deputy president pro tem.[36]

Byrd soon made it clear that he would not operate in the permissive style of his predecessor. "He is going to run this place more like LBJ than Mike Mansfield," a Senate insider told *Newsweek*. That was an overstatement; Byrd never achieved Johnson's dominance of the upper house in his career. His partisanship and his capacity for what John Tower of Texas called "flatulent indignation" sometimes grated on his colleagues in both parties. Nonetheless, Byrd would prove to be an efficient steward of Democratic fortunes over the next thirteen years.[37]

The Republicans conducted a more spirited contest, between Howard Baker of Tennessee and Robert Griffin of Michigan. Baker had tried twice before to challenge Hugh Scott for the leadership and lost each time. When Scott declared in the late winter of 1976 that he would not be returning to the Senate, jockeying broke out to be the next minority leader. Baker was in a position where he had to win or be relegated to subordinate status within the Republican ranks. Robert Griffin had been the minority whip for seven years and should have had the advantage, but he had not gathered the necessary votes and lacked the skills that Baker possessed to win over wavering members. Baker was a conservative, the son-in-law of Everett Dirksen, and an affable leader who would perform well in public settings. When the votes were counted, Baker eked out a 19–17 victory. The winner told the press, "I wish the President well. I hope he prospers and succeeds but we must exercise our constitutional authority to agree or disagree."[38]

Jimmy Carter did not get off to a promising start with either Republicans or Democrats in the upper house. The new president and his top aides came to Washington convinced that they had little to learn from the leaders on Capitol Hill. The White House devoted scant attention to congressional relations and treated lawmakers as political inferiors. The result was immediate resistance and displeasure from the veteran legislators. The Democratic majority soon experienced signs of strain.[39]

By 1977 James Allen had refined his technique to perfect the post-cloture filibuster. He did not so much talk a bill to death as inflict procedural wounds that produced inordinate delays. Soon liberal colleagues saw what Allen was doing as something they could try as well. The Senate is very imitative, and when a parliamentary action succeeds it quickly gets adopted by all sides. Robert Byrd watched what Allen was accomplishing, and he knew that steps had to be taken to rein in the post-cloture filibuster. His opportunity came in September 1977 over a bill to deregulate natural gas. In the debate on that measure, Lloyd Bentsen and James Pearson offered a substitute that would over time have ended price controls on new natural gas discoveries. The Senate then invoked cloture on the Bentsen-Pearson bill. At that point, two liberal senators, Howard Metzenbaum of Ohio and James Abourezk of South Dakota, commenced a post-cloture filibuster that went on for twelve days. Byrd recruited Vice President Walter Mondale in his position as president of the Senate to help him in the effort to restrict these post-cloture tactics. Mondale recognized Byrd, who then called up the dilatory amendments one after the other. The vice president declared them out of order and would not allow senators to appeal his rulings. When a furor erupted, Byrd took to the floor to tell his colleagues and Mondale that it was "long past time, Mr. President, to stop this filibuster, and to stop the abuse of the Senate and its rules."[40]

Byrd prevailed, and precedents were adopted that put restrictions on the right of senators to engage in the post-cloture tactics that Allen had made famous. These changes were codified into Senate rules in 1979. However, the devils that Allen had unleashed were not easily tamed. The Alabaman had shown ways to bend the rules to keep talkathons going, and the ingenuity of other senators ensured that there would be fresh post-cloture filibusters in the future. He had several willing disciples in Jesse Helms of North Carolina and Orrin Hatch of Utah, who learned well what Allen had to teach. The capacity of the Senate to function efficiently had been permanently impaired.

The difficulties that the Carter administration suffered during its first year made the Democrats in the Senate more vulnerable to the well-organized and resurgent Republicans. Though winning control of the upper house still seemed out of reach, the Grand Old Party anticipated gains in the 1978 elections. One issue that appeared to be promising for the Republicans came when the White House negotiated two treaties with Panama returning control of the Canal to that country and allowing the United States to provide military defense for the waterway. The Carter administration contended that the United States could not defend the Canal against the Panamanians and that the 1903 treaty that Theodore Roosevelt had imposed was now a relic of a vanished era. It was time to turn the Canal over to its proper owner. Conservative Republicans, led by presidential candidate Ronald Reagan, regarded the pacts as a sellout of American interests. A loud and powerful lobby came into existence that tried to stymie the treaties in the Senate in 1978. James Allen was one of the leaders in the upper house in the campaign against approval of the Panama initiatives.[41]

For one of the few times during his troubled presidency, to gain approval of the treaties, Jimmy Carter mounted a well-focused lobbying campaign. The White House enlisted prominent Americans to endorse the pacts and made their case to the media with skill. The president sold his position to senators such as Russell Long of Louisiana, who then helped to bring along wavering legislators. Frank Church, now chairman of the Foreign Relations

Committee, led the battle on the floor against the conservative attacks from Allen and Republicans such as Paul Laxalt of Nevada and Orrin Hatch.[42]

The struggle during the winter and spring of 1978 finally resulted in the approval of both treaties by identical votes of 68 to 32. Robert Byrd helped in fashioning language about the treaties that wooed Howard Baker and just enough Republicans to produce victory. The majority leader's tactics allowed time for momentum to build behind the pacts. Frank Church, now the chair of the Foreign Relations Committee, played a central part in the approval of the treaties. The White House and the Democrats had survived a major test, but, as it turned out, at a serious political cost to the majority party. The Republican right had been energized and would demonstrate its power in the congressional elections that followed.[43]

By 1978 the Carter presidency and Senate Democrats faced restive voters and worsening electoral prospects. Inflation, rising energy prices, and an increasing tax burden fueled discontent with Washington and incumbents. Carter seemed an inept president who could not work well even with members of his own party. Republicans coalesced behind the idea of cutting income taxes, a strategy on which they would rely for the rest of the century. One irritant for the administration was removed when a heart attack claimed the life of James Allen in June 1978. On the hustings, however, the resurgent Republicans were the party with the momentum going into the fall balloting.

When the votes were counted, the GOP had a net gain of three seats so that the Democratic advantage now stood fifty-nine to forty-one. More important, the tone of the upper house became more conservative. Moderate Republicans were defeated when Clifford Case lost to the Democrat Bill Bradley in New Jersey and Paul Tsongas ousted the two-term Republican incumbent Edward Brooke in Massachusetts. Robert Griffin lost in Michigan to his Democratic challenger, Carl Levin. The Republicans added conservative newcomers in Thad Cochran of Mississippi, Gordon Humphrey of New Hampshire, and Larry Pressler from South Dakota. William Cohen was a moderate GOP addition from Maine. Nancy Kassebaum of Kansas, daughter of one-time presidential candidate Alf Landon, brought a female presence back to the chamber. If the Republicans nominated a strong presidential candidate in 1980, their prospects for regaining control of the Senate, so improbable after the 1976 election, might become a reality.[44]

With the uninspiring Carter administration sowing discord and restiveness among the Democrats, the Republicans built up their organizational strength during the concluding years of the decade. Superior fund-raising techniques added to the emerging advantage for the GOP. Direct-mailing committees with a conservative bent, developed by such masters of the art as Richard Viguerie, produced impressive results for challengers to liberal Democratic senators who would be up for reelection in 1980. Political action committees with a single-issue focus mounted aggressive advertising campaigns against their targets. With names such as the Committee for a Survival of Free Congress and the National Conservative Political Action Committee, these groups softened up the liberals in advance of the election itself. Some Republicans questioned the effectiveness of these endeavors, but in 1979–80 they worked better than anyone realized going into the voting.[45]

Both the Democrats and the Carter administration gave their rivals ample ammunition as the 1980 contest neared. Edward Kennedy challenged the president for the nomination, but his initial television appearance of the campaign revealed an inarticulate and unconvincing figure. Kennedy proved to be a nuisance to the incumbent; his sharp attacks wounded the president. He did not, however, succeed in shaking Carter's hold on the party. The takeover of the American embassy in Tehran by Iranian militants, and the captivity of more than fifty hostages, provided a continuing narrative that ate away at Carter's political standing in the nation. With interest rates rising and inflation rampant, many Americans felt less prosperous and confident than they had earlier in the 1970s.[46]

On the Republican side Ronald Reagan of California defeated his rivals and gained the nomination easily, promising lower taxes and greater defense spending to restore the country to its former preeminence. He was the party's strongest choice, and its senatorial candidates found they had a powerful force at the top of their ticket whose popularity lifted the campaigns of Republicans good and bad throughout the fall of 1980. The result was that longtime liberal senators found themselves under assault and in danger of losing their elections as the campaign progressed. Those incumbents who came from states where the Republicans usually did well in presidential contests found themselves in the most difficulty.

As the campaign neared its end, a Republican takeover of the Senate seemed imminent. In Idaho, Frank Church was in a tight race with his rival, Steve Symms. Birch Bayh in Indiana, George McGovern in South Dakota, Gaylord Nelson in Wisconsin, Warren Magnuson in Washington, and John C. Culver in Iowa faced similar problems. All these Democrats went down before the Reagan tide in 1980.[47]

Other Democrats faced more personal dilemmas. Herman Talmadge, a conservative southern Democrat, encountered voter unhappiness because of his alcoholism, marital problems, and assorted ethical issues. The Senate had "denounced" his conduct in October 1979. Harrison Williams of New Jersey, another senator with a drinking problem, had been caught up in the "Abscam" scandal in which the Justice Department targeted venal lawmakers. Williams was indicted and later convicted for involvement in a crooked mining scheme. With the combination of ethical lapses and ideological currents running against them, the Democrats were embattled. The electorate wanted conservatives and voted that way.[48]

On Election Day in 1980 the Republicans and Ronald Reagan triumphed. Most of the endangered Democrats, except for Alan Cranston in California, were defeated, and the GOP picked up twelve seats to gain a majority with fifty-three members. A happy Howard Baker greeted his colleagues with the salutation "Mr. Chairman." A happy Mark Hatfield woke up on the day after the election and told his wife, "You are now sleeping with a committee chairman." After twenty-five years of Democratic control since the 1954 election, the Republicans were back in charge. John Tower told the press, "We have to show our ability to manage well the Senate's affairs."[49]

The capacity of the Senate to play a constructive role in national politics had significantly slipped during the 1970s. The increasing effect of outside money on campaigns and the resulting emphasis on the "money chase" meant that legislative business often took second place to the insatiable demands of fund-raising and reelection. Leaders in both parties discovered that it was more difficult to discipline their members and produce coherent programs. Having come to the upper house usually through their own efforts rather than the support of their parties, senators operated as freelance politicians. Republicans, however, resolved to be more disciplined, to assist the presidency of Ronald Reagan. That collective determination would be tested during the 1980s, when the Senate experienced the consequences of the polarization and partisanship that the 1970s had brought to the upper house.

## CHAPTER FIFTEEN

# A Ruder Senate

DURING THE 1980S, THE SENATE ECHOED WITH COMPLAINTS ABOUT THE loss of the civility and mutual understanding that had once characterized the chamber. Much of this nostalgia was misplaced; the upper house had always been combative and partisan. Memories softened the hard edges of senatorial history. The episodes of alcoholism, womanizing, and graft faded into obscurity. So too did the partisan tensions of the McCarthy era and the 1960s. What remained was a legend of a collegial time and place when politicians worked together for the national good. Nonetheless, there were, in the griping of senators in both parties, recurrent themes that the Senate was changing, and not for the better. The Senate, said Howard Baker of Tennessee as he prepared to leave office in 1984, "cannot fight a guerrilla war over every issue every time." In fact, that was what the Senate had begun to do during the 1980s as single-issue groups pressed lawmakers to fight to the last ditch for a particular cause or idea.[1]

The six-year term, which once stretched out for a new member with time to think and reflect, was now a marathon run where the new senator had to begin fund-raising upon taking office. "Senators, like representatives, now seem to be running continuously for reelection," observed a *Newsweek* staffer in 1983. The average senator was caught in a never-ending round of asking for money, lining up donors, and providing favors for well-heeled constituents. Money sloshed around Capitol Hill in amounts that for some observers evoked memories of the corrupt old days of the late nineteenth century.[2]

In this hectic atmosphere of perpetual campaigning, the older values of collegiality and comity, though rarer than senatorial memory had it, eroded to the point of virtual disappearance. "Everyone seems a lot ruder these days," observed a Senate insider in 1983. "There's no sense of institutional pride and respect for and veneration of the Senate as an institution."[3]

The election of 1980 that brought Ronald Reagan to the White House and the Republicans back to control of the Senate opened the modern era in the history of the upper house. The shift to the right and the cohesion of the GOP majority under Howard Baker from 1981 through 1984 shaped the policy choices that the nation faced for the remainder of the century. Although control moved back to the Democrats in 1986 for eight years, neither party thereafter held a sixty-vote majority that could defeat a filibuster. Accordingly, Democrats and Republicans sometimes had to put aside their mutual animosity as they struggled to achieve a super-majority that eluded both parties. The outcome of these battles often left the impression of a legislative body at war with itself and the best interests of the nation.

During the early years of the Reagan presidency, Howard Baker worked with impressive skill to hold his disparate coalition together. The rumpled, easygoing Baker showed an affable face to the public, but he could be very tough in private, as the Reagan White House and his colleagues both learned. The Republican Conference ranged from such moderates as Mark Hatfield of Oregon and Lowell Weicker of Connecticut to such conservatives as Jesse Helms of North Carolina and Strom Thurmond of South Carolina. Helms, in particular, carried on the tradition of James Allen with a greater flare for publicity and more tenacity in the quest for his policy goals.[4]

Flush with Reagan's victory, militant senators wanted to engage hot-button issues such as limits on abortion and a return of government-sanctioned prayer to the public schools. Baker knew that debating these volatile issues would only help the Democrats. The opposition would argue that the Republicans were intolerant and small-minded. Since the Reagan administration's top priority was the president's economic package, Baker steered his members toward issues on which they could all agree.

Baker, who was fifty-six and had presidential ambitions, had watched his father-in-law, Everett Dirksen, as minority leader in the 1960s. He had also seen the contrasting styles of Mike Mansfield and Robert Byrd as leaders of his Democratic rivals. Although he was as conservative as the mainstream of his party, Baker was a pragmatic realist more interested in results than ideological crusades. The majority leader took care to schedule sessions so that members had the long weekends they needed for fence mending at home. Partisan warfare continued, but the internal workings of the chamber operated with considerable efficiency under the emollient Baker. The Reagan White House appreciated what Baker accomplished; Reagan's chief of staff, James Baker, said, "Before we do anything we pick up the phone and get Howard Baker's judgment on what will or won't fly."[5]

The Republicans needed Howard Baker's talents as leader. Combined with Reagan's effectiveness in working with Congress, they got the new president off to a successful start in 1981. Democrats, shaken by the loss of power, were off stride against a popular president, especially after Reagan survived an assassination attempt in late March. Thus the president's economic program moved through both houses with unusual speed in the summer of 1981. The "Reagan revolution" of lower taxes, higher defense spending, and smaller government appeared to be a political juggernaut in the first year of his presidency.

Reagan's campaign to improve the economy went by the term "supply-side economics." Faced with inflation, high interest rates, and protests against the tax burden on individual Americans, Reagan and his team argued that the nation needed tax cuts to stimulate the economy and increased defense spending to meet the challenge of a resurgent Soviet Union bent on the destruction of the United States. The supply-siders contended that as tax cuts sparked the economy they would in turn lead to greater business expansion and increased tax revenues that would, over time, offset loss of government funds. It was an alluring proposition since it seemed to provide immediate relief for the voters, enhanced protection for the nation, and a long-term solution for the mounting budget deficit. The only flaw in the supply-side theory was that it did not work.

Some Republicans realized that at the time. New Hampshire senator Warren Rudman later described what the president offered as a "wonderfully seductive theory, because it promised so much and asked no pain or sacrifice in return." Howard Baker said in private that it was a "riverboat gamble." But in the euphoria of Reagan's 1980 triumph and the aftermath of the attempt on his life, hard economic calculations deferred to the pursuit of partisan success. The Senate, not for the last time, had now abandoned its role as a brake on unwise ideas. The members decided instead to enable a president in thrall to a misguided theory. The next two decades

would see the upper house attempt in various ways to escape the consequences of its 1981 folly, but the lure of lower taxes almost invariably outpaced any enduring pretense to fiscal responsibility.[6]

After Reagan made a personal pitch on national television for his economic program on July 27, 1981, the House endorsed his tax package in
the key vote. The upper house then concurred by a vote of 89 to 11. Had the
economy improved and the budget deficit receded, the president would have
won his bet. Since inflation was not yet under control, the combination of
higher defense spending and tax cuts swelled the deficit to an estimated $84
billion for the coming fiscal year. That result frightened Republican senators
and sparked negotiations in 1982 to work out a budget measure that provided some tax increases and spending reductions to offset revenues lost a
year earlier. Baker and his senators had taken a step back toward his party's
traditional opposition to large deficits at least for the moment.[7]

The persistence of economic pain, especially higher unemployment,
made the congressional elections difficult for the Republicans in 1982.
They lost two dozen seats in the House while the partisan balance in the
Senate remained unchanged. Since there had been some vulnerable Democratic seats going into the election cycle, this stalemate frustrated GOP
hopes for an electoral realignment. The White House took the opportunity
to punish a senator who had been critical of the president's policies. They
opposed a third term for Robert Packwood of Oregon as chair of the National Republican Senatorial Committee. The liberal, pro-abortion Packwood had been an irritant to the administration with his defection from
the majority on social issues. His rival, Richard Lugar of Indiana, was a reliable conservative. Lugar prevailed in the intra-party contest.[8]

After the 1982 election, the economy turned upward and prospects for
President Reagan's reelection improved. Meanwhile, Howard Baker announced in January 1983 that he would not stand for a fourth term in 1984.
He wanted to build a base for a presidential run in 1988, and he knew that
more time in the Senate would defeat that goal.

Before he left office, Baker pursued a long-standing personal ambition of
allowing Senate sessions to be televised. The House had started showing its
sessions on the cable network C-SPAN in 1979, improving the reputations
of those members who performed well for the camera. As Americans saw
the House in action, the Senate seemed less consequential in the legislative
process. Traditionalists in the upper chamber contended that lawmakers

would perform for the audience and thus lower the quality of debates and deliberations. Despite his best persuasive efforts, Baker departed in 1984 with the Senate still determined to resist television.[9]

It was during the summer of 1986 that the members decided that television and radio coverage of their debates would be allowed. For seven years the House of Representatives had been the public face of Congress and the Senate had been overshadowed. Such a condition could not long continue. Resistance persisted during the first half of the 1980s. Senators feared that their colleagues would perform for the cameras while many less-talented speakers would not do well on the small screen. By 1986, however, it was evident that the Senate was suffering in the war for public coverage.

Soon the viewers on C-SPAN 2 were introduced to the daily rhythms of Senate sessions. They learned of the importance of unanimous consent agreements, by which the modern chamber did much of its regular business. The role of the two leaders in structuring debate and the flow of legislation also came into focus. Then there were the quorum calls that came and went, often for no apparent reason. Viewership of the Senate lagged behind the House in part simply because the upper chamber had less going on most of the time.[10]

One constant irritant for Howard Baker had been the divisive tactics of conservatives within his own caucus. For Jesse Helms, his North Carolina colleague, John P. East, and a cadre of committed Republican senators, the Senate was an arena where they could pursue their social agenda against abortion, the Supreme Court's ban on organized prayer in the public schools, and other issues that activated the conservative base of the Republicans. As one of Baker's aides told a *Newsweek* reporter, "These guys don't want to make a deal, they want to make their point."[11]

In the minds of Helms and his associates, the Senate was a vehicle for social change. If their incessant amendments made members cast difficult votes on social issues, so much the better. Like Robert La Follette, Sr., eighty years earlier with his roll calls, Helms's goal was to create a voting record that would play badly in negative commercials against a liberal incumbent. Helms was quite willing to use the chamber's rules for his own advantage but felt less commitment to the institutional mores when they interfered with his ambitions. Senatorial courtesy and the conventions of Washington prevented Helms from being labeled what he was, an advocate of racism who opposed civil rights measures, tolerance of homosexuals, and the Martin

Luther King national holiday. (Helms charged in the 1980s that "Dr. King's action-oriented Marxism . . . is not compatible with the concepts of this country.") Through his years in the chamber, Helms advanced his noxious doctrines, and no Republicans ever truly repudiated him. Some of them feared the North Carolinian and his ability to rouse conservatives; more GOP members agreed with Helms's essential doctrines but were reluctant to be as blatant about hard-edged conservatism as he was.[12]

To succeed Howard Baker as their leader, the Republicans selected Robert Dole of Kansas. A decorated war hero who had suffered grievous wounds in Italy during World War II, Dole had come to the Senate in 1969 after several House terms and was soon recognized as a skilled legislator and hard-edged partisan. The Kansan had been Gerald Ford's running mate in 1976 and had not been an asset in that role. A quip about "Democrat wars" in his debate with Walter Mondale underscored Dole's "mean" image. In the Senate, however, respect for Dole's abilities won over some skeptics. His desire for the White House burned, but he also craved power in the upper house. Dole easily bested his major intra-party rivals in late November 1984. Like others who dreamed of a permanent GOP majority, Dole hoped that Republicans could "make 1986 another stepping stone on the path of realignment."[13]

With Dole's elevation he had to relinquish chairmanship of the Finance Committee, and that cleared the way for Robert Packwood to move up. The White House distrusted the mercurial Oregonian, who was beginning to be talked about around the Senate both for his independent stands and for his oafish tactics toward women. "He's the kind of a guy who will walk across the street to get into a fight," observed one White House insider. With issues of tax reform and tax simplification very much in the spotlight, Packwood would soon become even more of a Senate player.[14]

Despite the rout of the Democrats in the contest between Ronald Reagan and Walter Mondale, the opposition party picked up two seats in the upper house to trail the Republicans by fifty-three to forty-seven. One notable Republican victim had been the moderate Charles Percy of Illinois, who fell to a liberal, Paul Simon. The Republicans would have more seats to defend in 1986, when the beneficiaries of the Reagan tide in 1980 would face the voters. Many of those lucky winners were less than stellar senators, and there was a good chance for Democratic gains in two years.[15]

Reagan had not waged an issue-oriented campaign in 1984. The emphasis had been on "Morning in America" and feel-good evocations of the president's virtues. Accordingly, his second term lacked the central focus that had characterized the presidency in 1981. After James Baker's move to the Treasury Department, Donald Regan became White House chief of staff. Regan was abrasive and dictatorial in pressing his case with lawmakers, and so the upper house became less tractable and more inclined to pursue its own agenda on domestic issues.[16]

The ever-growing deficit was a major point of contention. The campaign promise of 1980 to balance the budget within four years and then eliminate the deficit seemed a fading dream as the red ink accumulated. Sentiment grew among fiscally conservative Republicans to take independent action. Warren Rudman remembered his state of mind early in 1985: "I was frustrated by the president's ever-rising budget deficits, which I saw as a political betrayal and an economic disaster."[17]

Dole and his Republican troops first endeavored to tackle the politically sensitive topics of entitlements and Social Security. Working through the Budget Committee and its chair, Pete Domenici of New Mexico, they devised a package that combined a one-year freeze on Social Security benefits, a slowdown in defense spending, and cuts in various domestic programs. The vote in May 1985 produced an early-morning session with the Republican initiative trailing by one vote as the roll call neared its end. One Republican senator, Pete Wilson of California, recovering from an emergency operation, was wheeled in on a gurney. He cast his favorable vote, produced a tie, and Vice President George H. W. Bush provided the deciding tally to adopt the package.[18]

Any euphoria that Senate Republicans might have felt vanished two months later. Reagan worked out a deal with House Speaker Thomas P. "Tip" O'Neill that ended any chance of changing Social Security. For Reagan, that retreat avoided a confrontation over a subject that Republicans regarded as politically dangerous. For O'Neill, it safeguarded a sacrosanct Democratic program. The losers were the Senate Republicans. Dole and his colleagues felt betrayed, but there was little they could do in the face of Reagan's popularity and Democratic opposition. Some other approach to the deficit issue would have to be found.

The simplest solution would have been to make spending cuts and raise taxes to achieve a balanced budget, but by the mid-1980s, neither party had the will to pursue a responsible course. Instead, legislators turned to gimmicks to make themselves do what they should have done in the first place.

The most notable such procedural panacea was the Gramm-Rudman-Hollings effort to force the Congress to balance the budget. Texan Phil

Gramm and Warren Rudman devised the plan. Gramm had been elected to the Senate in 1984 after service in the House first as a Democrat and then as a newly converted Republican. A former economics professor at Texas A&M University, Gramm had a sharp mind and aggressive political instincts. He was also a publicity seeker and the quip in Washington was that the most dangerous place in the city was between Gramm and a camera. In his race for the upper house against Lloyd Doggett, Gramm had used a small contribution made by a gay group to his Democratic rival to paint Doggett as out of step with mainstream Texas values. With Reagan so popular in Texas, Gramm would likely have won in any case, but the homosexual issue, however unfair to the very conventional Doggett, was too tempting for Gramm not to use. The result was a sweeping victory over an opponent whom a Gramm staffer later described as "liberal, unknown, under-financed, running not only against Phil Gramm, but against Ronald Reagan and a conservative tide."[19]

What Gramm and Rudman—and eventually Ernest F. "Fritz" Hollings, a Democratic sponsor—devised was an elaborate scenario that mandated presidential cuts in the budget annually with a mechanism for withholding, or "sequestering," from the Congress appropriated funds when the deficit rose above a specified level. Rudman believed that "the threat of automatic cuts would force Congress and the White House to compromise on a responsible budget." In theory, Gramm-Rudman-Hollings, known in technical language as the Balanced Budget and Emergency Deficit Control Act of 1985, was supposed to mandate reductions in both defense and non-defense spending. The Supreme Court overturned part of the enforcement mechanism as unconstitutional in 1986 because it violated the doctrine of separation of powers. A second Gramm-Rudman-Hollings law in 1987 remedied the procedural defect but did little to instill political will in the Senate. Deficits kept growing as the 1980s ended, and Congress found ways to avoid the plain message of the measure they had adopted for themselves. The framers of Gramm-Rudman-Hollings had been ingenious in shaping what looked like a serious effort at fiscal restraint. But it was no substitute for genuine action to produce a balanced budget. Like so much action in the chamber during the 1980s, symbolic accomplishments trumped the national interest.[20]

In 1986, however, the Senate produced one genuine step forward in economic policy. The tax reform measure of 1986 did, for a brief period, rationalize and simplify how the federal government obtained revenue from its citizens. The impulse to reform the tax code brought together Republicans who wanted to reduce marginal tax rates and Democrats who sought to remove loopholes and breaks for the wealthy and special interests. In 1985 an improbable coalition of Congressional Republicans, the White House, and reform-minded Democrats such as former basketball star Bill Bradley of New Jersey, pushed a measure through the House and on to the Finance Committee, where Robert Packwood and his colleagues took it up. A man with a drinking problem and unresolved sexual anxieties that led him to make unwelcome advances to women, Packwood was also a smart lawmaker who wanted legitimate tax reform to go to the floor from his committee.[21]

The usual process of logrolling and trading of favors started in the Finance deliberations of April and May 1986. It looked as if the erstwhile reform bill was going to end up as another example of congressional greed gone crazy. Faced with losing control of his committee and a political disaster, however, Packwood, in a rare moment of statesmanship, decided to support tax simplification, a lower top rate, and the elimination of many loopholes. To everyone's surprise, the initiative worked as members of the committee recognized the economic logic of what their chairman was proposing. The bill swept through the Finance Committee and later the Senate. By August the Tax Reform Act of 1986 was law. Subsequent legislation over the next two decades, however, would drain the 1986 measure of most of its reform effect. Nonetheless, its passage showed that the Senate could govern when it chose to do so.[22]

The Senate also acted wisely in the adoption of the Goldwater-Nichols Act in the spring. Spearheaded by Goldwater of Arizona and Alabama representative William Nichols, the measure reorganized the Pentagon's chain of command to provide more direct accountability for the armed services and more unity among the various branches in fighting wars. Goldwater, who was retiring in 1987, said that the measure was "the only goddamn thing I've done in the Senate that's worth a damn. I can go home happy."[23]

For the Democrats, 1986 turned out to be the last year for a substantial election victory in the struggle for control of the Senate. The weak incumbents who rode Reagan's coattails in 1980 now had to face the voters on their own merits. Burdened with the usual waning of enthusiasm for the party in power after six years in office, the Republicans were repudiated. The Democrats gained eight seats to establish a 55–45 majority. Among the newcomers were Tom Daschle of South Dakota, Brock Adams of Washington, and Bob Graham of Florida. What had seemed a Republican high tide at the start of the decade had momentarily ebbed.[24]

The return of the Democrats to control of the chamber provided the backdrop for a judicial confirmation battle that intensified partisan bitterness and poisoned the process of evaluating federal judges for the rest of the century. Ronald Reagan and his allies saw dominance of the Supreme Court as one of their key goals in order to achieve their policy objectives. The nomination of Sandra Day O'Connor as the first female justice had sailed through the upper house in 1981. Although she was conservative, liberals had no real grounds to oppose her selection because of her strong qualifications. In 1986, Antonin Scalia, his impressive intellectual merits evident to all sides, was confirmed 98–0 to replace William Rehnquist as associate justice. Rehnquist in turn was nominated as chief justice to succeed the retiring Warren Burger. It was a controversial nomination because of his role in the Saturday Night Massacre of Watergate and his role in preventing African-American voters from casting ballots in Arizona. Edward Kennedy and Howard Metzenbaum of Ohio sought to block Rehnquist's promotion, even to the point of a filibuster—the first time that Democrats had relied on that tactic to block a judicial appointment. After cloture was invoked, Rehnquist was approved despite thirty-three votes against him, seven more than the twenty-six senators who had opposed the nomination of Charles Evans Hughes in 1930. Both parties had now used filibusters against Supreme Court nominees. An intense fight over the next high court nominee appeared likely.[25]

The next year saw one of the bitterest and most consequential confirmation battles in the Senate's history: the nomination of Robert Bork to replace retiring justice Lewis Powell in July 1987. Over the course of the twentieth century, the upper house had never settled on a standard for approving Supreme Court nominees. Senators from the party of the president making the nominations argued that the chamber should examine the professional qualifications of the person picked, determine whether there was evidence of competence to discharge judicial duties, and place less weight on ideology or personal beliefs about the law. Those in opposition contended that the Senate had a duty to scrutinize the opinions of the person nominated to see if they fit within generally accepted standards of what a jurist should believe. The second group wanted to make ideology a test but had to do so gingerly and with care lest they be labeled as having a "litmus test" for a Supreme Court candidate. There was an ample amount of hypocrisy in this philosophical dispute, since senators tended to shift positions depending on the state of politics when the nomination was made. Like so much else in the Senate, rules and customs were to be observed except when political expediency required that they be broken.

To the Republicans, Robert Bork seemed an ideal nominee. He had taught in the Yale Law School for many years before becoming an appeals court judge in the District of Columbia, a customary stepping-stone for nominees to the high court. The fifty-eight-year-old Bork had a distinguished record of publications in law journals and had published extensively on such issues as antitrust law. He had served in the Nixon Justice Department and had carried out the firing of Watergate special prosecutor Archibald Cox in the celebrated Saturday Night Massacre of 1973, but that was a political action that Republicans could easily defend as part of Bork's duty as an agent of the president. So from the GOP point of view, Bork met the basic test of legal competence and should have been routinely confirmed after the usual hearings before the Judiciary Committee.[26]

That Bork's legal writings had led him to oppose the 1964 Civil Rights Act, the right of privacy in sexual matters, and the *Roe v. Wade* decision about abortion placed him well within the mainstream of conservatism. To liberals, however, Bork represented the darker side of the Reagan revolution. Led by Edward Kennedy, they mounted a vigorous opposition to his confirmation. The statement that Kennedy made in the Senate soon became famous for setting the tone of what followed. "Robert Bork's America is a land in which women would be forced into back alley abortions, blacks would sit at segregated lunch counters, rogue police could break down citizens' doors in midnight raids, school children could not be taught about evolution, writers and artists could be censored at the whim of government, and the doors of the federal courts would be shut on the fingers of millions of citizens for whom the judiciary is—and is often the only—protector of the individual rights that are the heart of democracy."[27]

Thrown off stride by the attacks of Kennedy and liberal interest groups, the Reagan White House failed to mount a convincing defense of Bork for the Senate. The bearded, introspective jurist proved to be his own worst enemy in the hearings. He conveyed a sense of bloodless detachment about constitutional issues and an aloofness from the everyday lives of Americans whose rights he would be evaluating. Potential support among conservative Democrats in the chamber did not materialize, and the result was the defeat of his nomination by a vote of forty-two in favor to fifty-eight against. After another potential nominee faltered, the president named Anthony Kennedy, who was easily confirmed.[28]

The Bork confirmation fight reverberated through the Senate for years, and its impact can still be felt. A new word entered the language of the upper house—to be "borked." It meant to Republicans that a qualified nominee had been unfairly rejected by bogus appeals to public opinion. A colleague of Orrin Hatch told the Utah senator that "he was so angry about what had happened that he vowed never again to follow the rule of giving the presumption to a president's nominee. From now on, he would base his vote to confirm or reject nominees on their political preferences." GOP members were bent on having their revenge, and since in their minds the Democrats had broken the rules of Senate culture on confirmations, they thought they were justified in doing whatever it took to defeat Democratic judicial selections in the future. After Bork, a progressive decline in comity and civility shaped the confirmation process. Few senators stopped to think about whether a politicized judiciary served the larger national interest.[29]

For the Senate, the two years before the 1988 presidential election were consumed with the aftermath of the Iran-*contra* scandal. In that controversy, the White House had authorized the sale of arms to Iran in return for the eventual release of American hostages held in Lebanon. In the process, money from the arms sales was diverted to assist the *contra* rebels against the government of Nicaragua, deemed to be a pro-Communist state. Most important, a clandestine foreign policy apparatus, not answerable to Congress or any part of the government, had pursued a reckless and unwise venture.

Senators and former senators played prominent parts in the unfolding of the story. John Tower, who had left the Senate in 1985, and Edmund Muskie, who had left in 1980, probed the conduct of the administration at the behest of the White House. Howard Baker came to the administration to serve as White House chief of staff to clean up the mess his predecessors had made in the scandal. A joint House-Senate committee looked into the affair in televised hearings that shed more heat than light on what had happened. Although Ronald Reagan and his aides had probably done things that qualified as impeachable offenses, neither Republicans nor Democrats wanted to see President Reagan impeached. With less than two years to go in his term, the consensus was to let the remainder of his term unfold and elect a new president in 1988. As a result, the hearings never achieved the iconic status of the Watergate panel fourteen years earlier.[30]

While the parties sought partisan advantage, ethical questions about the modern Senate remained to haunt the members as well. The cost of state-wide campaigns rose steadily during the eighties, to the point that in major contests expenditures of $3 million or $4 million became routine. In a large state such as Texas, Republican Phil Gramm projected that he needed more than $13 million for his reelection effort in 1990. To provide enough money for a reelection effort, an incumbent had to gather several thousand dollars every day of a six-year term. Receptions, dinners, and other events, not to mention direct telephone solicitation of potential givers, had to be part of any daily schedule.[31]

The need to find money and the amounts of dollars that became involved produced a lowering of the ethical tone of the chamber during the 1980s. When Lloyd Bentsen of Texas became chairman of the Finance Committee after the 1986 elections, he announced a series of breakfast meetings for lobbyists. Those in attendance were expected to provide campaign contributions of $10,000 for the opportunity to make their case on issues. The press dubbed the process "Eggs McBentsen," and the astute chairman quickly canceled the whole venture. The episode was only a minor ripple, but it illustrated how Washington had institutionalized the perpetual round of hitting up donors for the long green.[32]

What emerged was a process where senators got large contributions from special interests, and those favored groups had a sympathetic hearing on policy matters in the upper house. During the early 1980s, for example, Congress deregulated the savings and loan industry to make it easier for thrifts to realize greater returns from their loans and to attract a wider range of potential customers. In the process, lawmakers opened up the business to unscrupulous operators who exploited the weaknesses in the law to bilk billions from unwary depositors. The legislation sped through in part because the savings and loan industry affected so many members and could provide badly needed funds for campaigns. There was nothing illegal about what took place, but the Senate became more of a cash register for contributions and influence than a deliberative body considering laws on their merits.[33]

The case of the "Keating Five" provided a window into the ways in which the Senate operated in the shadowy and often unsavory world of finance and influence. Charles Keating was the operator of savings and loans in California, Arizona, Michigan, and elsewhere who thrived by duping guileless customers out of their savings. Through these schemes he financed a lavish lifestyle. He also dabbled in politics as an outspoken foe of pornography. By 1987, however, Keating's tactics and his criminal activities had attracted the attention of federal regulators. He turned to his friends on Capitol Hill to find ways to get the investigators to end their probe.[34]

These efforts involved meetings with four Democratic senators, Alan Cranston of California, John Glenn from Ohio, Donald Riegle of Michigan, and Dennis DeConcini of Arizona, and one Republican, John McCain of Arizona. Both Glenn and McCain had less to do with the controversy that followed than did their three colleagues, but the label of the "Keating Five" stuck in the popular mind. Cranston, DeConcini, and Riegle took a more active role in steering regulators away from Keating, and they also benefited to a greater degree than did the two others from the lavish campaign contributions that the savings and loan mogul steered their way. Cranston in particular saw hundreds of thousands of dollars from Keating flow into his campaign coffers and for voter registration projects in California. These funds received the closest scrutiny from the Senate Ethics Committee once the scandal came to light in 1989.[35]

The Keating Five scandal produced an inquiry that stretched into 1991 before it was resolved. McCain, DeConcini, Riegle, and Glenn were found to have engaged in inappropriate conduct. Cranston was given a more serious letter of reprimand. With his reelection prospects under a cloud because of the probe, he decided to leave politics in 1992.

The ways in which a scoundrel such as Keating was able to exercise influence on the regulatory process were typical in that similar behavior was happening on Capitol Hill all the time. When exposed to the public, these revelations brought cries of outrage from other senators and protestations that such methods were not customary. In fact, too often they were, and the real problem for the "Keating Three" who were most involved was that they had been caught.

The 1988 presidential election saw current and former senators pursuing the nomination in each party. Gary Hart, who had left the chamber in 1987, watched his chances for the Democratic nomination collapse when his philandering proved so blatant that press accounts made it a subject of national ridicule. On the Republican side, Robert Dole challenged Vice

President George H. W. Bush for the top spot. Victory in the Iowa caucuses gave the Kansan momentum going into the New Hampshire primary. In that contest, Bush's superior organization and anti-tax stand produced a decisive win that turned the tide against Dole. Testy in the wake of his defeat, he returned to the Senate and campaigned as a loyal Republican for what became the ticket of Bush and Indiana Senator J. Danforth "Dan" Quayle.

The Democratic nominee, Governor Michael Dukakis of Massachusetts, also looked to the upper house for his running mate, Lloyd Bentsen of Texas, who had considerably more experience in the upper house than the youthful Quayle. The two senators met in the single vice presidential debate. In an effort to blunt charges that he had a shallow record of accomplishment, Quayle asserted that he had as much experience as John F. Kennedy had when he ran for president in 1960. Alerted during debate preparations that his rival might make such a claim, Bentsen was ready: "Senator, I served with Jack Kennedy. I knew Jack Kennedy. Jack Kennedy was a friend of mine. Senator, you are no Jack Kennedy." The incident made for riveting television but did not affect the outcome of the election, which Bush won easily.[36]

The 1988 elections produced no change in the political alignment of the chamber, with fifty-five Democrats facing forty-five Republicans once again. For the majority Robert Byrd stepped down as the leader to become president pro tempore and take over the chairmanship of the Appropriations Committee. Devoted to obtaining ever more projects and appropriations for West Virginia, Byrd traded the aggravations of floor leadership for the pleasures of pork dispensing. To succeed him the party turned to George J. Mitchell of Maine. Soft-spoken with a pleasing manner, the bespectacled Mitchell was also a tenacious partisan who could turn a wry phrase. Asked what the powers of the majority leader were, he quipped, "You have the power to kiss 99 asses." In his race, he had promised to make the operations of the Senate more disciplined; lack of discipline is a perennial complaint that each new leader addresses and in time finds difficult to remedy.[37]

The first business of the Bush administration was to pick a cabinet, and few observers expected much controversy in that process. After all, since Lewis Strauss's rejection in 1959 no nominee for a cabinet position had been turned down. The presumption was that President Bush's choices would receive easy approval, and that impression seemed confirmed when the president-elect indicated his intention to name John G. Tower as secretary of defense. Yet the Tower confirmation struggle became another marker of the extent to which the Senate had relinquished its claims to collegiality and civility.

At an initial glance, Tower seemed a shoo-in. The first Republican senator from the South since Reconstruction when he was elected from Texas in 1961, the diminutive, dapper Tower had served four terms before retiring in 1984. He was well versed in defense issues after a long tenure on the Armed Services Committee, where he was justly regarded as a staunch ally of the military. His time as chairman of the committee reinforced that impression. From the outside, it looked as if Tower could count on the support of the current chair, Sam Nunn, a Georgia Democrat who was also pro-defense. There was every likelihood that Tower's confirmation would sail through the Senate.[38]

Circumstances were deceiving, however. Tower had made enemies during his time as committee chair because of his imperious manner and abrupt disdain for some fellow senators and their staffers. Since leaving the chamber, he had more than prospered as a consultant for various defense-related industries as much through his presumed influence as his expertise. These revelations bothered Nunn and his senior staff. There were also persistent tales of womanizing and drunken episodes when Tower had behaved badly. Despite these potential snags, the conventional wisdom in Washington after Bush's formal announcement was that Tower could overcome these handicaps.

Over the next several months, however, the nomination unraveled. Nunn moved to opposition in part because of worries about Tower's conflict-of-interest problems and his issues with liquor. An attack from conservative activist Paul Weyrich on Tower as a drinker and womanizer fueled the controversy. The actual merits of the case remain clouded years after Tower was rejected. The senator mounted a vigorous defense, as his memoirs reveal, and he received powerful support from John McCain and other Republicans, but in early March 1989, the Senate rejected its former member 53 to 47.[39]

What the Tower fight revealed was the unpleasant reality behind the facade of the Senate's public image. Cross-currents of personal venom and stored-up animosities provided the backdrop for the battle over Tower's candidacy. In the process, the public was treated to healthy doses of gossip, innuendo, and backbiting. Senators sometimes engage in juvenile behavior at odds with the gravity of their responsibilities. If the stories of Tower's lurid antics were to be believed, members had stood by while a petty bully harassed staffers, drank too much, and abused the public trust in his consulting ventures. On the other hand, if Tower was as blameless as his defenders suggested, then he was the victim of liars and fabricators who had no business holding elective office. In either case, the presence of dysfunctional personalities in the chamber seemed striking and troubling.

By the close of the 1980s, the intensifying partisanship and the souring atmosphere in the chamber led some senators to think about retirement. After he departed in 1987, Gary Hart called the upper house as he had known it earlier in the decade "a kind of controlled madhouse." The place, he argued, was "largely occupied by political careerists." An influx of Republicans who had served previously in the House brought the highly polarized tactics of that body across the Capitol. These new members believed that Senate procedures were only to be respected to the degree that they resulted in a partisan victory. Otherwise, it was appropriate for a Senate majority to treat the minority with the same disdain that operated in the House. As he witnessed this development, Republican Warren Rudman began to think midway through his second term whether he wanted to run for a third. "The confrontational, take-no-prisoners attitude" that these new Republicans "brought to the Senate was not one with which I was completely comfortable." The perception that an older, more civil Senate was giving way to a body of greater partisanship and less civility became a conventional judgment as the 1990s opened. To adopt that nostalgic position required forgetting about the troubled past of the institution, especially the events of the previous decade.[40]

The accumulated nastiness and scandals of the 1980s, from the Bork nomination to the Keating Five to the Tower confirmation struggle, could have raised larger issues about what the Senate was becoming as a legislative body. For most members, as the 1990s began, it was more of business as usual. That process led to another ten-year period when the Senate slipped further in public esteem and failed to meet its political responsibilities. By the end of the century, civility and a sense of common purpose had vanished from much of what the Senate did.

## CHAPTER SIXTEEN

# Republican Ascendancy
## at Century's End

D URING THE 1990S THE SENATE MOVED IN CONTRADICTORY DIRECTIONS. After many decades as a virtually all-male institution, the upper house witnessed the election of women in significant numbers for the first time. The trend left men still very much in charge, but gender diversity had finally come to the chamber. The other development involved a further deterioration of civility, comity, and ethical standards. Partisanship became more pronounced, political advantage counted for more than the national interest, and serious problems of basic honesty proliferated. By the end of the twentieth century, the Senate, for all the trappings of modernity, acted in ways that harked back to the discredited practices of the Gilded Age chamber.

The pervasive role of the mass media, and particularly the rise of cable television—with C-SPAN 2 and the twenty-four-hour news channels— accelerated these developments. Senators now had a way to publicize themselves on a daily basis, and the more adroit used the omnipresent cameras to make themselves national figures. But the dependence on the media also intensified the reliance on constant fund-raising to fend off potential opponents or defeat actual challengers. Most lawmakers spent only two or three days in Washington each week. For the rest, they pressed the flesh, accepted checks, and wooed constituents.

With the return of the Republicans to control of Congress in 1995, the Senate began to resemble the House of Representatives in its folkways and performance. Less taken with traditions of the upper house, Republicans who had been trained in the majoritarian ethos of the House insisted that Senate procedures should surrender to partisan victories. In judicial appointments, investigations, and policy decisions, the Senate did not act to cool the passions of the lower house. If anything, it heightened these emotions. The world's most exclusive club still required a high fee to enter its halls. Inside, however, a distinctive senatorial style of measured debate, careful procedure, and matured legislation seemed a relic of a dowdy past before pundits and consultants had reshaped American politics.

The presidency of George H. W. Bush provides one responsible episode in Senate history and one of its least edifying spectacles, both in 1991. The chamber witnessed a serious debate during the crisis arising from Iraq's invasion of Kuwait in 1990. Having forestalled Iraq's ambitions to move into Saudi Arabia, the Bush administration asked Congress to authorize its military campaign to oust the armed forces of Saddam Hussein from Kuwait. While the White House was intent on going to war no matter what happened on Capitol Hill, the president and his aides believed that congressional endorsement would enhance international support for liberating Kuwait.[1]

The debate occurred on January 10–11, 1991, with the decisive vote on the following day. On the whole, the Democrats proved skeptical of the need for war with Iraq. A majority favored allowing economic sanctions against the Hussein regime to operate. All but two Republicans backed the president's position. Such high-profile Democrats as George Mitchell, the majority leader, and Sam Nunn, chair of the Armed Services Committee, opposed the White House. Nine Democrats, most notably Albert Gore, Jr., gave Bush their votes. The final tally was fifty-two in favor and forty-seven against, a very close result for what was in fact a war resolution. It was generally agreed that the Senate conducted itself well in the Gulf War debate. Issues had been fully aired, and passions had not spilled over into intemperate language on either side. Of course, had the vote gone the other way, conservative denunciation of the Senate Democrats would have been intense. Whatever credit the chamber earned from the Gulf War episode disappeared when another controversial Supreme Court nomination was announced later that year.[2]

In the summer of 1991, the first African-American Supreme Court justice, Thurgood Marshall, in failing health, announced that he was retiring. As his successor, President Bush nominated another African American,

Clarence Thomas, who sat on the court of appeals for the District of Columbia. The conservative Thomas was, according to Bush, "the most qualified candidate" for the Supreme Court. Mindful of what had happened to Robert Bork in 1987, the White House mounted a vigorous media campaign in favor of Thomas.[3]

Thomas went through the hearings of the Senate Judiciary Committee in September 1991 without undue incident. Concerned about his relatively sparse résumé of judicial opinions and legal writing, as well as his conservative record as head of the Equal Employment Opportunity Commission (EEOC), Democrats opposed Thomas. The Judiciary Committee deadlocked on a seven-to-seven vote, but the nomination thus went to the floor for a projected confirmation debate on October 8, 1991. Out of public view, however, Anita Hill, herself an African American, was claiming that Thomas had sexually harassed her in the early 1980s when she had worked at the EEOC. As word spread of Hill's allegations, the issue arose of whether the Judiciary Committee should reopen its hearings.[4]

The opponents of Thomas, led by congressional women, persuaded Senate leaders in both parties to delay the confirmation vote for a week so that Hill's charges could be aired. In their public statements, many male senators came across as obtuse about the issue of sexual harassment and its effect on women. Chairman Joseph Biden of Delaware and his Republican counterpart, Orrin Hatch of Utah, thus saw their committee become the focus of national attention when the hearings opened before a large television audience.[5]

The Hill-Thomas hearings remain a contentious historical event with little agreement about the basic facts at issue. For Hill's partisans, her testimony was convincing. To her critics, most notably Hatch and Arlen Specter of Pennsylvania on the Republican side, Hill was lying and Thomas was truthful. Both sides approached the matter from a partisan framework where victory, and not historical accuracy, was the standard. The case thus developed into a fresh occasion for polarizing sentiments within the Senate.[6]

After the Hill-Thomas hearings had ended, the full Senate voted fifty-two to forty-eight to confirm the jurist for the Supreme Court—the narrowest margin for any successful nominee in the Court's history. The debate over Thomas led to some additional rancor within the chamber as members indulged in biting personal references. In debate, Hatch referred, for example, to the Chappaquiddick episode in which Edward Kennedy had been involved in 1969 to underscore the alleged weakness of Democratic criticism.

The outcome in favor of Thomas did nothing to quell bitterness about the nomination process. In fact, the Bork and Thomas cases seemed to demonstrate that the more political and corrosive one side could be the better their chances of winning on the Senate floor. That lesson would be relearned in other judicial nominations to come during the 1990s.[7]

The battle over Clarence Thomas also underscored how much of the Senate remained a male preserve. The 1980s had seen only minimal improvement in the election of women to the chamber. In the 1970s, Nancy Landon Kassebaum, a Kansas Republican, won a seat that led to an eighteen-year career. Paula Hawkins of Florida rode the Reagan tide to a single term from 1981 to 1987. Then Barbara Mikulski, a Maryland Democrat, began a tenure that saw her win a fourth term in 2004. That made a total of six women—Margaret Chase Smith and Maurine Neuberger being the others—who had served at least one term since Hattie Caraway's victory in 1932. For the most part, the upper house still operated as an elite men's club.

Among the staff of the Senate in the 1980s, women were marginalized. Male condescension was routine. Sexual harassment flourished. Robert Packwood, Republican of Oregon, made a habit of approaching women with unwanted physical advances. Brock Adams, a Washington Democrat, provoked similar charges. Extramarital affairs were common, including those involving Edward Kennedy, Gary Hart, John Tower, and David Durenberger of Minnesota. Senators regularly instructed the nation on moral values. Their own lives operated by a different standard. If pressed about rumors of sexual harassment, male senators responded that every senator was responsible to the voters. It was not up to the members to enforce rules for proper behavior. There was, it is true, an Ethics Committee, but it was a toothless body. Senators could have imposed more exacting standards upon themselves. Instead, lawmakers avoided thinking about the prevalence of sexual harassment in Congress and the view of women that permitted the practice to flourish.

By the early 1990s, political circumstances produced constructive change. Pundits dubbed 1992 "the year of the woman" because more female candidates were seeking Senate seats than in anyone's memory, and in fact four women, all Democrats, were elected to the chamber. From California came Dianne Feinstein, whom the voters chose to fill out the term of Pete Wilson, who had been elected governor. Barbara Boxer won the other California seat of the retiring and scandal-tainted Alan Cranston. Patty Murray secured the place in Washington being vacated by Brock Adams after the sexual harassment allegations against him clouded his reelection chances. In Illinois, Carol Moseley-Braun, an African American, defeated Alan Dixon in the Democratic primary, based in part on Dixon's vote to approve Clarence Thomas. Suddenly, the Senate had five women members and more would be elected in 1993, 1994, and 1996. In 2005, there were fourteen women serving as senators.[8]

The increasing number of Senate women, while a salutary occurrence, did not elevate the tone of the chamber in any notable respect. The new female members waged partisan warfare with as much gusto as their male counterparts. They did, however, broaden the range of issues being discussed and the human experiences of the membership at large. Once the number of female senators had expanded, it was hard to recall why it had taken so long to have the upper house more reflect the gender diversity of the United States as a country.

The 1992 election also led to further revelations about the troubled tenure of Robert Packwood and his treatment of women. News stories came out shortly after the voting about his chronic and blatant advances to female staffers in Washington and in Oregon. These disclosures could not be hushed up as readily as in the past. The case went to the Ethics Committee, which interviewed numerous witnesses. When it was disclosed that Packwood had kept an extensive diary of his years in Congress, his colleagues insisted in November 1993 that he turn over the documents to the panel. During 1994 and into 1995, the issue of Packwood's treatment of women revealed more about how insensitive the chamber's members could be on this issue. The Ethics Committee recommended in September 1995 that Packwood be expelled. The senator resigned. His peers had turned a blind eye to the Oregon senator's drinking and sexual assaults until the public learned of his antics. Only then did his enablers turn into his critics. Packwood's departure represented a public affirmation of the Senate's newfound belief in a more equitable workplace for women.[9]

The 1992 presidential election opened a period of significant change in how the Senate related to the occupant of the White House. In the 1988 election campaign, George H. W. Bush had made a "no new taxes" pledge that proved crucial to his victory over Michael Dukakis. Then, as budget problems pressed for solution in 1989 and 1990, the White House decided to strike deals with congressional Democrats that involved raising revenues.

Bush suffered from Republican outrage over this reversal of policy, and the party went into the elections of 1990 in some confusion. The Democrats gained one Senate seat as voters concentrated on the impending war in the Persian Gulf. The decisive military victory of the United States made Bush enormously popular, and it seemed his reelection was assured. Potential Democratic candidates, such as Senator Lloyd Bentsen of Texas, who had beaten Bush in the 1970 Senate race, and New York Governor Mario Cuomo, decided not to challenge the incumbent.[10]

Yet there were danger signs for Bush. The economy had soft spots, and polls showed an electorate worried about rising government deficits and a sluggish job market. An omen of Bush's troubles appeared in a special Senate election in Pennsylvania called to elect a successor to a Republican, John Heinz, who had died in an aviation accident on April 4, 1991. The Republicans wheeled out an imposing candidate in Richard Thornburgh, Bush's attorney general. His Democratic rival was Harris Wofford, the interim incumbent, who was little known in the state. Few expected a Democratic victory, since Thornburgh was a former governor, but the Democrats emphasized the hot issue of national health insurance, and their candidate won a surprisingly decisive victory. The episode suggested that the popular president and his policies were more vulnerable than they appeared.[11]

In the 1992 election, Bill Clinton defeated President Bush and the third-party challenger, billionaire Ross Perot. The Democrats added another seat to enjoy an apparent 57–43 advantage. In a sign of trouble to come, however, a Democratic incumbent, Wyche Fowler of Georgia, failed to attain an absolute majority in the general election and was unseated by the Republican, Paul Coverdell, in the runoff a month later. That result proved to be a signal of things to come for the Democrats. Their national advantage rested on seats in southern states that were more and more likely to go Republican when incumbent Democrats retired. The erosion of the Senate's once-formidable Democratic base in Dixie accelerated during the presidency of Bill Clinton.[12]

The new Democratic president and the Senate found themselves at odds from the outset of his administration. Within his own party, Clinton had to deal with the skepticism of such stalwarts as Daniel P. Moynihan of New York, chair of the Finance Committee. Convinced that he knew more about the nation's needs than did Clinton, Moynihan had little patience with the new president's emphasis on health-care reform. Moynihan's priority was reshaping the welfare system. Moreover, the egotistical New Yorker and the Clintons simply did not get along on a personal and policy level. Since he chaired the Finance Committee, Moynihan proved a major barrier to the initiative about reforming the medical system that Hillary Clinton championed in 1993–94.[13]

But Clinton's main problem was with the opposition party. Though he had dealt with a legislature in Arkansas as governor, there had been few Republicans in that body. In Washington, the Republicans regarded the new president as a usurper who had won the 1992 race through demagoguery and deceit. Since he had garnered only a plurality of the popular vote in the three-way race, the issue of his legitimacy also arose among Republicans prone to regard any Democratic president as questionable. Robert Dole, the minority leader, said that because Clinton did not "even win by a majority" the incoming president also lacked "a clear mandate there." Dole's novel argument about presidential legitimacy represented the views of many of his Republican colleagues.[14]

As a result, the minority in the upper house decided that they would oppose any and all efforts to deal with the budget that came from the Clinton White House, especially if such a proposal had any hint of new taxes. As Pete Domenici of New Mexico informed a Democratic friend, "We've been told by the leadership that we just can't support anything with a tax increase in it." Conservative elements of the GOP decided to oppose the Clintons over their proposal to change the health-care system. Instead of improving or modifying what the Clintons sought to do, the Republicans chose to reject any effort of any kind to address the question of medical care for all Americans. In the short term, that judgment produced large political gains for the GOP.[15]

As the new administration stumbled through its first year, Republicans looked for the opportunity to retake the Senate and the House in 1994. They stood united against any negotiations with the White House on substantive policy issues. As a result, the Clinton deficit-reduction plan encountered GOP intransigence and the defection of conservative Democrats. So close was the struggle in the Senate that the administration could only assemble a tenuous fifty votes in favor of Clinton's initiative. Vice President Al Gore then cast a tie-breaking vote to approve the plan in the Senate. Republicans predicted that the measure would lead to economic disaster and high unemployment, but in fact economic good times soon followed. The health-care plan, complex and cumbersome, never overcame a prolonged filibuster that the White House and the Senate could not break.

Robert Dole, a masterful legislative tactician, led his forty-one minority colleagues with great skill and cohesion in his determination to thwart Clinton's major initiatives. With his eye on the 1996 Republican nomination, Dole was building support as a possible challenger to Clinton's policies. With southern Democrats becoming more vulnerable to Republican challenges every year, the balance in the Senate swung toward the Grand Old Party even before the 1994 campaign was launched.

When Kay Bailey Hutchison won a special election in Texas in 1993 to fill the seat that Lloyd Bentsen vacated to join the Clinton cabinet as secretary of the treasury, her victory forecast Democratic troubles in the months that followed. Democratic senator Richard Shelby of Alabama crossed the aisle to the GOP during the first year of the new administration. These developments preceded a Republican resurgence in 1994. Conservative talk-radio hosts, particularly Rush Limbaugh, assailed the Democratic Congress every weekday and built sentiment behind sweeping out the incumbents. The Republican base was angry and thus motivated to cast votes against the Clintons. In the hard-nosed world of Senate campaigns, the Republicans had the money, superior organization, and the advantage of a coherent national message of lower taxes and smaller government.[16]

A Republican triumph ensued when ballots were cast in November 1994. The party gained eight seats and retook control of the Senate. Only in Virginia did an incumbent Democrat, Charles Robb, the son-in-law of Lyndon Johnson, hold his seat against a challenge, from Colonel Oliver North, who had gained national fame in the Iran-*contra* episode. Over in the House the "Contract with America" and Newt Gingrich swept the Republicans into power for the first time in four decades. The newly elected members shifted the party to the right in the Senate. Conservatives such as Rick Santorum of Pennsylvania and John Kyl of Arizona brought over from the House the blunter and more aggressive tactics they had learned in Gingrich's seminars on hardball methods. Civility and decorum were not virtues in the eyes of the Republican right. Power was to be exercised to achieve policy goals, and the Democratic minority would just have to adapt to the new regime in the chamber. Even Republican moderates would be disciplined if they resisted what the new majority sought to accomplish.[17]

The Republican triumph in 1994 brought Robert Dole to the post of majority leader again after an eight-year hiatus. The Kansan intended to leverage the visibility he would gain in opposing Bill Clinton to help his quest for the GOP presidential nomination in 1996. Sensing the imminent defeat of his own party, George Mitchell announced his retirement in 1994. The Democrats chose a relative newcomer, Thomas Daschle of South Dakota, as their leader. The youthful Daschle, who had only served for eight years, beat out Christopher Dodd of Connecticut by a single vote. The key ballot came from Colorado's Ben Nighthorse Campbell, who two weeks later switched to the Republicans. Over the next ten years Daschle proved to be an adept manager of his caucus and an irritant to the Republicans. Soft-spoken and ingratiating, Daschle defended the Democratic positions with unassuming skill.[18]

Both party leaders operated in a body where the rules of political warfare were still evolving. The use of the filibuster, or the mere threat of such a move, had established itself as a customary way of doing business. A senator with a purpose to filibuster simply had to state an intention to do so. Actual talking on the floor for a protracted period of time was almost never done anymore except for very visible and politically sensitive topics such as abortion, civil rights, or defense. In the daily business of the chamber, "unanimous-consent" agreements, negotiated between the two leaders, had developed into a common parliamentary device building on the historical examples of how first Lyndon Johnson and then Robert Byrd had employed the technique. Another delaying tactic that derived from the unanimous consent agreement was the "hold." A single senator, by indicating opposition to a proposed agreement or piece of legislation, could frustrate it through a hold. The existence of a hold, clandestine and anonymous as it was, could further delay action on any number of subjects. In his farewell address to the Senate in 1996, David Pryor of Arkansas recalled that "another senator's staff had arranged to place a hold on a piece of legislation I was proposing, and that senator wasn't even aware it had been done!"[19]

On judicial nominations, which had always been very political and tied up with patronage, senators had the privilege of opposing nominees from their own states whom they found objectionable. The members indicated their approval or disapproval on a blue piece of paper, known in the chamber as a "blue slip." In the 1990s, when Bill Clinton was president, the chair of the Judiciary Committee, Orrin Hatch, operated on the principle that the enmity of a single senator from a nominee's home state would be enough to stall that candidate from a floor vote and confirmation. In some instances, the potential to filibuster a nomination would be considered.

Out of the Clinton presidency and the battles over judicial selections came a system that viewed these choices as "a matter of intense partisan and ideological concern for all the court levels," according to one scholar of the process.[20]

The Senate Republicans did not have a legislative blueprint comparable to their House counterparts in 1995 with the Contract with America, but they moved forward on a number of similar fronts. One key goal for the GOP was a balanced budget constitutional amendment that would write into the fundamental law the party's commitment at that time to fiscal discipline. Since a two-thirds vote of the members was required, the balanced budget forces needed all the Republicans plus some Democratic defectors. As the date for the decisive vote approached in 1995, the outcome was yet undecided. To the surprise and dismay of Dole and his allies, the chairman of the Appropriations Committee, Mark Hatfield of Oregon, indicated plans to vote against the amendment because it did not produce real cuts in the budget that the Senate should have made on their own.

Despite appeals to his deeply held religious values and other less subtle pressures on him from Dole and the conservatives, Hatfield stood his ground, and the budget amendment failed by a single tally. Rick Santorum and the other hard-liners raised the question of whether Hatfield should remain the chair of Appropriations. "I was nothing but a poor excuse for a Republican, they said," Hatfield remembered. The Republican Conference discussed the matter for several hours before deciding that Hatfield, who was retiring in 1996, should not be punished, but the Republicans did change their rules to instill greater discipline and ideological unity. Henceforth, committee chairs would have to win the approval of the entire conference through a secret ballot. The autonomy of committee chairs was slowly being eroded. If these once-powerful members did not adhere to the party message, they could be ousted.[21]

Robert Dole's strategy of running for president from the leadership post failed in 1995–96. The House enacted many provisions of the Contract with America, such as the balanced-budget amendment, only to see them encounter roadblocks in the tangle of Senate procedures and delay. Recognizing the force of Gingrich's reminder that the Senate was not going to go away, Republicans began to contemplate further efforts to make the upper house behave more like the larger branch of Congress. Meanwhile, Dole told friends, "I am now the rational voice of the Republican Party." The leader's senior aide, Sheila Burke, turned into a target for GOP conservatives looking for sinister, moderate influences on the majority leader. Meanwhile, Dole had trouble forging an identity as a national figure and finding policy positions that appealed to a broad spectrum of the electorate.[22]

For Dole and the Republicans the end of 1995 brought political embarrassment. House Republicans decided to shut down the federal government as a means of seizing an advantage over Bill Clinton and the Democrats. The move was a disaster for the congressional majority. The public blamed the Republicans for closed government offices, parks, and museums. Dole and the Senate Republicans tried to distance themselves from what had happened, but with only limited success. With his presidential campaign needing a lift in the spring of 1996, Dole resigned his seat to pursue the White House full time. It was the end of an important career that underscored how difficult it was to use the Senate as a springboard to the presidency.[23]

To replace Dole, the Republicans elected Trent Lott of Mississippi as their new leader. He had earlier beaten Dole's personal choice, Alan Simpson of Wyoming, to be named Republican whip, and Lott was thus the logical choice in the GOP hierarchy to move up. More conservative and more combative even than Dole, Lott relied on the support of the former House members who demanded a more confrontational approach to Clinton and his party. Lott believed, as he would later say in 2002, that the nation had gone wrong when Strom Thurmond failed to win the White House in 1948 on the racist appeal of the Dixiecrats. The ascension of the Mississippian showed how southern senators had abandoned their Democratic allegiance to embrace a Republican Party that shared their narrow view of the place of African Americans in society.[24]

The reelection of Bill Clinton in 1996 did not threaten the Republican grip on the upper House. In fact, the GOP added three seats to establish a 55–45 advantage. Bitterness between the White House and the Senate intensified as Republicans looked to take down the president they despised and to set up their chances to win a national victory in 2000. In 1997, however, the two sides worked out an agreement to balance the federal budget that, in the good economic times of the 1990s, helped to produce surpluses for the next three years. Nonetheless, the underlying hostility between Clinton and his senatorial adversaries remained just below the surface of political life.[25]

Clinton had proved an elusive target for the Republicans. During his first term the Banking Committee had conducted extensive hearings in 1995 into the involvement of the president and his wife in an Arkansas land deal and related issues grouped under the term "Whitewater." To investigate the private financial activities of a president before he took office was something new in the nation's history, but the Republicans claimed the right to conduct their inquiry because of public interest in the issue and possible wrongdoing of the Clintons. The probe, spearheaded by the panel's chair, Alphonse D'Amato of New York, had been partisan and in the end nonproductive. No "smoking gun" had emerged that linked the Clintons to actual misdeeds of the past in their pre-presidential careers. Republicans remained frustrated. They knew Bill and Hillary Clinton were guilty of something. Finding out just what represented the challenge.[26]

The opposition believed that Clinton's lavish fund-raising in 1996 offered them a chance to nail him with serious charges of actual crimes. The presidential race had seen the Democrats canvass the world for money, including some illegal donations from China. Fred Thompson of Tennessee, who had been a Republican attorney for the Watergate Committee two decades earlier, was the choice to chair the probe. The Democrats succeeded in setting a time limit for the inquiry so that the proceedings would not extend into the 1998 election year. The White House fought back in the media to make the hearings seem partisan. As a result, although much information about foreign contributions, especially from China, was revealed, the investigation did not produce the disaster for the Clinton administration that some Republicans had hoped to see. Once again, "Slick Willie," as his critics called him, had eluded the Senate.[27]

Beginning in August 1994, the Clintons were being investigated by an independent counsel, Kenneth Starr, originally appointed to look into Whitewater. That same year, a former Arkansas state employee named Paula Jones filed a sexual harassment lawsuit against the president for actions he had allegedly taken while governor. A year later Clinton embarked on a sexual relationship with a White House intern, Monica Lewinsky. Word of this involvement reached first Starr's office in late 1997 and then the news media in early 1998. Suddenly the president seemed vulnerable. Had he broken a law and perjured himself? The possibility of an impeachment of the president and an ensuing trial in the Senate now seemed likely.[28]

Like the rest of the nation, senators watched during 1998 as Clinton at first denied any sexual relations with Lewinsky and then, faced with DNA evidence, had to admit that he had in fact had "improper" contact with her. The independent counsel believed that Clinton had lied under oath in the

Jones case, and he referred his findings to the House for consideration of impeachment. Those hearings opened as the congressional elections drew near. Although public opinion seemed inclined to favor Clinton, House Republicans determined to push ahead with an effort to bring their longtime foe to the processes of congressional justice.

Republicans also expected that Clinton's problems would result in electoral gains that would cement their hold on power. In another surprise in a year of stunning developments, the Democrats captured five seats in the House while the balance in the Senate was unchanged. Despite these results, the House leadership pressed on with impeachment, and two charges against Clinton were adopted in December 1998. One specified that he had lied to the grand jury of the independent counsel; the other alleged that he had obstructed justice in his actions toward Monica Lewinsky during the Starr investigation. With the House action, the case went to the Senate for trial on January 7, 1999.[29]

The House proceedings had been rancorous and partisan—in short, behavior that senators expected from the other body but were too dignified to practice on their own. The upper house was determined to maintain decorum and present a statesmanlike handling of the case. The problem was that the proponents of impeachment expected that their case would be won on its intrinsic merits. In the House the Republicans did not need Democratic votes to accomplish their goal. In the Senate, however, the anti-Clinton forces required sixty-seven votes to find the president guilty. So even if all fifty-five Republicans stood united, twelve Democrats had to be lured across the aisle to oust the president.[30]

To be sure, the Democrats had rallied behind the president in part because of the unseemly tactics that the House majority had employed. Converting a quarter of the president's party to conviction would not have been an easy task. But the Republicans never mounted a concerted effort to win over such potential defectors as Robert Byrd, Joseph Lieberman of Connecticut, and Daniel Patrick Moynihan, all of whom disliked Clinton. In the polarized Senate, the Republicans had forgotten about reaching across the aisles and had few clues to help them in doing so. So the proceedings in the upper house turned into a ritual that allowed both sides to vent their feelings in a display of political theater.

Only later would the national costs of this episode and the complicity of the Senate come into focus. For more than a year national leaders diverted themselves with a probe of President Clinton's sexual and moral failings. Meanwhile, threats of terrorism were gathering in ways that would reveal themselves in September 2001 with terrifying results. Caught up in their dance of partisanship, no senators asked whether the ouster of a president in such circumstances served the national interest at a time of mounting international danger.

Republican lawmakers also made much in this period of the need to uphold "the rule of law" as it applied to the president, despite all the potentially adverse consequences to the United States. Within a few years these same legislators would value that principle at a discount when it came to a Republican chief executive whose administration faced credible accusations of prisoner abuse, corruption in spending projects, and outright lying to Congress. Members of the Senate have always altered principles when political goals shifted, but rarely did this philosophical expediency appear in such sharp relief. The Clinton impeachment had the trappings of a solemn constitutional moment, but at its core it illustrated more about how endemic partisanship had trivialized American politics.

The Senate voted to acquit Clinton on both impeachment articles on February 12, 1999. On the perjury allegation, the vote was forty-five in favor and fifty-five against. Ten Republicans voted for acquittal. For the article involving obstruction of justice, the Senate split 50–50. The pro-impeachment forces could not muster a simple majority on either count. Predictably, both Democratic and Republican lawmakers congratulated themselves on the decorum of the trial and how it had enhanced the reputation of the chamber. These judgments bore little relation to the reality of how the Senate had performed. The Republicans had toyed with a constitutional process. The Democrats had stood aside from a real debate about whether Clinton should remain in office. Most of all the nation had suffered as real dangers mounted while the Senate indulged in its political gamesmanship.

As the 1990s closed, the Senate did engage in its way the perennial issue of campaign finance and its perceived excesses. By this time complaints about the gusher of funds flowing in and around Capitol Hill had intensified to a popular clamor. The 1996 election had concentrated attention on Democratic transgressions in gathering campaign funds, but there was ample evidence that Republicans were masters of the art as well. The bugaboo for politicians was what was known as "soft money," funds donated outside the legislative limits and the rules of the toothless Federal Elections Commissions. These moneys, used in theory for party-building activities, television advertising, and get-out-the-vote efforts, were subject to numerous and flagrant abuses. As John McCain wrote, "The soft money loophole has made a mockery of all campaign finance laws."[31]

Control of access to soft money, much of which came from corporations and labor unions, enabled the parties to enforce discipline in Congress and thus strengthened partisanship. Advocates of the existing order of things argued that campaign contributions were a kind of free speech, based on the Supreme Court decision in *Buckley v. Valeo* (1976) that laid down that principle. There thus had emerged a powerful array of special interests in the 1990s in both parties that wanted to maintain the status quo in fundraising. The Republicans, because of their base of small givers on the one hand and their ties to corporate largesse on the other, had the most to lose from change. Democrats were more inclined to favor reform, but not when it threatened their access to funds from unions, trial lawyers, and environmentalists. Privately, most politicians agreed that the fund-raising system was corrupt and broken, but changing how senators raised money for their expensive campaigns would not be a simple endeavor, as proponents of cleaner politics learned in the 1990s.

The legislative proposal that the upper house debated in the fall of 1999 was an offshoot of the Shays-Meehan campaign finance bill that passed the House in mid-September. The Senate backers of reform, most notably McCain and Russell Feingold, a Wisconsin Democrat, sought to outlaw soft money but did not address the vexing subject of campaign advertising that promoted voting based on issues rather than advocating a particular candidate. Of course, in practice the campaign spots were tailored so that it was clear how a candidate stood on the issues, and the voters could easily be implored to cast their ballots in the right way. This concession to the free speech argument did little to quell opposition, and battle lines were drawn over soft money itself.[32]

When McCain made his familiar argument that soft money had corrupted Congress, his foes struck back by challenging him to identify "corrupt" senators. A testy exchange with several Republicans followed as McCain was pressed to say which one of his colleagues was guilty of such behavior. McCain could not make a direct charge about the integrity of his fellow members without becoming a pariah to his colleagues. Of course, the focus on the presence or absence of individual wrongdoing missed the point.

The Senate had become so permeated with the fund-raising, pork-barrel politics, and special-interest influences that an objective evaluation of the merits of controversial legislation, never easy to accomplish at any time, had become almost impossible. McCain correctly cited the telecommunications bill of 1996, which strongly favored the cable television industry over the interests of consumers, as an example of how the business of influence actually operated.[33]

In 1999 the McCain-Feingold measure reached a dead end from a filibuster and the failure to achieve cloture. The pro-reform coalition never came close to achieving the sixty votes required to end debate. Once again, the inability of a majority of members to enact a bill within the Senate's rules on extended debate had stymied action on a serious national problem.

The election of 2000 saw senators and former senators from both parties seeking presidential nominations. Bill Bradley of New Jersey, the former basketball star with the New York Knickerbockers who had served from 1979 to 1997 in the Senate, contested the Democratic nomination with Vice President Al Gore and lost. Joseph Lieberman of Connecticut, the first Jew to be part of a major party ticket, became Gore's running mate, a role in which he was singularly ineffective and inept. On the Republican side, John McCain challenged George W. Bush for the nomination. The senator's campaign of "straight talk" won a surprise victory in the New Hampshire primary, but he was defeated when the Bush campaign used hardball tactics, including attacks on his wife and adopted Asian daughter, to drive McCain's poll numbers down. The self-confessed maverick from Arizona was no match for the ruthless Bush effort with its superior organization.

In 2000 the most celebrated senatorial race seemed to be shaping up in New York as the year opened. First Lady Hillary Clinton was being groomed as a Democratic candidate for the seat of the retiring Daniel Patrick Moynihan. Faced with the prospect that the popular mayor of New York City, Rudolph Giuliani, might run for the GOP, Democrats implored Mrs. Clinton, a non–New Yorker, to make the race. She agreed to do so while Giuliani had to deal with damaging revelations about his tangled personal life and failing marriage. The news in the spring of 2000 that he had prostate cancer removed the mayor from the contest. The Republicans selected a Long Island congressman, Rick Lazio, to oppose the first lady. Helped by the coattails of Al Gore, who carried the state decisively against George W. Bush, Hillary Clinton gained the Senate victory in a moment that added more glamour and celebrity to the chamber.

The final set of elections to the Senate for the twentieth century, though overshadowed by the prolonged fight about the Bush-Gore presidential contest, produced a result not seen since 1881 when the two parties had split evenly. The Democrats added five seats to their total from victories in Florida, Georgia, Michigan, Missouri, and Washington. In addition to Hillary Clinton, two more women senators were elected in the balloting. A 50–50 tie now existed in the Senate for the two parties. Since George W. Bush won the presidency, Vice President Richard Cheney's vote would allow the Republicans to organize the chamber after January 20, 2001. The even partisan balance raised new issues of comity and organization for the members to ponder as the new century began. Tom Daschle and Trent Lott opened negotiations to see how this situation, unknown in modern times, would play out. As Don Nickles, the Republican whip observed, "It's difficult for me to see how two people can drive a car at the same time." But Lott and Daschle had to develop some means of conducting an evenly divided Senate as the new Bush presidency opened in January 2001.[34]

Their task would be complicated because of the developments of the decade that had just ended. With additional women among its membership, the Senate had moved toward a more diverse representation. The likelihood of more Hispanics and African Americans being elected to the Senate in the future would in time also produce salutary changes. On the other hand, the partisanship and rancor of the 1990s had left wounds and a desire for political revenge among Republicans and Democrats. The enduring question was whether the Senate had undergone permanent changes. The experience of a century of lawmaking and partisan contention provided grounds for optimism that the Senate would endure in its historic role. At the same time, there were legitimate fears that the upper house in 2000 no longer fulfilled the role that the Framers of the Constitution had envisioned for it.

# Conclusion:
# The Senate and Its Future

THE POLITICAL STASIS OF LATE 2000 AND EARLY 2001 DID NOT ENDURE. The brief period of equipoise does, however, provide an opportunity to reflect on how much the Senate had changed since that December day in 1900 when the chamber was filled with dignitaries and flowers during the presidency of William McKinley.

Renovation and air-conditioning had altered the look of the Senate, but the procedures and seating within the chamber would have been familiar to a lawmaker from the Gilded Age. Republicans were on the left of the chamber from the presiding officer's point of view, the Democrats on the right. The two party leaders were more in evidence in modern times than would have been the case a hundred years before. The rituals of addressing the chair, praising fulsomely colleagues in debate (especially those a senator disliked), and periodic quorum calls, all these had little changed since the days of Nelson Aldrich and Arthur Pue Gorman.

More striking changes had occurred outside the room where the Senate met. In 1900 the *Congressional Directory* listed about 125 employees of the upper house (that number might have been closer to 200 if members' secretaries had been included). A century later, more than eight thousand people worked for the Senate. The budget for operating the chamber and maintaining the staff stood at more than half a billion dollars annually. Three sizable office buildings, the Richard Russell, the Everett Dirksen, and the Philip

Hart, provided stately accommodations for the members and space for the ever-growing cadre of staff.

For the senators themselves, their salaries stood at $162,100 in 2005, with the party leaders receiving higher sums. The chamber now enjoyed the presence of fourteen women elected to the Senate, the highest number in the body's history. Only thirty-three women, including the current fourteen, had held seats in the institution since its founding.

Over the course of the century, the upper house had, with great reluctance, been made more accessible. The number of secret executive sessions had been reduced, and documents about the history of the body had also been made public. C-SPAN 2 brought the proceedings of the Senate to the public.

Citizens and journalists now have reasonably ready access to information about bills and debate from on-line sources that Congress itself provides. Yet reporting about the inner workings of the Senate in both print media and on television is far less informative and thorough than it was in 1900. An interested reader, even in smaller cities, received in William McKinley's day more analysis, albeit from a partisan perspective, about how the Senate worked, than a modern follower of the news obtains. More open in some respects, the Senate is by the same token more opaque than it was in December 1900 during a time when newspapers covered political affairs more closely than now.

What of the modern Senate in debate? The advent of television has not brought the undue histrionics that had been forecast, but neither has the presence of cameras raised the level of discourse. Political oratory has been in steady decline over the course of the past century, if the Senate is any indication. Most senators read speeches that staff has written for them. In hearings members often rely on questions that their aides have prepared. The prepackaged speeches of today, the ebbing away of genuine deliberation, and the dominance of partisanship have meant that actual interchanges of views and philosophy rarely occur. Fewer modern senators can think on their feet or make a sustained argument without supporting information or props. "We're just no longer a debating forum," said Robert C. Byrd in October 2004.[1]

It is hard to overstate this loss to American political life. With the House tightly structured and the presidency disdainful of real discussion, the Senate is the last place in American government where disputed issues can be aired before they become law. As debate becomes more constricted there as well, something indispensable about the historical Senate is passing out of political life. If extended relevant discussion is not the major reason for the continued existence of the Senate, it is hard to see what is.

In the spring of 2001, Republican James "Jim" Jeffords of Vermont announced that he had become an independent and would vote with the Democrats on procedural issues, thereby putting an end to the evenly divided Senate that had emerged from the 2000 elections. With a slim 50–49–1 majority, the Democrats under Tom Daschle of South Dakota took over control of the chamber. Despite their advantage, the opposition party could not stop the large tax cuts that President George W. Bush sought in 2001, as several key Democrats endorsed what the new chief executive proposed.[2]

The terrorist attacks of September 11, 2001, changed the political landscape. Bush's poll numbers soared as the nation rallied around the president. Caught up in the patriotic fervor, the Senate hastily adopted measures such as the Patriot Act, which eroded civil liberties. The White House and the Republicans played the patriotism card for its maximum electoral value in the congressional races of 2002. In several races, Republicans suggested that Democratic candidates were either soft on terrorism or were doing the bidding of the nation's enemies. As a result, the Republicans gained two seats to reestablish their control in the chamber.[3]

The GOP leadership shifted after Majority Leader Trent Lott's gaffe in praising the retiring Strom Thurmond on his one-hundredth birthday. Lott's suggestion that the nation would have been better off if Thurmond had been elected president in 1948 evoked a storm of protest over his implicit racism. The outrage of Internet weblogs and bloggers who kept the controversy hot led to Lott's resignation. The Republicans then elected William H. "Bill" Frist of Tennessee as his successor.[4]

A physician and heart surgeon and a politician with a leadership style that wavered between subservience to the White House and arrogance toward his colleagues, Frist had barely concealed ambitions to be the Republican presidential candidate in 2008. The key to that prize was building up his party's majority in the upper house. To that end, he went into Daschle's home state in 2004 to campaign for the Republican challenger to the minority leader. This represented a breach of longtime protocol. Senate leaders did not interfere in each other's election struggles. Frist's strategy proved successful; Daschle was defeated in a close race. Harry Reid of Nevada succeeded Daschle as the Democratic leader in early 2005.

The 2004 presidential election also underscored the continuing difficulties of seeking the White House from the Senate. Though the defeat of the Democratic nominee, Senator John Kerry of Massachusetts, and his running mate, Senator John Edwards of North Carolina, had many causes, one special area of vulnerability for Kerry was his twenty-year voting record, which gave the Republicans ample opportunity to paint him as prone to change his mind on issue after issue.

As the Democrats filibustered some of Bush's judicial nominees in 2003 and 2004, Republicans contemplated significant changes in the chamber's rules. They were further emboldened in the wake of the election of 2004, in which the Republicans gained four seats for a total of fifty-five. Overlooking their own filibuster that had doomed the chances of Abe Fortas in 1968 to be chief justice, Republicans asserted that Democratic filibusters against judicial appointees had no prior precedent. Frist pronounced himself in favor of what became known as the "nuclear option" on filibusters. Under this scenario, the Republicans, using their majority status, would change the rules. A simple majority of fifty-one senators would be needed to approve a prospective judge, instead of the sixty votes required to end a filibuster. The Democrats responded that they would use all the obstructive tactics at their command if the Republicans attempted such a move. A compromise in May 2005 preserved the filibuster for the moment; the fundamental issue of the "nuclear option" remained unresolved.[5]

During the four years after 2000, the Senate seemed increasingly dysfunctional and out of touch with the purposes of the Framers of the Constitution. When the upper house confronted the issue of authorizing the president to take military action against Iraq in the autumn of 2002, no great debate over national priorities ensued. In a desultory session that often strayed from the issue at hand to discuss parochial matters, lawmakers debated the order in which they should speak with more fervor than whether war in Iraq was wise and necessary. Republicans followed the then popular President Bush into an Iraq involvement. The Democrats, fearful of an aroused electorate, muted their skepticism about the projected war. By March 2003, the Bush administration had taken the country into a conflict in Iraq that achieved military victory over the regime of Saddam Hussein only to confront a violent insurgency; resistance to American rule intensified throughout the remainder of 2003 and into 2005. The Senate never probed in sufficient depth the issue of national war aims and the prospect for success of the administration's policies toward Iraq.[6]

Equally disheartening was the Senate's failure to respond to the allegations of torture at Abu Ghraib prison in Iraq in the spring of 2004. The Senate Armed Services Committee took a brief look at the episode and then backed away from a further inquiry. Republicans in control of the committee did not want to embarrass the administration in an election year. Their pusillanimity contrasted with events half a century earlier, when Richard Russell and the Armed Services Committee conducted a significant probe into American strategy in the Far East in the wake of the firing of General Douglas MacArthur in April 1951. Senators had once boasted of their independence from the executive. The tacit endorsement by the Armed Services Committee of torture and barbarism as instruments of national policy showed how much the Senate had changed in modern times.

Indeed, in the first five years of the twenty-first century, the Senate seemed to be driven primarily by partisanship and pork. The Republican majority moved in lockstep with the White House and tolerated few signs of dissent within its ranks. Democrats had seldom been more divided and less effectual.

Many of the Senate's other flaws became more visible as well. The incessant pursuit of reelection accelerated the already out-of-control fundraising process, which gave lobbyists and special interests ever greater influence with the members. Enactment of the McCain-Feingold campaign-reform legislation in 2002 did little to improve this situation. The ethical tone of the Senate also coarsened in ways that Gilded Age members would have understood. Nepotism, cozy ties with businesses, and illicit campaign contributions marred the records of senators of both parties. Members who came to the chamber without personal wealth transformed their new power and influence into financial opportunities in ways that Lyndon Johnson would have admired. The "millionaires club" of the early twentieth century received a new lease on life a century later.[7]

The passage of a measure to change bankruptcy laws in the winter of 2005 showed the Senate's extraordinary deference to business interests and large contributors. Written to assist the powerful credit-card industry, the law attracted the united support of Republicans and key defections from Democrats who represented states where credit-card firms and insurance companies were dominant. The debate on the proposed legislation was designed to avoid attracting public notice and the bill passed easily once proponents invoked cloture to end a filibuster.[8]

In purely practical terms, the modern Senate, like the House, seems incapable of performing its constitutionally assigned tasks in an orderly manner in any given year. Appropriation bills rarely are finished on time, continuing resolutions substitute for completed legislation on budget issues, and deadlines for mandated actions regularly slip away. In the expedient process, members craft raids on the treasury and enact measures that do little to advance the national interest.

Perhaps not surprisingly, contemporary criticisms of the Senate and its members have come to sound very much like those levied in the time of Nelson Aldrich and "The Four." A majority of modern senators are wealthy and live far removed from the everyday experience of their voters. Higher salaries and abundant fringe benefits, including very generous medical insurance beyond the reach of the average citizen, further insulate even the most folksy lawmakers from the realities of life. No David Graham Phillips has come forward to level allegations of systemic corruption in the Senate, but modern muckrakers would likely find a receptive audience for such a campaign.

The Framers of the Constitution envisioned a Senate that would function as a wise and judicious check on both executive power and the House of Representatives. They did not imagine a body that would act as a rubber stamp for an incumbent president. Nor would they have been pleased to see the Senate so focused on allocating federal appropriations to contributors and constituents. While the members paid lip service to their constitutional obligations, they had largely forsaken them as a practical matter. By 2005, the Senate had become more often an impediment to democratic government rather than a place to express sober second thought on national priorities. The upper house had outlived its usefulness as a restraint on popular excesses and had emerged as an enemy of effective governance.

The reasons for this stem from the structure of the Senate as well as broader shifts in American politics. The power of individual states and their senators to skew the system was built into the chamber from the start. The emergence of the filibuster in the nineteenth century and the readiness to employ that tactic in the twentieth enhanced a minority's ability to delay and obstruct. Particularly in the area of race relations, the filibuster proved to be a national disaster that delayed justice for decades. So encrusted with rules and procedural barriers did the Senate become as a result of the filibuster that often members forgot why they were elected in the first place. Too often, senators have shown excessive concern for rules and procedures for their own sake rather than as a means of accomplishing the nation's business.

The way in which senators were elected also had a dramatic impact on the conduct of the upper house. The adoption of the Seventeenth Amendment radically changed the nature of political campaigns. The relentless demands of the "permanent campaign" have led some senators and pundits to advocate a return to the original manner of electing individuals to the upper house through state legislatures. It seems improbable that this could happen. For better or worse, citizens are going to elect senators. The problem with direct elections is not the basic democratic idea but rather the failure of the nation's political leadership to put in place safeguards against campaign contributors and special interests manipulating elections. Public financing of Senate elections with a firm cap on outside contributions would be one way to restore a semblance of competitive balance for those seeking high national office.[9]

The trends that have made the Senate more like the House of Representatives reflect the impatience with constitutional procedures and the concept of checks and balances. Politicians value winning above other considerations, and rules that establish minority rights in the Senate seem obstacles to be surmounted or subverted rather than salutary safeguards to be available when the other party has a majority. Debate and discussion, which lack the celebrity appeal of sound bites for cable television, seem increasingly irrelevant in a fast-paced world. In March 2005, for example, the Senate and the House found time to pass a bill intervening in the case of an incapacitated woman in Florida within a matter of days. The Senate's skewed sense of priorities, not to mention its cavalier attitude toward serious federalism matters such as the role of the states in shaping laws on the treatment of people in these end-of-life situations, revealed how trivialized the upper house had allowed itself to become in the constitutional system.

Should the Senate be retained as part of the American system of government? A few critics have argued that it should be abolished altogether.[10] This is of course highly unlikely and probably not desirable. In some specific instances, the mere existence of a second house has improved legislation. On occasion, the House of Representatives may have passed weaker legislation in the knowledge that the upper house would tinker with its work. With a more powerful lower chamber, such as the British House of Commons, and the Senate in a diminished role, Congress might actually pass better laws. Whether the gerrymandered House of modern times is adequate to that task is the subject for other books.

The Senate seems likely to persist as an element of American government into the future despite its evident weaknesses as a legislative institution. To remove it from the scene would require a reshaping of the Constitution, an unlikely occurrence in a conservative nation. So "the most exclusive club" will go on, probably much as it has in the past, as a mixture of infuriating slowness mixed with occasional spasms of positive achievement. Whether the upper house in its current form is sufficient to preserve democratic government now seems more doubtful than when the Senate assembled in December 1900 amidst the pageantry and flowers.

# Notes

## Introduction

1. Madison is quoted in Richard Allan Baker, *The Senate of the United States: A Bicentennial History* (Robert E. Krieger, 1988), p. 113.

2. Ross K. Baker, *House and Senate: Third Edition* (W. W. Norton, 2001), p. 228.

3. Donald R. Matthews, *U.S. Senators and Their World* (University of North Carolina Press, 1960), p. 13.

## Chapter One

1. "The Day in the Senate," *Washington Post*, 4 December 1900.

2. Marcus A. Hanna to Albert J. Beveridge, 10 November 1900, Albert J. Beveridge Papers, Manuscript Division, Library of Congress.

3. George H. Haynes, *The Senate of the United States: Its History and Practice*, 2 vols. (Houghton Mifflin, 1938), 2, pp. 917–18.

4. Ibid., p. 918 (both quotations); Robert Connington, "Keeping Cool in the Senate," *Harper's Weekly*, 12 August 1911, p. 7, gives a good picture of working conditions in the chamber during that summer.

5. "Day in the Senate."

6. E. Anthony Rotundo, *American Manhood: Transformations in Masculinity from the Revolution to the Modern Era* (Basic Books, 1993), pp. 62–74.

7. Finley Peter Dunne, *Mr. Dooley in Peace and in War* (Small, Maynard, 1898), p. 9.

8. Ray Stannard Baker, *American Chronicle* (Charles Scribner's Sons, 1945), p. 90.

9. David J. Rothman, *Politics and Power: The United States Senate, 1869–1901* (Harvard University Press, 1966), p. 244.

10. For the political environment of the Senate in 1900, see Lewis L. Gould, *The Presidency of William McKinley* (University Press of Kansas, 1980), pp. 160–64, 244–47.

11. Lewis L. Gould, *Grand Old Party: A History of the Republicans* (Random House, 2003), pp. 114–38.

12. Michael McGerr, *A Fierce Discontent: The Rise and Fall of the Progressive Movement in America* (Free Press, 2003), pp. 3–39.

13. Jerome Clubb, "Congressional Opponents of Reform, 1901–1913" (Ph.D. diss., University of Washington, 1963), indicates the political alignments at the start of the new century.

14. Henry Loomis Nelson, "The Overshadowing Senate," *Century Magazine* 65(1902–3):504; Rothman, *Politics and Power*, p. 243.

15. A good brief summary of the nature of the Senate as the Framers conceived it is in Richard Allen Baker, *The Senate of the United States: A Bicentennial History* (Robert E. Krieger, 1988), pp. 3–22; Haynes, *Senate of the United States*, 1, pp. 3–38, has a more detailed treatment; Frances E. Lee and Bruce I. Oppenheimer, *Sizing up the Senate: The Unequal Consequences of Equal Representation* (University of Chicago Press, 1999), looks at the impact on the modern institution of each state's having the same number of senators.

16. Sara A. Binder and Steven S. Smith, *Politics or Principle? Filibustering in the United States Senate* (Brookings Institution, 1997), p. 4.

17. Baker, *The Senate of the United States*, pp. 23–52; Webster quoted in Robert C. Byrd, *The Senate 1789–1989: Addresses on the History of the United States Senate* (Government Printing Office, 1988), 1, p. 114.

18. Merrill D. Peterson, *The Great Triumvirate: Webster, Clay, and Calhoun* (Oxford University Press, 1987).

19. Binder and Smith, *Politics or Principle?*, pp. 37–39, 56, 74–75.

20. Eric Foner, *Reconstruction: America's Unfinished Revolution, 1863–1877* (Harper & Row, 1988), pp. 333–37.

21. For examples of how senatorial contests in state legislatures worked, see "Reform in Senatorial Elections," *The Outlook*, 25 February 1911, 389, 392; Rothman, *Politics and Power*, pp. 162–87.

22. Rothman, *Politics and Power*, pp. 174–75.

23. *Washington Post*, 2 June 1906; "Mr. Addicks As Viewed at Home," *Literary Digest*, 6 December 1902; for a brief account of Addicks, see Carol E. Hoffecker, *Honest John Williams: U.S. Senator from Delaware* (University of

Delaware Press, 2000), pp. 30–31; Lewis L. Gould, *Wyoming: From Territory to Statehood* (High Plains Publishing, 1989), pp. 186–91, 194–96.

24. H. Wayne Morgan, *From Hayes to McKinley: National Party Politics, 1877–1896* (Syracuse University Press, 1969), p. 464; William P. Frye to James H. Wilson, 20 March 1899, James H. Wilson Papers, Manuscript Division, Library of Congress.

25. "Electing Senators by Popular Vote," *The Nation* 74(1902): 222; Charles James Fox, "Direct Election of United States Senators," *The Arena* 27(1902): 455–67.

26. Raymond Smock, "Black Members: Nineteenth Century," in Donald C. Bacon, Roger H. Davidson, and Morton Keller, eds., *The Encyclopedia of the United States Congress*, 4 vols. (Simon & Schuster, 1995), 1, pp. 170–72.

27. Rothman, *Politics and Power*, pp. 140–43; Walter P. Webb and Terrell Webb, eds., *Washington Wife: Journal of Ellen Maury Slayden from 1897 to 1919* (Harper & Row, 1963), p. 27.

28. Nelson, "Overshadowing Senate," p. 515; Rothman, *Politics and Power*, pp. 121–26.

29. Henry Cabot Lodge, "The Senate," *Scribner's Magazine* 34(1903): 549; Gould, *Presidency of William McKinley*, p. 35.

30. Gould, *Presidency of William McKinley*, pp. 212, 213.

31. H. Wayne Morgan, *William McKinley and His America* (Syracuse University Press, 1963), p. 450.

32. On Cleveland's problems with the Supreme Court, see Morgan, *From Hayes to McKinley*, pp. 463–64.

33. Julius Caesar Burrows to James Gallup, 24 December 1896, collection of author; Francis E. Warren to Willis Van Devanter, 10 March 1897 and 11 March 1897, Willis Van Devanter Papers, Manuscript Division, Library of Congress, are classic examples of a senator's handling of a patronage case.

34. Gould, *Presidency of William McKinley*, p. 240.

35. William Lilley III and Lewis L. Gould, "The Western Irrigation Movement, 1878–1902: A Reappraisal," in Gene M. Gressley, ed., *The American West: A Reorientation* (University of Wyoming Publications, 1966), p. 73.

36. William P. Frye to William E. Chandler, 6 September 1898, William E. Chandler Papers, New Hampshire Historical Society, Concord.

37. Gould, *Presidency of William McKinley*, pp. 244–51.

38. Theodore Roosevelt to Cecil Spring Rice, 16 March 1901, *The Letters of Theodore Roosevelt*, 8 vols., ed. Elting E. Morison (Harvard University Press, 1951–1954), 3, p. 14.

39. Murat-Halstead to Albert Halstead, 23 November 1901, Halstead family papers, Cincinnati Historical Society, Cincinnati.

## Chapter Two

1. Condit Crane, "In the Seats of the Mighty," *The Outlook* 61(1899): 27.

2. Frederick H. Pauls, "Sessions of Congress," in Donald C. Bacon, Roger H. Davidson, and Morton Keller, eds., *The Encyclopedia of the United States Congress*, 4 vols. (Simon & Schuster, 1995), 4, p. 1804.

3. Claude G. Bowers, *Beveridge and the Progressive Era* (Literary Guild, 1932), pp. 139, 158; Alan Lesoff, *The Nation and Its City: Politics, "Corruption," and Progress in Washington, D.C., 1861–1902* (Johns Hopkins University Press, 1994), pp. 160–63.

4. On the Maltby Building, see Dorothy Ganfield Fowler, *John Coit Spooner: Defender of Presidents* (University Publishers, 1961), p. 215; A. J. Halford, comp., *Official Congressional Directory: Fifty-sixth Congress [second session, beginning December 3, 1901]* (Government Printing Office, 1901), p. 197.

5. Albert J. Beveridge to Orville H. Platt, 1 August 1903, Orville H. Platt Papers, Connecticut Historical Society, Hartford; Joseph B. Foraker, *Notes of a Busy Life*, 2 vols. (Stewart & Kidd, 1916), 2, pp. 328–54.

6. Aldrich's railroad holdings are discussed in Anthony Rosmond, "Nelson Aldrich, Theodore Roosevelt and the Tariff: A Study to 1905" (Ph.D. diss., University of North Carolina at Chapel Hill, 1974), pp. 36–38; James Richard Parker, "Senator John C. Spooner, 1897–1907" (Ph.D. diss., University of Maryland, 1972), pp. 183–84; on Warren's activities, Francis E. Warren to William C. Deming, 11 March 1907, 20 March 1907, Francis E. Warren Papers, American History Center, University of Wyoming, Laramie; Robert Harrison, *Congress, Progressive Reform, and the New American State* (Cambridge University Press, 2004), p. 62, has the quip about Warren; Henry Loomis Nelson, "The Overshadowing Senate," *Century Magazine* 65(1902–1903): 515, has the $60,000 per year remark.

7. Louis Ludlow, *From Cornfield to Press Gallery: Adventures and Reminiscences of a Veteran Washington Correspondent* (W. W. Roberts, 1924), p. 164; J. Franklin Little, Senate Page, 1910–1912, transcript of Oral History Interview, Senate Historical Office, Washington, D.C., p. 8; on Charles Culberson's drinking problems, see R. E. Cowart to Thomas S. Henderson, 30 November 1910, Thomas S. Henderson Papers, Center for American History, University of Texas at Austin; on Beveridge and his drinking issue, William Howard Taft to Horace Taft, 4 February 1911, William Howard Taft Papers, Manuscript Division, Library of Congress.

8. Ludlow, *From Cornfield to Press Gallery*, p. 163; Little, interview, p. 31; Dan Balz, "GOP Nominee Fights Calls to Exit Contest," *Washington Post*, June 23, 2004, discusses the personal problems of the Republican senatorial candidate in Illinois.

9. Crane, "In the Seats of the Mighty," p. 38; Clarence L. Cullen, "How Wolcott's Passion for Play Ruined a Brilliant Career," *New York Times*, 19 March 1905.

10. David J. Rothman, *Politics and Power: The United States Senate, 1869–1901* (Harvard University Press, 1966), p. 153; Parker, "Senator John C. Spooner," p. 155; Henry L. West, "The Place of the Senate in Our Government," *The Forum* 31(1901): 429.

11. John Braeman, *Albert J. Beveridge: American Nationalist* (University of Chicago Press, 1971), pp. 43–51.

12. Bowers, *Beveridge and the Progressive Era*, pp. 184–87; the quotation is on p. 186.

13. George H. Haynes, *The Senate of the United States, Its History and Practice*, 2 vols. (Houghton Mifflin, 1938), 1, pp. 187–88.

14. James K. Jones to William Jennings Bryan, 18 December 1899, box 23, William Jennings Bryan Papers, Manuscript Division, Library of Congress; George Fred Williams to Moreton Frewen, 15 November, 1899, Moreton Frewen Papers, Library of Congress.

15. David S. Barry, *Forty Years in Washington* (Little, Brown, 1924), p. 78.

16. David A. Shannon, ed., *Beatrice Webb's American Diary, 1898* (University of Wisconsin Press, 1963), p. 31; *Houston Chronicle*, 2 January 1918; Bob Charles Holcomb, "Senator Joe Bailey: Two Decades of Controversy" (Ph.D. diss., Texas Tech University, 1968).

17. Joseph Simpson to Jonathan Bourne, 21 December 1889, Jonathan Bourne Papers, University of Oregon, Eugene; "The 'Big Five' Who Run the U.S. Senate," *New York Times*, 13 March 1905.

18. Rosmond, "Nelson Aldrich, Theodore Roosevelt and the Tariff," p. 26; "'Big Five' Who Run the U.S. Senate" (first two quotations); Nathaniel Wright Stephenson, *Nelson Aldrich: A Leader in American Politics* (Charles Scribner's Sons, 1930) is the only published biography.

19. Orville H. Platt to Henry R. Reed, 13 February 1905, Orville H. Platt Papers, Connecticut Historical Society, Hartford; for contemporary estimates of Aldrich, see Willard French, "Senator Aldrich," *The Independent* 67(1909): 588–91, and Judson C. Welliver, "Aldrich: Boss of the Senate," *Hampton's Magazine* 22(1909): 39–46.

20. Shelby M. Cullom, *Fifty Years of Public Service* (A. C. McClurg, 1911), p. 216; Edwina Carol Smith, "Conservatism in the Gilded Age: The Senatorial

Career of Orville H. Platt" (Ph.D. diss., University of North Carolina at Chapel Hill, 1976), pp. 2–3; Louis A. Coolidge, *An Old-Fashioned Senator: Orville H. Platt of Connecticut* (G. P. Putnam's Sons, 1914).

21. Leland Sage, *William Boyd Allison: A Study in Practical Politics* (State Historical Society of Iowa, 1956), gives a good sense of Allison's cautious and enigmatic personality; Barry, *Forty Years in Washington*, p. 106.

22. On the "Iowa Idea," see Ralph Mills Sayre, "Albert Baird Cummins and the Progressive Movement in Iowa" (Ph.D. diss., Columbia University, 1958), pp. 153–55, 167–70; Richard Cleveland Baker, *The Tariff Under Roosevelt and Taft* (Democrat Printing Co., 1941), pp. 15–16, 30–33.

23. Fowler, *Spooner*, p. 215.

24. Parker, "Senator Spooner," pp. 4–5, 19–20.

25. Geoffrey G. Drutchas, "Gray Eminence in a Gilded Age: The Forgotten Career of Senator James S. McMillan of Michigan," *Michigan Historical Review* 28(2002): 92–93.

26. Thomas Collier Platt to William Boyd Allison, 26 July 1899, William Boyd Allison Papers, box 334, Iowa State Department of History and Archives, Des Moines; on the committee structure of The Four and their allies, see Rothman, *Politics and Power*, pp. 46–61.

27. Theodore Roosevelt to Joseph B. Bishop, 23 March 1905, in Elting E. Morison et al., eds., *The Letters of Theodore Roosevelt*, 8 vols. (Harvard University Press, 1951–54), 4, p. 1144; the quotation about Senator Hale is from the George von Lengerke Meyer Diary, 17 April 1908, Manuscript Division, Library of Congress.

28. Aldrich is quoted in the *American Economist*, 8 November 1901.

29. George W. Smalley to Moreton Frewen, 16 June 1902, Frewen Papers.

30. Stephenson, *Aldrich*, pp. 194–99; Lewis L. Gould, *The Presidency of Theodore Roosevelt* (University Press of Kansas, 1991), pp. 65–66.

31. *New York Herald*, 10 January 1905.

32. Franklin L. Burdette, *Filibustering in the Senate* (Princeton University Press, 1940), p. 76.

33. *Harper's Weekly* 47(1903): 467–68.

34. For the political context of Gorman's strategy, see Richard H. Collin, *Theodore Roosevelt's Caribbean: The Panama Canal, the Monroe Doctrine, and the Latin American Context* (Louisiana State University Press, 1990), pp. 292, 295–96.

35. Donald A. Ritchie, ed., *Minutes of the Senate Democratic Conference, Fifty-eighth Congress through Eighty-eighth Congress, 1903–1964* (Government Printing Office, 1998), pp. 1–3. John R. Lambert, *Arthur Pue Gorman* (Louisiana State University Press, 1953), pp. 303–4.

36. John R. Lambert, Jr., "The Autobiographical Writings of Senator Arthur Pue Gorman," *Maryland Historical Magazine* 58(1963): 237.

37. John Morton Blum, *The Republican Roosevelt* (Harvard University Press, 1954), pp. 38–54, is the classic statement about the Roosevelt-Hanna rivalry.

38. James S. Clarkson to A. B. Humphrey, 20 September 1902, James S. Clarkson Papers, Manuscript Division, Library of Congress; James P. Hornaday to Delavan Smith, 7 June 1904, Charles W. Fairbanks Papers, Lilly Library, Indiana University at Bloomington.

39. Roosevelt to William Howard Taft, 19 March 1903, Morison et al., *Letters of Theodore Roosevelt*, vol. 3, p. 450.

40. Jonathan P. Dolliver to S. W. Rathbun, 6 September 1904, Jonathan P. Dolliver Papers, State Historical Society of Iowa, Iowa City; Orville H. Platt, speech given at Providence, Rhode Island, 13 October 1904, copy in Orville H. Platt Papers, Connecticut Historical Society, Hartford.

41. John Coit Spooner to Elisha W. Keyes, 25 December 1904, John Coit Spooner Papers, Manuscript Division, Library of Congress.

42. Haynes, *The Senate of the United States*, 1, pp. 99–104.

43. On Joseph Burton's legal problems, see Robert Sherman La Forte, *Leaders of Reform: Progressive Republicans in Kansas, 1900–1916* (University Press of Kansas, 1974), pp. 39–40; on the Oregon land frauds and Senator Mitchell, see Thomas Roger Wessel, "Republican Justice: The Department of Justice Under Roosevelt and Taft, 1901–1913" (Ph.D. diss., University of Maryland, 1972), pp. 144–49.

44. "The Senate's Loss of Public Confidence," *World's Work* 9(1905): 6118.

## Chapter Three

1. Theodore Roosevelt to Lyman Abbott, 10 January 1905, in Elting E. Morison, et al., eds., *The Letters of Theodore Roosevelt*, 8 vols. (Harvard University Press, 1951–54), 4, p. 1100; *New York Herald*, 27 February 1905.

2. Theodore Roosevelt to Shelby M. Cullom, 10 February 1905, *Letters*, 4, p. 1118; Lewis L. Gould, *The Presidency of Theodore Roosevelt* (University Press of Kansas, 1991), p. 149.

3. Diary entry, 6 February 1905, James R. Garfield Papers, Manuscript Division, Library of Congress; Jacob H. Gallinger to James O. Lyford, James O. Lyford papers, New Hampshire Historical Society, Concord; Mortimer Durand to Marquess of Lansdowne, 10 March 1905, Marquess of Lansdowne Papers, Foreign Office 800/144, Public Record Office, Kew.

4. *Washington Post*, "In Defense of Mitchell," 1 July 1905, and "Mitchell Found Guilty," 4 July 1905; on Burton, "Unworthy Senators," *Independent*

59(1905): 1291–92; Mortimer Durand to Marquess of Lansdowne, 30 November 1905, Foreign Office 5/2580, Public Record Office, Kew.

5. *Washington Post*, 13 January 1905; Charles Hopkins Clark to Orville H. Platt, 10 February 1905, Orville H. Platt Papers, Connecticut Historical Society, Hartford; "The Senate's Loss of Public Confidence," *The World's Work* (1905): 6118.

6. Newell Dwight Hilles to Jonathan P. Dolliver, 9 June 1905, Jonathan P. Dolliver Papers, Iowa Historical Society, Iowa City; on Depew, see "Depew to Quit Yale," *New York Times*, 5 April 1906, and "Depew Picture of Despair," *Washington Post*, 6 July 1906.

7. Elisha W. Keyes to John Coit Spooner, 25 January 1906, John Coit Spooner Papers, Manuscript Division, Library of Congress.

8. Nancy C. Unger, *Fighting Bob La Follette: The Righteous Reformer* (University of North Carolina Press, 2000), is the best one-volume treatment of the senator's life; Browning verse mentioned in Robert M. La Follette to William Kent, 15 February 1912, William Kent Papers, Sterling Memorial Library, Yale University, New Haven.

9. Robert M. La Follette, *La Follette's Autobiography: A Personal Narrative of Political Experiences* (Robert M. La Follette Company, 1911), p. 372.

10. For contemporary assessments of La Follette, see William Bayard Hale, "La Follette, Pioneer Progressive," *The World's Work* (1911): 14599, and "Mr. La Follette as Seen from the Gallery," *The Outlook*, 3 February 1912, p. 255; Herbert Parsons to Joseph Deutsch, 22 March 1911, box 19, Herbert Parsons Papers, Columbia University Library, New York.

11. Gould, *Presidency of Theodore Roosevelt*, pp. 150–51.

12. Theodore Roosevelt, *The Works of Theodore Roosevelt*, vol. 15, *State Papers as Governor and President, 1899–1909* (Charles Scribner's Sons, 1926), p. 226.

13. Orville H. Platt to Wilbur F. Day, 15 February 1905, Orville H. Platt Papers, Connecticut Historical Society, Hartford.

14. Gould, *Presidency of Theodore Roosevelt*, pp. 156–57; Robert Harrison, *Congress, Progressive Reform and the New American State* (Cambridge University Press, 2004), pp. 50–62, is excellent on the background of the legislation and the forces at play in the congressional debates.

15. Dolliver to J. J. Ryan, 26 January 1906, Jonathan P. Dolliver Papers, Iowa Historical Society, Iowa City.

16. Dolliver to Shelby M. Cullom, 26 February 1906, Jonathan P. Dolliver Papers, Iowa Historical Society, Iowa City.

17. David Graham Phillips, *The Treason of the Senate*, edited with an introduction by George E. Mowry and Judson Grenier (Quadrangle Books, 1964), p. 59.

18. David S. Barry, "The Loyalty of the Senate," *New England Magazine* 35(1906): 165–76; Donald A. Ritchie, *Press Gallery: Congress and the Washington Correspondents* (Harvard University Press, 1991), pp. 187–94.

19. Roosevelt to George William Alger, 20 March 1906, *Letters*, 5, p. 189.

20. Theodore Roosevelt, "The Man with the Muckrake," *The Works of Theodore Roosevelt*, vol. 16, *American Problems* (Charles Scribner's Sons, 1926), pp. 415–24.

21. Unger, *Fighting Bob La Follette*, pp. 144–45, describes the scene and includes the famous quotation. Spooner maintained that La Follette "was not hazed by the Senate"; see John Coit Spooner to Elisha W. Keyes, 4 June 1906, Elisha W. Keyes Papers, Wisconsin State Historical Society, Madison.

22. Spooner to Keyes, 25 June 1906, Elisha W. Keyes Papers, Wisconsin State Historical Society, Madison. Mark Sullivan, *Our Times*, vol. 3, *Pre-War America* (Charles Scribner's Sons, 1930), pp. 260–61.

23. "A Congress That Made History," *Collier's*, 14 July 1906, 9.

24. Belle Case La Follette and Fola La Follette, *Robert M. La Follette: June 14, 1855–June 18, 1925*, 2 vols. (Macmillan, 1952), 1, p. 212.

25. Cullom to Spooner, 19 October 1907, John Coit Spooner Papers, Manuscript Division, Library of Congress; La Follette and La Follette, *Robert M. La Follette*, 1, p. 217.

26. Mortimer Durand to Edward Grey, 27 December 1906, Foreign Office 371/357, Public Record Office, Kew.

27. John D. Weaver, *The Brownsville Raid* (Texas A&M University Press, 1992), pp. 131–34.

28. Mabel Boardman to William Howard Taft, 18 November 1907, William Howard Taft Papers, Manuscript Division, Library of Congress.

29. David Sarasohn, *The Party of Reform: Democrats in the Progressive Era* (University of Mississippi Press, 1989), pp. 24–25.

30. Gould, *Presidency of Theodore Roosevelt*, pp. 203–4.

31. Henry White to Henry Cabot Lodge, 1 May 1908, Henry Cabot Lodge Papers, Massachusetts Historical Society, Boston.

32. Claude G. Bowers, *Beveridge and the Progressive Era* (Literary Guild, 1932), p. 282.

33. Gould, *Presidency of Theodore Roosevelt*, pp. 277–78.

34. Unger, *Fighting Bob La Follette*, pp. 182–83.

35. Franklin L. Burdette, *Filibuster in the Senate* (Princeton University Press, 1940), pp. 84–91.

36. Robert C. Byrd, *The Senate 1789–1989: Addresses on the History of the United States Senate*, 2 vols. (Government Printing Office, 1991), 2, pp. 108–10.

37. Lodge commented on the reaction of one senator to Taft's working style in Lodge to Roosevelt, 27 December 1909, Henry Cabot Lodge Papers, Massachusetts Historical Society, Boston. Charles D. Hilles, "Memorandum for the President," 25 November 1912, series 6, case file 149, William Howard Taft Papers, Manuscript Division, Library of Congress, indicates that these problems persisted through the end of the administration.

38. Robert Connington, "Keeping Cool in the Senate," *Harper's Weekly*, 12 August 1911, p. 7; Albert J. Beveridge to L. G. Rothschild, 28 June 1909, Albert J. Beveridge Papers, Manuscript Division, Library of Congress.

39. Lewis L. Gould, *Reform and Regulation: American Politics from Roosevelt to Wilson* (Waveland Press, 1996), pp. 113–17.

40. Lewis L. Gould, "Western Range Senators and the Payne Aldrich Tariff," *Pacific Northwest Quarterly* 64(1973): 49–56.

41. Richard Cleveland Baker, *The Tariff Under Roosevelt and Taft* (Democrat Printing Co., 1941), pp. 93, 95; U.S. Senate, *Congressional Record*, 61st Cong., 1 Sess. (22 April 1909), pp. 1454, 1461; William Allen White, *The Autobiography of William Allen White* (Macmillan, 1946), p. 426.

42. Beveridge quoted in *Springfield Republican* (Massachusetts), 14 July 1909; William Howard Taft, *Presidential Addresses and State Papers* (Doubleday, Page, 1910), p. 222. Joseph L. Bristow to Albert B. Cummins, 30 October 1909, Joseph L. Bristow Papers, Kansas Historical Society, Topeka.

43. Bristow to F. S. Jackson, 18 February 1910, Joseph L. Bristow Papers, Kansas Historical Society, Topeka.

## Chapter Four

1. L. Ethan Ellis, *Reciprocity 1911: A Study in Canadian-American Relations* (Yale University Press, 1939), pp. 116–19.

2. George H. Haynes, *The Senate of the United States*, 2 vols. (Houghton Mifflin, 1938), 1, pp. 135–37.

3. Joel Arthur Tarr, *A Study in Boss Politics: William Lorimer of Chicago* (University of Illinois Press, 1971).

4. Ibid., p. 233; Haynes, *The Senate of the United States*, 1, pp. 131–35.

5. Larry J. Easterling, "Senator Joseph L. Bristow and the Seventeenth Amendment," *Kansas Historical Quarterly* 41(1975): 493–94.

6. Easterling, "Senator Joseph L. Bristow," p. 496; Howard W. Allen, Aage R. Clausen, and Jerome M. Clubb, "Political Reform and Negro Rights in the Senate," *Journal of Southern History* 37(1971): 191–92.

7. Easterling, "Senator Joseph L. Bristow," pp. 503–6.

8. Ibid., p. 503. For a critique of the movement for the direct election of senators, see C. H. Hoebke, *The Road to Mass Democracy: Original Intent and the Seventeenth Amendment* (Transaction, 1995).

9. William S. Kenyon to George D. Perkins, 29 April 1911, George D. Perkins Papers, Iowa State Department of History and Archives, Des Moines; Wendy A. Wolff and Donald Ritchie, eds., *Minutes of the Senate Republican Conference, Sixty-second Through Eighty-eighth Congress* (Government Printing Office, 1999), pp. 18–20.

10. Virginia Floy Haughton, "John Worth Kern and Wilson's New Freedom: A Study of a Senate Majority Leader" (Ph.D. diss., University of Kentucky, 1973), p. 33. On Senator Bailey's trouble, see Lewis L. Gould, *Progressives and Prohibitionists: Texas Democrats in the Wilson Era* (Texas State Historical Association, 1992), pp. 18–23.

11. Tarr, *Study in Boss Politics*, pp. 293–305; "Lorimer Out," *The Literary Digest*, 27 July 1912, 134.

12. Henry Cabot Lodge to Mrs. Parkman, 1 March 1913, copy in author's files.

13. Woodrow Wilson to A. Mitchell Palmer, 5 February 1913, Woodrow Wilson, *The Papers of Woodrow Wilson*, 69 vols., ed. Arthur S. Link (Princeton University Press, 1966–94), 27, p. 149.

14. Howard W. Allen, *Poindexter of Washington: A Study in Progressive Politics* (Southern Illinois Press, 1981), pp. 85–93; Wythe W. Holt, Jr., "The Senator from Virginia and the Democratic Floor Leadership: Thomas S. Martin and Conservatism in the Progressive Era," *Virginia Magazine of History and Biography* 83(1975): 3–21.

15. See Haughton, "John Worth Kern and Wilson's New Freedom"; Claude G. Bowers, *The Life of John Worth Kern* (Hollenbeck Press, 1918); and Walter J. Oleszek, "John Worth Kern: Portrait of a Floor Leader," in Richard Baker and Roger H. Davidson, eds., *First Among Equals: Outstanding Senate Leaders of the Twentieth Century* (Congressional Quarterly, 1991), pp. 7–37.

16. Donald A. Ritchie, ed., *Minutes of the Senate Democratic Conference: Fifty-eighth Congress Through Eighty-eighth Congress, 1903–1964* (Government Printing Office, 1998), pp. 51–72; Haughton, "John Worth Kern and Wilson's New Freedom," p. 142.

17. On Kern's problems with absenteeism, see Haughton, "John Worth Kern and Wilson's New Freedom," pp. 143–45.

18. On Ham Lewis, see "The New Senators from Illinois," *Literary Digest*, 12 April 1913, 860; and David Kenney and Robert E. Hartley, *An Uncertain Tradition: U.S. Senators from Illinois, 1818–2003* (Southern Illinois Press, 2003), pp. 102–5.

19. Ritchie, *Minutes of the Senate Democratic Conference*, p. 59; "Rome Rolls Round Again," *The Nation*, 24 November 1920, 583.

20. Betty Glad, *Key Pittman: The Tragedy of a Senate Insider* (Columbia University Press, 1986), p. 42.

21. A. Maurice Low, "The South in the Saddle," *Harper's Weekly*, 8 February 1913, 20; Joel Williamson, *The Crucible of Race: Black-White Relations in the American South Since Emancipation* (Oxford University Press, 1984), p. 379.

22. George F. Sparks, ed., *A Many-Colored Toga: The Diary of Henry Fountain Ashurst* (University of Arizona Press, 1962), pp. 26–27.

23. Woodrow Wilson to Mary Allen Hulbert, 8 April 1913, Wilson, *Papers*, vol. 27, p. 273; U.S. Senate, *Congressional Record*, 63 Cong. 1 Sess. (7 April 1913), pp. 58, 60.

24. Ritchie, *Minutes of the Senate Democratic Conference*, p. 119.

25. Woodrow Wilson, "A Statement on Tariff Lobbyists," Wilson, *Papers*, 27, p. 473; "Expose the Lobby," *Washington Post*, 30 May 1913.

26. U.S. Senate, *Maintenance of a Lobby to Influence Legislation*, 63 Cong., 1 Sess., 4 vols. (Government Printing Office, 1913); "Query a 'Disgrace': Thornton Resents Senate Inquiry as to His Property," *Washington Post*, 5 June 1913.

27. "President Wilson, the Democratic Party and the New 'Competitive' Tariff," *The Independent*, 9 October 1913, 62.

28. George H. Haynes, "The Changing Senate," *North American Review*, August 1914, 223.

29. Gifford Pinchot to G. F. Robinson, 29 December 1914, original in author's files.

30. "From the Diary of Nancy Saunders Toy," 3 January 1915, Wilson, *Papers*, 32, p. 10.

31. Milton R. Merrill, *Reed Smoot: Apostle in Politics* (Utah State University Press, 1999), p. 246; John W. Weeks to James T. Williams, 15 January 1915, James T. Williams Papers, Duke University Library, Durham; Henry Cabot Lodge to James Lord Bryce, 14 January 1915, Lord Bryce Papers, Bodleian Library, Oxford.

32. Ruth Warne Towne, *Senator William J. Stone and the Politics of Compromise* (Kennikat Press, 1979), pp. 165–66; Franklin L. Burdette, *Filibustering in the Senate* (Princeton University Press, 1940), p. 111; Charles S. Thomas, "The Shackled Senate," *North American Review* 202(1915): 424–31 (Thomas was a Colorado senator who made the case for filibuster reform).

33. Henry Cabot Lodge to Moreton Frewen, 16 August 1915, Henry Cabot Lodge Papers, Massachusetts Historical Society, Boston; Lodge to John St. Loe

Strachey, 20 May 1915, John St. Loe Strachey Papers, House of Lords Record Office, London.

34. A. L. Todd, *Justice on Trial: The Case of Louis D. Brandeis* (McGraw-Hill, 1964).

35. Joseph P. Harris, *The Advice and Consent of the Senate: A Study of the Confirmation of Appointments by the United States Senate* (Greenwood, 1968), pp. 99, 111.

36. Towne, *Senator William J. Stone and the Politics of Compromise*, pp. 173–79; Haughton, "John Worth Kern and Wilson's New Freedom," pp. 275–81.

37. James E. Watson to Victor Rosewater, 15 November 1916, Victor Rosewater Papers, American Jewish Historical Society, Cincinnati; George C. Roberts, "Woodrow Wilson, John W. Kern, and the 1916 Indiana Election: Defeat of a Senate Majority Leader," *Presidential Studies Quarterly* 10(1980): 63–73.

38. John Milton Cooper, *Breaking the Heart of the World: Woodrow Wilson and the Fight for the League of Nations* (Cambridge University Press, 2001), p. 20.

39. "An Address to a Joint Session of Congress," 26 February 1917, Wilson, *Papers*, 41, pp. 283–87.

40. Henry Cabot Lodge to Theodore Roosevelt, 27 February 1917, in Henry Cabot Lodge, ed., *Selections from the Correspondence of Theodore Roosevelt and Henry Cabot Lodge, 1884–1918*, 2 vols. (Charles Scribner's Sons, 1925), 2, p. 497.

41. Nancy C. Unger, *Fighting Bob La Follette: The Righteous Reformer* (University of North Carolina Press, 2000), pp. 243–46; Thomas W. Ryley, *A Little Group of Willful Men: A Study of Congressional-Presidential Authority* (Kennikat Press, 1975), pp. 103–15.

42. Woodrow Wilson, "A Statement," 4 March 1917, Wilson, *Papers of Woodrow Wilson*, 41, p. 320; "The Most Reprehensible Filibuster in History," *Current Opinion* 62(April 1917): 229.

43. "Closure At Last," *New York Times*, 9 March 1917; Burdette, *Filibustering in the Senate*, pp. 127–28; Ritchie, *Minutes of the Senate Democratic Conference*, pp. 258, 259.

## Chapter Five

1. John A. Garraty, *Henry Cabot Lodge: A Biography* (Alfred A. Knopf, 1953), p. 336.

2. Richard Lowitt, *George W. Norris: The Persistence of a Progressive, 1913–1933* (University of Illinois Press, 1971), p. 74; Nancy Unger, *Fighting*

*Bob La Follette: The Righteous Reformer* (University of North Carolina Press, 2000), pp. 249–50.

3. "A Review of the World: The Case of Senator La Follette," *Current Opinion* 53(1917): 289–90; Unger, *Fighting Bob La Follette*, pp. 254–57.

4. Unger, *Fighting Bob La Follette*, pp. 258–61; Thomas H. Smith, "The Senatorial Career of Atlee Pomerene" (Ph.D. diss., Kent State University, 1966), pp. 229–41.

5. Lowitt, *George W. Norris*, p. 88.

6. Hiram Johnson to Hiram Johnson, Jr., and Archibald W. Johnson, 6 April 1917, in Robert E. Burke, ed., *The Diary Letters of Hiram Johnson*, 7 vols. (Garland, 1983). There is no pagination for this series and letters can only be cited by date.

7. Seward Livermore, *Politics Is Adjourned: Woodrow Wilson and the War Congress* (Wesleyan University Press, 1966), p. 56.

8. Martin L. Fausold, *James Wadsworth, Jr.: The Gentleman from New York* (Syracuse University Press, 1975), p. 106.

9. Hiram Johnson to Hiram Johnson, Jr., and Archibald W. Johnson, 30 April 1917, in Burke, *Diary Letters of Hiram Johnson*, vol. 1.

10. Sara Hunter Graham, *Woman Suffrage and the New Democracy* (Yale University press, 1996), p. 117.

11. Ibid., pp. 125–27.

12. Woodrow Wilson, "An Address to a Joint Session of Congress, 27 May 1918," *The Papers of Woodrow Wilson*, 69 vols., ed. Arthur S. Link (Princeton University Press, 1966–94), 48, p. 164. Theodore Roosevelt to Arthur Lee, 5 April 1917, Papers of Lord Lee of Fareham, Courtauld Institute, London; Henry Cabot Lodge to Theodore Roosevelt, 27 April 1917, Henry Cabot Lodge Papers, Massachusetts Historical Society, Boston.

13. Lewis L. Gould, *Reform and Regulation: American Politics from Roosevelt to Wilson* (Waveland Press, 1996), p. 199.

14. Ibid., pp. 199–200.

15. George H. Haynes, *The Senate of the United States: Its History and Practice*, 2 vols. (Houghton Mifflin, 1938), 2, p. 921; Forrest Maltzman, Lee Sigelman, and Sara Binder, "Leaving Office Feet First: Death in Congress," *PS: Political Science and Politics*, 1 December 1996, pp. 65–671, examines the causes behind congressional fatalities.

16. Wilson to Thomas Riley Marshall, 15 March 1918, and Wilson to Joseph Edward Davies, 18 March 1919, in Wilson, *Papers*, 47, p. 52; Herbert F. Margulies, *Senator Lenroot of Wisconsin: A Political Biography, 1900–1929* (University of Missouri Press, 1977), p. 245.

17. Livermore, *Politics Is Adjourned*, p. 159; James K. Vardaman to Douglass Robinson, 24 August 1918, Vardaman's Weekly On-Line, www.hhtc.org/vw/son.html.

18. Gould, *Reform and Regulation*, p. 159; John Milton Cooper, *Breaking the Heart of the World: Woodrow Wilson and the Fight for the League of Nations* (Cambridge University Press, 2001), pp. 30–31.

19. W. D. Jamieson, "Why You Should Give Earnest Attention Right Now to Electing a Democratic Congress," pamphlet, published by Democratic National Committee, Minnie Fisher Cunningham Papers, Houston Metropolitan Research Center, Houston; "An Appeal for a Democratic Congress," in Wilson, *Papers*, 51, p. 382; Fausold, *James Wadsworth, Jr.*, p. 108.

20. Henry Cabot Lodge to William Allen White, 16 November 1918, William Allen White Papers, Manuscript Division, Library of Congress.

21. Livermore, *Politics Is Adjourned*, pp. 225–241.

22. George F. Sparks, ed., *A Many-Colored Toga: The Diary of Henry Fountain Ashurst* (University of Arizona Press, 1962), p. 90.

23. Cooper, *Breaking the Heart of the World*, pp. 33–34.

24. William C. Widenor, *Henry Cabot Lodge and the Search for an American Foreign Policy* (University of California Press, 1980), p. 208; for Lodge's interpretation of their animosity, see Henry Cabot Lodge, *The Senate and the League of Nations* (Charles Scribner's Sons, 1925).

25. Lodge to Arthur Balfour, 25 November 1918, Arthur Balfour Papers, no. 49742, British Library, London.

26. Hiram Johnson to Hiram Johnson, Jr., 16 February 1919, in Burke, *Diary Letters of Hiram Johnson*, vol. 3.

27. Lodge, *Senate and the League of Nations*, pp. 119–20; Cooper, *Breaking the Heart of the World*, pp. 50–57, is excellent on the Round Robin.

28. Ralph Stone, *The Irreconcilables: The Fight Against the League of Nations* (University Press of Kentucky, 1970), p. 63; Cooper, *Breaking the Heart of the World*, p. 67.

29. Warren G. Harding to Malcolm Jennings, 28 January 1916, Malcolm Jennings Papers, box 1, reel 261, Warren G. Harding Papers, microfilm edition, Ohio Historical Society, Columbus; Cooper, *Breaking the Heart of the World*, p. 57; Marian C. McKenna, *Borah* (University of Michigan Press, 1961), pp. 152–57.

30. Hiram Johnson to Archibald Johnson, 16 March 1919, in Burke, *Diary Letters of Hiram Johnson*, vol. 3.

31. Herbert F. Margulies, *The Mild Reservationists and the League of Nations Controversy in the Senate* (University of Missouri Press, 1989), is definitive on its subject.

32. Cooper, *Breaking the Heart of the World*, p. 95, note 68.

33. Ibid., pp. 111–18.

34. Sparks, *A Many-Colored Toga*, pp. 98–99; Johnson to Hiram Johnson, Jr., and Archibald Johnson, 23 August 1919, in Burke, *Diary Letters of Hiram Johnson*, vol. 3.

35. Stone, *The Irreconcilables*, p. 129; Margulies, *Mild Reservationists*, pp. 94–98.

36. Cooper, *Breaking the Heart of the World*, pp. 198–212, covers the controversy about Wilson's illness in a comprehensive and insightful manner.

37. Margulies, *Mild Reservationists*, pp. 155–56, makes clear how narrow the cloture decision actually was.

38. Cooper, *Breaking the Heart of the World*, p. 262.

39. David H. Stratton, *Tempest over Teapot Dome: The Story of Albert B. Fall* (University of Oklahoma Press, 1998), pp. 170–73. Cooper, *Breaking the Heart of the World*, pp. 285–88, provides a thorough recounting of the visit of the "smelling committee" to the White House.

40. Cooper, *Breaking the Heart of the World*, pp. 288, 289.

41. *New York Times*, 9 March 1920; Cooper, *Breaking the Heart of the World*, p. 373.

42. Margulies, *Senator Lenroot*, pp. 323–29.

43. Belle Case La Follette and Fola La Follette, *Robert M. La Follette, June 14, 1855–June 18, 1925*, 2 vols. (Macmillan, 1953), 2, p. 1020.

## Chapter Six

1. LeRoy Ashby, *The Spearless Leader: Senator Borah and the Progressive Movement in the 1920s* (University of Illinois Press, 1972), p. 34; William C. Widenor, "Henry Cabot Lodge: The Astute Parliamentarian," in Richard A. Baker and Roger H. Davidson, eds., *First Among Equals: Outstanding Senate Leaders of the Twentieth Century* (Congressional Quarterly, 1991), pp. 52–56; George Rothwell Brown, *The Leadership of Congress* (Bobbs-Merrill, 1922), pp. 254–56.

2. Mark O. Hatfield et al., *Vice Presidents of the United States, 1789–1993* (Government Printing Office, 1997), pp. 377–378; the Curtis endorsement of Lucky Strike cigarettes appeared in *The American Magazine*, August 1927, p. 123.

3. Frank R. Kent, "Senator James E. Watson: The Professional Public Servant," *Atlantic Monthly* 159(1932): 184–90. For the senator's anecdotal and often unreliable recounting of his public career, see James E. Wason, *As I Knew Them* (Bobbs-Merrill, 1936).

4. Evans C. Johnson, *Oscar W. Underwood: A Political Biography* (Louisiana State University Press, 1988), pp. 291–341, is favorable, but unconvincing, on its subject's record as minority leader.

5. Donald C. Bacon, "Joseph Taylor Robinson: The Good Soldier," in Richard A. Baker and Roger H. Davidson, eds., *First Among Equals: Outstanding Senate Leaders of the Twentieth Century* (Congressional Quarterly, 1991), p. 70; for a not particularly penetrating look at Robinson's Senate record, see Cecil Edward Weller, Jr., *Joe T. Robinson: Always a Loyal Democrat* (University of Arkansas Press, 1998).

6. Ray Thomas Tucker [Anonymous], *The Mirrors of 1932* (Brewer, Warren & Putnam, 1931), pp. 130, 132; Elliott Thurston, "Joseph T. Robinson-Presidential Possibilities-III," *The Forum* 86(1931): 252–56.

7. Arthur M. Schlesinger, Jr., *The Crisis of the Old Order, 1919–1933* (Houghton Mifflin, 1957), p. 376; "Reverberations of the Dawes Slam," *The Literary Digest*, 21 March 1925, p. 11.

8. "Rome Rolls Round Again," *The Nation* 110(1920): 583.

9. Hiram Johnson to Hiram Johnson, Jr., and Archibald W. Johnson, 6 April 1917, in Robert E. Burke, ed., *The Diary Letters of Hiram Johnson*, 7 vols. (Garland, 1983), vol. 2; Robert C. Byrd, with Wendy Wolff, *The Senate 1789–1989: Addresses on the History of the United States Senate*, 2 vols. (Government Printing Office, 1991), 2, p. 355.

10. Richard Langham Riedel, *Halls of the Mighty: My 47 Years at the Senate* (Robert B. Luce, 1969), p. 16.

11. Norman D. Brown, *Hood, Bonnet, and Little Brown Jug: Texas Politics, 1921–1928* (Texas A&M Press, 1984), pp. 88–89, 107–8.

12. Drew Pearson and Robert S. Allen, "The Capitol Underworld," in *Katharine Graham's Washington*, ed. Katharine Graham (Vintage Books, 2002), pp. 208–9; Bacon, "Joseph Taylor Robinson," pp. 73–74; Kristie Miller, *Ruth Hanna McCormick: A Life in Politics, 1880–1944* (University of New Mexico Press, 1992), pp. 149–51.

13. "Republican Absenteeism," *Washington Post*, 24 May 1922.

14. George H. Haynes, *The Senate of the United States: Its History and Practice*, 2 vols. (Houghton Mifflin, 1938), 2, p. 942. For Tillman's action, see U.S. Senate, *Congressional Record*, 63 Cong., 2 Sess. (9 March 1914): 4531–32.

15. For the origins of the Ladies of the Senate, see George F. Sparks, ed., *A Many-Colored Toga: The Diary of Henry Fountain Ashurst* (University of Arizona Press, 1962), p. 171. Byrd and Wolff, *The Senate, 1789–1989*, 2, pp. 513–15. Joel Williamson, *The Crucible of Race: Black-White Relations in the American South Since Emancipation* (Oxford University Press, 1984), pp. 124–30, 303, 461.

16. *New York Times*, 7 January 1923.

17. Ashby, *Spearless Leader*, pp. 17–20.

18. Robert S. Allen, *Washington Merry-Go-Round* (Horace Liveright, 1931), p. 214.

19. Richard L. Neuberger, *Our Promised Land* (Macmillan, 1938), p. 179.

20. Ashby, *Spearless Leader*, p. 4.

21. Robert David Johnson, *The Peace Progressives and American Foreign Relations* (Harvard University Press, 1995), p. 168.

22. Ashby, *Spearless Leader*, pp. 107–8.

23. Herbert F. Margulies, *Senator Lenroot of Wisconsin: A Political Biography, 1900–1929* (University of Missouri Press, 1977), pp. 380–88.

24. Donald R. McCoy, *Calvin Coolidge: The Quiet President* (Macmillan, 1967), pp. 361–63.

25. Marian C. McKenna, *Borah* (University of Michigan Press, 1961), p. 244.

26. Hiram Johnson to Hiram Johnson, Jr., and Archibald W. Johnson, 12 January 1929, in Burke, *Diary Letters of Hiram Johnson*, vol. 5.

27. Nancy C. Unger, *Fighting Bob La Follette: The Righteous Reformer* (University of North Carolina Press, 2000), pp. 262–303.

28. James H. Shideler, *Farm Crisis, 1919–1923* (University of California Press, 1957), pp. 46–75.

29. Ibid., pp. 155–65; for a discussion of the complexities behind the term "farm bloc," see Patrick J. O'Brien, "A Reexamination of the Senate Farm Bloc, 1921–1933," *Agricultural History* 47(1973): 248–63.

30. Steve Neal, *McNary of Oregon: A Political Biography* (The Press of the Oregon Historical Society, 1985), pp. 95–106.

31. For a richly detailed discussion of Norris's role, see Richard Lowitt, *George W. Norris: The Persistence of a Progressive, 1913–1933* (University of Illinois Press, 1971), pp. 138–319.

32. David H. Stratton, *Tempest over Teapot Dome: The Story of Albert B. Fall* (University of Oklahoma Press, 1998), pp. 229–30, is a good introduction to the controversy.

33. J. Leonard Bates, *Senator Thomas J. Walsh of Montana: Law and Public Affairs from TR to FDR* (University of Illinois Press, 1999), pp. 212–44, looks into Walsh's role. Martin R. Ansell, *Oil Baron of the Southwest: Edward L. Doheny and the Development of the Petroleum Industry in California and Mexico* (Ohio State University Press, 1998), pp. 228–29, is an excellent introduction to one of the major players in the scandal.

34. Franklin. L. Burdette, *Filibustering in the Senate* (Princeton University Press, 1940), pp. 132–33.

35. George C. Rable, "The South and the Politics of Antilynching Legislation, 1920–1940," *Journal of Southern History* 51(1985): 203–5; Robert L. Zangrando, *The NAACP Crusade Against Lynching, 1909–1950* (Temple University Press, 1980), pp. 54–61.

36. Claudine L. Ferrell, *Nightmare and Dream: Antilynching in Congress, 1917–1922* (Garland, 1986), pp. 275–300; U.S. Senate, *Congressional Record*, 67 Cong., 3 Sess. (29 November 1922), p. 390. In 2005, two senators, George Allen of Virginia, a Republican, and Mary Landrieu of Louisiana, a Democrat, introduced a resolution to apologize for the Senate's record on legislation to control lynching in the 1920s and 1930s. "Senators Introduce Lynching Apology," *New York Times*, 2 February 2005; Peter Hardin, "Lynching Apology Being Revived," *Richmond Times-Dispatch*, 2 February 2005. The Senate adopted a resolution apologizing for its record on lynching in June 2005. Sheryl Gay Stolberg, "Senate Issues Apology Over Failure on Lynching Law," *The New York Times*, 14 June 2005.

37. David Robertson, *Sly and Able: A Political Biography of James F. Byrnes* (W. W. Norton, 1994), pp. 101–13, is excellent on Baruch and his influence on the Senate Democrats. Jordan Schwarz, *The Speculator: Bernard M. Baruch in Washington, 1917–1965* (University of North Carolina Press, 1981), is an outstanding biography.

38. "Proposes Cloture by Majority Vote," *Washington Post*, 14 March 1923; "Rules of the Senate," *Washington Post*, 14 March 1923. See also the remarks of Oscar W. Underwood in U.S. Senate, *Congressional Record*, 67 Cong., 3 Sess (19 February 1923): 3964.

39. Hatfield et al., *Vice Presidents of the United States*, "Charles G. Dawes," pp. 359–69; U.S. Senate, *Congressional Record*, 69 Cong., Special Sess. (5 March 1925): 3–4; "Reverberations of the Dawes Slam," pp. 10–11; "Dawes Takes His Case to the People," *The Literary Digest*, 9 May 1925, pp. 14–15; Oliver Peck Newman, "'Cloture' in the Senate," *American Review of Reviews* 71(9125): 623–26; George Wharton Pepper, *In the Senate* (University of Pennsylvania Press, 1930), pp. 97–100.

40. Hiram Johnson to Hiram Johnson, Jr., 4 March 1925, in Burke, *Diary Letters of Hiram Johnson*, vol. 4; for both quotations, see Haynes, *Senate of the United States*, 1, pp. 417–18.

41. "The Senate's War on the President," *The Literary Digest*, 28 March 1925, p. 7. On the Warren nomination battle, see Joseph P. Harris, *The Advice*

*and Consent of the Senate: A Study of the Confirmation of Appointments by the United States Senate* (Greenwood, 1968), pp. 119–24; Harry Barnard, *Independent Man: The Life of Senator James Couzens* (Charles Scribner's Sons, 1958; reprint, Wayne State University Press, 2002), pp. 175–77.

42. Burdette, *Filibustering in the Senate*, pp. 146–47; Haynes, *Senate of the United States*, 1, pp. 408–409.

43. Haynes, *Senate of the United States*, 1, pp. 137–140.

44. Ibid., p. 144, note 1; Lowitt, *George W. Norris*, p. 161.

45. Augustine Lonergan to Morris Sheppard, 10 August 1936, and Edwin A. Halsey to Morris Sheppard (enclosing a copy of the Federal Corrupt Practices Act to show how the act worked in practice), 3 October 1926, Morris Sheppard Papers, Center for American History, University of Texas at Austin; Haynes, *Senate of the United States*, 1, pp. 159–60.

46. "Smith and Vare Barred Out," *The Literary Digest*, 24 December 1927, pp. 10–11; for a speech by Norris reviewing the Vare controversy, see U.S. Senate, *Congressional Record*, 69 Cong., 2 Sess. (22 December 1926), pp. 917–21; Lowitt, *George W. Norris*, pp. 386–95.

47. On the efforts of one senator to stem the flow of campaign contributions, see Richard Lowitt, *Bronson Cutting: Progressive Politician* (University of New Mexico Press, 1992), pp. 144–45, 163.

## Chapter Seven

1. Jordan A. Schwarz, *The Interregnum of Despair: Hoover, Congress, and the Depression* (University of Illinois Press, 1970), p. 6.

2. Theodore Joslin, *Hoover Off the Record* (Doubleday, Doran, 1935), p. 163.

3. Schwarz, *Interregnum of Despair*, p. 49. For Watson's view of Hoover, see James E. Watson, *As I Knew Them* (Bobbs-Merrill, 1936), pp. 242–79.

4. Schwarz, *Interregnum of Despair*, p. 56; Ray T. Tucker, *Sons of the Wild Jackass* (L. C. Page, 1932), p. 29.

5. Elliott Thurston, "Joseph T. Robinson: Presidential Possibilities," *The Forum* 86(1931): 252–56; Donald C. Ritchie, "Joseph Taylor Robinson: The Good Soldier," in Richard A. Baker and Robert H. Davidson, eds., *First Among Equals: Outstanding Senate Majority Leaders of the Twentieth Century* (Congressional Quarterly, 1991), pp. 77–79.

6. Betty Glad, *Key Pittman: The Tragedy of a Senate Insider* (Columbia University Press, 1986), pp. 129–36; Schwarz, *Interregnum of Despair*, p. 68.

7. A Washington Correspondent, "The Progressives of the Senate," *American Mercury* 16(1929): 385, 386.

8. Richard Lowitt, *George W. Norris: The Persistence of a Progressive, 1913–1933* (University of Illinois Press, 1971), covers his subject's career in great depth; Tucker, *Sons of the Wild Jackass*, pp. 43–69, has an illuminating chapter about Norris.

9. "The Progressives of the Senate," p. 386; Patrick J. Maney, *Young Bob: A Biography of Robert M. La Follette, Jr.* (Wisconsin State Historical Society, 2002), is a sympathetic and informed study.

10. Richard Lowitt, *Bronson M. Cutting: Progressive Politician* (University of New Mexico Press, 1992), p. 202.

11. Kenneth W. Goings, *"The NAACP Comes of Age": The Defeat of Judge John J. Parker* (Indiana University Press, 1990), p. 43; Hiram Johnson to Archibald Johnson, 15 February 1930, in Robert E. Burke, ed., *The Diary Letters of Hiram Johnson*, 7 vols. (Garland, 1983), vol. 5.

12. Richard L. Watson, Jr., "The Defeat of Judge Parker: A Study in Pressure Groups and Politics," *The Mississippi Valley Historical Review* 50(1963): 218.

13. Goings, *"NAACP Comes of Age,"* pp. 21–36; Watson, "Defeat of Judge Parker," p. 222.

14. Milton R. Merrill, *Reed Smoot: Apostle in Politics* (Utah State University Press, 1990), pp. 329–43; Alfred Pearce Dennis, "The Diligent Senator Smoot," *The World's Work*, May 1930, pp. 62–64.

15. Schwarz, *Interregnum of Despair*, pp. 13, 17.

16. Kristie Miller, *Ruth Hanna McCormick: A Life in Politics, 1890–1944* (University of New Mexico Press, 1992), pp. 207–34; Hiram Johnson to Archibald Johnson, 9 April 1930, in Burke, *Diary Letters of Hiram Johnson*, vol. 5.

17. Lowitt, *George W. Norris*, pp. 472–73, 485–86.

18. John Robert Moore, *Senator Josiah William Bailey of North Carolina: A Political Biography* (Duke University Press, 1968), pp. 62–75; Richard L. Watson, Jr., "A Southern Democratic Primary: Simmons v. Bailey in 1930," *North Carolina Historical Review* 41(1965): 21–46.

19. Maney, *Young Bob*, pp. 83–84; Schwarz, *Interregnum of Despair*, pp. 30–38.

20. Schwarz, *Interregnum of Despair*, pp. 52–54; quotation is on p. 52.

21. Diane D. Kincaid, ed., *Silent Hattie Speaks: The Personal Journal of Senator Hattie Caraway* (Greenwood Press, 1979), pp. 4–11.

22. T. Harry Williams, *Huey Long* (Random House, 1969), pp. 460–80; William Ivy Hair, *The Kingfish and His Realm: The Life and Times of Huey P. Long* (Louisiana State University Press, 1991), pp. 196–205, explores this phase of Long's career from contrasting perspectives.

23. Kincaid, *Silent Hattie Speaks*, p. 130; Hair, *Kingfish and His Realm*, pp. 246–248; Williams, *Huey Long*, p. 587.

24. Williams, *Huey Long*, pp. 589, 591; Allen Drury, *A Senate Journal, 1943–1945* (McGraw-Hill, 1963), p. 225.

25. Schwarz, *Interregnum of Despair*, p. 198.

26. Lowitt, *George W. Norris*, p. 557; Harry Barnard, *Independent Man: The Life of Senator James Couzens* (Wayne State University Press, 2002); Ronald L. Fineman, *Twilight of Progressivism: The Western Republican Senators and the New Deal* (Johns Hopkins University Press, 1981), pp. 33–47.

27. Hiram Johnson to Hiram Johnson, Jr., 4 December 1932, in Burke, *Diary Letters of Hiram Johnson*, vol. 5.

28. Steve Neal, *McNary of Oregon: A Political Biography* (Press of the Oregon Historical Society, 1985), pp. 125, 135–36.

29. Mark O. Hatfield, as told to Diane N. Solomon, *Against the Grain: Reflections of a Rebel Republican* (White Cloud Press, 2001), pp. 118–19.

30. Gilbert C. Fite, *Richard B. Russell, Jr.: Senator from Georgia* (University of North Carolina Press, 1991), pp. 168, 181, 183.

31. Ibid., 171–73, 201, 207; confidential source on Russell's suicidal thoughts.

32. Ronald L. Heinemann, *Harry Byrd of Virginia* (University Press of Virginia, 1996), is a well-documented, full biography.

33. Ibid., p. 230.

34. Rixey Smith and Norman Beasley, *Carter Glass: A Biography* (Longmans, Green, 1939), pp. 345, 346–47; Williams, *Huey Long*, p. 627.

35. William E. Leuchtenberg, *Franklin D. Roosevelt and the New Deal, 1932–1940* (Harper & Row, 1963), pp. 48–51.

36. Richard Lowitt, *George W. Norris: The Triumph of a Progressive, 1933–1944* (University of Illinois Press, 1978), pp. 16–25.

37. Leuchtenburg, *Roosevelt and the New Deal*, pp. 55–56; James E. Sargent, *Roosevelt and the Hundred Days: Struggle for the Early New Deal* (Garland, 1981), pp. 124, 198–99.

38. J. Joseph Hutmacher, *Senator Robert F. Wagner and the Rise of Urban Liberalism* (Atheneum, 1968), p. 112.

39. Ibid., pp. 148–51; Arthur M. Schlesinger, Jr., *The Coming of the New Deal* (Houghton Mifflin, 1959), pp. 99–102; Patrick Maney, "The Forgotten New Deal Congress," in Julian E. Zelizer, ed., *The American Congress: The Building of Democracy* (Houghton Mifflin, 2004), pp. 451–53.

40. George F. Sparks, ed., *A Many-Colored Toga: The Diary of Henry Fountain Ashurst* (University of Arizona Press, 1962), p. 333.

41. E. Pendelton Herring, "First Session of the 73rd Congress," *American Political Science Review* 27(February 1934): 82.

42. Alben Barkley, *That Reminds Me* (Doubleday, 1954), p. 144.

43. Robert T. Johnson, "Charles McNary and the Republican Party" (Ph.D. diss., University of Wisconsin, 1967), pp. 170–76.

44. Hiram Johnson to Hiram Johnson, Jr., 22 December 1934, in Burke, *Diary Letters of Hiram Johnson*, vol. 6. Maney, *Young Bob*, pp. 152, 153; Lowitt, *Bronson M. Cutting*, pp. 307–12.

45. Heinemann, *Harry Byrd of Virginia*, pp. 165–66.

## Chapter Eight

1. Hiram Johnson to Hiram Johnson, Jr., 22 February 1935, in Robert E. Burke, ed., *The Diary Letters of Hiram Johnson*, 7 vols. (Garland, 1983), vol. 6; Richard Lowitt, *George W. Norris: The Triumph of a Progressive, 1933–1944* (University of Illinois Press, 1978), pp. 28, 169–70. For a good sense of how a senatorial office handled constituent mail, see Robert Jackson to Edith H. Parker, 5 October 1937, Edith H. Parker Papers, Center for American History, University of Texas at Austin (hereinafter Parker Papers).

2. Wayne S. Cole, *Senator Gerald P. Nye and American Foreign Relations* (University of Minnesota Press, 1962), pp. 79–96; Jon Edward Wiltz, *In Search of Peace: The Senate Munitions Inquiry, 1933–1936* (Louisiana State University Press, 1963).

3. Marian McKenna, *Borah* (University of Michigan Press, 1961), pp. 349–52.

4. Hiram Johnson to Hiram Johnson, Jr., 21 January 1935, in Burke, *Diary Letters of Hiram Johnson*, vol. 6; Richard Coke Lower, *A Bloc of One: The Political Career of Hiram Johnson* (Stanford University Press, 1993), pp. 284–85; Lowitt, *George W. Norris*, pp. 73–74.

5. Betty Glad, *Key Pittman: The Tragedy of a Senate Insider* (Columbia University Press, 1986), p. 235.

6. Huey Long, "Share Our Wealth," *Congressional Record*, 15 May 1935, pamphlet, in author's files; William Ivy Hair, *The Kingfish and His Realm: The Life and Times of Huey P. Long* (Louisiana State University Press, 1991), p. 283; J. Edgar Hoover to Marvin McIntyre, 1 and 4 September 1934, Huey Long FBI File, File 62-32509-32, Federal Bureau of Investigation, Freedom of Information Act.

7. Roger T. Johnson, "Charles L. McNary and the Republican Party" (Ph.D. diss., University of Wisconsin, 1967), p. 194; Marian C. McKenna, *Franklin Roosevelt and the Great Constitutional War: The Court-Packing Crisis of 1937* (Fordham University Press, 2002), p. 113.

8. William E. Leuchtenburg, *Franklin D. Roosevelt and the New Deal* (Harper & Row, 1963), pp. 143–66, offers the best summary of the dramatic events of the summer of 1935.

9. David McKean, *Tommy the Cork: Washington's Ultimate Insider from Roosevelt to Reagan* (Steerforth Press, 2004), pp. 59–66; Joseph Alsop and Turner Catledge, *The 168 Days* (Doubleday, Doran, 1938), pp. 36–37, 81–82.

10. Martha H. Swain, *Pat Harrison: The New Deal Years* (University Press of Mississippi, 1978), pp. 110–17; James T. Patterson, *Congressional Conservatism and the New Deal: The Growth of the Conservative Coalition in Congress, 1933–1939* (University of Kentucky Press, 1967), pp. 72–76.

11. T. Harry Williams, *Huey Long* (Random House, 1969), pp. 864–872; Hair, *Kingfish and His Realm*, pp. 310–11.

12. David Robertson, *Sly and Able: A Political Biography of James F. Byrnes* (W. W. Norton, 1994), pp. 191–93.

13. Alsop and Catledge, *The 168 Days*, provides a vivid, fast-paced narrative account of the Court-packing controversy. William E. Leuchtenburg, *The Supreme Court Reborn: The Constitutional Revolution in the Age of Roosevelt* (Oxford University Press, 1995), pp. 82–162, is an excellent account.

14. Cecil Edward Weller, Jr., *Joe T. Robinson: Always a Loyal Democrat* (University of Arkansas Press, 1998), pp. 163–65; Burton K. Wheeler, *Yankee from the West* (Doubleday, 1962), pp. 319–40. On the defection of another liberal senator, see Gene M. Gressley, "Joseph C. O'Mahoney, FDR, and the Supreme Court," *Pacific Historical Review* 40(1971): 183–202.

15. Steve Neal, *McNary of Oregon: A Political Biography* (Press of the Oregon Historical Society, 1985), pp. 164–66.

16. The disorganization of the White House in handling the Senate is evident in Alsop and Catledge, *The 168 Days*, pp. 106–14; McKenna, *Roosevelt and the Great Constitutional War*, pp. 317–20, 365–77, shows how effective the opposition to Roosevelt's plan was.

17. Wheeler, *Yankee from the West*, pp. 332–33.

18. McKenna, *Roosevelt and the Great Constitutional War*, pp. 453–60; Leuchtenburg, *Supreme Court Reborn*, pp. 144–45.

19. Wheeler, *Yankee from the West*, p. 357.

20. The Harrison-Barkley leadership contest has been covered from many perspectives. Swain, *Pat Harrison*, pp. 154–55; Polly Ann Davis, *Alben W. Barkley: Senate Majority Leader and Vice President* (Garland, 1979), pp. 14–34; and Robertson, *Sly and Able*, pp. 263–266, offer useful treatments. Alben Barkley, *That Reminds Me* (Doubleday & Co., 1954), gives the personal perspective of the winner.

21. McKenna, *Roosevelt and the Great Constitutional War*, pp. 508, 510, prints the text of the letter (the Johnson quote is on p. 521).

22. Barkley, *That Reminds Me*, p. 156; John Bankhead to Barkley, 20 July 1937, Barkley to Bankhead, 28 July 1937, Alben Barkley papers, Political File, 1932–1937, box VII, "Election, Senate Majority Leader," Alben Barkley Papers, University of Kentucky, Lexington.

23. Davis, *Alben W. Barkley*, p. 17; Donald Ritchie, "Alben W. Barkley: The President's Man," in Richard A. Baker and Roger Davidson, eds., *First Among Equals: Outstanding Senate Leaders of the Twentieth Century* (Congressional Quarterly, 1991), pp. 129, 137.

24. Davis, *Alben W. Barkley*, pp. 41–42.

25. U.S., Senate, *Congressional Record*, 75 Cong. 1 Sess. (11 August 1937), 8694–97; J. Joseph Hutmacher, *Senator Robert F. Wagner and the Rise of Urban Liberalism* (Atheneum, 1968), pp. 238–39; Robert L. Zangrando, *The NAACP Crusade Against Lynching, 1909–1950* (Temple University Press, 1980), pp. 145–46.

26. Hutmacher, *Senator Robert F. Wagner*, pp. 239–40.

27. Leuchtenburg, *Supreme Court Reborn*, p. 211.

28. Leuchtenburg, *Supreme Court Reborn*, is excellent on the Black broadcast; Robert Jackson to Edith Parker, 5 October 1937, Parker Papers.

29. Robertson, *Sly and Able*, pp. 267–268; Patterson, *Congressional Conservatism*, pp. 200–207.

30. Patterson, *Congressional Conservatism*, pp. 200–207; John Robert Moore, *Senator Josiah William Bailey of North Carolina: A Political Biography* (Duke University Press, 1968), pp. 144–59.

31. Gilbert C. Fite, *Richard B. Russell, Jr., Senator from Georgia* (University of North Carolina Press, 1991), pp. 167–68; George C. Rable, "The South and the Politics of Antilynching Legislation, 1920–1940," *The Journal of Southern History* 51(1985): 217.

32. Patterson, *Congressional Conservatism*, pp. 234–46.

33. Claude Denson Pepper, with Hays Gorey, *Pepper: Eyewitness to a Century* (Harcourt Brace Jovanovich, 1987), pp. 71, 73.

34. Robert S. Allen, *Washington Merry-go-Round* (Horace Liveright, 1931), p. 20; Harold L. Ickes, *The Secret Diary of Harold L. Ickes*, vol. 2, *The Inside Struggle, 1936–1939* (Simon & Schuster, 1954), p. 95; Caroline H. Keith, *"For Hell and a Brown Mule": The Biography of Senator Millard E. Tydings* (Madison Books, 1991), pp. 343–54; Eleanor Davies Tydings Ditzen, *My Golden Spoon: Memoirs of a Capital Lady* (Madison Books, 1997), pp. 148–153.

35. Keith, *"For Hell and a Brown Mule,"* p. 340.

36. Capra's dramatic story of making Mr. *Smith Goes to Washington* is recounted in Frank Capra, *The Name Above the Title: An Autobiography* (Macmillan, 1971), pp. 254–320; a more balanced version is in Joseph McBride, *Frank Capra: The Catastrophe of Success* (Simon & Schuster, 1992), pp. 401–3, 415–24. Charles Wolfe, "Mr. *Smith Goes to Washington:* Democratic Forums and Representational Forms," in Robert Sklar and Vito Zaarrio, eds., *Frank Capra: Authorship and the Studio System* (Temple University Press, 1998), pp. 190–221.

37. *Christian Science Monitor*, 17 October 1939; Otis Ferguson, "Mr. Capra Goes Some Place," *The New Republic*, 1 November 1939.

38. Hendrik Hertzberg, *Politics: Observations and Arguments, 1966–2004* (Penguin, 2004), p. 542.

## Chapter Nine

1. Marian C. McKenna, *Borah* (University of Michigan Press, 1961), p. 354; Richard Coke Lower, *The Political Career of Hiram Johnson* (Stanford University Press, 1993), p. 322; Wayne S. Cole, *Senator Gerald P. Nye and American Foreign Relations* (University of Minnesota Press, 1962), pp. 187–89.

2. Betty Glad, *Key Pittman: The Tragedy of a Senate Insider* (Columbia University Press, 1986), pp. 204–6, 280–83, 286.

3. Hiram Johnson to Hiram Johnson, Jr., 16 July 1939, in Robert E, Burke, ed., *The Diary Letters of Hiram Johnson* (Garland, 1983), vol. 7.

4. McKenna, *Borah*, pp. 362–63.

5. James T. Patterson, *Mr. Republican: A Biography of Robert A. Taft* (Houghton Mifflin, 1972), is the standard biography. Also useful is William S. White, *The Taft Story* (Harper & Bros., 1954), which has some good insights from a close observer of Taft. Robert A. Taft, *The Papers of Robert A. Taft*, 3 vols., ed. Clarence E. Wunderlin, Jr., et al. (Kent State University Press, 1997–2003), provides selections from Taft's letters and speeches.

6. Richard Norton Smith, *Thomas E. Dewey and His Times* (Simon & Schuster, 1982), p. 278; Milton S. Mayer, "Men Who Would Be President," *The Nation*, 11 May 1940, pp. 587–90. The standard biography is C. David Tompkins, *Arthur H. Vandenberg: The Evolution of a Modern Republican* (University of Michigan Press, 1970).

7. Patterson, *Mr. Republican*, p. 217.

8. Steve Neal, *McNary of Oregon: A Political Biography* (Press of the Oregon Historical Society, 1985), pp. 183–88.

9. Patterson, *Mr. Republican*, p. 241.

10. Burton K. Wheeler, with Paul F. Healy, *Yankee from the West* (Doubleday, 1962), p. 27; Johnson to Hiram Johnson, Jr., 9 March 1941, in Burke, *Diary Letters of Hiram Johnson*, vol. 7.

11. David Robertson, *Sly and Able: A Political Biography of James F. Byrnes* (W. W. Norton, 1994), pp. 296–97, 298–99.

12. H. G. Nicholas, ed., *Washington Despatches, 1941–1945: Weekly Political Reports from the British Embassy* (Weidenfeld & Nicolson, 1981), p. 64. Robert Dallek, *Lone Star Rising: Lyndon Johnson and His Times, 1908–1961* (Oxford University Press, 1991), p. 215; Robert A. Caro, *The Years of Lyndon Johnson: The Path to Power* (Alfred A, Knopf, 1983), pp. 675–740, is a detailed account of the campaign from an anti-Johnson perspective.

13. Edith Parker told me the story about Tom Connally and the war declaration on several occasions during the 1970s. Connally mentioned the drive, but not his companion, in his memoir, *My Name is Tom Connally* (Thomas Y. Crowell, 1954), p. 248.

14. Isaiah Berlin, *Flourishing: Letters 1928–1946*, edited by Henry Hardy (Chatto & Windus, 2004), p. 456; Nicholas, *Washington Despatches*, pp. 18–19, 26–27.

15. On Guffey, see Joseph F. Guffey, *Seventy Years on the Red Fire Wagon: From Tilden to Truman Through New Freedom and New Deal* (privately printed, 1952), pp. 159–64; John W. Malmsberger, *From Obstruction to Moderation: The Transformation of Senate Conservatism, 1938–1952* (Susquehanna University Press, 2000), pp. 73–99.

16. Patrick Maney, *Young Bob: A Biography of Robert M. La Follette, Jr.* (Wisconsin Historical Society Press, 2000), pp. 273–74; Robert M. La Follette, Jr., "A Senator Looks at Congress," *Atlantic Monthly*, July 1943, 91–92.

17. The best source on the Walsh episode is Lawrence R. Murphy, "The House on Pacific Street: Homosexuality, Intrigue, and Politics During World War II," *Journal of Homosexuality* 12(1985): 27–47. There is also useful information in Anthony Tommasini, *Virgil Thomson: Composer on the Aisle* (W. W. Norton, 1997), pp. 355–57.

18. "Statements Made in Senate Clearing Walsh of Charges," *New York Journal American*, 21 May 1942, David I. Walsh file, *Journal American* morgue, Center for American History, University of Texas at Austin.

19. Harold Ickes to Lady Bird Johnson, box 16, Harold Ickes Papers, Manuscript Division, Library of Congress; Taft, *Papers*, 2, p. 303.

20. Roland Young, *Congressional Politics in the Second World War* (Columbia University Press, 1956), pp. 12–17; John Morton Blum, *V Was for Victory: Politics*

*and American Culture During World War II* (Harcourt Brace Jovanovich, 1975), pp. 221–34.

21. Young, *Congressional Politics in the Second World War*, p. 84; Gilbert C. Fite, *Richard B. Russell, Jr., Senator from Georgia* (University of North Carolina Press, 1991), pp. 180–81; Polly Ann Davis, *Alben W. Barkley: Senate Majority Leader and Vice President* (Garland, 1979), pp. 114–15; U.S. Senate, *Congressional Record*, 77 Cong., 2 Sess. (17 November 1942), 8905–8, indicates the passions that Barkley's move aroused among southern senators.

22. Davis, *Alben W. Barkley*, pp. 118–20; Nicholas, *Washington Despatches*, p. 118.

23. Richard B. Russell to Cobb C. Torrance, 31 May 1944, Richard B. Russell Papers, series V, box 108, file 6, #2, Fair Employment Practices Commission, 1944–1949, University of Georgia Library, Athens.

24. U.S. Senate, *Congressional Record*, 78 Cong. 1 Sess. (7 December 1943), 16344–45; Guffey, *Seventy Years on the Red Fire Wagon*, pp. 148–53.

25. Roland L. Heinemann, *Harry Byrd of Virginia* (University Press of Virginia, 1996), p. 287; Robert Taft to Harry Byrd, 21 November 1945, Taft to Stanley M. Row, 21 December 1946, Taft to Sidney B. Thompson, 5 April 1947, all cited in Taft, *Papers*, 3, pp. 96, 235, 268.

26. Wendy Wolff and Donald A. Ritchie, eds., *Minutes of the Senate Republican Conference, Sixty-second through Eighty-eighth Congress, 1911–1964* (Government Printing Office, 1999), pp. 344–46, 354–56.

27. Frank McNaughton to Eleanor Welch, 17 June 1944, Frank McNaughton Papers, box 6, 9–30 June 1944, Harry S. Truman Library, Independence, Missouri.

28. Alonzo Hamby, *Man of the People: A Life of Harry S. Truman* (Oxford University Press, 1995), p. 260; Nicholas, *Washington Despatches*, pp. 50, 391–92.

29. Robert H. Ferrell, *Choosing Truman: The Democratic Convention of 1944* (University of Missouri Press, 1994), is a good guide to the extensive literature on the selection of Truman as the vice-presidential candidate.

30. Allen Drury, *A Senate Journal, 1943–1945* (McGraw-Hill, 1963); Davis, *Alben W. Barkley*, pp. 119–33.

31. For the Roosevelt quotation, see Blum, *V Was for Victory*, p. 243.

32. John Morton Blum, ed., *The Price of Vision: The Diary of Henry A. Wallace, 1942–1946* (Houghton Mifflin, 1973), p. 301; Alben Barkley, *That Reminds Me* (Doubleday, 1954), p. 173. On the tax-veto episode, see also George W. Robinson, "Alben Barkley and the 1944 Tax Veto," *The Register of the Kentucky Historical Society* 67(1969): 197–210, and James K. Libbey, *"Dear Alben": Mr. Barkley of Kentucky* (University Press of Kentucky, 1979), pp. 85–88.

33. Barkley, *That Reminds Me*, p. 176; Drury, *Senate Journal*, p. 90.

34. For the quotation see Donald A. Ritchie, ed., *Minutes of the Senate Democratic Conference, Fifty-eighth through Eighty-eighth Congress* (Government Printing Office, 1998), pp. 370–71; "Caucus of Democratic Senators, Resolution of Confidence," 24 February 1944, Alben Barkley Papers, box 21; Drury, *Senate Journal*, p. 93; Blum, *Price of Vision*, p. 302.

35. Blum, *Price of Vision*, p. 488; Connally, *My Name Is Tom Connally*, p. 269; Lewis L. Gould, "Thomas Terry ('Tom') Connally," in John A. Garraty, ed., *Dictionary of American Biography: Supplement Seven, 1961–1965* (Charles Scribner's Sons, 1981), p. 138.

36. Arthur H. Vandenberg, Jr., and Joe Alex Morris, eds., *The Private Papers of Senator Vandenberg* (Houghton Mifflin, 1952), is a good source for the senator's thinking.

37. Nicholas, *Washington Despatches*, p. 269.

38. Randall Bennett Woods, *Fulbright: A Biography* (Cambridge University Press, 1995), pp. 88–100; William B. Pickett, *Homer E. Capehart: A Senator's Life* (Indiana Historical Society, 1990), pp. 88–94; Mason Drukman, *Wayne Morse: A Political Biography* (Press of the Oregon Historical Society, 1997), pp. 135–42.

39. Drury, *Senate Journal*, p. 334; Vandenberg and Morris, *Private Papers*, p. 135; James Reston, *Deadline: A Memoir* (Random House, 1989), pp. 158–59.

## Chapter Ten

1. Frank Madison [pseudonym], *A View from the Floor: The Journal of a U.S. Senate Page Boy* (Prentice Hall, 1967), p. 152.

2. Jack Gould, "The X of the Campaign-TV 'Personality,'" *The New York Times Magazine*, 22 June 1952, pp. 14, 40, 42.

3. Charles L. Fontenay, *Estes Kefauver: A Biography* (University of Tennessee Press, 1980), is a careful portrait of Kefauver as a politician.

4. William Howard Moore, *The Kefauver Committee and the Politics of Crime, 1950–1952* (University of Missouri Press, 1974), is the best treatment of the committee's work.

5. For an example of how the Kefauver committee probed in the president's home state, see *Hearings before the Special Committee to Investigate Organized Crime in Interstate Commerce, Eighty-first Congress, Second Session, Pursuant to S. Res. 202, Part 4 Missouri* (Government Printing Office, 1950).

6. Patrick J. Maney, *Young Bob: A Biography of Robert M. La Follette, Jr.* (Wisconsin Historical Society Press, 2002), pp. 275–78; Merlo Pusey, "Revise Congress," *The Forum* 105(1946): 618; Richard Lee Strout, "Let's Modernize

Congress," *The New Republic*, 18 March 1946, p. 369. The most detailed examination of these congressional problems was George B. Galloway, *Congress at the Crossroads* (Thomas Y. Crowell, 1946).

7. Maney, *Young Bob*, pp. 278–86.

8. Robert C. Byrd, with Wendy Wolff, *The Senate 1789–1989: Addresses on the History of the United States Senate* (Government Printing Office, 1991), 2, pp. 433–36.

9. Patricia L. Schmidt, *Margaret Chase Smith: Beyond Convention* (University of Maine Press, 1996), pp. 200–202; Janann Sherman, *No Place for a Woman: A Life of Senator Margaret Chase Smith* (Rutgers University Press, 2000), pp. 90–93.

10. Sherman, *No Place for a Woman*, p. 282.

11. Madison, *View from the Floor*, p. 45; Byrd, *The Senate*, p. 386.

12. "Ladies Invited," *Newsweek*, 5 August 1946, 22.

13. Katharine Graham, *Katharine Graham's Washington* (Random House, 2002), p. 641.

14. Eleanor Davies Tydings Ditzen, *My Golden Spoon: Memoirs of a Capital Lady* (Madison Books, 1997), p. 89; Lewis L. Gould, *Lady Bird Johnson and the Environment* (University Press of Kansas, 1988), p. 23.

15. Ellen Proxmire, *One Foot in Washington: The Perilous Life of a Senator's Wife* (Robert B. Luce, 1963), p. 28.

16. John F. Kennedy's romantic activities have been well documented; see Robert Dallek, *An Unfinished Life: John F. Kennedy, 1917–1963* (Little Brown, 2003), pp. 194–95. Gilbert C. Fite, *Richard B. Russell, Jr., Senator from Georgia* (University of North Carolina Press, 1991), pp. 200–201; Fontenay, *Estes Kefauver*, pp. 340–45; Louis Hurst, as told to Frances Spatz Leighton, *The Sweetest Little Club in the World* (Prentice Hall, 1980), pp. 109–11.

17. Gayle B. Montgomery and James W. Johnson, with Paul G. Manolis, *One Step from the White House: The Rise and Fall of Senator William F. Knowland* (University of California Press, 1998), pp. 221–24; Helen Knowland, *Lady Baltimore* (Dodd, Mead, 1949).

18. Robert Dallek, *Flawed Giant: Lyndon Johnson and His Times, 1961–1973* (Oxford University Press, 1998), pp. 186–87, 408.

19. David K. Johnson, *The Lavender Scare: The Cold War Persecution of Gays and Lesbians in the Federal Government* (University of Chicago Press, 2004), p. 80.

20. Rick Ewig, "McCarthy Era Politics: The Ordeal of Senator Lester Hunt," *Annals of Wyoming* 55(1984): 9–21; James K. Kiepper, *Styles Bridges: Yankee Senator* (Phoenix, 2001), pp. 145–47; Johnson, *Lavender Scare*, p. 141.

21. Kiepper, *Styles Bridges*, p. 146. The governor of Wyoming appointed a successor for Hunt who served until O'Mahoney won the Senate election in the fall.

22. Todd Steven Burroughs, "Who Is This Man, Louis Lautier?" www.Black PressUSA.com/History/Timeline_Essayasp.

23. Hubert Humphrey, *The Education of a Public Man: My Life and Politics* (Doubleday, 1976), p. 121; Robert Parker, with Richard Rashke, *Capitol Hill in Black and White* (Dodd, Mead, 1986), pp. 57–58.

24. Menu of United States Senate Restaurant, 10 September 1949, original in author's files; Leverett Saltonstall, "Notes of a Novice Senator," *The American Mercury* 68(1946): 234.

25. Byrd, *The Senate*, p. 234.

26. Gould, *Lady Bird Johnson and the Environment*, p. 141.

27. Jack Gould conveyed the remark to me in the 1960s and confirmed it in the 1980s. Johnson biographers go into the issue of his wealth at length. For a good brief guide, see Dallek, *Lone Star Rising*, pp. 409–15. John L. Bullion, *In the Boat with LBJ* (Republic of Texas Press, 2001), pp. 86–102, explores the subject from the perspective of Johnson's tax lawyer.

28. The charges against Bridges are explored in Kiepper, *Styles Bridges*, pp. 183–97, 198–99.

29. Francis Case to John Griffin, 2 February 1956; John M. Neff to Francis Case, 4 February 1956; Francis Case to John Cowles, 15 May 1956, all in Old File Drawer 63, Francis Case Papers, Dakota Wesleyan University, Mitchell, South Dakota. Richard Chenoweth, "Francis Case: A Political Biography" (Ph.D. diss., University of Nebraska, 1977), pp. 176–87.

30. Madison, *View from the Floor*, p. 37.

31. Dallek, *Lone Star Rising*, pp. 498–99; Chenoweth, "Francis Case," pp. 179–82.

32. Richard L. Neuberger, "Mistakes of a Freshman Senator," in Steve Neal, ed., *They Never Go Back to Pocatello: The Selected Essays of Richard Neuberger* (Press of the Oregon Historical Society, 1988), pp. 242–55; Stephen K. Bailey and Howard D. Samuel, "A Day in the Life of a Senator: The Congressional Office, 1952," *Commentary* 31(1952): 433–41.

33. Donald R. Matthews, *U.S. Senators and Their World* (University of North Carolina Press, 1960), p. 84.

34. Ibid., pp. 83–85; Proxmire, *One Foot in Washington*, pp. 28, 41–42, 113–14, 164–65.

35. Matthews, *U.S. Senators and Their World*, p. 77; Neal, ed., *They Never Go Back to Pocatello*, p. 293.

36. Bobby Baker, with Larry L. King, *Wheeling and Dealing: Confessions of a Capitol Hill Operator* (W. W. Norton, 1978), p. 38.

37. Fontenay, *Estes Kefauver*, pp. 328, 395, 396; Robert Mann, *Legacy to Power: Senator Russell Long of Louisiana* (Paragon House, 1992), pp. 287–89; Byron C. Hulsey, *Everett Dirksen and His Presidents: How a Senate Giant Shaped American Politics* (University Press of Kansas, 2000), pp. 22, 148–49, 189; Roger Biles, *Crusading Liberal: Paul H. Douglas of Illinois* (Northern Illinois University Press, 2002), pp. 118–19, discusses Thomas C. Hennings; Randall Bennett Woods, *Fulbright: A Biography* (Cambridge University Press, 1995), p. 188, mentions McClellan's alcoholism.

38. Graham, *Katharine Graham's Washington*, p. 718; Madison, *View from the Floor*, pp. 30–31, 75, 132, 147, 152–53; Francis R. Valeo, *Mike Mansfield, Majority Leader: A Different Kind of Senate, 1961–1976* (M. E. Sharpe, 1999), p. 43.

39. Hulsey, *Everett Dirksen and His Presidents*, p. 65.

40. Marvin E. Stromer, *The Making of a Political Leader: Kenneth S. Wherry and the United States Senate* (University of Nebraska Press, 1969); Catherine Marshall, *A Man Called Peter* (McGraw-Hill, 1951), pp. 223–24.

41. *A Man Called Peter* (Twentieth-Century Fox, 1955; VHS, 2003).

42. Jon Meacham, "The Insider," *Stanford Alumni Magazine*, January–February 1999; Allen Drury, *Advise and Consent* (Doubleday, 1959).

43. Johnson, *Lavender Scare*, pp. 141–42; Myrna Oliver, "Pulitzer Prize Author Allen Drury Dies at 80," *Los Angeles Times*, 2 September 1998.

44. William S. White, *Citadel* (Harper & Bros., 1956), p. 68.

45. Ibid., pp. 69–75.

46. Matthews, *U.S. Senators and Their World*, p. 90.

## Chapter Eleven

1. James T. Patterson, *Mr. Republican: A Biography of Robert A. Taft* (Houghton Mifflin, 1972), pp. 312–13.

2. William E. Jenner to Lewis W. Fletcher, 29 May 1946, original in author's files.

3. James T. Patterson, *Grand Expectations: The United States, 1945–1974* (Oxford University Press, 1996), pp. 117–26, 179–95, offers an excellent survey of these issues.

4. For a critical look at Truman's performance and the overall record of American society on race during the postwar years, see Carol Anderson, "Clutching at Civil Rights Straws: A Reappraisal of the Truman Years and the

Struggle for African-American Citizenship," in Richard S. Kirkendall, ed., *Harry's Farewell* (University of Missouri Press, 2004), pp. 75–100.

5. Gilbert C. Fite, *Richard B. Russell, Jr.: Senator from Georgia* (University of North Carolina Press, 1991), pp. 224–38.

6. Ibid., pp. 227–28.

7. Patterson, *Mr. Republican*, p. 371.

8. Hubert Humphrey, *The Education of a Public Man: My Life and Politics* (Doubleday, 1976), p. 459.

9. Contrasting treatments of Johnson and the infamous 1948 election race against Coke Stevenson can be found in Robert Caro, *The Years of Lyndon Johnson: Means of Ascent* (Alfred A. Knopf, 1990), pp. 179–412, which is very critical of Johnson, and Robert Dallek, *Lone Star Rising: Lyndon Johnson and His Times, 1908–1960* (Oxford University Press, 1991), pp. 299–398, which supplies a more even-handed analysis.

10. Donald A. Ritchie, ed., *Minutes of the Senate Democratic Conference: Fifty-eighth Congress Through Eighty-eighth Congress, 1903–1964* (Government Printing Office, 1998), pp. 410–11, 423–24, 426; Marvin E. Stromer, *The Making of a Political Leader: Kenneth S. Wherry and the United States Senate* (University of Nebraska Press, 1969), pp. 97–102.

11. Polly Ann Davis, *Alben W. Barkley: Senate Majority Leader and Vice President* (Garland, 1949), pp. 282–86; Alben Barkley, "Original Intent of Cloture Petition," *Vital Speeches of the Day*, April 1949, p. 327.

12. "No Time to Go Fishing," *New Republic*, 21 March 1949, p. 3; Roger Biles, *Crusading Liberal: Paul H. Douglas of Illinois* (Northern Illinois University Press, 2002), pp. 57–58.

13. Humphrey, *Education of a Public Man*, p. 124.

14. Anne Hodges Morgan, *Robert S. Kerr: The Senate Years* (University of Oklahoma Press, 1977), pp. 55–75; Dallek, *Lone Star Rising*, pp. 57–58.

15. William B. Pickett, *Homer E. Capehart: A Senator's Life* (Indiana Historical Society, 1990), p. 118.

16. Robert Griffith, *The Politics of Fear: Joseph R. McCarthy and the Senate* (University of Massachusetts Press, 1970, 1987), is critical of how the Senate handled the McCarthy problem. David Oshinsky, *A Conspiracy So Immense: The World of Joe McCarthy* (Free Press, 1983), is a fair-minded treatment. Arthur Herman, *Joseph McCarthy: Reexamining the Life and Legacy of America's Most Hated Senator* (Free Press, 2000), is a recent effort to rehabilitate the Wisconsin lawmaker.

17. Griffith, *Politics of Fear*, p. 49.

18. Margaret Chase Smith, *Declaration of Conscience*, ed. William C. Lewis, Jr. (Doubleday, 1972), p. 14; Janann Sherman, *No Place for a Woman: A Life of Senator Margaret Chase Smith* (Rutgers University Press, 2000), pp. 104–26.

19. Griffith, *Politics of Fear*, pp. 65–68.

20. For a lengthy and perceptive examination of McCarran's career and his legacy, see Michael J. Ybarra, *Washington Gone Crazy: Senator Pat McCarran and the Great American Communist Hunt* (Steerforth Press, 2004).

21. Eleanor Davies Tydings Ditzen, *My Golden Spoon: Memoirs of a Capital Lady* (Madison Books, 1997), pp. 315–342, looks at the 1950 campaign from the perspective of Tydings's wife; Griffith, *Politics of Fear*, pp. 65–74.

22. Brian Lewis Crispell, *Testing the Limits: George Armistead Smathers and Cold War America* (University of Georgia Press, 1999), pp. 65–67.

23. On the 1950 election results, see Griffith, *Politics of Fear*, pp. 122–31. On Johnson's election as whip, see Dallek, *Lone Star Rising*, pp. 389–91.

24. Oshinsky, *A Conspiracy So Immense*, p. 180.

25. Fite, *Richard B. Russell, Jr.*, pp. 256–59.

26. Patterson, *Mr. Republican*, pp. 578–587.

27. Charles L. Fontenay, *Estes Kefauver: A Biography* (University of Tennessee Press, 1980), pp. 208–29.

28. Fite, *Richard B. Russell, Jr.*, pp. 271–300.

29. On the Checkers speech, see Tom Wicker, *One of Us: Richard Nixon and the American Dream* (Random House, 1991), pp. 87–108.

30. Thomas J. Whalen, *Kennedy Versus Lodge: The 1952 Massachusetts Senate Race* (Northeastern University Press, 2000), p. 155.

31. Mason Drukman, *Wayne Morse: A Political Biography* (Press of the Oregon Historical Society, 1997), pp. 191–96; Robert Alan Goldberg, *Barry Goldwater* (Yale University Press, 1995), pp. 92–98.

32. Patterson, *Mr. Republican*, p. 586.

33. Dallek, *Lone Star Rising*, pp. 422–25.

## Chapter Twelve

1. George A. Smathers, Oral History, 24 October 1989, interview no. 3, p. 56, Senate Historical Office; Robert Dallek, *Lone Star Rising: Lyndon Johnson and His Times, 1908–1960* (Oxford University Press, 1991), p. 474.

2. For Johnson's lack of strong commitments to attacking Republicans and behaving like a partisan Democrat, see Lewis L. Gould, "Never a Deep Partisan: Lyndon Johnson and the Democratic Party, 1963–1969," in Robert A.

Divine, ed., *The Johnson Years*, 3 vols. (University Press of Kansas, 1994), 3, pp. 21–52.

3. Bobby Baker, with Larry L. King, *Wheeling and Dealing: Confessions of a Capitol Hill Operator* (W. W. Norton, 1978), provides Baker's self-serving, but often informative, account of his relationship with Johnson.

4. Dallek, *Lone Star Rising*, pp. 426–32.

5. For Johnson's wooing of Humphrey, see Carl Solberg, *Hubert Humphrey: A Biography* (W. W. Norton, 1984), pp. 160–64.

6. George Reedy Memo, February 1957, Senate Papers, box 420 ("Reedy Memo"), Lyndon B. Johnson Library, Austin, Texas.

7. Gayle B. Montgomery and James W. Johnson, with Paul G. Manolis, *One Step from the White House: The Rise and Fall of Senator William F. Knowland* (University of California Press, 1998), pp. 155–56, 160–61, 187–88. William S. White, Oral History Interview, 21 July 1978, page 18, Lyndon Baines Johnson Library, Austin, Texas.

8. For these events, see David M. Oshinsky, *A Conspiracy So Immense: The World of Joe McCarthy* (Free Press, 1983), pp. 395–401.

9. White, Oral History Interview, p. 10.

10. Robert Griffith, *The Politics of Fear: Joseph R. McCarthy and the Senate* (University of Massachusetts Press, 1970, 1987), pp. 270–71.

11. Dallek, *Lone Star Rising*, pp. 456–57; Griffith, *Politics of Fear*, pp. 296–98.

12. John W. Finch to Francis Case, 16 November 1954, Older Drawer 62, Francis Case Papers, Dakota Wesleyan University, Mitchell, South Dakota.

13. Lyndon Johnson and Sam Rayburn to Dwight D. Eisenhower, 9 October 1954, White House Central File—President's Personal File, 20-X-16, box 638, Speech of 8 October 1954, Dwight D. Eisenhower Library, Abilene.

14. Oshinsky, *Conspiracy So Immense*, pp. 483–507.

15. Dallek, *Lone Star Rising*, pp. 470–78.

16. Ibid., pp. 483–91.

17. Ronald L. Heinemann, *Harry Byrd of Virginia* (University Press of Virginia, 1996), p. 334.

18. Tony Badger, "Southerners Who Refused to Sign the Southern Manifesto," *The Historical Journal* 42(1999): 517.

19. Ibid., pp. 518–34; Kyle Longley, *Senator Albert Gore, Sr.: Tennessee Maverick* (Louisiana State University Press, 2004), pp. 123–24; Dallek, *Lone Star Rising*, p. 497.

20. On the 1956 battle between Kefauver and Kennedy see Charles Fontenay, *Estes Kefauver: A Biography* (University of Tennessee Press, 1980), pp. 266–79;

Robert Dallek, *An Unfinished Life: John F. Kennedy, 1917–1963* (Little, Brown, 2003), pp. 205–10.

21. The literature on the 1957 civil rights law is too large to list in detail here. Dallek, *Lone Star Rising*, pp. 517–26, is a good brief treatment. Gilbert C. Fite, *Richard B. Russell, Jr.: Senator from Georgia* (University of North Carolina Press, 1991), pp. 336–43, is good on how the southerners interacted with Johnson. Roger Biles, *Crusading Liberal: Paul H. Douglas of Illinois* (Northern Illinois Press, 2002), pp. 116–26, shows Johnson in a less favorable light. Robert Caro, *Master of the Senate* (Alfred A. Knopf, 2002), pp. 848–1012, is the most elaborate treatment of the law from Johnson's point of view, albeit one that is very critical of Johnson.

22. Dallek, *Lone Star Rising*, pp. 520–21.

23. Fite, *Richard B. Russell, Jr.*, pp. 337–40.

24. LeRoy Ashby and Rod Gramer, *Fighting the Odds: The Life of Senator Frank Church* (Washington State University Press, 1994), pp. 74–82.

25. Ibid., pp. 89–90.

26. Nadine Cohadas, *Strom Thurmond and the Politics of Southern Change* (Simon & Schuster, 1993), pp. 292 (quotation), 293–97. Long denied and carefully hidden during his lifetime, Thurmond's relationship with a young black woman came to light only after his death. David Mattingly, "Strom Thurmond's Family Confirms Paternity Claim," CNN, 16 December 2003; "Woman: I'm Thurmond's daughter," CBS News.com, 13 December 2003.

27. Ellen Proxmire, *One Foot in Washington: The Perilous Life of a Senator's Wife* (Robert B. Luce, 1963), pp. 3–10.

28. Richard Russell to Dwight D. Eisenhower, 26 September 1957, Little Rock School Integration Crisis, On-Line Documents, Dwight D. Eisenhower Library. http://www.eisenhower.archives.gov/dl/LittleRock/TelegramRussell toDDE92657pg1.pdf.

29. For the background of the 1958 election, see Dominic Sandbrook, *Eugene McCarthy: The Rise and Fall of Postwar American Liberalism* (Alfred A. Knopf, 2004), pp. 82–88; Michael B. O'Brien, *Philip Hart: The Conscience of the Senate* (Michigan State University Press, 1995), pp. 68–75.

30. Montgomery and Johnson, *One Step from the White House*, pp. 228–38.

31. Michael Foley, *The New Senate: Liberal Influence on a Conservative Institution* (Yale University Press, 1980), pp. 23–28.

32. Byron C. Hulsey, *Everett Dirksen and His Presidents: How a Senate Giant Shaped American Politics* (University Press of Kansas, 2000). Hulsey's study is excellent on Dirksen's political career, role in the Senate, and national influence.

33. Ibid., p. 2.

34. Ibid., p. 114.

35. Wendy Wolff and Donald A. Ritchie, eds., *Minutes of the Senate Republican Conference, Sixty-second Congress Through Eighty-eighth Congress, 1911–1964* (Government Printing Office, 1999), pp. 819–20; Hulsey, *Everett Dirksen and His Presidents*, p. 118.

36. Dallek, *Lone Star Rising*, pp. 539–40.

37. Ibid., p. 547; Bernard Asbell, *The Senate Nobody Knows* (Doubleday, 1978), pp. 120–21.

38. Proxmire, *One Foot in Washington*, p. 25; Alfred Steinberg, *Sam Johnson's Boy: A Close-up of the President from Texas* (Macmillan, 1968), pp. 495–97.

39. Hulsey, *Everett Dirksen and His Presidents*, p. 118; Clinton B. Anderson, with Milton Viorst, *Outsider in the Senate: Senator Clinton Anderson's Memoirs* (World Publishing, 1970), pp. 184–221; Richard Allan Baker, *Conservation Politics: The Senate Career of Clinton P. Anderson* (University of New Mexico Press, 1982), pp. 118–19.

40. James C. Olson, *Stuart Symington: A Life* (University of Missouri Press, 2003), pp. 348–58.

41. Solberg, *Hubert Humphrey*, pp. 199–212.

42. Sean J. Savage, *JFK, LBJ, and the Democratic Party* (State University of New York Press, 2004), pp. 39–56.

43. Dallek, *Lone Star Rising*, pp. 559–68.

44. Ibid., pp. 574–82.

45. Don Oberdorfer, *Senator Mansfield: The Extraordinary Life of a Great American Statesman and Diplomat* (Smithsonian Books, 2003), pp. 156–57.

46. Donald A. Ritchie, ed., *Minutes of the Senate Democratic Conference: Fifty-eighth Congress Through Eighty-eighth Congress* (Government Printing Office, 1998), pp. 577–79. Longley, *Senator Albert Gore, Sr.*, p. 159; Francis R. Valeo, *Mike Mansfield, Majority Leader: A Different Kind of Senate, 1961–1976* (M. E. Sharpe, 1999), pp. 12–14; Albert Gore, Sr., *Let the Glory Out: My South and Its Politics* (Hill Street Press, 2000), p. 148 (Gore quotations).

## Chapter Thirteen

1. Ross K. Baker, "Mike Mansfield and the Birth of the Modern Senate," in Richard A. Baker and Roger H. Davidson, eds., *First Among Equals: Outstanding Senate Leaders of the Twentieth Century* (Congressional Quarterly, 1991), p. 274; Donald A. Ritchie, "The Senate of Mike Mansfield," *Montana* 48(1998): 50–62.

2. The best biographical sources on Mansfield are Francis R. Valeo, *Mike Mansfield, Majority Leader: A Different Kind of Senate, 1961–1976* (M. E. Sharpe,

1999); Donald A. Ritchie, "Advice and Dissent: Mike Mansfield and the Vietnam War," in Randall B. Woods, ed., *Vietnam and the American Political Tradition: The Politics of Dissent* (Cambridge University Press, 2003), pp. 171–203; and Don Oberdorfer, *Senator Mansfield: The Extraordinary Life of a Great American Statesman and Diplomat* (Smithsonian Books, 2003), p. 147.

3. Donald A. Ritchie, ed., *Minutes of the Senate Democratic Conference: Fifty-eighth Through Eighty-eighth Congress, 1903–1964* (Government Printing Office, 1998), p. 577; Oberdorfer, *Senator Mansfield*, pp. 154–56.

4. On Mansfield's style of leadership and its effect on his colleagues in both parties, see Valeo, *Mike Mansfield, Majority Leader*, pp. 31–44. A contemporary assessment appears in Randall B. Ripley, *Power in the Senate* (St. Martin's Press, 1969), pp. 92–96.

5. Harold E. Hughes, with Dick Schneider, *The Man from Ida Grover: A Senator's Personal Story* (Chosen Books, 1979), pp. 14–19, 264–66; "Hollings Spills It, Sort Of. Just Who Were the Drunks in 1966," *The Hill*, 24 November 2004; U.S. Congress, Senate, *The Impact of Alcoholism: Hearings Before the Special Subcommittee on Alcoholism and Narcotics of the Committee on Labor and Public Welfare, United States Senate, July 23, 24, and 25, 1969*, Ninety-first Congress, First Session (Government Printing Office, 1969), pp. 2–5.

6. Michael O' Brien, *Philip Hart: The Conscience of the Senate* (Michigan State University Press, 1995); Robert G. Kaufman, *Henry M. Jackson: A Life in Politics* (University of Washington Press, 2000); Patrick Cox, *Ralph W. Yarborough: The People's Senator* (University of Texas Press, 2001).

7. John G. Tower, *Consequence: A Personal and Political Memoir* (Little Brown, 1991), pp. 19–25.

8. Robert Alan Goldberg, *Barry Goldwater* (Yale University Press, 1995), pp. 149–57; Byron C. Hulsey, *Everett Dirksen and His Presidents: How a Senate Giant Shaped American Politics* (University Press of Kansas, 2000), pp. 149–58; Frederick Logevall, "A Delicate Balance: John Sherman Cooper and the Republican Opposition to the Vietnam War," in Woods, *Vietnam and the American Political Tradition*, pp. 237–58.

9. Randall Bennett Woods, *Fulbright: A Biography* (Cambridge University Press, 1998), pp. 244–49.

10. Ellen Proxmire, *One Foot in Washington: The Perilous Life of a Senator's Wife* (Robert B. Luce, 1963), pp 99, 101.

11. Richard Langham Riedel, *Halls of the Mighty: My 47 Years at the Senate* (Robert B. Luce, 1969), pp. 285–86.

12. Robert Dallek, *An Unfinished Life: John F. Kennedy, 1917–1963* (Little, Brown, 2003), pp. 328–30, 493, 604–6; Howard K. Smith, *Events Leading Up to My*

*Death: The Life of a Twentieth Century Reporter* (St. Martin's Press, 1996), p. 298, has some acerbic quotes about Kennedy's legislative program from his Republican critics. George Smathers, Oral History, 5 September 1989, interview no. 4, p. 90, Senate Historical Office, discusses senators' reactions to Kennedy as president.

13. Nigel Bowles, *The White House and Capitol Hill: The Politics of Presidential Persuasion* (Clarendon Press, 1987), pp. 18–25; Kenneth E. Collier, *Between the Branches: The White House Office of Legislative Affairs* (University of Pittsburgh Press, 1997), pp. 67–78; Sean J. Savage, *JFK, LBJ, and the Democratic Party* (State University of New York Press, 2004), pp. 96–97, 106–7, 109–10.

14. James MacGregor Burns, *The Deadlock of Democracy: Four Party Politics in America* (Prentice Hall, 1963, 1967); Joseph S. Clark, *Congress: The Sapless Branch* (Harper & Row, 1964); Julian E. Zelizer, *On Capitol Hill: The Struggle to Reform Congress and Its Consequences, 1948–2000* (Cambridge University Press, 2004), pp. 85–86.

15. For a more favorable assessment of the Kennedy administration's legislative record, see Savage, *JFK, LBJ and the Democratic Party*, pp. 116–17; Dallek, *An Unfinished Life*, pp. 707–8; on Mansfield, see Valeo, *Mike Mansfield, Majority Leader*, pp. 79–89.

16. Hulsey, *Everett Dirksen and His Presidents*, p. 177.

17. Ibid., pp. 177–80.

18. Carol E. Hoffecker, *Honest John Williams: U.S. Senator from Delaware* (University of Delaware Press, 2000), pp. 179–85.

19. Valeo, *Mike Mansfield, Majority Leader*, pp. 77–78; Oberdorfer, *Senator Mansfield*, pp. 203–5.

20. Valeo, *Mike Mansfield, Majority Leader*, pp. 182–85.

21. Michael Beschloss, ed., *Taking Charge: The Johnson White House Tapes, 1963–1964* (Simon & Schuster, 1997), pp. 49 (Dirksen), 59 (Russell).

22. On Johnson's motivation concerning civil rights relative to the Senate, see Robert Dallek, *Flawed Giant: Lyndon Johnson and His Times, 1961–1973* (Oxford University Press, 1998), pp. 112–13; Nick Kotz, *Judgment Days: Lyndon Baines Johnson, Martin Luther King Jr., and the Laws That Changed America* (Houghton Mifflin, 2005), pp. 24–41.

23. Hulsey, *Everett Dirksen and His Presidents*, pp. 187–89.

24. Valeo, *Mike Mansfield, Majority Leader*, pp. 135–36, 140–144; Gilbert C. Fite, *Richard B. Russell, Jr., Senator from Georgia* (University of North Carolina Press, 1991), pp. 407–13.

25. Hulsey, *Everett Dirksen and His Presidents*, p. 189; Carl Solberg, *Hubert Humphrey: A Biography* (W. W. Norton, 1984), pp. 221–27; Hubert H. Humphrey, *The Education of a Public Man* (Doubleday, 1976), pp. 273–286.

26. Nadine Cohodas, *Strom Thurmond and the Politics of Southern Change* (Simon & Schuster, 1993), p. 349.

27. Hulsey, *Everett Dirksen and His Presidents*, p. 196; Humphrey, *Education of a Public Man*, p. 283.

28. There is a vast literature on the Tonkin Gulf Resolution, the events that surrounded its introduction, and the senatorial debate that it sparked. A good recent survey of how individual senators reacted is in Woods, *Vietnam and the American Political Tradition*, pp. 58–59, 187–88, 210, 245–46. The two senators who voted against the resolution are profiled in Robert David Johnson, *Ernest Gruening and the American Dissenting Tradition* (Harvard University Press, 1998), pp. 252–54, and Mason Drukman, *Wayne Morse: A Political Biography* (Press of the Oregon Historical Society, 1997), pp. 408–13.

29. Dallek, *Flawed Giant*, pp. 143–56; Eric Alterman, *When Presidents Lie: A History of Official Deception and Its Consequences* (Viking, 2004), pp. 160–212.

30. Woods, *Fulbright*, pp. 349–55.

31. Drukman, *Wayne Morse*, pp. 410–11.

32. Solberg, *Hubert Humphrey*, pp. 244–58; Dominic Sandbrook, *Eugene McCarthy: The Rise and Fall of Postwar American Liberalism* (Alfred A. Knopf, 2004), pp. 110–16.

33. Dallek, *Flawed Giant*, pp. 196–221.

34. Woods, *Fulbright*, pp. 376–85, discusses Fulbright's response to the Dominican Republic intervention.

35. Ibid., pp. 402–14.

36. George D. Aiken, *Aiken: Senate Diary, January 1972–January 1975* (Stephen Greene Press, 1976), p. x.

37. Mark O. Hatfield, as told to Diane N. Solomon, *Against the Grain: Reflections of a Rebel Republican* (White Cloud Press, 2001), pp. 106–8; J. Lee Annis, *Howard Baker: Conciliator in an Age of Crisis* (Madison Books, 1995), pp. 30–37.

38. Jeff Shesol, *Mutual Contempt: Lyndon Johnson, Robert Kennedy, and the Feud That Defined a Decade* (W. W. Norton, 1997), pp. 397–403.

39. Sandbrook, *Eugene McCarthy*, p. 156.

40. Ibid., p. 162.

41. Lewis L. Gould, *1968: The Election That Changed America* (Ivan Dee, 1993), pp. 33–59; Hulsey, *Everett Dirksen and His Presidents*, pp. 248–51.

42. Hulsey, *Everett Dirksen and His Presidents*, pp. 251–53; Thomas Francis Clarkin, "The Fair Housing Act of 1968" (Master's thesis, University of Texas at Austin, 1993).

43. Lucas A. Powe, Jr., *The Warren Court and American Politics* (Belknap Press of Harvard University Press, 2000), pp. 467–69.

44. Fite, *Russell*, pp. 467–81; Dallek, *Flawed Giant*, pp. 556–64; Hulsey, *Everett Dirksen and His Presidents*, pp. 257–67.

45. On Mansfield's and Fulbright's attitudes toward Richard Nixon, see Woods, *Fulbright*, pp. 503–6; Oberdorfer, *Senator Mansfield*, pp. 348–53.

46. On Nixon and the Senate, see H. R. Haldeman, *The Haldeman Diaries: Inside the Nixon White House* (G. P. Putnam's Sons, 1994), pp. 48, 67, 81, 113; Richard Reeves, *President Nixon: Alone in the White House* (Simon & Schuster, 2001), p. 576 (Nixon quotation). Bill Christofferson, *The Man from Clear Lake: Earth Day Founder Senator Gaylord Nelson* (University of Wisconsin Press, 2004), pp. 302–12.

47. For the Kennedy-Long contest, see Adam Clymer, *Edward M. Kennedy: A Biography* (William Morrow, 1999), pp. 131–33; Robert Mann, *Legacy of Power: Russell Long of Louisiana* (Paragon House, 1992), pp. 291–95.

48. Dean J. Kotlowski, "Unhappily Yoked? Hugh Scott and Richard Nixon," *Pennsylvania Magazine of History and Biography* 125(2001): 233–66.

49. On the ABM battle, see Clymer, *Edward M. Kennedy*, pp. 134–35; Kaufman, *Henry M. Jackson*, pp. 210–12; Haldeman, *Haldeman Diaries*, p. 48.

50. Stanley I. Kutler, *The Wars of Watergate: The Last Crisis of Richard Nixon* (Alfred A. Knopf, 1990), pp. 140–44.

51. Haldeman, *Haldeman Diaries*, p. 113. Melvin Small, *The Presidency of Richard Nixon* (University Press of Kansas, 1999), p. 169.

52. Reeves, *President Nixon*, p. 161.

53. Walter Kravitz, "The Advent of the Modern Congress: The Legislative Reorganization Act of 1970," *Legislative Studies Quarterly* 15(1990): 375–99.

54. Vincent Canby, "'Candidate,' a Comedy About the State of Politics, Opens," film review, *New York Times*, 30 June 1972.

## Chapter Fourteen

1. J. Lee Annis, *Howard Baker: Conciliator in an Age of Crisis* (Madison Books, 1995), p. 72.

2. Bernard Asbell, *The Senate Nobody Knows* (Doubleday, 1978), p. 80 (Muskie quote); William S. Cohen, *Roll Call: One Year in the United States Senate* (Simon & Schuster, 1981), p. 225 (Javits quote).

3. For the background of the Cooper-Church Amendment, see Gustaf J. Brock, "'Congress Must Draw the Line': Senator Frank Church and the

Cooper-Church Amendment of 1970," *Idaho Yesterdays* 35(1991): 27–36; LeRoy Ashby and Rod Gramer, *Fighting the Odds: The Life of Senator Frank Church* (Washington State University Press, 1994), pp. 308–30; Frederik Logevall, "A Delicate Balance: Johnson Sherman Cooper and the Republican Opposition to the Vietnam War," in Randall Bennett Woods, ed., *Vietnam and the American Political Tradition: The Politics of Dissent* (Cambridge University Press, 2003), pp. 253–56.

4. Brock, "'Congress Must Draw the Line,'" p. 32.

5. Ashby and Gramer, *Fighting the Odds*, pp. 328–30.

6. Patrick Cox, *Ralph W. Yarborough: The People's Senator* (University of Texas Press, 2001), pp. 255–57. The challenge that Yarborough faced from Lloyd M. Bentsen, Jr., is discussed in Lloyd M. Bentsen, Oral History, 27 November 1989, pp. 110–29, Center for American History, University of Texas at Austin; Kyle Longley, *Senator Albert Gore, Sr.: Tennessee Maverick* (Louisiana State University Press, 2004), pp. 223–29. The strategy of the Nixon White House toward the Senate is outlined in H. R. Haldeman, *The Haldeman Diaries: Inside the Nixon White House* (G. P. Putnam's Sons, 1994), pp. 148, 173, 183, 203.

7. On the impact of the Muskie television appearance in 1970, see Haldeman, *Haldeman Diaries*, p. 206, and Richard Reeves, *President Nixon: Alone in the White House* (Simon & Schuster, 2001), p. 271; Lowell P. Weicker, Jr., with Barry Sussman, *Maverick: A Life in Politics* (Little, Brown, 1995), pp. 35–37; Cox, *Ralph W. Yarborough*, pp. 263–64; Longley, *Senator Albert Gore, Sr.*, pp. 238–39.

8. For the 1971 Byrd-Kennedy contest, see Adam Clymer, *Edward M. Kennedy: A Biography* (William Morrow, 1999), pp. 171–73.

9. Byrd's own account of his life is in Robert C. Byrd, and Wendy Wolff, ed., *The Senate, 1789–1989: Addresses on the History of the United States Senate*, vol. 2 (Government Printing Office, 1991), pp. 541–72.

10. The 1972 presidential election is discussed in Jules Witcover, *Party of the People: A History of the Democrats* (Random House, 2003), pp. 579–88.

11. Patricia L. Schmidt, *Margaret Chase Smith: Beyond Convention* (University of Maine Press, 1996), p. 329.

12. Richard T. McCulley, "'Plowing a Straight Furrow': John C. Stennis and the Reform Politics of the U.S. Senate," paper delivered at the American Historical Association Annual Meeting, January 1999, pp. 11–12. Robert A. Katzmann, "War Powers Resolution," in Donald C. Bacon, Robert H. Davidson, and Morton Keller, eds., *The Encyclopedia of the United States Congress*, 4 vols. (Simon & Schuster, 1995), 4, pp. 2100–2102.

13. Don Oberdorfer, *Senator Mansfield: The Extraordinary Life of a Great American Statesman and Diplomat* (Smithsonian Books, 2003), pp. 432–33; Stanley I. Kutler, *The Wars of Watergate: The Last Crisis of Richard Nixon* (Alfred A. Knopf, 1990), pp. 255–56; Annis, *Howard Baker*, pp. 65–66.

14. Kutler, *Wars of Watergate*, is an excellent, comprehensive history of this complex episode. Also useful is Keith W. Olson, *Watergate: The Presidential Scandal That Shook America* (University Press of Kansas, 2003), pp. 70–72, 89–101.

15. Weicker, *Maverick*, pp. 90–98; Annis, *Howard Baker*, pp. 82–83; J. Anthony Lukas, *Nightmare: The Underside of the Nixon Years* (Viking Press, 1976; Ohio University Press, 1999), pp. 443–44.

16. Eric Patashnik, "Congress and the Budget Since 1974," in Julian E. Zelizer, ed., *The American Congress: The Building of Democracy* (Houghton Mifflin, 2004), pp. 673–76; Bernard Asbell, *The Senate Nobody Knows* (Doubleday, 1978), p. 144 (Muskie quotation).

17. Clymer, *Edward M. Kennedy*, pp. 202–4.

18. Ibid., pp. 209–10.

19. Ashby and Gramer, *Fighting the Odds*, pp. 443–50; Lewis L. Gould, *Grand Old Party: A History of the Republicans* (Random House, 2003), p. 403.

20. Randall Bennett Woods, *Fulbright: A Biography* (Cambridge University Press, 1995), pp. 658–59.

21. Donn Tibbetts, *The Closest U.S. Senate Race in History: Durkin v. Wyman* (Lew A. Cummings, 1976), p. 55; "John A. Durkin v Louis C. Wyman (NH) (1974–1975)," in Anne M. Butler and Wendy Wolff, *United States Senate: Election, Expulsion and Censure Cases, 1793–1990* (Government Printing Office, 1995), pp. 421–25.

22. William F. Hildenbrand, Oral History, 28 March 1985, Senate Historical Office, pp. 76, 136 (quotation).

23. Richard T. McCulley, unpublished history of the Senate Armed Services Committee, pp. 326–32, courtesy of the author.

24. Christopher J. Bailey, *The Republican Party in the U.S. Senate, 1974–1984: Party Change and Institutional Development* (St. Martin's Press, 1988), p. 75; Carl T. Curtis and Regis Courtemanche, *Fifty Years Against the Tide* (Regnery Gateway, 1986), pp. 396–99; "Senate Steering Committee, General Description, 1979–1980," in John P. East Papers, East Carolina Manuscript Collection, J. Y. Joyner Library, East Carolina University, Greenville, North Carolina.

25. Bailey, *Republican Party in the U.S. Senate*, pp. 41–46.

26. Sarah A. Binder and Steven S. Smith, *Politics or Principle: Filibustering in the United States Senate* (Brookings Institution Press, 1997), pp. 165–66.

27. "Senator James Allen Dies; Alabamian Led Canal Pact Fight," *New York Times*, 12 June 1978; Elbert L. Watson, *Alabama United States Senators* (Strode Publishers, 1982), pp. 146–49; "James B. Allen," Alabama Academy of Honor, www.archives.state.al.us/famous/academy/J-allen.html (quotation).

28. Asbell, *Senate Nobody Knows*, p. 101; for a description of how Allen searched for assistance and then trained like-minded new conservative senators, see Orrin Hatch, *Square Peg: Confessions of a Citizen Senator* (Basic Books, 2002), pp. 21, 28–29.

29. For a good analysis of Allen's technique from a fellow senator, see Byrd, *The Senate, 1789–1989*, 2, p. 154.

30. "Reformers Consider Filibuster Compromise," *Congressional Quarterly*, 1 March 1975, pp. 448–49; for Nelson Rockefeller's discussion of his role in the controversy, see Cabinet Meeting, 12 March 1975, box 4, James E. Connor Files, Gerald R. Ford Library, Ann Arbor. "Nelson Aldrich Rockefeller," in Mark O. Hatfield, et al., eds., *Vice Presidents of the United States, 1789–1993* (Government Printing Office, 1997), p. 510, discusses Rockefeller's actions and Floyd M. Riddick, Oral History, August 25, 1978, p. 217, indicates that Rockefeller was working on his own in making his ruling.

31. Chris Mooney, "Back to Church," *The American Prospect*, 5 November 2001 (*Wall Street Journal* quotation), on-line edition; Frank J. Smist, Jr., *Congress Oversees the United States Intelligence Community* (University of Tennessee Press, 1999), pp. 25–81.

32. Ashby and Gramer, *Fighting the Odds*, pp. 468–71.

33. For other discussions of the Church committee and its work, see John Tower, *Consequences: A Personal and Political Memoir* (Little, Brown, 1991), pp. 133–37; John Prados, *Lost Crusader: The Secret Wars of CIA Director William Colby* (Oxford University Press, 2003), pp. 297–300.

34. Witcover, *Party of the People*, pp. 595–98.

35. Don Oberdorfer, *Senator Mansfield: The Extraordinary Life of a Great American Statesman and Diplomat* (Smithsonian Books, 2003), p. 543; Ross K. Baker, "Mike Mansfield and the Birth of the Modern Senate," in Richard A. Baker and Roger H. Davidson, eds., *First Among Equals: Outstanding Senate Leaders of the Twentieth Century* (Congressional Quarterly, 1991), p. 294. Mansfield went on to serve with distinction as ambassador to Japan.

36. Both quotations are in Lindsay to Nation, Parker, Goldman, 6 January 1977, U.S. Congress—Senate Leaders, *Newsweek* Archives, Center for American History, University of Texas at Austin.

37. Ibid.; Tower, *Consequences*, p. 112.

38. Lindsay to Nation, Parker, Goldman, 6 January 1977; Annis, *Howard Baker*, pp. 105–6. While the Senate was selecting its leaders, it was also completing a reorganization of its committee structure. For a contemporary analysis of that process, see Judith H. Parris, "The Senate Reorganizes Its Committees, 1977," *Political Science Quarterly* 94(1979): 319–37.

39. On Carter's relations with Congress, see Gary M. Fink and Hugh Davis Graham, eds., *The Carter Presidency: Policy Choices in the Post–New Deal Era* (University Press of Kansas, 1998), pp. 12–13, 97, 123; Bailey, *The Republican Party in the U.S. Senate*, pp. 112–13.

40. Byrd, *The Senate, 1789–1989*, 2, pp. 155–56.

41. Annis, *Howard Baker*, pp. 112–27; Bailey, *Republican Party in the U.S. Senate*, pp. 114–15.

42. Ashby and Gramer, *Fighting the Odds*, pp. 542–50.

43. Ibid., pp. 549–50.

44. Bailey, *Republican Party in the U.S. Senate*, pp. 39–46.

45. David W. Reinhard, *The Republican Right Since 1945* (University Press of Kentucky, 1983), pp. 242–46.

46. Witcover, *Party of the People*, pp. 606–14.

47. Ashby and Gramer, *Fighting the Odds*, pp. 586–605; Shelby Scates, *Warren G. Magnuson and the Shaping of Modern America* (University of Washington Press, 1997), pp. 316–19.

48. Butler and Wolff, *United States Senate*, sv. "Herman E. Talmadge" and "Harrison A. Williams, Jr.," pp. 429–37.

49. Both quotations are in Lindsay (others filing separately) to Nation, Shepard, Alpern, Mayer, 13 November 1980, U.S. Congress—Senate, *Newsweek* Archives, Center for American History, University of Texas at Austin.

## Chapter Fifteen

1. J. Lee Annis, Jr., *Howard Baker: Conciliator in an Age of Crisis* (Madison Books, 1995), p. 194.

2. Fineman/Washington to Nation/Reese, Sheils, 17 March 1983, U.S. Congress—Senate, *Newsweek* Archives, Center for American History, University of Texas at Austin (hereinafter *Newsweek* Archives).

3. Ibid.

4. Baker's own view of his role is evident in Howard H. Baker, Jr., "The View from Both Ends of the Avenue," *Presidential Studies Quarterly* 20(1990): 489–92; Annis, *Howard Baker*, is excellent on Baker's years as leader.

5. Annis, *Howard Baker*, p. 170.

6. Warren B. Rudman, *Combat: Twelve Years in the U.S. Senate* (Random House, 1996), p. 67; Annis, *Howard Baker*, p. 172.

7. John W. Sloan, *The Reagan Effect: Economics and Presidential Leadership* (University Press of Kansas, 1999), pp. 143–46, 148–51.

8. Richard Lugar to John P. East, 27 September 1982, 5 and 17 November 1982, 3 December 1982; Robert Packwood to East, 29 September 1982, John P. East Papers, East Carolina Manuscript Collection, J. Y. Joyner Library, East Carolina University, Greenville, North Carolina; Mark Kirchmeier, *Packwood: The Private and Public Life from Acclaim to Outrage* (HarperCollins West, 1995), p. 167; Jeffrey H. Birnbaum and Alan S. Murray, *Showdown at Gucci Gulch: Lawmakers, Lobbyists and the Unlikely Triumph of Tax Reform* (Vintage Books, 1988), p. 186.

9. Annis, *Howard Baker*, pp. 116, 192; Robert C. Byrd, with Wendy Wolff, ed., *The Senate, 1789–1989: Addresses on the History of the United States Senate* (Government Printing Office, 1991), 2, pp. 614–15.

10. Ronald Garay, "Broadcasting of Congressional Proceedings," in Donald C. Bacon, Roger H. Davidson, and Morton Keller, eds., *The Encyclopedia of the United States Congress* (4 vols., Simon & Schuster, 1995), 1, p. 199. Fred R. Harris, *Deadlock or Decision: The U.S. Senate and the Rise of National Politics* (Oxford University Press, 1993), pp. 146–51.

11. Fineman/Washington to Nation/Reese, Sheils, 17 March 1983, *Newsweek* Archives.

12. Ernest B. Furguson, *Hard Right: The Rise of Jesse Helms* (W. W. Norton, 1986), pp. 177 (quotation), 188–206; Jesse Helms to John P. East, 12 January 1982, John P. East Papers; Annis, *Howard Baker*, pp. 185–86.

13. DeFrank/Clift Wash to Nation, Starr, 29 November 1984, U.S. Congress—Senate Leaders, *Newsweek* Archives; Robert Dole to John P. East, 23 November 1984, John P. East Papers. Richard Ben Cramer, *What It Takes: The Way to the White House* (Vintage Books, 1992, 1993), pp. 227–31, 237–39, 394–400, is excellent on Dole's background.

14. De/Frank Clift to Nation, Starr, 29 November 1984, U.S. Congress—Senate Leaders, *Newsweek* Archives.

15. Borger/Washington to Nation/Sheils, Starr, 21 November 1984, U.S. Congress—Senate Leaders, *Newsweek* Archives.

16. William E. Pemberton, *Exit with Honor: The Life and Presidency of Ronald Reagan* (M. E. Sharpe, 1997), pp. 144–45.

17. Rudman, *Combat*, p. 65.

18. Ibid., pp. 76–78.

19. "Press Office 1988 Annual Report," Phil Gramm Papers, box 3R 37, Center for American History, University of Texas at Austin. A former Gramm employee gave these documents to the *Dallas Morning News* and the newspaper donated the materials to the University of Texas.

20. James A. Thurber, "Balanced Budget and Emergency Deficit Control Act," in Bacon et al., *Encyclopedia of the United States Congress*, 1, pp. 129–130; Rudman, *Combat*, pp. 82–106, is the best published account of the development of Gramm-Rudman-Hollings by one of its architects.

21. The most detailed treatment of the 1986 tax legislation is Birnbaum and Murray, *Showdown at Gucci Gulch*; Kirchmeier, *Packwood*, pp. 178–79.

22. Kirchmeier, *Packwood*, pp. 180–81; Birnbaum and Murray, *Showdown*, pp. 204–9, 288–91.

23. Robert Alan Goldberg, *Goldwater: A Biography* (Yale University Press, 1995), p. 326; James R. Locher, *Victory on the Potomac: The Goldwater-Nichols Act Unifies the Pentagon* (Texas A&M University Press, 2002).

24. On the results of the 1986 elections, see Adam Clymer, *Edward Kennedy: A Biography* (William Morrow, 1999), p. 406.

25. Norman Vieria and Leonard Gross, *Supreme Court Appointments: Judge Bork and Politicization of Senate Confirmations* (Southern Illinois Press, 1998), pp. 3–10; Clymer, *Edward Kennedy*, pp. 403–5; Ethan Bronner, *Battle for Justice: How the Bork Nomination Shook America* (W. W. Norton, 1989), pp. 15–30.

26. There is no biography of Robert Bork. Bronner, *Battle for Justice*, pp. 56–76, discusses his life and early career. Vieria and Gross, *Supreme Court Appointments*, pp. 12–21, covers the same ground. For Republican attitudes toward Bork's candidacy, see Orrin Hatch, *Square Peg: Confessions of a Citizen Senator* (Basic Books, 2002), pp. 130–35, and Arlen Specter, with Charles Robbins, *Passion for Truth: From Finding JFK's Single Bullet to Questioning Anita Hill to Impeaching Clinton* (William Morrow, 2000), pp. 319–21.

27. Clymer, *Edward Kennedy*, p. 418, has the famous Kennedy quotation.

28. Bronner, *Battle for Justice*, pp. 343–52.

29. Hatch, *Square Peg*, p. 137; Vieria and Gross, *Supreme Court Appointments*, pp. 247–54.

30. On the Iran-*contra* scandal and the role of the Senate, see Rudman, *Combat*, pp. 107–51; Annis, *Howard Baker*, pp. 196–203; John G. Tower, *Consequences: A Personal and Political Memoir* (Little, Brown, 1991), pp. 270–89; Miller/Wash to Martz/Nation, 18 December 1986, U.S. Congress—Senate/Select Committee on Intelligence, *Newsweek* Archives, has some interesting background on the Senate and the case.

31. Phil Gramm Reelection Campaign, "Preliminary 1990 Campaign Revenue Projections," Phil Gramm Papers, box 3R 37.

32. For a discussion of the Bentsen episode see Jack DeVore, interview with Lewis L. Gould, 31 August 1994, pp. 19–20, Center for American History, University of Texas at Austin.

33. Michael Binstein and Charles Bowden, *Trust Me: Charles Keating and the Missing Billions* (Random House, 1993), pp. 160–62; Charles Lewis and the Center for Public Integrity, *The Buying of Congress* (Avon Books, 1998), pp. 16–17; Elizabeth Drew, *The Corruption of American Politics: What Went Wrong and Why* (Overlook Press, 1999), p. 164; Pemberton, *Exit with Honor*, pp. 129–130; Harris, *Deadlock or Decision*, p. 81.

34. Rudman, *Combat*, pp. 195–241, considers the investigation of the five senators. Bill Miller, "Chapter V: The Keating Five," *Arizona Republic*, 3 October 1999, looks at McCain's role in the case. John McCain, *Worth the Fighting For: A Memoir* (Random House, 2002), pp. 160–205, provides his defense of his actions in the matter; for the documents and testimony in the case, see U.S. Congress, Senate Select Committee on Ethics, hearing 101–1214, *Preliminary Inquiry into Allegations Regarding Senators Cranston, DeConcini, Glenn, McCain, and Riegle* (5 vols., Government Printing Office, 1991).

35. Rudman, *Combat*, pp. 207–17.

36. DeVore interview, 31 August 1994, gives the background for Bentsen's devastating remark to Dan Quayle; see also Herbert S. Parmet, *George Bush: The Life of a Lone Star Yankee* (Scribner, 1997), p. 354.

37. Ross K. Baker, *House and Senate: Third Edition* (W. W. Norton, 2001), p. 93.

38. George N. Green and John L. Kushma, "John Tower," in Kenneth E. Nedrickson and Michael L. Collins, eds., *Profiles in Power: Twentieth Century Texans in Washington* (Harland Davidson, 1993), pp. 197–227.

39. Helen Dewar and Dan Balz, "Tracing the Steps in Tower's Downfall," *Washington Post*, 29 March 1989; "Sam Nunn Replies: We Are Not Being Unfair," *Washington Post*, 3 March 1989; McCain, *Worth the Fighting For*, pp. 121–57, mounts a vigorous defense of Tower.

40. Gary Hart, *The Good Fight: The Education of an American Reformer* (Random House, 1993), pp. 192, 237; Rudman, *Combat*, pp. 242–43.

## Chapter Sixteen

1. On the context in which the vote to authorize the use of force against Iraq over Kuwait occurred, see Herbert Parmet, *George Bush: The Life of a Lone*

*Star Yankee* (Scribner, 1997), p. 475; John Robert Greene, *The Presidency of George Bush* (University Press of Kansas, 2000), pp. 126–27.

2. On the Gulf War vote and the Senate's performance, see Mark O. Hatfield, with Diane N. Solomon, *Against the Grain: Reflections of a Rebel Republican* (White Cloud Press, 2001), pp. 197–99; Bill Turque, *Inventing Al Gore: A Biography* (Houghton Mifflin, 2000), pp. 239–40; Fred R. Harris, *Deadlock or Decision: The U.S. Senate and the Rise of National Politics* (Oxford University Press, 1993), pp. 244–47.

3. Norman Vieria and Leonard Gross, *Supreme Court Appointments: Judge Bork and the Politicization of Senate Confirmations* (Southern Illinois University Press, 1998), p. 201; Jane Mayer and Jill Abramson, *Strange Justice: The Selling of Clarence Thomas* (Houghton Mifflin, 1994), pp. 11–30.

4. Mayer and Abramson, *Strange Justice*, pp. 169–220. For positive assessments of Thomas's role in the confirmation process, see Ken Foskett, *Judging Thomas: The Life and Times of Clarence Thomas* (William Morrow, 2001), and Andrew Peyton Thomas, *Clarence Thomas: A Biography* (Encounter Books, 2001).

5. Mayer and Abramson, *Strange Justice*, pp. 244–57.

6. A convenient source for the hearing is Anita Miller, ed., *The Complete Transcripts of the Clarence Thomas–Anita Hill Hearings October 11, 12, 13, 1991* (Academy Chicago Publishers, 1994).

7. Mayer and Abramson, *Strange Justice*, p. 348. See Arlen Specter, with Charles Robbins, *Passion for Truth: From Finding JFK's Single Bullet to Questioning Anita Hill to Impeaching Clinton* (William Morrow, 2000), pp. 349–80, for his own remarks to Kennedy and Orrin Hatch's allusion to Kennedy's involvement in the fatal Chappaquiddick incident in 1969.

8. Barbara Mikulski et al., with Catherine Whitney, *Nine and Counting: The Women of the Senate* (William Morrow, 2000), pp. 46–47, 48–50.

9. Mark Kirchmeier, *Packwood: The Public and Private Life: From Acclaim to Outrage* (HarperCollins West, 1995), pp. 191–228.

10. Greene, *Presidency of George Bush*, p. 88; Dennis J. McGrath and Dane Smith, *Professor Wellstone Goes to Washington: The Inside Story of a Grassroots U.S. Senate Campaign* (University of Minnesota Press, 1995), examines the victorious election of the one senator the Democrats gained in 1991.

11. On the significance of the Wofford-Thornburgh race, see Greene, *Presidency of George Bush*, p. 166; Parmet, *George Bush*, p. 497.

12. The outcome of the 1992 presidential race is discussed in Greene, *Presidency of George Bush*, pp. 178–79; Earl Black and Merle Black, *The Rise of Southern Republicans* (Belknap Press of Harvard University Press, 2002), pp. 197–203, examines the Coverdell-Fowler race and what it implied for the Democrats.

13. Godfrey Hodgson, *The Gentleman from New York: Daniel Patrick Moynihan, a Biography* (Houghton Mifflin, 2000), pp. 349–61.

14. Bill Clinton, *My Life* (Alfred A. Knopf, 2004), p. 450.

15. Joe Klein, *The Natural: The Misunderstood Presidency of Bill Clinton* (Doubleday, 2002), p. 52.

16. Kim Fridkin Kahn and Patricia J. Kenner, *No Holds Barred: Negativity in U.S. Senate Campaigns* (Pearson/Prentice Hall, 2004), is a brief but informative look at the subject of modern Senate campaigning. On Kay Bailey Hutchison, see Mikulski et al., *Nine and Counting*, pp. 50–53, 80–84. On Limbaugh, see David Brock, *The Republican Noise Machine: Right-Wing Media and How It Corrupts Democracy* (Crown, 2004), pp. 262–66.

17. Elizabeth Drew, *The Corruption of American Politics: What Went Wrong and Why* (Overlook Press, 1999), pp. 36–38; Colton C. Campbell and Nicol C. Rae, eds., *The Contentious Senate: Partisanship, Ideology, and the Myth of Cool Judgment* (Rowman & Littlefield, 2001), pp. 8–9, 10–11.

18. Tom Daschle, with Michael D'Orso, *Like No Other Time: The 107th Congress and the Two Years That Changed America Forever* (Crown Publishers, 2003), pp. 79–81.

19. Norman Ornstein, ed., *Lessons and Legacies: Farewell Addresses from the Senate* (Addison Wesley, 1997), p. 158.

20. Elizabeth A. Palmer, "Nominating Judges: President vs. Senate," in Scott Montgomery, ed., *Inside Congress: A CQ Reader 107th Congress* (CQ Press, 2002), p. 126; Orrin Hatch, *Square Peg: Confessions of a Citizen Senator* (Basic Books, 2002), pp. 125–26.

21. Hatfield's situation is discussed in Drew, *Corruption of American Politics*, pp. 36–37, and Hatfield, *Against the Grain*, pp. 174–77 (quotation on page 177).

22. Eleanor Clift and Tom Brazaitis, *War Without Bloodshed: The Art of Politics* (Simon & Schuster, 1996, 1997), p. 431.

23. On the debacle of closing down the government and later Dole's departure from the Senate, see Klein, *The Natural*, pp. 145–49, 158; Clift and Brazaitis, *War Without Bloodshed*, pp. 375–76.

24. Karen Tumulty, "Trent Lott's Segregationist College Days," *Time*, 12 December 2002; "Lott Apologizes Anew for Comments," CNN.com, 14 December 2002; Black and Black, *The Rise of Southern Republicans*, pp. 302–4.

25. Clinton, *My Life*, pp. 752–73; Klein, *The Natural*, pp. 158–60.

26. Joe Conason and Gene Lyons, *The Hunting of the President: The Ten-Year Campaign to Destroy Bill and Hillary Clinton* (St. Martin's Press, 2000), pp. 189–200.

27. Drew, *Corruption of American Politics*, pp. 3–18, 101–15, provides the most extensive treatment of the fund-raising probe in the Senate.

28. Nicol C. Rae and Colton C. Campbell, *Impeaching Clinton: Partisan Strife on Capitol Hill* (University Press of Kansas, 2004), pp. 20–22, 76–83.

29. There is already a wide-ranging literature on the Clinton impeachment and trial in the Senate. Haynes Johnson, *The Best of Times: The Boom and Bust Years of America Before and After Everything Changed* (Harcourt, 2001, 2002), pp. 411–29; Rae and Campbell, *Impeaching Clinton*, pp. 122–50; Jeffrey Toobin, *A Vast Conspiracy: The Real Story of the Sex Scandal That Nearly Brought Down a President* (Random House, 1999), pp. 363–91; Peter Baker, *The Breach: Inside the Impeachment and Trial of William Jefferson Clinton* (Scribner, 2000), pp. 279–412.

30. Specter, *Passion for Truth*, pp. 437–538, illustrates the lack of any clear Republican strategy in the Clinton impeachment proceedings.

31. John McCain, with Mark Salter, *Worth the Fighting For: A Memoir* (Random House, 2002), p. 353; Diana Dwyre and Victoria A. Farrar-Myers, *Legislative Labyrinth: Congress and Campaign Finance Reform* (CQ Press, 2001), pp. 1–34.

32. McCain and Salter, *Worth the Fighting For*, pp. 213–21.

33. U.S., Senate, *Congressional Record*, 106 Cong. 1 Sess., 1999, 12585–86, 12592; McCain discusses these events in *Worth the Fighting For*, pp. 361–62.

34. Daschle, *Like No Other Time*, pp. 36–42, discusses these negotiations.

### Conclusion: The Senate and Its Future

1. Mary Lynn F. Jones, "Byrd's-Eye View: Robert Byrd Explains Why He's Ashamed of the Current Congress," *The American Prospect*, Online Edition, accessed 13 October 2004.

2. Tom Daschle, with Michael D'Orso, *Like No Other Time: The 107th Congress and the Two Years That Changed America Forever* (Crown Publishers, 2003), pp. 62–72, discusses Jeffords's change of allegiance; James M. Jeffords, with Yvonne Daley and Howard Coffin, *An Independent Man: Adventures of a Public Servant* (Simon & Schuster, 2003), pp. 253–77, provides his own account of his decision.

3. Daschle, *Like No Other Time*, pp. 225–26, examines the 2002 Senate races.

4. Frist is profiled in William H. Frist and J. Lee Annis, Jr., *Tennessee Senators, 1911–2001* (Madison Books, 2001), pp. 243–61.

5. On the case for the "nuclear option," see Orrin G. Hatch, "Crisis Mode: A Fair and Constitutional Option to Beat the Filibuster Game," *National Review*

*Online*, 12 January 2005; on the case against, see Ralph G. Neas, "The Nuclear Option in the Senate: A Preemptive Strike for Absolute Power," news release, People for the American Way, 1 February 2005; Charles Babington, "GOP Moderates Wary of Filibuster Curb," *Washington Post*, 16 January 2005, and Norman Ornstein, "GOP Should Handle Filibusters the Old-Fashioned Way," *Roll Call*, 17 November 2004; Alexander Bolton, "Frist Aims Nuke at the Dems," *The Hill*, 19 January 2005; "Partisans Fume As Senate Disdains 'Nuclear Option,'" *USA Today*, 24 May 2005.

6. For a scathing portrayal of the Senate's October 2002 debate on authorizing President Bush to use force against Iraq, see Winslow T. Wheeler, *The Wastrels of Defense: How Congress Sabotages U.S. Security* (Naval Institute Press, 2004), pp. 14–15, 202–29.

7. The case of Senator Ted Stevens, an Alaska Republican and chair of the Appropriations Committee, attracted brief attention in 2003 and then faded away. See Chuck Neubauer and Richard T. Cooper, "Senator's Way to Wealth Was Paved with Favors," *Los Angeles Times*, 17 December 2003; "Alaskan Outrage," *Washington Post*, 29 December 2003; "Senate Ethics and 'Stevens' Money,'" *New York Times*, 27 December 2003; Paul Jacob, "The Appearance of Corruption," townhall.com, 18 January 18 2004;  Donna Cassata, "Disclosure Forms Offer Glimpses of Senators' Personal Finances," Philly.com, 15 June 2005; Gail Russell Chaddock, "In the Stock Market, U.S. Senators Beat Averages," *Christian Science Monitor*, 7 March 2004. For a more general picture of the Washington atmosphere in 2005, see Elizabeth Drew, "Selling Washington," *New York Review of Books*, 23 June 2005.

8. Jim VanderHei, "Business Sees Gains in GOP Takeover," *Washington Post*, 27 March 2005.

9. Bruce Bartlett, "The Problem with the 17th," Townhall.com, 12 May 2004; Lewis Gould, "Alan Keyes's Daffy Idea to Repeal the 17th Amendment," *History News Network*, 23 August 2004.

10. Richard Rosenfeld, "What Democracy? The Case for Abolishing the Senate," *Harper's Magazine*, May 2004.

# Suggestions for Further Reading

## General

IT WOULD BE IMPOSSIBLE TO COMPILE A FULL BIBLIOGRAPHY OF THE UNITED States Senate in a single volume. The comments that follow are designed to direct those with an interest in other books about the Senate to the more accessible and helpful volumes. Naturally, some worthwhile books will be omitted, for which I apologize in advance. The notes to the chapters indicate how wide a range of reading is available for students of Senate history.

There is no full-scale scholarly or popular history of the United States Senate. Richard Alan Baker, *The Senate of the United States: A Bicentennial History* (Malabar, Fla.: Robert E. Krieger, 1988), is a reliable brief treatment with illustrative documents. Robert C. Byrd, *The Senate, 1789–1989: Addresses on the History of the United States Senate*, 2 vols. (Washington, D.C.: Government Printing Office, 1988, 1991), contains the speeches that Senator Byrd gave to his colleagues on Senate history. The books are a goldmine of information and reflect the hard work of Byrd's researchers. Given the format, however, they are more a collection of essays about the Senate than a unified narrative. Robert C. Byrd and Wendy Wolff, eds., *The Senate, 1789–1989: Historical Statistics, 1789–1992* (Washington, D.C.: Government Printing Office, 1993), provides a convenient source of information for every aspect of Senate history. George H. Haynes, *The Senate of the United States: Its History and Practice*, 2 vols. (Boston, Mass.: Houghton Mifflin, 1938), is a standard work on the institution that contains much relevant and incisive data about how the Senate evolved. Now, however, it is very dated; generally it can be found only in research libraries. For more assistance with Senate topics, interested readers should visit the Senate Historical Office at www.senate.gov/ artandhistory. The on-line resources there will take the researcher into every phase of Senate history, and the staff is cooperative and very professional.

## Chapter One

David J. Rothman, *Politics and Power: The United States Senate, 1869–1901* (Cambridge, Mass.: Harvard University Press, 1966), is a richly detailed look at the Senate on the eve of the twentieth century. John Braeman, *Albert J. Beveridge: American Nationalist* (Chicago: University of Chicago Press, 1971), provides a portrait of how men became senators and the culture they encountered when they arrived in Washington. Nathaniel Wright Stephenson, *Nelson W. Aldrich: A Leader in American Politics* (New York: Charles Scribner's Sons, 1930), is somewhat overwritten but is nonetheless a valuable biography of the dominant figure in the Senate in 1900.

## Chapter Two

Robert Harrison, *Congress, Progressive Reform, and the New American State* (New York: Cambridge University Press, 2004), is a very well researched and perceptive examination of Congress during the first decade of the twentieth century. Lewis L. Gould, *The Presidency of Theodore Roosevelt* (Lawrence: University Press of Kansas, 1991), considers the president's relations with Capitol Hill throughout his two terms. David Sarasohn, *The Party of Reform: Democrats in the Progressive Era* (Jackson: University of Mississippi Press, 1989), has much of interest on the Senate Democrats. Donald A. Ritchie, ed., *Minutes of the Senate Democratic Conference: Fifty-eighth Congress Through Eighty-eighth Congress, 1903–1964* (Washington, D.C.: Government Printing Office, 1998), is of continuing usefulness for the party in the Senate.

## Chapter Three

James Holt, *Congressional Insurgents and the Party System, 1909–1916* (Cambridge, Mass.: Harvard University Press, 1967), explores the roots of factionalism among congressional Republicans during the Roosevelt-Taft years. Nancy C. Unger, *Fighting Bob La Follette: The Righteous Reformer* (Chapel Hill: University of North Carolina Press, 2000), traces the rise to prominence of the Wisconsin senator. Joel Arthur Tarr, *A Study in Boss Politics: William Lorimer of Chicago* (Urbana: University of Illinois Press, 1971), is excellent on the dispute over Lorimer's election and his ultimate ouster from the Senate.

## Chapter Four

There is no published biography of John Worth Kern, but a good introduction exists in the essay about him by Walter J. Oleszek in Richard A. Baker and Roger H. Davidson, eds., *First Among Equals: Outstanding Senate Leaders of the Twentieth Century* (Washington, D.C.: Congressional Quarterly, 1991). This volume belongs in any library devoted to the Senate and its history. Wendy Wolff and Donald A. Ritchie, eds., *Minutes of the Senate Republican Conference: Sixty-second Through Eighty-eighth Congress, 1911–1964* (Washington, D.C.: Government Printing Office, 1999), is often dry but contains indispensable information about the inner deliberations of the Grand Old Party in the Senate. William C. Widenor, *Henry Cabot Lodge and the Search for an American Foreign Policy* (Berkeley: University of California Press, 1980), is excellent on the Republican response in the Senate to the programs and policies of the administration of Woodrow Wilson.

## Chapter Five

John Milton Cooper, Jr., *Breaking the Heart of the World: Woodrow Wilson and the Fight for the League of Nations* (New York: Cambridge University Press, 2001), is a model study of this legislative battle and a delight to read as well. Herbert F. Margulies, *The Mild Reservationists and the League of Nations Controversy in the Senate* (Columbia: University of Missouri Press, 1989), examines an important faction in the fight about the League. Robert E. Burke, ed., *The Diary Letters of Hiram Johnson*, 8 vols. (New York: Garland Publishing, 1983), consists of the letters that Johnson wrote home to his family. Cranky, insightful, and gossipy, Johnson traced the foibles of his colleagues over almost three decades in an indispensable source for Senate history.

## Chapter Six

Three biographical studies are valuable for the Senate in the 1920s. Leroy Ashby, *The Spearless Leader: Senator Borah and the Progressive Movement in the 1920s* (Urbana: University of Illinois Press, 1972), explores well the contradictions in Borah's thinking and political style. Herbert Margulies, *Senator Lenroot of Wisconsin: A Political Biography, 1900–1929* (Columbia: University of Missouri Press,

1977), is a superb study of the influential regular Republican lawmaker. Richard Lowitt, *George W. Norris: The Persistence of a Progressive, 1913–1933* (Urbana: University of Illinois Press, 1971), provides copious detail about one of the Senate's most productive mavericks from the Middle West.

## Chapter Seven

For the Senate during the early years of the Depression, Jordan Schwarz, *The Interregnum of Despair: Hoover, Congress, and the Depression* (Urbana: University of Illinois Press, 1970), is excellent. Richard Lowitt, *Bronson M. Cutting: Progressive Politician* (Albuquerque: University of New Mexico Press, 1992), examines one of the institution's most intriguing personalities. Steve Neal, *McNary of Oregon: A Political Biography* (Portland: Press of the Oregon Historical Society, 1985), is an engaging portrait of a man who enjoyed the respect and affection of Democrats and Republicans alike.

## Chapter Eight

James T. Patterson, *Congressional Conservatism and the New Deal: The Growth of the Conservative Coalition in Congress, 1933–1939* (Lexington: University of Kentucky Press, 1967), has a well-deserved status as a classic. Martha Swain, *Pat Harrison: The New Deal Years* (Jackson: University of Mississippi Press, 1978), traces the evolution of a key southern Democrat from friend to foe of Franklin D. Roosevelt. David Robertson, *Sly and Able: A Political Biography of James F. Byrnes* (New York: W. W. Norton, 1994), is very illuminating on the southern conservatives and their attitudes.

## Chapter Nine

Gilbert C. Fite, *Richard B. Russell, Jr., Senator from Georgia* (Chapel Hill: University of North Carolina Press, 1991), is an excellent biography. Although I disagree with some of its interpretation, it is an indispensable work. James T. Patterson, *Mr. Republican: A Biography of Robert A. Taft* (Boston: Houghton Mifflin, 1972), is another outstanding contribution to Senate history. Patrick J. Maney, *Young Bob: A Biography of Robert M. La Follette, Jr.* (Madison: Wisconsin Historical Society Press, 2003; reprint, Columbia: University of Missouri Press, 1978), shows how a thorough examination of the life of a single senator can illuminate the whole institution. Allen Drury, *A Senate Journal, 1943–1945* (New York: McGraw Hill, 1963), is an absorbing firsthand account of the wartime Senate.

## Chapter Ten

In addition to the works by William S. White, Donald R. Matthews, and Allen Drury discussed in this chapter, the Senate in the postwar era is depicted in Ellen Proxmire, *One Foot in Washington: The Perilous Life of a Senator's Wife* (Washington, D.C.: Robert B. Luce, 1963). Janann Sherman, *No Place for a Woman: A Life of Senator Margaret Chase Smith* (New Brunswick, N.J.: Rutgers University Press, 2000), provides insight into the extent of masculine dominance of the Senate in these years. Hubert H. Humphrey, *The Education of a Public Man: My Life and Politics* (Garden City, N.Y.: Doubleday, 1976), is an absorbing memoir.

## Chapter Eleven

David M. Oshinsky, *A Conspiracy So Immense: The World of Joe McCarthy* (New York: Free Press, 1983), and Robert Griffith, *The Politics of Fear: Joseph R. McCarthy and the Senate* (Amherst: University of Massachusetts Press, 1987), are insightful about McCarthy's role in the chamber. Anne Hodges Morgan, *Robert S. Kerr: The Senate Years* (Norman: University of Oklahoma Press, 1977), is a model Senate biography of an influential lawmaker in the 1950s.

## Chapter Twelve

Biographies of Lyndon Johnson have become almost as controversial as their subject. Contrasting views of his record are offered in Robert Dallek, *Lone Star Rising: Lyndon Johnson and His Times, 1908–1960* (New York: Oxford University Press, 1991), and Robert Caro, *Master of the Senate* (New York: Random House, 2002). Byron C. Hulsey, *Everett Dirksen and His Presidents: How a Senate Giant Shaped American Politics* (Lawrence: University Press of Kansas, 2000), shows with great skill how Republicans operated in the upper house during the 1950s and 1960s.

## Chapter Thirteen

Francis R. Valeo, *Mike Mansfield, Majority Leader: A Different Kind of Senate, 1971–1976* (Armonk, N.Y.: M. E. Sharpe, 1999), written by a key Mansfield aide, is illuminating and informative. Michael Foley, *The New Senate: Liberal Influence on a Conservative Institution, 1959–1972* (New Haven: Yale University Press, 1980), is excellent on the political and institutional changes of the

1960s. Randall Bennett Woods, *Fulbright: A Biography* (New York: Cambridge University Press, 1995), is a superb biography of an important senator in the foreign policy debates of the Vietnam era.

## Chapter Fourteen

Barbara Sinclair, *The Transformation of the U.S. Senate* (Baltimore: Johns Hopkins University Press, 1989), looks at the way the institution developed in the 1970s and 1980s. Bernard Asbell, *The Senate Nobody Knows* (Garden City, N.Y.: Doubleday, 1978), tracks more than a year of Senator Edmund S. Muskie's life in the Senate to provide a compelling look at the institution from the inside. LeRoy Ashby and Rod Gramer, *Fighting the Odds: The Life of Senator Frank Church* (Pullman: Washington State University Press, 1994), is a detailed and thoughtful examination of a key Senate liberal.

## Chapter Fifteen

Memoirs of senators illuminate the 1980s. Warren Rudman, *Combat: Twelve Years in the U.S. Senate* (New York: Random House, 1996), is very informative and even-handed. John G. Tower, *Consequences: A Personal and Political Memoir* (Boston: Little, Brown, 1991), is Tower's response to his Senate critics, and he takes his revenge and then some. Adam Clymer, *Edward M. Kennedy: A Biography* (New York: William Morrow, 1999), is full of valuable information about the controversies that roiled the Senate in the 1980s.

## Chapter Sixteen

The 1990s are too recent for any real historical perspective at this point. Colton C. Campbell and Nicol C. Rae, eds., *The Contentious Senate: Partisanship, Ideology and the Myth of Cool Judgment* (Lanham, Md.: Rowman & Littlefield, 2001), is a collection of perceptive essays on the modern Senate. Julian E. Zelizer, *On Capitol Hill: The Struggle to Reform Congress and Its Consequences* (New York: Cambridge University Press, 2004), places the modern Congress and its efforts to reform in historical context. Winslow T. Wheeler, *The Wastrels of Defense: How Congress Sabotages U.S. Security* (Annapolis, Md.: Naval Institute Press, 2004), is a scathing attack on the Senate that does for the modern institution what David Graham Phillips tried to accomplish a century ago in *The Treason of the Senate*, edited with an introduction by George E. Mowry and Judson Grenier (Chicago: Quadrangle Books, 1964).

# Acknowledgments

Many people helped me write this book. For health reasons that limit my ability to travel, I depended on the efforts of other scholars and students to assist me with research into selected senatorial collections. I owe thanks for completing those tasks to Andre Fleche at the University of Virginia, Teri Daniel at Washington and Jefferson College, and Matthew Brenckle at East Carolina University. Jason dePreaux of the University of Texas at Austin did excellent work in the materials at the Center for American History. Thomas Appleton, Jr., kindly spent time in the Alben Barkley papers at the University of Kentucky, to my great benefit.

Friends and colleagues shared research materials with me as well. For those kindnesses I am indebted to Thomas Appleton, Jr., Charles Calhoun, Bill Childs, Thomas Clarkin, Stacy Cordery, Gene Gressley, the late Sara Hunter Graham, Byron Hulsey, the late Herbert F. Margulies, Anne Hodges Morgan, H. Wayne Morgan, F. Duane Rose, Katherine Sibley, Mark E. Young, and Nancy Beck Young. Nancy was especially gracious in sharing with me sources from her extensive research in presidential libraries and congressional collections. The late Jack DeVore, Mary Finch Hoyt, Ellen Proxmire, and Margaret Shannon provided timely interviews and helpful leads.

Among librarians, I owe special thanks to Laurie Langland of Dakota Wesleyan University for her extraordinary kindness with regard to providing copies of materials from the Francis Case and George McGovern Papers. Heather Moore at the Senate Historical Office helped me secure many of the photographs in the book. The Margaret Chase Smith Library, the Center for Legislative Archives of the National Archives, and the University of Kentucky Library provided illustrations, for which I am grateful. I also gained from the cooperation of the dedicated staff at the Prints and Photographs Collection at the Library of Congress. Ellen Peterson, Ralph Elder, Brenda Gunn, and their colleagues at the Center for American History, University of Texas at Austin, have assisted my work in vital ways. For many years, Gene Gressley, then at the University of Wyoming, enabled me to delve into the collections on that state's United States senators, which first interested me in the upper house of Congress. Don E. Carleton, the director of the Center for American History, has been a valuable collaborator in my writing for a quarter of a century. His skill and energy as a collector of vital historical manuscripts is unsurpassed and I am grateful to him for access to the *Newsweek* Archives.

Senator Lloyd M. Bentsen, Jr., has not been involved with this book. In 1989, however, he invited me to supervise a project to record an oral history of his life. That endeavor provided me with an inside look at the workings of the Senate that I could have achieved in no other way. His aide, Mike Levy, facilitated the completion of that endeavor.

I am indebted to several scholars and friends who have read portions of the manuscript and am especially grateful for their wise and thoughtful criticisms and suggestions. John M. Blum, Charles Calhoun, Richard T. McCulley, Chip Rossetti, R. Hal Williams, and Nancy Beck Young were valuable guides to a better book, but they are not responsible for any errors that may remain in this narrative. My agent, Jim Hornfischer, helped get this manuscript to the right publisher, provided good suggestions about improving what I had written, and is a source of ebullient encouragement to his authors.

Patricia Schaub has been an indispensable research assistant in the writing of this book. She has provided me with materials that it would have been difficult for me to obtain on my own, and she has responded with enthusiasm and dedication to every request for information.

Lara Heimert of Basic Books supplied enthusiastic support, valuable suggestions, and a rigorous editorial supervision to this book in its final stages. Her unstinting efforts improved the manuscript in ways that are reflected on every page.

Carol Smith of Basic Books provided excellent editorial guidance and abundant patience through the rigors of the publication process.

My health problems of recent years have received the professional and personal attention of medical practitioners who merit recognition. I would like to thank Larry Breedlove, Christi Eubank, David M. Ferguson, Martin S. Stocker, and Elizabeth Sylvester for their patience and thoughtfulness with my infirmities and the high quality of care they have supplied to me.

Karen Gould has gone through her own difficult personal trials while this book was being written. She has remained a source of inspiration and affection whose loving influence can be seen in everything I have written for the past thirty-five years.

None of the people who have helped me should be held accountable for any errors of fact or interpretation that appear in this book. Any shortcomings are my sole responsibility.

*Lewis L. Gould*
*Austin, Texas*
*May 2005*

# Index

Abortion, 266, 278, 281, 287, 303

Abourezk, James, 272

Abscam scandal, 276

Absenteeism, 98

Abu Ghraib prison, 317

Acheson, Dean, 171, 207

Adams, Brock, 299

Adams, Sherman, 226

Adamson Act, 67

Addicks, J. Edward, 10

*Advise and Consent* (film/novel), 153, 182, 190–191

African Americans, 7, 43, 54, 76, 101, 120, 129, 140, 147, 165, 197, 201, 225, 250, 260, 286, 296–298, 305

  African-American reporters, 183

  African-American senators, 11, 248

  Great Migration to cities of the North, 60–61, 107

  *See also* Civil rights; Lynchings; Race issues; Slavery

Agriculture, 67, 78, 104, 165

  Agricultural Adjustment Act, 130, 141

  Agricultural Appropriation Act, 41, 43

Aiken, George D., 247

Alaska, 236

Alcoholism, 76, 97, 98, 116, 128, 156, 173, 180, 187, 189, 205, 235, 252, 276

Aldrich, Nelson, 19, 22–23, 25, 26, 29, 33, 35, 38, 39, 48, 49, 54, 318

  and Albert J. Beveridge, 45

  and ICC, 41

  impression on Senate, 50

Aldrich-Vreeland bill, 45–46, 152

Alien Acts, 74

Allen, James Browning, 264, 266–268, 272, 273, 278

  death of, 274

Allison, William Boyd, 24, 25, 29, 35, 38, 43

  and ICC, 41

America First, 161

American Bar Association, 66

American Federation of Labor, 120

*American Mercury*, 116

Anderson, Jack, 185, 237

Antiballistic missile system, 253

Anti-lynching legislation.

    *See under* Lynchings

Anti-Saloon League, 75

Anti-Semitism, 66, 79

Antitrust legislation, 44, 63

Appointments, 13. *See also* Nominations

Argentina, 15

Arizona, 27, 46

Army, 14, 161, 217

Ashurst, Henry Fountain, 81–82, 132

Associated Press, 74

Atomic bomb, 203. *See also* Treaties, nuclear test ban treaty

Atomic Energy Commission, 229

Bailey, Joseph Weldon, 21, 22, 39, 41, 55, 140

Bailey, Josiah, W., 122, 129, 133, 149, 167

Baker, Howard H., Jr., 248, 257, 262, 263, 263(photo), 272, 274, 276, 277, 278–279, 288

  presidential candidacy of, 280

  and television coverage of Senate, 280–281

Baker, James, 279, 283

Baker, Ray Stannard, 4

Baker, Robert "Bobby" Gene, 215–216, 220, 238–239

Balanced Budget and Emergency Deficit Control Act of 1985, 284

Balfour, Arthur, 83

Ballinger, Gifford, 49

Banking system, 44, 45, 50, 51, 61, 62, 63, 109, 123, 129, 130, 138

Bankruptcy laws, 317

Barkley, Alben, 144, 145(photo), 145–146, 150, 153, 163, 164, 165, 199, 231

  and change in filibuster rule, 201–202

  and Smith-Connally bill, 169

Barry, David S., 39

Baruch, Bernard M., 108

Bayh, Marvella, 180

Beer-Wine Revenue Act, 130

Bentsen, Lloyd M., 259, 270, 272, 289, 291, 300, 302

Berlin, Isaiah, 163

Beveridge, Albert J., 18–19, 20, 21, 27, 43, 44, 47, 48, 49–50

  and Nelson Aldrich, 45

Biden, Joseph, 297

Bilbo, Theodore G., 149, 165

Bipartisanship, 172, 193, 198

Black, Hugo L., 131, 147–148

Blackmun, Harry, 254

Boardman, Mabel, 43

Borah, William E., 85, 94, 99–103, 107, 116, 126, 132, 137, 155, 258

  death of, 159

  and World War II, 157

Bork, Robert, 286–288, 298

*Boston Herald,* 110

Boxer, Barbara, 298

Bradley, Bill, 274, 285, 310

Brandegee, Frank, 76, 98

Brandeis, Louis D., 65–66

Brewster, Ralph Owen, 180

Bribery, 10, 54, 106, 216.

  *See also* Corruption

Bricker amendment, 189

Bridges, Styles, 183, 185, 190

Bristow, Joseph L., 49, 54, 55

Brooke, Edward, 248, 274

*Brown v. Board of Education,* 220, 222

Brownsville, Texas, 42–43

Bruce, Blanche K., 11

Bryan, William Jennings, 46, 58

*Buckley v. Valeo,* 309

Budget, 108, 136, 148, 149, 240, 263–264, 279, 280

  balanced budget constitutional amendment, 304

  and Gramm-Rudman-Hollings bill, 283–284

  surpluses in, 305

Bulkeley, Morgan, 34

Bumpers, Dale, 265

Burke, Sheila, 304–305

Burns, James MacGregor, 237

Burrows, Julius Caesar, 14

Burton, Joseph R., 31, 34

Bush, George H. W., 259, 283, 291, 296, 297, 299–300

Bush, George W., 310, 315

Butterfield, Alexander, 262

Byrd, Harry Flood, 127, 128–129, 133, 134, 167, 216, 222, 240, 254

Byrd, Robert, 215(photo), 260, 269, 271, 272, 273, 274, 291, 303, 307, 314

Byrnes, James F., 108, 132, 161–162

Calhoun, John C., 7, 8, 103

Cambodia, 258, 259

Campaign finance, 110, 111, 177, 185–186, 254, 258, 262, 264, 266, 275, 276, 277, 289, 295, 306, 308–309, 310, 317, 319

Campbell, Ben Nighthorse, 303

Canada, 53, 56

*Candidate, The* (film), 255

Cannon, Joseph G., 27, 43, 49

Capitol, 18, 60, 178

Capper, Arthur, 126

Capra, Frank, 152

Caraway, Hattie, 99, 124–126, 172

Carswell, G. Harold, 254

Carter, Jimmy, 257, 270, 272, 273, 275

Carter, Thomas H., 15

Case, Francis, 185–186, 219

Cattle hides, 47, 48

CBS News, 242, 247

Celebrities, 188

Central Intelligence Agency (CIA), 269–270

Chamberlain, George E., 75

Chandler, A. B. "Happy," 150

Chandler, William E., 39

Chavez, Dennis, 133–134, 198

*Chicago Tribune*, 109

Child labor, 23, 44, 67, 101

China, 195, 203, 207, 208, 306

Church, Frank, 225, 257, 258, 264, 273–274, 275

Church Committee, 269–270

CIA. *See* Central Intelligence Agency

CIO. *See* Congress of Industrial Organizations

*Citadel* (White), 192

Citizenship (national), 9

Civil rights, 71, 165, 172, 192, 195, 197, 201, 210, 221–222, 235, 237, 250, 281, 303

Civil Rights Bill of 1964, 240–243, 260, 287

Civil Rights Law of 1957, 223–225, 232

*See also* Race issues; *under* Johnson, Lyndon B.

Civil War, 9, 21

Civility, 128, 271, 277, 288, 292, 293, 295, 302

Clark, Bennett Champ, 173

Clark, William A., 10

Clay, Henry, 7, 8, 103

Clayton Antitrust Act, 63

Clayton-Bulwer Pact, 13

Clements, Earle, 216

Cleveland, Grover, 10, 12, 13–14, 21

Clinton, Bill, 300–301, 305–308

Clinton, Hillary, 301, 306, 310

Cloture, 8, 65, 70, 71, 88–89, 102, 106, 108, 109, 165, 198, 201, 240, 242, 243, 250, 310, 317

changing cloture rule, 266, 268–269. *See also* Filibusters, regulating/changing rules for *See also* Filibusters, post-cloture filibusters

Coal, 47, 48, 49, 141

Cohen, Benjamin V., 139

Cohen, William, 274

Cohn, Roy, 217

Cold War, 194, 195, 198

*Collier's* magazine, 42

Colombia, 28

Communism, 149, 182–183, 191, 195, 196, 197, 203, 207, 219, 220, 246, 247, 288. *See also* Subversion

Compromise, 45, 51, 88

Compromise of 1850, 7, 8

Congress
56th, 14–57
58th, 28
65th, 68
71st, 122, 123
80th, 198–199
Congressional Budget Office, 264
special sessions, 56, 57, 61, 69, 107, 148, 159
*See also* House of Representatives; Senate

Congress of Industrial Organizations (CIO), 148

Congressional Budget and Impoundment Act, 264

*Congressional Government* (Wilson), 57

*Congressional Record*, 239

Connally, Tom, 162, 165, 171, 180

Conscription, 161

Conservatives, 24, 65–66, 129, 133, 134, 150, 151, 153, 164, 165, 191, 211, 238, 251, 265, 272, 274, 275, 276, 278, 280, 281
Conservative Manifesto (1937), 149
right-wing pressure groups, 266
talk-radio hosts, 302
*See also* Senate, conservative Club in

Constitution, 8, 53, 105, 146, 316, 318, 320
balanced budget constitutional amendment, 304
Constitutional Convention, 6, 9, 11
Eighteenth Amendment, 76, 97
equal rights amendment for women, 178, 266

Seventeenth Amendment, 63, 110, 319. *See also* Elections, direct election of senators

Thirteen/Fourteenth/Fifteenth Amendments, 9, 60

Containment policy, 198, 209, 247

Contract with America, 302, 304

Coolidge, Calvin, 91, 93, 100–101, 102, 104, 105, 106, 108, 131

Cooper, John Sherman, 227, 236, 253, 258

Cooper-Church Amendment, 257, 258–259

Copeland, Royal, 118(photo)

Corcoran "Tommy the Cork," 139, 145

Corporations, 5–6, 27, 61, 63, 125, 149, 309
senators as agents for, 35

Corruption, 10, 11, 31, 53, 80, 106, 277, 309
Federal Corrupt Practices Acts of 1911/1925, 110–111, 185
*See also* Bribery

*Cosmopolitan*, 39

Costello, Frank, 176

Costigan, Edward P., 147

Cotton, 56, 78

Coughlin, Father Charles E., 137, 138

Couzens, James, 126

Coverdell, Paul, 300

Cox, Archibald, 287

Crane, Condit, 17

Cranston, Alan, 276, 290, 298

Credit-card industry, 317

CREEP. *See* Republican Party, Committee to Reelect the President

Crime, 177, 251, 259, 306

C-SPAN and C-SPAN 2, 280, 281, 295, 314

Cuba, 3, 12, 14, 26

Culberson, Charles A., 19, 76, 97

Cullom, Shelby M., 42, 55

Cummins, Albert B., 70
Curtis, Charles T., 94, 95(illus.), 114, 115(photo), 266
Cutting, Bronson, 117, 127, 132, 133–134
Czolgosz, Leon, 16

D'Amato, Alphonse, 306
Daschle, Tom, 286, 303, 311, 315
Daugherty, Harry M., 106
Dawes, Charles G., 108–109
*Deadlock of Democracy, The* (Burns), 237
Dean, John W., 262
Debt, 264
DeConcini, Dennis, 290
Defense spending, 279, 280, 283, 284
Deficits, 279, 280, 283, 284, 300, 301
Deflation, 117, 130
Delaware, 10
Democratic Party, 4, 10, 12, 21–22, 28, 55–56, 57, 63, 94–96, 112, 133, 255, 271, 317
   and frugality, 60
   National Convention of 1936, 140
   and 1932 election, 127
   and 1958 election, 226
   and 1986 elections, 285–286
   and Panama Canal, 28–29
   Policy Committee, 216
   Senatorial Campaign Committee, 108
   and small government, 5–6, 117
   and the South, 12, 21–22, 30, 54, 60, 61, 79. *See also* Senate, southerners in
   Steering Committee, 59, 216
   support for Theodore Roosevelt, 43
Denby, Edwin, 106
Depew, Chauncey M., 35, 39
Depressions
   of 1890s, 4, 12
   of farmers in 1919–1923, 104
   *See also* Great Depression

Dewey, Thomas E., 160, 172, 199
Dingley Tariff of 1897, 12, 48
Dirksen, Everett McKinley, 179–180, 189, 207, 227, 233, 235–236, 238, 241(photo), 250, 251, 278
   and civil rights, 240–241, 242, 243
   death of, 252
   press conferences of, 235
District of Columbia, 18, 19, 47
Dodd, Thomas, 259
Doheny, Edward L., 106
Dole, Robert, 282, 290–291, 301
   presidential candidacy of, 302–303, 304–305
Dolliver, Jonathan P., 30, 38, 43, 45, 47, 48, 50
Domenici, Pete, 301
Dominican Republic, 246
Douglas, Helen Gahagan, 207
Douglas, Paul, 192, 199, 247
Douglas, Stephen A., 8
Drury Allen, 126, 153, 169, 173, 182, 190–191
Dubois, Fred, 20
Dunne, Finley Peter, 3–4
Durkin, John A., 265
Dustin, Frances, 180
Dyer, Leonidas C., 106, 107, 109

East, John P., 281
Eastland, James O., 224, 262
Economy Act of 1933, 130, 132
Education, 202, 220, 224, 246, 287
   prayer in public schools, 278, 281
Eisenhower, Dwight D., 179–180, 185, 209, 214, 217, 223, 227, 229, 238
   and Joseph McCarthy, 212
   and school integration crisis, 226
Elections, 10, 12
   of 1904, 27, 29, 30
   of 1906, 43
   of 1908, 46, 58

Elections (*continued*)
of 1910, 49, 50, 53
of 1914, 63–64
of 1916, 67, 68
of 1918, 74, 76, 77, 79–81
of 1920, 91–92, 93, 96
of 1922, 107, 110
of 1924, 100–101, 103, 106, 140
of 1928, 112, 119
of 1930, 114, 120, 121
of 1932, 126–127, 140
1932 Louisiana special election, 124
of 1934, 133, 134, 135
of 1936, 141
of 1938, 149, 150, 151
1941 special election, 162
of 1942, 163, 164–165, 166
of 1944, 166–167, 169, 172–173
of 1946, 196, 199
of 1948, 199–200, 225
of 1950, 206, 207, 218
of 1952, 177, 209, 210, 211
of 1954, 183, 219
of 1956, 222–223
of 1958, 213, 226–227, 259
of 1960, 224, 228, 229–231
of 1964, 245–246
of 1966, 247–249
of 1968, 251
of 1970, 259
of 1972, 261, 262
of 1974, 264–265
of 1976, 270, 271
of 1980, 275, 276, 278
of 1982, 280
of 1986, 285–286
of 1988, 290–291
of 1990, 300
of 1992, 298–299, 300
of 1994, 302
of 1996, 305, 308
of 2000, 310, 311, 315
of 2002, 315
of 2004, 316
direct election of senators, 11, 30–31,
    53, 54–55, 63, 64, 110, 114, 319
election fraud, 200
honesty in, 110. *See also*
    Campaign finance
primaries, 30–31, 53, 110, 111,
    206–207, 209, 230, 291, 299
and voting by military personnel in
    the field, 166–167
Electoral College, 116
Electric utility industry, 105
Emergency Banking Relief Act, 130
Employment Act of 1946, 196
Energy prices, 274
Environmental issues, 131, 246, 252
Equitable Life Assurance Company, 35
Ervin, Sam, 262, 263(photo)
Espionage Act, 74
Ethical issues, 19, 34, 276, 289, 295, 317.
    *See also* Senate, Ethics Committee
Europe, 34, 100

Fair Employment Practices Commission
    (FEPC), 128, 166, 173, 174, 198
Fair Labor Standards Act, 149
Fairbanks, Charles W., 29, 46
Fall, Albert B., 89, 105
Farm Bloc, 104, 114
Fascism, 136–137
Federal Bureau of Investigation, 138
Federal Elections Commission, 308–309
Federal Power Commission, 185, 202
Federal Reserve Act, 50, 53, 63, 71
Federal Reserve Board, 123
Federal Theater Project, 153
Federal Trade Commission, 63, 109
Feingold, Russell, 309, 310
Felton, Rebecca, 98, 100(photo)
FEPC. *See* Fair Employment Practices
    Commission

Filibusters, 8–9, 15, 27, 28, 45, 56, 61, 64, 69, 84, 101, 102, 105, 139–140, 147, 153, 174, 198, 224, 251, 260, 264, 278, 302, 303, 310, 317
and judicial appointments, 286, 316
"nuclear option" on, 316
post-cloture filibusters, 268, 269, 272–273
regulating/changing rules for, 46, 65, 70–71, 109–110, 201–202, 228, 266, 268–269
*See also* Cloture; *under* Race issues
Finestein, Dianne, 298
Flanders, Ralph, 218
Fletcher, Duncan U., 136
Florida, 206–207
Foraker, Joseph B., 19, 42–43, 44
Ford, Gerald, 257, 264, 270
Ford, Henry, 79, 80, 110
Foreign Military Sales Act, 258
Foreign policy, 6, 12, 26, 34, 66, 83, 100, 105, 137, 155, 156, 157, 237, 245, 270, 288
bipartisanship in, 172, 198, 209
*See also* Senate, Foreign Relations Committee
Fortas, Abe, 250–251, 316
Fowler, Wyche, 300
France, 15, 64, 66, 82, 101, 103, 159
Free silver, 21
Frist, William H. "Bill," 315, 316
Frye, William P., 1–2, 10, 15, 25
Fulbright, J. William, 125, 172, 233, 236, 244, 245, 246, 251, 260, 264–265
Fund-raising. *See* Campaign finance

Gallinger, Jacob H., 34, 80
Garfield, James R., 34
Garner, John Vance, 146–147, 149
George, Walter, 129, 150, 186, 216, 222
Germany, 68, 69, 137, 155. *See also* World War I; World War II

Gingrich, Newt, 302
Giuliani, Rudolph, 310
Glass, Carter, 133, 140, 162
Glass-Stegall Act, 123
Glenn, John, 290
Gold standard, 12, 21, 130
Goldwater, Barry, 211, 227, 233, 236, 243, 244, 245, 265, 270
Goldwater-Nichols Act, 285
Gore, Albert, Jr., 296, 301, 310
Gore, Albert, Sr., 222, 231, 259
Gore, Thomas P., 46, 66, 133
Gorman, Arthur Pue, 21, 28, 29
Gossip, 20, 292
Government spending, 5, 118, 124, 129, 130, 135, 136, 148, 149, 167, 284. *See also* Defense spending
Graham, Bob, 286
Gramm, Phil, 283–284, 289
Great Britain, 13, 59, 64, 66, 85, 101, 117, 159–160, 161, 319
Great Depression, 112, 113, 116, 122, 123, 124, 129, 135, 155
Great Society, 246
Greece, 198
Greenfield, Meg, 189
Griffin, Robert, 253, 272, 274
Gruening, Ernest, 245, 246, 251
Guffey, Joseph, 163, 167
Guffey Coal Act, 141
Gulf War, 296, 300

Hale, Eugene, 25, 26
Halleck, Charles, 235
Halstead, Murat, 16
Hanna, Marcus A., 25, 29
Harding, Warren G., 63, 85, 91, 92
death of, 106
Harris, Mary, 58
Harrison, Pat, 108, 132, 136, 139, 144, 145(photo), 149
Hart, Gary, 290, 293, 298

Hart, Philip A., 226, 235

*Hartford Courant,* 34–35

Hatch, Orrin, 273, 297, 303

Hatfield, Mark, 128, 247, 276, 278, 304

Hawaii, 236

Hawkins, Paula, 298

Hayne, Robert, 7

Haynes, George H., 2, 63

Haynesworth, Clement, 253

Hay-Pauncefote Treaty, 13

Health care system, 200, 202, 300,
     301, 302

Hearst, William Randolph, 137

Hells Canyon Dam (Idaho), 224

Helms, Jesse, 273, 278, 281

Hepburn Bill, 38, 39, 41, 42, 50

Hersh, Seymour, 269

Hertzberg, Hendrik, 153

Highway Beautification Act of 1965, 184

Hill, Anita, 297

Hill, Lister, 150, 163, 207, 267

Hiss, Alger, 203

Hitchcock, Gilbert M., 89

Hitler, Adolf, 134, 155

Hoar, George Frisbie, 4, 11, 25

Holds, 303

Hollings, Ernest F. "Fritz," 284

Home Loan Bank Act, 123

Homosexuals, 164, 182–183, 191, 196,
     203, 281, 284

Hoover, Herbert, 94, 96, 112, 113–114,
     119, 121, 122–123, 124, 131, 158

House of Representatives, 6, 12, 38, 55,
     57, 61, 80, 121, 147, 151, 157, 165,
     224, 237, 246, 255, 264, 280, 293,
     305, 309
   and African-American reporters, 183
   compared with Senate, 20, 193, 281,
     295–296, 304, 319
   declaration of war by, 73
   and impeachment of Bill Clinton, 307
   Judiciary Committee, 142
   and Payne bill, 47–48

Speaker of the House, 5, 27, 43
   television coverage of, 176, 280
   and Watergate scandal, 265

Hruska, Roman, 254

Hughes, Charles Evans, 68, 119, 143, 286

Hughes, Harold, 235

Hull, Cordell, 157, 172

Humphrey, Hubert, 182, 184, 199, 212,
     216, 229, 230, 231, 234, 235, 242,
     243, 250, 261, 271
   and 1964 election, 245–246

Hunt, Lester C., Jr., 182, 183

Hutchison, Kay Bailey, 302

Hyde, James Hazen, 35


ICC. *See* Interstate Commerce
     Commission

Ickes, Harold, 151, 164

Impeachment, 6, 9, 13, 288, 306, 307

Income tax, 53, 61, 126, 274

Independents, 211, 315

Indiana, 57, 67

Industrialism, 4–5

Inflation, 21, 37, 104, 130, 274, 279, 280

Intelligence issues, 257, 269–270

Interest rates, 279

Internal Revenue Service, 138

Internal Security Act of 1950, 206

Internationalists, 155, 160, 171, 198,
     199, 209

Internet, 315

Interstate Commerce Commission (ICC),
     33, 37, 49
   judicial review of orders of, 39,
     41, 50

Iowa, 24

Iran, 275
   Iran-*contra* scandal, 288–289

Iraq, 316. *See also* Gulf War

Isolationism, 83, 90, 100, 101, 116, 136,
     137, 161, 171. *See also* Senate,
     isolationists in

Italy, 137

Jackson, Henry M. "Scoop," 235, 238, 253, 260, 261, 270

Jamaica, 15

Japan, 101, 155

Javits, Jacob, 180, 236, 257, 261

Jefferson, Thomas, 7

Jeffords, James "Jim," 315

Jews, 65–66, 137, 156, 190, 310

Johnson, Andrew, 9

Johnson, Hiram, 74, 75, 76, 84, 85, 97, 101, 102, 103, 109, 116, 119, 121, 126–127, 133, 135, 137, 144, 161, 180

Johnson, Lady Bird, 180, 181, 184

Johnson, Lyndon B., 68, 96, 162, 185, 186, 187, 189, 191–192, 200, 207, 238, 303

candidacy for presidency, 220, 221, 222, 228, 230, 250

candidacy for vice presidency, 230–231

and civil rights, 222, 223, 224, 230, 232. *See also* Civil rights, Civil Rights Bill of 1964

and the Club, 216

and Edmund Muskie, 228

health of, 221

Johnson administrations, 239–251

the "Johnson treatment," 213, 215(photo), 231

and Joseph McCarthy, 217–218, 220

and Leland Olds, 202

as a liar, 214, 245, 246

as minority/majority leader, 211, 212, 213, 214–216, 217, 218, 219, 220–221, 223, 228, 232, 271

and Richard Russell, 240, 251

sex life of, 182

withdrawal from presidential race, 250

Joint Chiefs of Staff, 208

Jones, Paula, 306, 307

Jones, Wesley L., 108

Judiciary, 7, 39, 50, 118–119, 250, 251, 253, 303–304, 316. *See also* Supreme Court

*Jungle, The* (Sinclair), 41

Jury trials, 225

Justice Department, 224

Kassebaum, Nancy Landon, 274, 298

Keating, Charles, 290

Keating Five, 289–290

Kefauver, Estes, 176, 182, 189, 199, 209, 222–223. *See also* Senate, Kefauver hearings in

Kellogg, Frank B., 81(photo), 103

Kennedy, Edward M., 252, 253, 259–260, 262, 264, 275, 286, 287, 297, 298

Kennedy, Joan, 180

Kennedy, John F., 103, 177, 181—182, 187, 210–211, 222–223, 227, 234

assassination of, 239, 240

candidacy for presidency, 229–230

and Joseph McCarthy, 219

Kennedy administration, 236–239

Kennedy, Robert F., 233, 235, 239, 246, 249

assassination of, 250

Kent, Frank R., 94

Kenyon, William S., 104

Kern, John Worth, 49–50, 55–56, 57–60, 58(photo), 62, 63, 66–67, 68, 71, 92

death of, 67

Kerr, Robert, 185, 188, 199, 202, 216

Kerry, John, 316

Kilgore, Harley, 189

King, Martin Luther, Jr., 250, 281–282

King, William H., 144

Knowland, William F., 182, 216, 217, 218, 223, 225, 226, 227

Knox, Frank, 138

Knox, Philander C., 81(photo)

Kopechne, Mary Jo, 260

Korean War, 206, 207

Ku Klux Klan, 148, 271
Kyl, John, 302

La Follette, Robert M., 25, 35–37,
    36(photo), 44, 45, 47, 48, 55, 62,
    80, 91, 92, 94, 102, 103–104, 105
    and Aldrich-Vreeland bill, 45–46
    and arming merchant ships, 69—70
    death of, 103
    and election of 1920, 50–51
    and Foreign Relations Committee, 86
    La Follette Seaman Act of 1915, 69,
        103–104
    third-party candidacy of, 103
    and voting records of his foes, 36–37,
        40, 41, 42, 266
    and World War I, 73–74
La Follette, Robert M., Jr., 103, 116–117,
    122, 123, 126, 196
Labor unions, 58, 67, 119, 148, 149, 169,
    199, 309
Ladies of the Senate, 98, 99(photo)
League of Nations, 71, 82, 85, 86, 100,
    137, 155, 159
    covenant of, 83, 86–87, 90
    See also Wilson, Woodrow, and peace
        treaty/League of Nations
Legislative Reorganization Acts of
    1946/1970, 178, 254
Lehman, Herbert, 192, 216
Lend-Lease, 161
Lenroot, Irvine, 79, 86, 91, 102
Lever Act of 1917, 78
Lewinsky, Monica, 306–307
Lewis, J. Hamilton, 59, 80, 121
Liberals/liberalism, 150, 162, 163, 165,
    169, 170, 173, 192, 196, 199, 200,
    201, 202, 210, 212, 216, 226, 228,
    229, 234, 235, 245, 249, 251, 252,
    258, 264, 272, 275, 280, 281, 284.
    See also Progressives
Lieberman, Joseph, 307, 310
Limbaugh, Rush, 302

Lippman, Walter, 173
Little, J. Franklin, 19
Little Rock, Arkansas, 226
Lobbyists, 62, 186, 237, 289, 317
Lodge, Henry Cabot, Jr., 210–211, 231
Lodge, Henry Cabot, Sr., 12, 13, 25, 27,
    34, 64, 69, 71, 81(photo), 102
    death of, 94
    as majority leader, 80, 86, 88, 93–94
    and "Round Robin" document, 84
    See also under Wilson, Woodrow
Long, Huey, 124–125, 126, 130, 137–138,
    139–140
    assassination of, 139
Long, Russell, 189, 252, 273
Lorimer, William, 54
Lott, Trent, 305, 311, 315
Louisiana Purchase, 7
"Loyalty of the Senate, The" (Barry), 39
Lucas, Scott, 201, 206, 207, 227
Ludlow, Louis, 19
Lugar, Richard, 280
Lusitania, 65
Lynchings, 98, 101, 197
    anti-lynching legislation, 61, 93,
        106–107, 128, 146–147, 149,
        162, 174

MacArthur, Douglas, 207–209, 317
Maltby Building (Washington, D. C.), 18
Man Called Peter, A (Marshall), 190
Mann-Elkins Act, 49
Mansfield, Mike, 67, 96, 189, 214,
    232, 233–235, 237–238, 239,
    241(photo), 241–242, 251, 262,
    268, 269
    not seeking reelection and tributes to,
        270–271
Marcy, Carl, 236
Marshall, George C., 207, 212
    Marshall Plan, 176, 198
Marshall, Peter and Catherine, 190
Marshall, Thomas Riley, 79, 88

Martin, Thomas S., 55, 57, 70

Maryland, 151

Mason, William E., 28

Matthews, Donald R., 193

McCain, John, 290, 292, 309–310

McCarran, Pat, 205–206

McCarthy, Abigail, 181

McCarthy, Eugene J., 226, 233, 249–250

McCarthy, Joseph R., 140, 179, 186, 188,
    196, 203–206, 204(photo), 207,
    211, 212, 234
  and Army hearings, 217, 218
  censure of, 218–220
  death of, 220, 225
  and Millard Tydings, 206

McClellan, John, 125, 186, 189

McClure, James, 266

McCormick, Medill, 80, 81(photo), 98

McCormick, Ruth Hanna, 121

McCumber, Porter J., 81(photo)

McFarland, Ernest, 207, 211

McGee, Gale, 259

McGovern, George, 261, 264, 275

McKinley, William, 12, 14, 26, 29,
    111, 314
  assassination of, 16
  and senate, 15–16

McMillan, James S., 25

McNamara, Robert, 245

McNary, Charles L., 81, 94, 104,
    115(photo), 126, 127, 142, 149,
    157, 160
  death of, 167

McPherson, Harry, 233

Meatpacking industry, 41

Media, 175, 180, 185, 273, 297, 306.
    *See also* Press; Television

Medicare, 246

Merchant marine, 2, 14, 64
  arming of, 68–70

Metzenbaum, Howard, 272, 286

Mexico, 34, 69, 89
  Mexican War of 1846–1848, 8

Middle class, 3, 4, 41, 55, 148, 150

Mikulski, Barbara, 298

Minimum wage, 220

Minneapolis *Tribune*, 96

Miscegenation, 128, 166

Mr. Dooley, 3–4

*Mr. Smith Goes to Washington* (film),
    152–153

Mitchell, George J., 291, 296, 303

Mitchell, John H., 31, 34

Mondale, Walter, 268, 272–273

Montana, 10

Moody, Blair, 182

Morse, Wayne, 172–173, 205, 211, 216,
    219, 235, 251
  and Tonkin Gulf Resolution,
    245, 246

Moseley-Braun, Carol, 299

Moses, George H., 81(photo), 109, 114,
    115(photo), 116, 127

"Mother Jones," 58

Moynihan, Daniel P., 300–301, 307

Muckrakers, 39, 40

Mudd, Roger, 242

Murray, James, 163

Murray, Patty, 298–299

Murrow, Edward R., 217

Muscle Shoals dam project, 105, 112,
    116, 130–131

Muskie, Edmund S., 226, 257, 259, 261,
    264, 288

NAACP *See* National Association
    for the Advancement of
    Colored People

*Nation, The*, 11, 96

National Association for the
    Advancement of Colored People
    (NAACP), 107, 120, 147

National Association of
    Manufacturers, 62

National defense, 235, 243. *See also*
    Defense spending

National Industrial Recovery Act, 131–132, 138, 141
National Labor Relations Act, 138
National Monetary Commission, 50
National Woman Suffrage Association, (NAWSA), 76
Natural gas, 185–186, 202, 272
Naval Limitation Pact, 101
Navy, 44, 45, 67
NAWSA. *See* National Woman Suffrage Association
Nelson, Gaylord, 252, 264, 275
Nepotism, 317
Neuberger, Maurine, 236, 247, 261, 298
Neuberger, Richard L., 101, 186, 188
Neutrality Act, 137, 155, 156, 159
New, Harry S., 81(photo)
New Deal, 105, 112, 122, 135, 140, 147, 149, 150, 153, 159, 160, 162, 164, 178, 196
    and coalition of southern Democrats and Republicans, 134, 162, 163, 165, 166, 167, 174, 198
    committee chairmanships during, 136
    loyalists in Senate, 163
    and 1946 elections, 199
    One Hundred Days of, 129–130, 132
    Second Hundred Days of, 138–139
New Frontier, 236, 237, 249
New Mexico, 27, 46, 133
*New Republic*, 202
Newberry, Truman H., 110
*Newsweek*, 180
*New York Herald*, 34
*New York Post*, 164
*New York Times*, 22, 70, 191
Nicaragua, 288
Nichols, William, 285
Nickles, Don, 311
Nine-Power Treaty, 101–102

Nixon, Richard, 207, 216, 219, 225, 231, 233, 250
    Checkers speech of, 210
    Nixon administration, 251–254, 262. *See also* Watergate scandal
Nominations, 13–14, 56, 198, 229, 303–304
    for cabinet, 13, 291–293
    *See also* Supreme Court, appointments/confirmations
Non-Partisan League, 73
Norbeck, Peter, 113
Norris, George, 69, 70, 73, 74, 104, 105, 110, 112, 116, 119, 127, 130–131, 135, 142, 163, 165
Norris, George W. (grocer), 121
Norris-La Guardia Act, 124
North, Oliver, 302
North Africa, 164
Northern Pacific Railroad, 24
Nunn, Sam, 292, 296
Nye, Gerald P., 126, 136, 137, 155, 156, 173

O'Connor, Sandra Day, 286
O'Daniel, W. Lee, 162
Ohio, 91
Oklahoma, 27
Olds, Leland, 202
O'Neill, Thomas P. "Tip," 283
Orators, 22, 99, 227, 314
Oregon, 31, 43

Pacific area, 101
Packwood, Robert, 280, 282, 285, 298, 299
Pages. *See under* Senate
Palmer, A. Mitchell, 64
Panama Canal, 13, 27, 28–29, 82, 273–273
Panic of 1893, 12, 24
Panic of 1907, 45

Parker, Alton B., 30
Parker, Edith, 180
Parker, John J., 119–120
Parsons, Herbert, 37
Partisanship, 4, 78, 151, 173–174, 193,
    254, 255, 271, 286, 293, 297, 299,
    304, 308, 309, 311, 314, 317
Patriot Act, 315
Patronage, 14, 16, 49, 114, 132, 303
Payne bill, 47–49, 50
Pearl Harbor attack, 162
Pearson, Drew, 237
Pearson, James, 268, 272
Penrose, Boies, 63–64, 91
Pentagon, 285
Pepper, Claude, 150, 163, 206–207
Percy, Charles, 282
Perot, Ross, 300
*Philadelphia Press*, 14
Philippines, 3, 12, 14
Phillips, David Gordon, 39
*Pilgrim's Progress* (Bunyan), 40
Pinchot, Gifford, 49, 64
Pittman, Key, 60, 76, 116, 137,
    145(photo), 156
Platt, Orville H., 2, 23–24, 29, 30, 33
    death of, 35
Platt, Thomas Collier, 25, 35, 39
Platt Amendment, 14
Pointdexter, Miles, 62
Poker games, 25
Political action committees, 266, 275
Political parties, 4, 55
    party whips, 59
    third parties, 10, 103, 200, 300. *See
        also* Progressive Party; State rights,
        States' Rights (Dixiecrat) ticket
    *See also* Democratic Party;
        Partisanship; Republican Party;
        Senate, majority leaders of
Poll tax, 165, 174
Populists, 12, 27

Poverty, 113, 214
Presidency
    cabinet, 20. *See also* Nominations,
        for cabinet
    and candidates' identification with the
        South, 210, 223
    inauguration date changed, 124
    power of relative to Congress, 61, 90
    presidential debates, 291
    presidents remaining within borders of
        United States, 82
    reorganizing, 149
    *See also under* Senate
Press, 6, 20, 34, 54, 85, 88, 100, 102, 106,
    111, 116, 135, 142, 146, 148, 165,
    186, 188, 205, 208, 237, 245, 269,
    289, 290, 314
Prices
    agricultural, 78, 104
    of consumer goods, 24, 37
    of energy, 274
Progressive Party, 56, 63, 103
Progressives, 25, 58, 59, 62, 63, 91, 105,
    107, 112, 116–118, 119, 124, 132,
    133, 227
    and 1932 election, 126–127
    *See also* La Follette, Robert M.;
        Progressive Party
Prohibition, 75–76, 97, 130
Prosperity, 4, 12, 63, 64, 113, 184, 196
Protestants, 190
Proxmire, Ellen, 181, 236
Proxmire, William, 225, 228
Pryor, David, 303
Public housing, 202, 220, 250
Public lands, 43–44, 49, 105, 131
Public opinion, 29, 38, 74, 88, 100, 111,
    132, 155, 217, 226, 243, 247, 288
Public utilities, 138
Puerto Rico, 3, 12
Pure Food and Drug Act, 41
Pusey, Merlo, 177

Quayle, J. Danforth "Dan," 291
Quorum calls, 46

Race issues, 6, 11, 21, 51, 54, 60–61, 119,
    120, 128, 129, 134, 165, 167, 174,
    197, 200, 237, 254, 259, 260, 315
  African-American reporters, 183
  and anti-Communism, 207
  and Democratic National Convention
    in 1936, 140
  and filibusters, 106, 107, 108, 147,
    149, 202, 225, 235, 240, 241–242,
    250, 318
  and menial jobs in Senate, 184
  See also African Americans;
    Civil rights; Lynchings;
    Segregation; Slavery
Railroads, 36, 51, 67
  regulating, 33, 35, 37, 38–39, 49
Rains, Claude, 152
Rayburn, Sam, 217
Reagan, Ronald, 273, 275, 276, 288
  assassination attempt on, 279
  Reagan revolution, 279, 287
  second term of, 282–283
Recessions, 150, 226
Reconstruction Finance Corporation
    (RFC), 123, 124
Reconstruction period, 9, 11, 60
Redford, Robert, 255
Reed, James, 73
Reed, Thomas B., 5
Reforms, 5–6, 11, 23, 30, 31, 44, 59, 62, 67,
    70, 76, 92, 134, 138, 139, 165, 170,
    174, 202, 255, 264, 282, 284–285
Regan, Donald, 283
Regulations, 17, 27, 44, 61, 108, 138,
    185–186, 202, 272, 289.
    See also Railroads, regulating;
    Trust regulation
Rehnquist, William, 286
Relief programs, 140, 148. See also
    Welfare system

Republican Party, 4, 5, 9, 10, 12, 17, 63,
    80, 91–92, 112, 121, 151, 255, 276,
    295–311, 317
  and 1932 election, 127
  and 1946 election, 196
  and 1958 election, 226
  and autonomy of committee
    chairs, 304
  Committee to Reelect the President
    (CREEP), 261
  leadership in 1929, 115(photo)
  moderates in, 236, 274, 278, 282, 302
  National Republican Senatorial
    Committee, 280
  party caucus/conference and major
    committees, 25, 168
  Republican National Convention in
    1940, 160
  Senate Steering Committee, 265
  and the South, 235, 243, 253, 300,
    302, 305
  and Supreme Court fight in 1937, 142
  unity in, 265, 278
Reston, James, 173
Revels, Hiram, 11
Revenue Act of 1932, 124
RFC. See Reconstruction Finance
    Corporation
Richard B. Russell Building, 60
Richberg, Donald, 148
Riedel, Richard, 97
Riegle, Donald, 290
Robinson, Joseph T., 68, 95–96, 97, 108,
    109, 112, 114–115, 119, 125, 132,
    137, 139, 142
  death of, 143
Rockefeller, Nelson A., 268
Roe v. Wade, 287
Rogers, Will, 99, 137
Rometsch, Ellen, 239
Roosevelt, Franklin Delano, 92, 96, 112,
    126–127
  characterized, 163

health/death of, 169, 173
promises not kept by, 132
relations with Senate, 129–130, 132,
    134, 136, 139, 141, 143, 144–145,
    148, 162, 164, 169
and Senate races, 150–151
State of the Union message in
    1944, 169
and Supreme Court. *See* Supreme
    Court, increase of number of judges
*See also* New Deal
Roosevelt, Theodore, 13, 17, 39–40, 78,
    82, 273
annual messages to Congress, 26, 44
and Benjamin Tillman, 21, 38–39
and The Four, 24, 27, 29–30, 33, 43
and Joseph B. Foraker, 42–43
and journalist muckrakers, 40
and Marcus A. Hanna, 29
and Progressive Party, 56
and regulating corporations/railroads,
    27, 33, 37, 38–39, 41, 43
and Robert M. La Follette, 74
as vice-president, 16
Root, Elihu, 49
Rudman, Warren, 279, 283, 284, 293
Rural Electrification Administration, 198
Russell, Richard B., 127–128,
    149, 165–166, 182, 197, 198,
    207, 212, 216, 222, 230, 235,
    254, 317
candidacy for president, 210
and civil rights bills, 224, 226, 242
death of, 260–261
and Hubert Humphrey, 202
Russell hearings of 1951, 208–209
*See also under* Johnson, Lyndon B.

Saltonstall, Leverett, 184
Santorum, Rick, 302, 304
*Saturday Evening Post*, 18
Savings and loan industry, 289, 290
Scalia, Antonin, 286

Scandals, 31, 54, 55, 93, 105–106,
    182–183, 185–186, 209, 226, 276
during Kennedy administration,
    238–239
Iran-*contra* scandal, 288–289
*See also* Watergate scandal
Schine, G. David, 217
Scott, Hugh, 252, 253, 264, 272
*See It Now* program, 217
Segregation, 6, 11, 60, 93, 107, 129,
    140, 152, 166, 183–184, 197, 221,
    235, 287
in public schools, 220, 224, 226
Senate
amenities of senatorial life, 60, 96, 97,
    184, 318
Appropriations Committee, 25, 86,
    291, 304
Armed Services Committee, 178, 208,
    262, 292, 317
Banking Committee, 305–306
behavior in, 2, 186–187, 313
Budget Committee in, 283
budget for operating, 313
changes in membership and working
    habits, 9, 46
chaplain of the Senate, 189–190
committee chairmanships in New
    Deal era, 136
Committee on Privileges and
    Elections, 218
Committee on Public Lands and
    Surveys, 105
compared with House, 20, 193, 281,
    295–296, 319
conservative Club in, 129, 134, 147,
    148, 149, 152, 184, 187, 192, 195,
    199, 203, 238, 254. *See also* New
    Deal, and coalition of southern
    Democrats and Republicans
constitutional functions of, 13
creation of, 6, 7
criticism of, 177–178, 237, 316–318

Senate *(continued)*

debates becoming more constricted in, 314–315

declaration of war by, 73, 162

drinking alcohol in, 19, 76, 97–98, 184, 187, 188–189, 235, 299

Ethics Committee, 290, 298, 299

as exclusive private club, 2, 4, 31, 35, 60, 108, 320

executive sessions, 208, 314

expanded membership of, 46

Finance Committee, 25, 86, 240, 249, 252, 282, 285, 289, 301

Foreign Relations Committee, 67, 81(photo), 86, 87, 89, 103, 116, 156, 157, 162, 171, 206, 208, 219, 236, 246–247, 258, 260

The Four group in, 22–25, 23(photo), 31, 318. *See also* Roosevelt, Theodore, and The Four

galleries, 40–41, 85, 99, 175, 178, 183

greatest members of, 103

Hispanic members, 134

Interstate Commerce Committee, 38

investigative powers of, 105

and Iraq in 2002, 316

"irreconcilables" in, 85, 88, 100

as isolated and removed from daily concerns, 4, 175, 318

isolationists in, 155–156, 156–157, 160, 164, 173. *See also* Isolationism

Judiciary Committee, 54, 66, 119, 120, 143, 144, 147, 224, 262, 287, 297

Kefauver hearings in, 176–177

majority leaders of, 57, 68, 70, 80, 93, 94–95, 98, 114, 144–145, 163, 168, 170, 189, 201, 231, 234, 252, 260, 271–272, 279, 282, 291, 302, 303, 305, 314, 315. *See also* Johnson, Lyndon, as minority/majority leader

"mild reservationists" in, 86

pages, 3(photo), 97, 175, 180

and presidency, 6, 12, 14, 25–26, 30, 31, 34, 37, 61, 64, 74–75, 93, 113–114, 153, 170, 253, 257, 299, 317, 318. *See also* Roosevelt, Franklin Delano, relations with Senate

president pro tempore, 1, 16, 114, 291

public credit for accomplishments of, 41–42

and regulation of business, 17. *See also* Regulations

reputation in 1990s, 293, 308

reputation in 1920s, 90, 96

Rules Committee, 25, 239, 265

Russell hearings of 1951, 208–209

salaries, 18, 97, 184, 236, 314, 318

Select Committee on Intelligence Activities, 269–270

Senate chamber, 2, 47, 78, 96–97, 98, 118(photo), 158(photo), 178

Senate Ladies Club, 181

Senate office buildings, 60, 96, 313–314

senatorial courtesy, 14

senators chosen by state legislatures, 7, 9–11, 53. *See also* Elections, direct election of senators

sessions of, 18, 105

and single-issue groups, 277

smoking in chamber, 98

and social inequities, 51

southerners in, 78, 93, 108, 115, 120, 123–124, 129, 134, 136, 140, 147, 152, 156, 173, 192, 195, 197, 198, 200, 222, 226, 242–243, 254. *See also* Democratic Party, and the South

staff/employees, 180, 187, 236, 254, 257–258, 313

television coverage of, 280—281, 314

and treaties, 6, 12–13, 34, 172, 189. *See also* Treaties, Treaty of Versailles

wealth of members, 12, 19, 185, 317, 318

women senators, 98–99, 121, 124–126, 178–180, 236, 274, 295, 297, 298–299, 311, 314

working habits of Senators, 186–187

Sex, 19, 128, 181–182, 188, 239, 287

sexual harassment, 285, 297, 298, 299, 306

*See also* Homosexuals

Shafroth, John, 61

Share Our Wealth Society, 126, 138

Shays-Meehan bill, 309

Shelby, Richard, 302

Sherman, James S., 49, 55

Shipstead, Henrik, 126

Shortridge, Samuel M., 107

Silver, 21, 104, 116, 130

Simmons, Furnifold M., 122

Simon, Joseph, 22

Sinclair, Upton, 41

Slavery, 7, 8, 9

Small government, 114, 135. *See also* *under* Democratic Party

Smathers, George, 181–182, 206–207, 213, 216, 234

Smith, Alfred E., 96, 112, 114, 122, 126

Smith, Ellison D. "Cotton Ed", 136, 140, 150

Smith, Frank L., 111

Smith, Margaret Chase, 178–180, 179(photo), 205, 229, 236, 261, 298

Smith-Connally bill, 169

Smoot, Reed, 64, 127

Social justice, 23, 51, 53, 58, 192

Social science, 193

Social Security, 138, 143, 283

Socialism, 4, 22, 37, 64, 159, 199, 203

Soft money, 308–309

Southern Manifesto, 222

Soviet Union, 195, 203, 226, 238. *See also* Cold War

Spanish American War, 3, 4, 12, 15, 16

Special interests, 31, 120, 285, 289, 309, 317, 319

Specter, Arlen, 297

Spooner, John Coit, 19, 20, 24–25, 29, 30, 35, 43, 53, 152

*Sputnik* satellite, 226

Stalemate, 237

Standard Oil Company, 19, 43

Starr, Kenneth, 306—307

State Department, 204

State rights, 5, 6, 7, 129, 135, 199

States' Rights (Dixiecrat) ticket, 200, 225

Stennis, John C., 261–262, 265

Stephenson, Isaac, 53–54

Stevenson, Adlai, 209–210, 222

Stevenson, Coke, 200, 214

Stewart, Jimmy, 152, 153

Stock market crash (1929), 113, 117, 131

Stone, William J., 46, 65, 67, 69, 70, 76

Strauss, Lewis, 179, 229

Strikes, 67, 105, 124, 150, 169

Subsidies, 5, 104

Subversion, 195, 196–197, 203, 204, 205–206, 217

Sugar, 26, 47, 48, 62, 109

Suicide, 98, 128

Supply-side economics, 279

Supreme Court, 6, 110, 138, 220, 222, 281, 284, 309

appointments/confirmations, 13, 65, 118–120, 147–148, 162, 250–251, 286–288, 296–298, 316

increase in number of judges, 135, 141–144

Symington, Stuart, 216, 229

Taft, Robert A., 103, 151, 157–159, 161, 164, 167–168, 174, 195, 198

candidacy for presidency, 160, 209

death of, 211, 216

Taft-Hartley Act, 199

Taft, William Howard, 31, 44, 46, 47, 48, 49, 53, 56, 66, 118–119

*Taft Story, The* (White), 192

Talmadge, Herman, 276

Tariffs, 5, 12, 15, 19, 22, 33, 45, 51, 59, 114
	and financial holdings of senators, 62
	Fordney-McCumber Tariff bill, 106
	lowering, 26, 44, 47, 61–62
	and Payne bill, 47–48, 50
	and prices of consumer goods, 24, 49
	reciprocal tariff agreement with Canada, 53, 56
	Smoot-Hawley Tariff bill, 120
	Underwood tariff bill, 61–62

Taxation, 78, 108, 117, 124, 126, 138, 139, 149, 167, 237, 240, 279, 280, 282, 301, 315
	and George H. W. Bush, 299–300
	Tax Reform Act of 1986, 184–185
	and World War II, 169
	*See also* Income tax

Teapot Dome scandal, 105–106

Telecommunications bill of 1996, 310

Television, 175–176, 188, 194, 210, 217, 230, 233, 242, 246–247, 297, 310
	increased role of, 254–255, 280–281, 295, 314

Tennessee Valley Authority, 131. *See also* Muscle Shoals dam project

Terrorist attacks of September 11, 2001, 269, 270, 308, 315

Texas, 200

Thomas, Clarence, 297–298, 299

Thompson, Fred, 306

Thornberry, Homer, 250

Thornburgh, Richard, 300

Thurmond, Strom, 200, 222, 225, 242, 278, 305, 315

Tillman, Benjamin "Pitchfork Ben," 21, 38–39, 48, 98

*Time*, 168

Tonkin Gulf Resolution, 244–245, 246, 249

Tower, John, 235, 265, 270, 288, 291–293, 298

Trade, 5, 16, 66, 103, 220. *See also* Tariffs

"Treason of the Senate, The" (Phillips), 39

Treasury Department, 109

Treaties
	arbitration treaties, 34
	nuclear test ban treaty, 238
	to outlaw war, 102–103
	for Panama Canal construction/control, 28–29, 273–274
	reciprocity treaties, 15–16, 26
	Treaty of Versailles, 85, 88–90, 137. *See also* Wilson, Woodrow, and peace treaty/League of Nations; World War I, peace treaty
	*See also under* Senate

Truman, Bess, 188

Truman, Harry S., 145, 168, 169, 173, 195, 209
	attacks on Congress by, 199
	and Douglas MacArthur, 207
	Fair Deal program of, 200–201, 202
	Truman Doctrine, 198–199

Trust regulation, 44, 57, 62, 63, 132

Tsongas, Paul, 274

Turkey, 198

Tydings, Eleanor, 181

Tydings, Millard, 129, 133, 149, 150–151, 206

Unanimous-consent agreement, 221, 281, 303

Underwood, Oscar W., 61, 94, 107

Unemployment, 105, 113, 117, 118, 121, 122, 123, 129, 131, 136, 148, 280, 301

United Mine Workers, 185

United Nations, 159, 163, 172

United States
  admission of states, 27, 46
  Middle West, 33, 35, 42, 78, 103
  role of government in, 5
  South, 6, 12, 60, 66, 107, 111, 135,
    150, 165, 195, 235. *See also*
    Democratic Party, and the South;
    Republican Party, and the South;
    Senate, southerners in
  West, 43–44, 66
  as world power, 3, 4, 6, 90
*U.S. Senators and Their World*
  (Matthews), 193

Van Devanter, Willis, 143
Vandenberg, Arthur, 149, 160, 171–172,
  198, 199
Vardaman, James K., 60, 79
Vare, William S., 111
Vetoes, 104, 131, 186
  overridden, 169, 170, 262
Vietnam War, 236, 243—245, 246—247,
  249–250, 252, 257, 258, 259, 261
  Tet Offensive, 250
Viguerie, Richard, 275
Volstead Act, 130. *See also* Prohibition
Voting rights, 9, 11, 54, 76, 286
  Voting Rights Act of 1965
  *See also* Women, woman suffrage

Wadsworth, James W., 59, 80
Wagner, Robert F., 122, 123, 131,
  146–147, 163
  Wagner Act, 138, 199
*Wall Street Journal*, 269
Wallace, Henry A., 169, 171, 173
Walsh, David I., 163–164
Walsh, Thomas J., 105–106
War of 1812, 7
War Powers Act of 1973, 257
War Powers Resolution, 261–262
Warren, Charles Beecher, 109

Warren, Earl, 250, 253
Warren, Francis E., 19
Washington, D. C. *See* District of
  Columbia
Washington, George, 7
Washington Naval Conference, 101
*Washington Post*, 10, 98, 178
Watergate scandal, 257, 261, 262, 263,
  264, 265, 269
  and Saturday Night Massacre,
  286, 287
Watkins, Arthur V., 218, 219
Watson, James E., 94, 114,
  115(photo), 127
Webb, Beatrice, 22
Webster, Daniel, 7, 8, 103
Weicker, Lowell, 259, 263, 278
Welfare system, 301. *See also*
  Relief programs
Welker, Herman, 183
West, Henry L., 20
Weyrich, Paul, 292
Wheat, 75, 78
Wheeler, Burton K., 103, 105, 142, 143,
  156, 161
Wherry, Kenneth, 190, 201, 202
White, George H., 11
White, Henry, 83
White, Walter, 107
White, William S., 191–192, 217
Whitewater affair, 306
Williams, Aubrey, 198
Williams, Harrison, 276
Williams, John J., 239
Williams, John Sharp, 73, 76, 97
Willkie, Wendell, 160
Wilson, Edith, 88
Wilson, Edmund, 117
Wilson, Pete, 283, 298
Wilson, Woodrow, 50, 53, 56–57, 64
  and congressional elections of
  1918, 79–80

Wilson, Woodrow (*continued*)
  and Foreign Relations Committee,
    87, 89
  hatred of, 71, 75, 80, 82
  health of, 87, 88, 89
  and Henry Cabot Lodge, 71, 72, 73,
    80, 82–83
  New Freedom of, 61, 63, 65
  and peace treaty/League of Nations,
    71, 80, 81–84, 86–88, 89–90, 171
  "peace without victory" address, 68
  reelection of, 68
  and separation of races, 60
  speaking tour of, 87–88
  and World War I, 65, 67, 68, 70,
    73, 78
Wisconsin, 53–54, 103
  Wisconsin Idea, 36
Wolcott, Edward O., 20
Women, 11–12
  female Supreme Court justice, 286
  as Senate staff members/pages,
    180, 187
  senators' wives, 180—181, 188
  woman suffrage, 75, 76–77, 98
  *See also* Constitution, equal rights
    amendment for women; Senate,
    women senators

Wool goods, 56
Working conditions, 23, 44
Workmen's compensation, 67
World Court, 102, 109, 136, 137, 155
World War I, 64, 66, 96, 106
  American entry into, 71, 73
  and neutral shipping, 68
  peace treaty, 77. *See also* Treaties,
    Treaty of Versailles; Wilson,
    Woodrow, and peace treaty/League
    of Nations
  and probe of arms industry, 136
  reparations, 103
  senators voting against, 73–74
  and Zimmerman Telegram, 69
  *See also under* Wilson, Woodrow
World War II, 153, 157, 164, 169,
    174, 187
  and arms embargo, 159
  rationing during, 163
  tax bill for, 169
  United States entry into, 162
Wyman, Louis, 265
Wyoming, 10

Yarborough, Ralph, 235, 259

Zwicker, Ralph, 218